# HAND TOOLS

## Their Ways and Workings

# HAND TOOLS

## THEIR WAYS AND WORKINGS

BY Aldren A. Watson

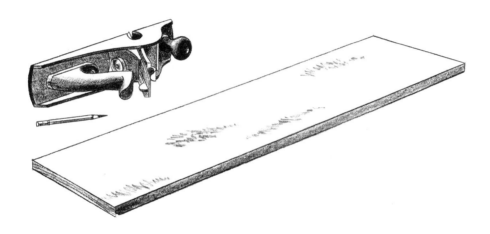

*Illustrations by the Author*

## LYONS & BURFORD
PUBLISHERS

BY ALDREN A. WATSON

*Hand Tools: Their Ways and Workings*
*Country Furniture*
*The Village Blacksmith*
*The Watson Drawing Book (with Ernest W. Watson)*
*Hand Bookbinding*

*Hand Tools: Their Ways and Workings*
was edited and designed by
T & A Foxe Ltd, North Hartland, Vermont

Printed in the United States of America

10   9   8   7   6   5   4   3   2   1

Library of Congress Cataloging-in-Publication Data

Watson, Aldren Auld, 1917–
    Hand tools : their ways and workings / by Aldren A. Watson ;
    illustrations by the author.
        p.   cm.
    Reprint. Originally published: Norton : New York, 1982.
    Includes index.
    ISBN 1-55821-224-8
    1. Tools.   I. Title.
TJ1195.W356   1996
    621.9′08—dc20                                      92-38762
                                                            CIP

*For Theodora*

# Contents

Preface

1 Discovery   *13*

2 Workbench & Vise   *15*

3 Anvil   *37*

4 Awl   *41*

5 Brace & Bits   *45*

6 Wire Brush   *83*

7 Chisels   *87*

8 Clamps   *105*

9 Drawknife   *123*

10 Hand Drill   *133*

11 File & Rasp   *141*

12 Hammer   *155*

13 Inshave   *167*

14 Jackknife   *171*

15 Level   *175*

16 Mallet   *185*

17 Marking Gauge   *189*

18 Mitering Tools   *195*

19 Nail Set   *203*

20 Planes   *207*

21 Pliers   *275*

22 Pry Bar   *279*

23 Rules   *283*

24 Sandpaper   *291*

25 Saws   *297*

26 Scrapers   *321*

27 Screwdriver   *327*

28 Spokeshave   *335*

29 Square   *341*

30 T-Bevel   *349*

31 Sharpening   *353*

Appendixes   *373*

A Toolmakers   *374*

B Tool Catalogs   *376*

C Workbench Plans   *380*

D Plans for Bench Tools   *385*

E Fitting a Hammer Handle   *401*

F Closet Workbench Plans   *404*

G Inventory of Typical Shop   *409*

Index   *413*

# Preface

Boatbuilder, carpenter, cabinetmaker, and furniture maker all use tools that are almost identical and interchangeable, whose design and function were fully evolved very early on and remain virtually unchanged today. A plane shaves wood no differently now than it did in 1780; a saw must still be held in a certain way, pushed, pulled, and otherwise manipulated according to a tried and time-proven set of principles.

Whether practiced as a trade, an avocation, or simply as a practical adjunct to daily existence, working wood with hand tools satisfies some elemental needs of the human animal—for manual work, development of innate skills, peace and quiet, and a sense of control over his temporal affairs. Listen to the sound of a sharp plane peeling tightly curled shavings from the edge of a board. Sniff the aroma of released oils by which oak and pine are instantly recognizable. Watch the color changes as the surface skin is cut away to the underlying layers. Satisfy the sense of touch by brushing the hand over a tool-worked surface, which with experience may become a reliable test of its flatness. And enjoy the feeling of independence when you sit down for a meal at the table you have built with your own hands.

*North Hartland, Vermont*                                        ALDREN A. WATSON

# Acknowledgments

*Thomas A.*

Wendy  Mary  Cameron  James

Peter  Tina  Alexander  Pete-Pete

Clyde  Deny  Julian  Amos

Linda  David  Georgia

Annie  Sam  Cammie  Caitlin

Toby  Nancy  Thomas B.

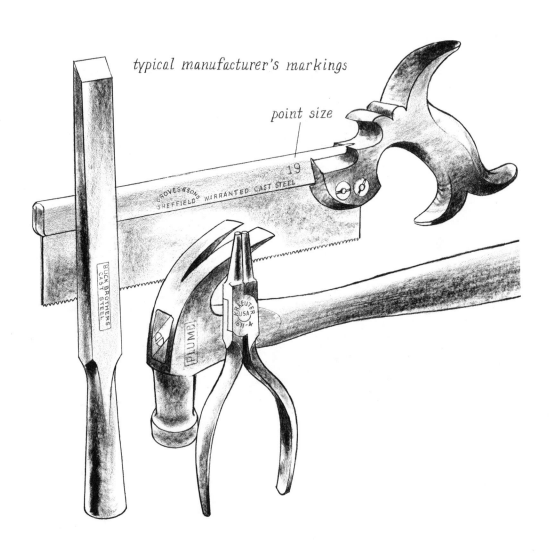

*typical manufacturer's markings*

*point size*

# 1

# Discovery

In one sense, tools are simply things of steel and wood, attractive to the eye, perhaps even beautiful in their efficient lines, functional design, and appealing contrasts of texture and color. In another, it might be imagined that they only wait to be taken up and used, when they will then automatically perform with the precision that their appearance implies. This is an illusion. Tools can indeed be made to perform extraordinary tasks, sometimes with such impressive dispatch that they seem to have life of their own. However, it is more realistic to see that a tool has no more and no less than a high potentiality for capacity performance. At the same time each one has its own peculiar ways and workings, individual quirks of personality, if you like. These traits must be discovered, at times only through dogged trial and error, and the knowledge of them applied with persistent discipline and an attitude of acceptance, for the tool will not change its ways. When a tool is picked up and used in recognition of these limitations, then its full capability can be exploited to your purposes, and the two of you will work agreeably in tandem. Thus there is a sharp distinction between working *with* your tools and merely working them on wood.

To my way of thinking the most practical means of acquiring this intimate understanding of the ways and workings of a tool is to take it apart, see how it is built and how its mechanism controls its performance. Sharpen the cutter iron, clean and oil the tool, and put it back together again. Then look into its adjustments, trying out each one of them on waste pieces of wood. Experiment, too, with the different handholds and the stance of your feet to determine what effect they have on the ease and efficiency of using the tool.

All of these factors operate in a cyclical fashion. As the potentialities and limitations of a tool are explored and understood, the quality of work tends to improve; and along with it grows the confidence that even more professional procedures are possible. As the tool begins to show signs of functioning more nearly as it was designed to perform, you may perceive that the implications of the phrase "in good hands this tool is capable of the finest work" is not after all beyond your reach.

Tools are expensive, and finding good ones is more difficult now than it was in the 1900s, when excellent tools were manufactured mainly for the professional who earned a living at the workbench. They were built of high-quality materials, properly machined, nicely finished, and fitted with comfortable handles. Toolmakers described their products in detail with clear illustrations and specifications in regularly issued catalogs, a number of which are available as reprints. Information from these sources, along with notes made on the cost of new models, can be useful when buying at auctions, flea markets, and from secondhand dealers. There are a great many of these older tools in circulation and they are generally a good investment, despite the fact that you may have to clean them up, put on new handles, or make other minor repairs.

When buying new tools, look for well-known names such as Craftsman, Diamond, Disston, Irwin, Jennings, Marples, Nicholson, Plumb, Record, Stanley, and Starrett. This is only a representative handful; a more complete list of manufacturers of both new and old tools is included in the Appendix. If at all possible, buy from a reputable local dealer rather than from a mail-order catalog, even though many of these companies carry a good range of tools and have satisfactory policies on return and refund. It is more advantageous—when you can—to see the real article, pick it up, heft it for size and comfort, and compare it with other brands in the store. The Appendix includes a list of tool manufacturers and distributors who publish catalogs.

To keep an expensive collection of tools in good working condition, and to safeguard your investment, you should store the tools ready to hand as well as safe from damage to their cutting edges. Simple wooden racks are inexpensive to build and provide good protection even for chisels and auger bits. And if they are designed to keep all your tools in plain sight, it is an easy matter to reach for the one you want, and just as convenient to put it back when you've finished with it.

# 2

# Workbench & Vise

A workbench and vise are the first, last, and most important tools without which all the others would be only half useful. The bench is the place to measure, set out the work, prepare the wood, and assemble it—the center of a shop. Without a bench there is no way or place to use a vise, and nearly every woodworking operation requires one. So indispensable is this pair of tools that the usefulness of one depends almost completely on the other.

The workshop should be a comfortable and convenient place in which to work—the one place you'd rather spend time in than anywhere else. And a good bench and vise to a large extent make it so. Good artificial lighting is another necessity. Have a fair-sized main fixture hung over the bench near the vise. An inexpensive one can be built in the form of an inverted trough with three or four ceramic sockets wired in line. Two or three scissor clamp spotlights and a 25-foot extension cord will complete a flexible system providing light of varying intensity in any part of the shop without the need of burning all of them at once.

Most factory-made benches come with at least one vise attached and are quite expensive, while some of the so-called German benches with two vises cost as much as an entire collection of planes. But for a fraction of such an outlay you can build, alone or with some help, an excellent bench that will save you enough money to buy a first-class vise and a good many tools besides. Plans and directions for a home-made bench are given in the Appendix.

# How Big a Bench?

Whatever your shop space, have a bench as long as you can fit in, with a top no more than 24 inches wide. In my estimation there is no advantage in a bench that you can't easily reach across, particularly if it must go against a wall. A long bench can be freestanding, but one that is shorter than 5 feet should be secured to the floor or to a wall in order to make it sufficiently solid. If you simply have no space for a workshop as such or if you live in an apartment, you might consider building a closet workbench similar to the one shown in the Appendix.

# Height of Bench

More important than length is the height of a bench, or more properly the height of *your* bench, for the bench ought to fit the person. Many of the old-time benches in professional shops were very low by our standards, often no more than 28 inches above the floor. With good reason: to work efficiently on wood it is preferable to be on top of the work, to take advantage of the natural mechanics of operating tools with hands, arms, and shoulders. If the bench is too high, you will be using only a fraction of your driving force, and then only with poor control over the tool. Moreover, working in the shop will always be needlessly tiring. While it may affect different parts of the anatomy, too low a bench is just as fatiguing and just as inefficient.

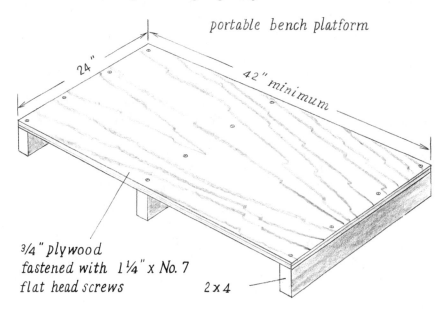

*portable bench platform*

24"

42" *minimum*

3/4" *plywood*
*fastened with  1¼" x No. 7*
*flat head screws*        2 x 4

The top of a bench should come to your wrist (give or take an inch) as you stand in a normally erect position with arms hanging down. Take plenty of time to determine the most comfortable height, for you will spend a lot of time working there. Have someone measure from floor to wrist, or else try out and measure tables, counters, cabinets—anything with a flat top—until you find something that fits, then use the dimensions of the one that does.

At the same time, think about the kind of work you expect to be doing. As one example, the top edge of a 12-inch board held in the vise for jointing will come about 8 inches above the top of the bench. If you gauged the height of the bench by this alone, it might well be too low for other kinds of work. It is therefore a matter of striking an average that will do reasonably well for everything. And if other people—especially shorter people—will be using the same bench, a practical solution is to build a low, portable platform for them to stand on.

# Construction

A bench should be as solid as a butcher's chopping block—no vibration when you pound on it, no shuck, and no creeping along the floor when you plane on it. In thinking of a factory-made bench, don't even consider buying it unless it passes these three tests. And if you should decide instead to build one, give some attention to the question of materials and construction. Use dry lumber. Stuff that has air-dried for a year or more is ideal, but kiln-dried material is about as good and more readily obtained. Green lumber will shrink, opening cracks in the top wide enough for nails and screws to fall through. Make the top of solid wood at least 2 inches thick. Three would be better. Two planks $2'' \times 12'' \times 6'$ will make up into a top approximately $22^1/_2$ inches wide. Maple, oak, and beech are the traditional woods for this purpose, but other less expensive species such as pine and fir are quite satisfactory. Joint the edges of all pieces smooth and true, and bolt $2'' \times 4''$ cleats on the underside for reinforcement.

The frame that supports the top should be just as rugged, with solid legs and good bracing. Assemble all the main structural members with machine bolts so that any loosening of joints due to shrinkage can conveniently be taken up. They are better than roundheaded carriage bolts which usually turn round and round when you try to tighten them.

Although the traditional workbench has a sunken tool tray along the back edge, I prefer a plain flat top that can be completely cleared off when extra space is needed.

LEVELING    When the bench is put in place, it should be made level. Use a carpenter's level to check the top in both directions and again on the front face to make sure it is plumb. This is especially important, since the vise should also be plumb and level. Put thin shims under each leg as needed. The thin ends of wood shingles, cut pieces of asphalt shingle, or dense cardboard make good shims. Don't

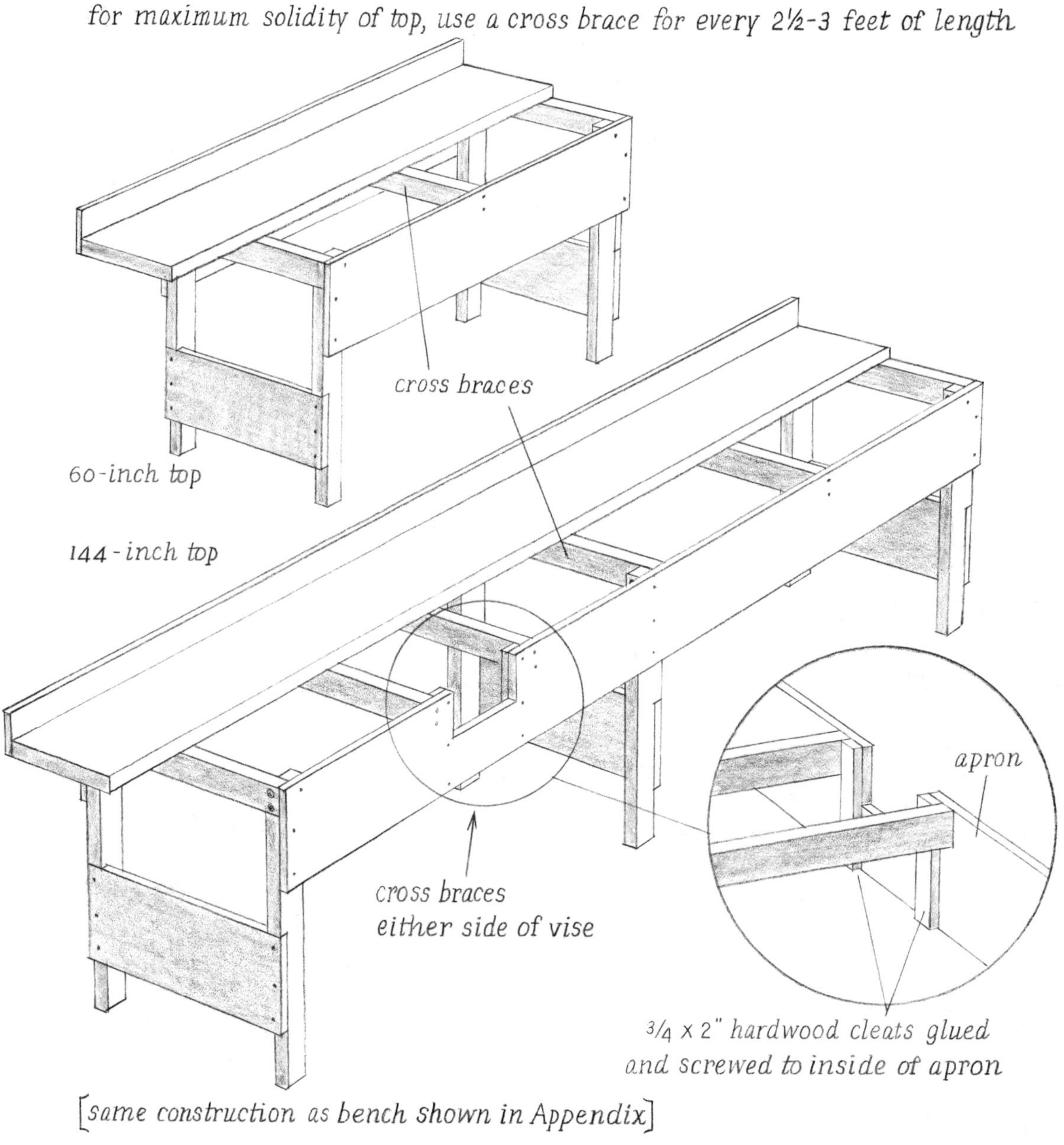

*for maximum solidity of top, use a cross brace for every 2½-3 feet of length*

*cross braces*

*60-inch top*

*144-inch top*

*cross braces either side of vise*

*apron*

*¾ x 2" hardwood cleats glued and screwed to inside of apron*

[*same construction as bench shown in Appendix*]

*a short bench should be secured
to the floor to make it solid*

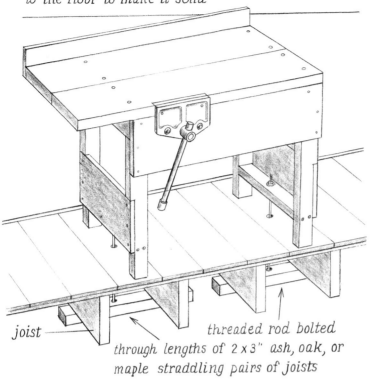

*joist*

*threaded rod bolted
through lengths of 2 x 3" ash, oak, or
maple straddling pairs of joists*

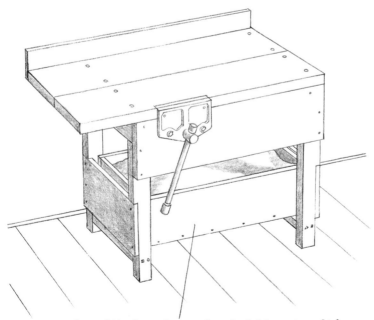

*wooden box filled with sand to hold bench solid*

use corrugated board. The bench should be completely solid with the floor, each of the legs carrying an equal weight. Test it by shucking it end-to-end and front-to-back. The shims should be painstakingly adjusted until all movement has been completely eliminated.

FINISHING THE BENCH    When all this is done, dress the top as smooth and flat as possible with a sharp plane set for a fine cut. This will be a test of how good a job you did with the shims, for planing puts a great deal of lengthwise stress on a bench. Go over the top with medium and fine grits of sandpaper, then clean off the dust with a brush or vacuum cleaner. Finally, paint the top and edges with three coats of sealer or hot linseed oil rubbed down between coats with fine steel wool.

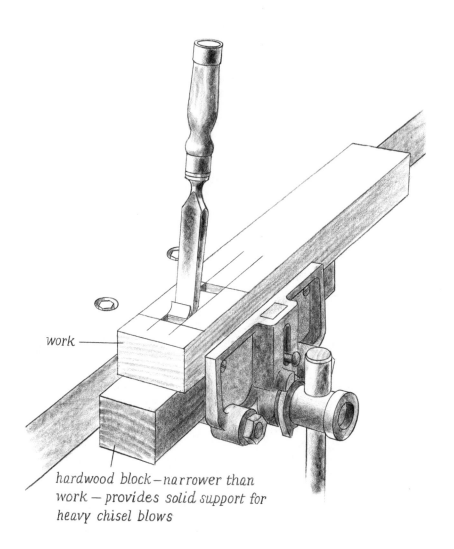

work —

hardwood block — narrower than
work — provides solid support for
heavy chisel blows

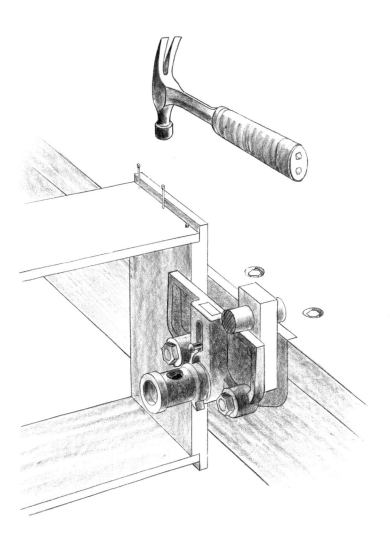

# Woodworking Vise

Every stick of wood that goes into a job must in one way or another be worked on with other tools: saw, plane, drill, brace and bit, screwdriver, hammer, chisels, spokeshave, or drawknife. A vise is the indispensable tool that holds the wood during these operations, as well as for holding a miter box, shooting board, and other pieces of bench equipment.

A good vise costs more than any other one tool. Yet you need one, use it every time you work at the bench, and open and close it a dozen times on every job. To withstand this kind of use, the vise must be heavy, strong, and above all quick and simple to operate.

Woodworking vises are of two kinds: quick-action and continuous screw. Both are made in several sizes, designated by width of jaw and opening capacity. For example, a 7"×8" vise has jaws 7 inches wide and will open a maximum distance of 8 inches.

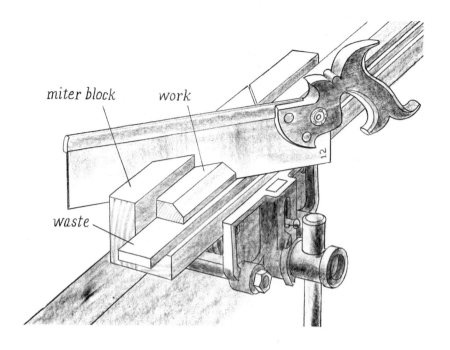

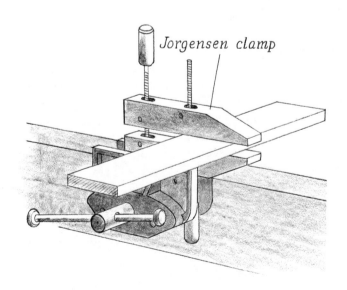

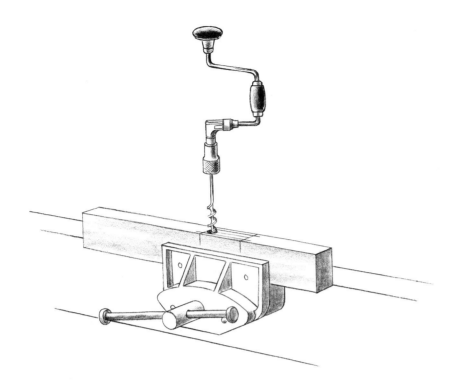

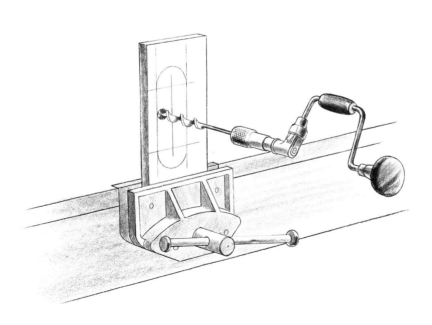

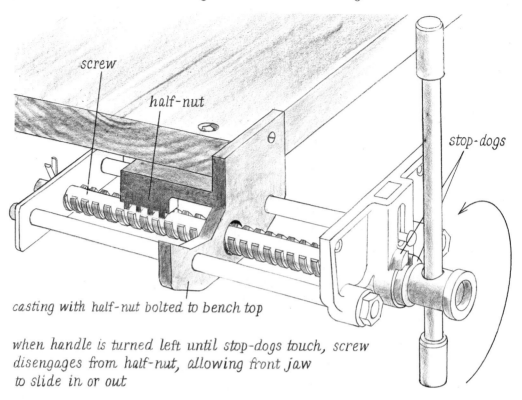

screw

half-nut

stop-dogs

casting with half-nut bolted to bench top

when handle is turned left until stop-dogs touch, screw disengages from half-nut, allowing front jaw to slide in or out

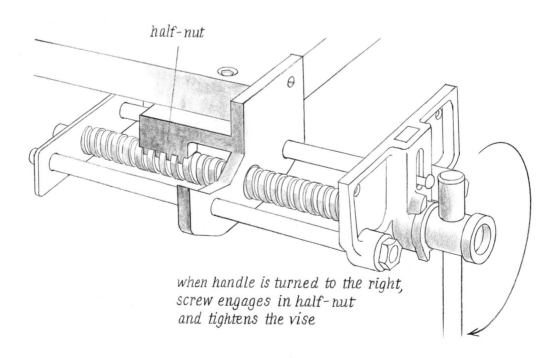

half-nut

when handle is turned to the right, screw engages in half-nut and tightens the vise

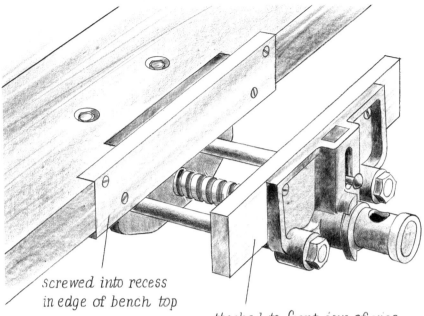

*screwed into recess
in edge of bench top*

*attached to front jaw of vise*

QUICK-ACTION VISE    This is the best kind. A milled groove runs
the full length of the screw, allowing the front jaw to *slide* in against
the work. A half-turn of the handle to the right then engages the screw
with a half-nut and tightens the vise. The vise is released just as fast:
turn the handle to the left until you feel the half-nut disengage, then
simply pull the front jaw toward you.

There are advantages to getting the biggest available model. A
$10'' \times 15''$ vise will handle all small stuff but it will also accommodate
a 12-inch board laid in flat. And this large model can also be used as a
clamp for gluing up many small jobs. Most vises have holes drilled
through the front jaw for attaching protective wooden faceplates, which
of course reduces the opening capacity of the vise. If you decide to
cover the jaws with wood, set the vise back in from the edge of the
bench and cut a recess for the wooden faceplate. Fit the wood to the
recess and attach it to the edge of the bench with screws, making sure
that it is flush with the edge, as shown in the illustration. I prefer to
protect the work with loose pieces of scrap wood, keeping the full
opening capacity in reserve for very wide stuff.

CONTINUOUS SCREW VISE    Just as its name implies, this type
has a continuous screw without a milled groove and without the quick-
action. It is slow and tedious to operate. The handle must be wound
round and round many times to close or open the vise, although when
you finally get there it holds just as tight. A continuous screw vise
costs about half as much, but in my estimation is not as sound an
investment.

*gluing up a paneled door*

*vise dog in raised position*

*bench dogs*

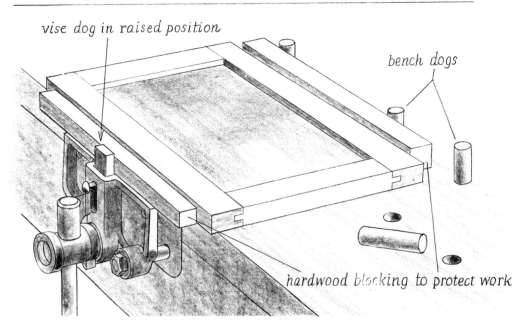

*hardwood blocking to protect work*

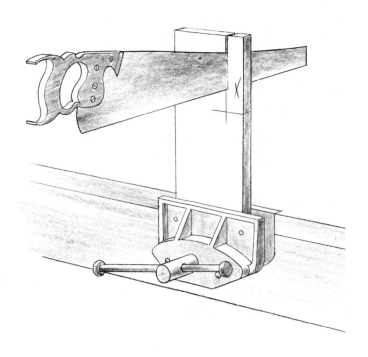

blocking of same thickness as the work
distributes pressure evenly, prevents
damaging the vise

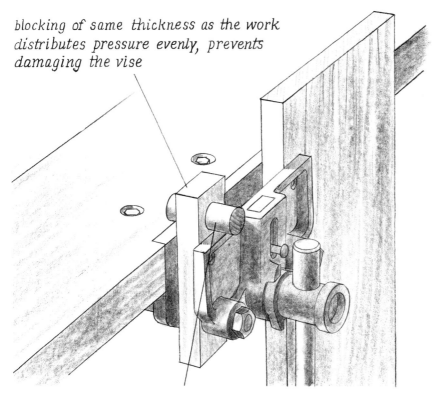

blocking with dowel won't drop on the floor
when vise pressure is released

without blocking,
a severe strain is put on the vise mechanism

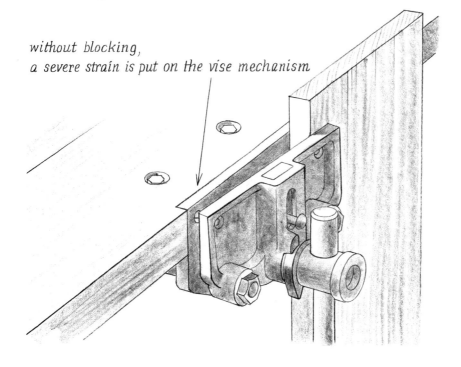

work clamped to overhanging end of bench

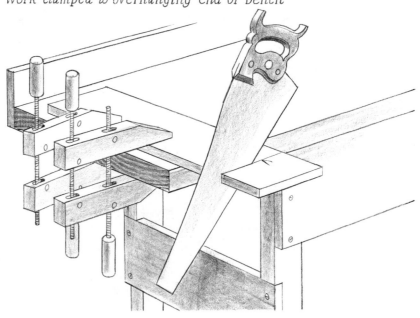

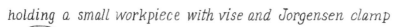

holding a small workpiece with vise and Jorgensen clamp

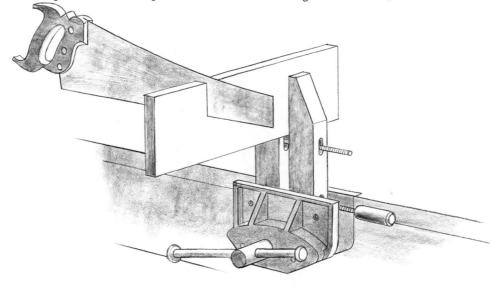

*swivel base machinist's vise*

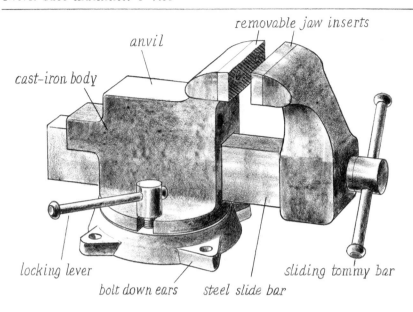

*anvil*

*removable jaw inserts*

*cast-iron body*

*locking lever*

*bolt down ears*     *steel slide bar*

*sliding tommy bar*

# Machinist's Vise

This is a metalworking tool used to hold rods, bolts, pipe, and other metal for bending, filing, forming, drilling, and hacksaw work. Although a machinist's vise is not, strictly speaking, a woodworking tool, it is often very useful and certainly an invaluable adjunct to a well-equipped shop. A good quality, heavy-duty vise can be bought for about a third the price of a comparable woodworking model. While the jaws of these vises are too thin and narrow for the best woodworking, it will serve as a temporary substitute by taking special care always to protect the work with pieces of waste wood.

Get a model that bolts to the bench and has these other features: a jaw opening of at least 5 inches, slide bar of steel rather than cast iron, removable jaw inserts, and a swivel base. The jaw inserts can be replaced with a pair of maple blocks. The swivel base allows turning the whole vise at right angles to the bench, which is especially handy for small work.

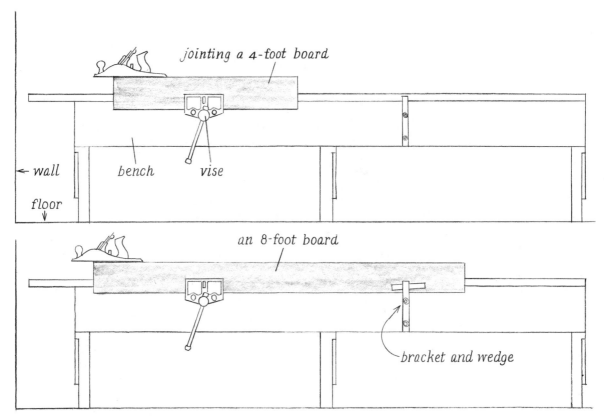

*jointing a 4-foot board*

wall

bench    vise

floor

*an 8-foot board*

*bracket and wedge*

*vise located to accommodate boards of as many different lengths as possible*

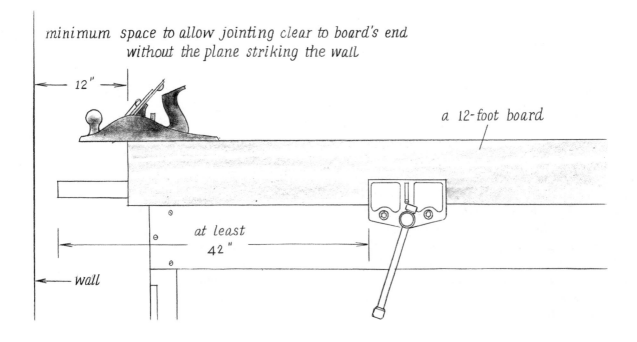

*minimum space to allow jointing clear to board's end*
*without the plane striking the wall*

12"

*a 12-foot board*

*at least*
*42"*

wall

INSTALLING A VISE    A woodworking vise should be located to accommodate boards of as many different lengths as possible. Most factory-made benches are built with the vise at one end or in some cases one at each end. But for a homemade bench the vise is more useful if it is located about 4 feet from one end, particularly if the bench butts against a wall or is close to it. In this position, short or long boards can be handily jointed clear to the end without the plane running off and striking the wall. In a large shop where the bench stands clear of all the walls, this may be no problem at all. In any case, when one end of a long board is put in the vise, some way should be provided to hold the other end steady, otherwise it will weave from side to side and make the work difficult.

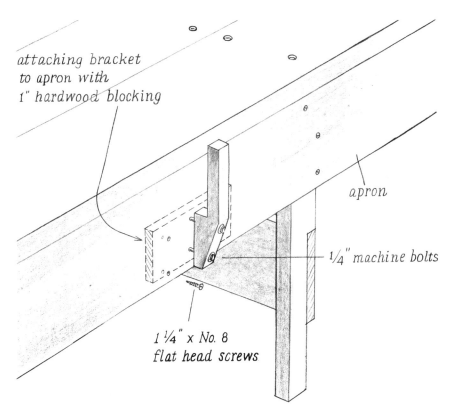

attaching bracket
to apron with
1″ hardwood blocking

apron

¼″ machine bolts

1 ¼″ x No. 8
flat head screws

A pair of vises on the front of the bench would be ideal, but lacking that, a notched bracket bolted to one bench leg will work fine. Have the notch of the bracket at the same level as the slide rails of the vise, and use a wedge to tighten the board in the bracket. Many of the old benches were equipped with similar holding devices, or fitted with a front apron in which numerous holes were bored for dowel pegs which served the same purpose.

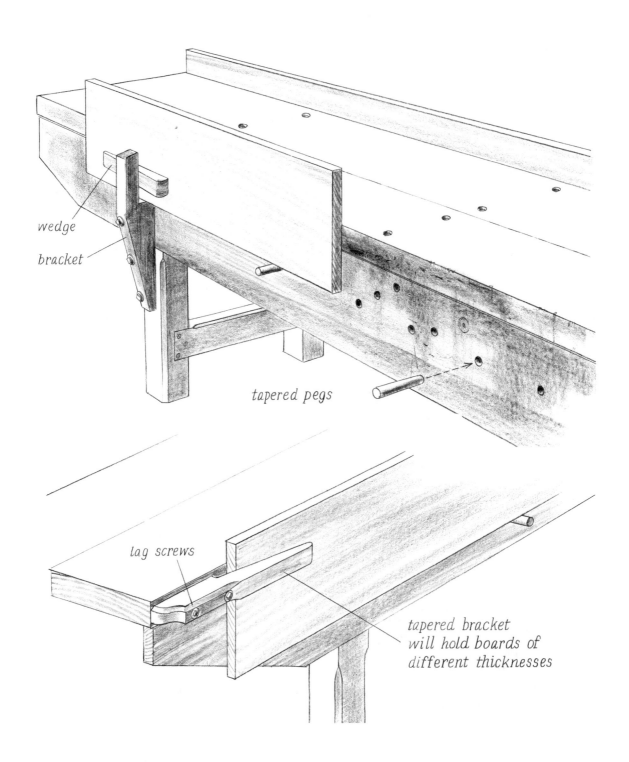

*wedge*

*bracket*

*tapered pegs*

*lag screws*

*tapered bracket
will hold boards of
different thicknesses*

*a handy place to bore trial auger holes*

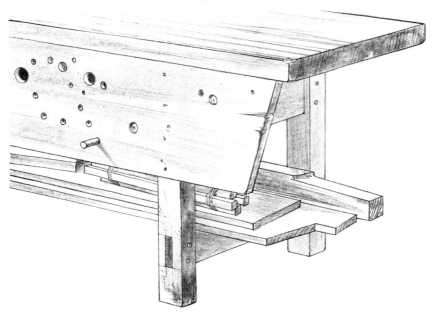

*holding work flat on the bench
for planing and sanding*

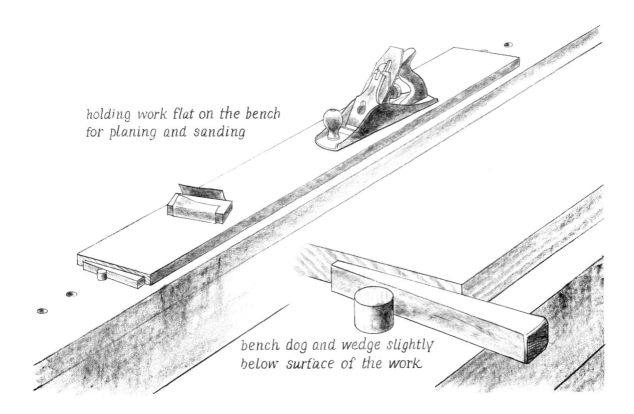

*bench dog and wedge slightly
below surface of the work*

vise and face of bench should be plumb

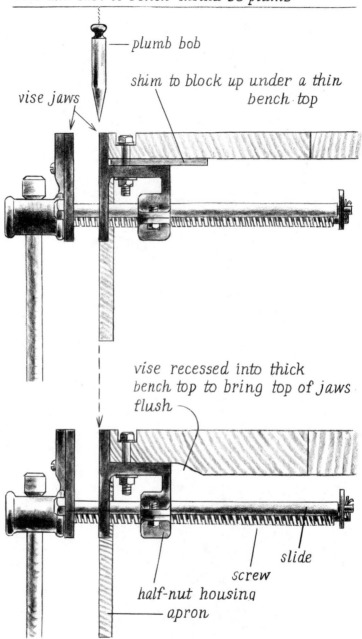

— plumb bob

shim to block up under a thin
bench top

vise jaws

vise recessed into thick
bench top to bring top of jaws
flush

slide

screw

half-nut housing

apron

ATTACHING THE VISE    Use the manufacturer's instructions and install the vise with the top edges of the jaws exactly flush with the top of the bench. Depending on the exact thickness of your bench top, you may either have to chisel out a recess for the vise casting or build up under it with blocking. In either case, take time and use shims of tin or sheet metal to bring it right.

The inside jaw should be mounted flush and smooth with the front edge of the bench, so that the edge of the bench in fact becomes an extension of the vise. This allows clamping a board in the vise without bending or crimping it when the vise is tightened.

*hold-down for shooting grooves and moldings*

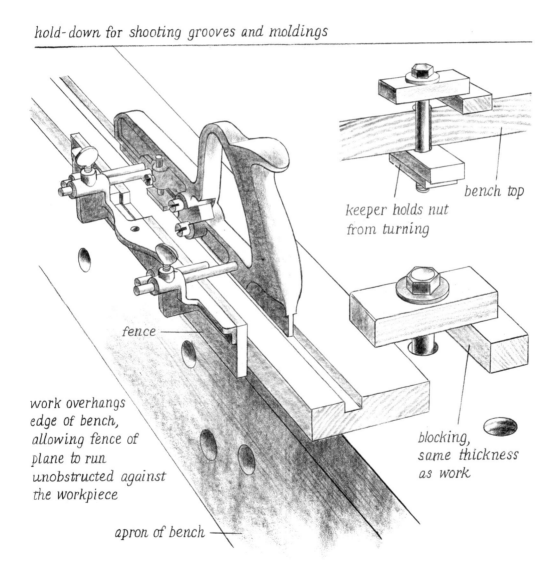

*keeper holds nut*
*from turning*

*bench top*

*fence*

*work overhangs*
*edge of bench,*
*allowing fence of*
*plane to run*
*unobstructed against*
*the workpiece*

*blocking,*
*same thickness*
*as work*

*apron of bench*

When installing a vise, it is more critical to have it plumb than it is to make it square with the bench top, although you should aim to do both. Using a plane on work held in the vise, and planing it square, is a skill that develops with the aid of instinct. If the vise is out of plumb, your planework may always tend to be out of square. A carefully installed vise saves untold hours of work in preparing good square edges.

Treat your bench and vise kindly and they will last a long time. As a surface on which to set out work and put it together, the top should be maintained flat, smooth, and without dents, gouges, and bruises.

Don't pound directly on the top; straighten nails, bolts, or metal on a separate ''beating block'' of 2-inch plank. Don't drill or bore holes in work laid flat on the bench; use a piece of scrap wood under the work or put it in the vise. Don't saw directly on the bench top; use a sawhorse or bench hook. Don't use the top for a chopping block; use the beating block. Don't use the top edges of a woodworking vise for an anvil; this practice deforms the vise which in turn spoils lumber. Don't attempt to bend thick iron in a woodworking vise.

# 3

# Anvil

A small bench anvil such as this 9-pounder has a dozen uses in a woodworking shop, and is also handy for household repair jobs. The striking face is used for hammering metal flat, and the chipping block, which is of harder steel, for cutting metal with a cold chisel. Both ends—horn and heel—can be used to good advantage either by standing the anvil on end, or by clamping the horn in the vise. Although provided with holes for bolting down, this little anvil is a lot more useful if left loose, since it is light enough to hold in one hand, or to carry about.

*setting glazier's points*

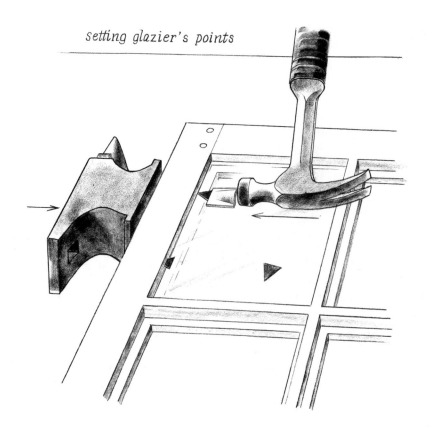

*for small glue jobs*

*clinching nails*

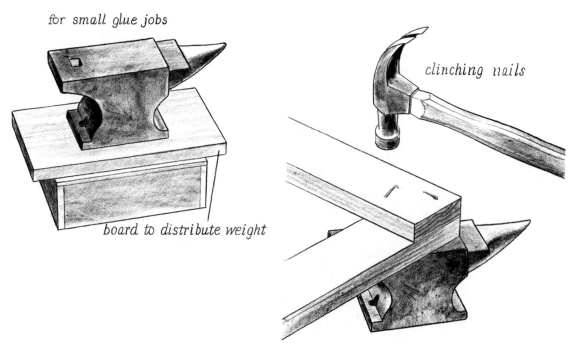

*board to distribute weight*

*used as a bucking iron*

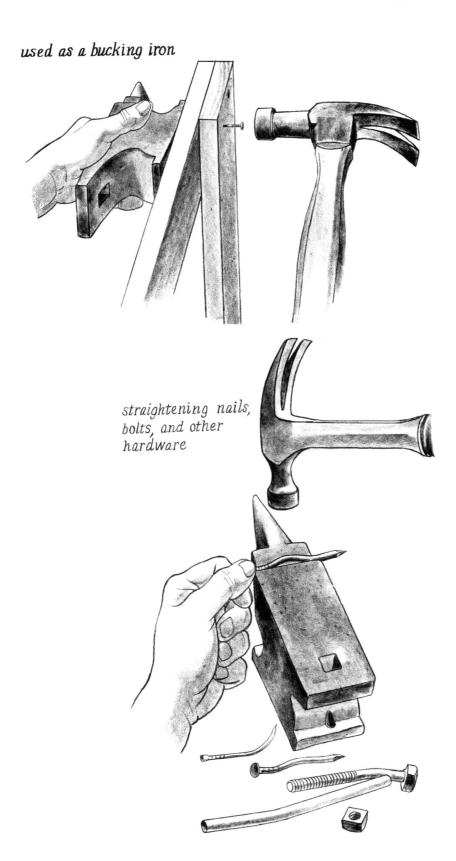

*straightening nails, bolts, and other hardware*

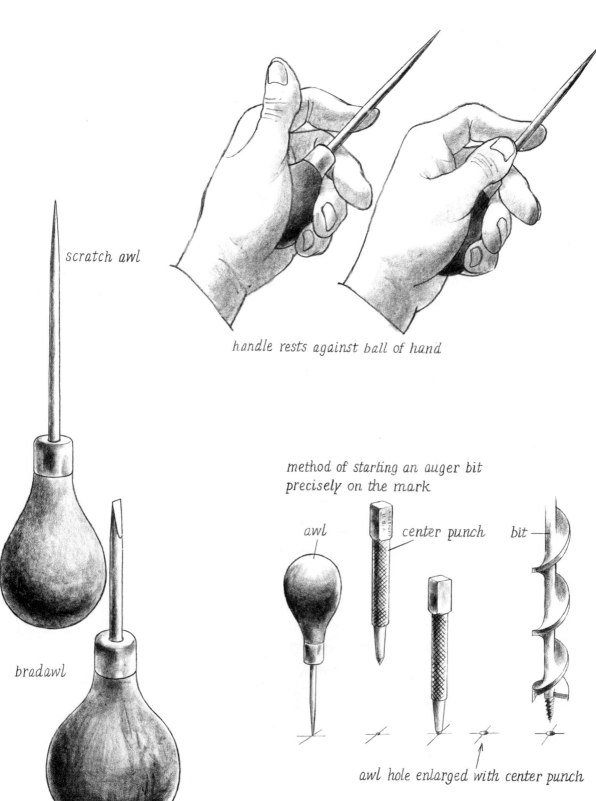

scratch awl

handle rests against ball of hand

bradawl

method of starting an auger bit
precisely on the mark

awl          center punch          bit

awl hole enlarged with center punch

# 4

# Awl

An awl is primarily a softwood tool traditionally used to make starting holes for nails, brads, and screws. Without a pilot hole, a driven nail often veers off when it strikes the hard annular rings of the wood. Thus the function of the awl is to make a straight-in hole, to engage sufficient length of the nail or screw so it can be driven the rest of the way without going crooked.

The simplest awl—called a scratch awl—has a round shank tapered to a sharp point, and resembles a shortened ice pick. The hole is made by the point puncturing the surface and the tapered shank spreading the wood fibers. In wood with a pronounced hard grain, the scratch awl tends to slip off the hard annular rings, making it difficult to locate the hole in a precise spot.

Here's where the bradawl with a chisel point works better. To start a bradawl, set the chisel point *across* the grain, push on the awl to *cut* the grain, then twist it back and forth as it is pushed in farther.

As a maker of pilot holes, the usefulness of the awl is pretty much limited to brads, small nails, and small screws. Larger holes for bigger fasteners are more satisfactorily made with a hand drill.

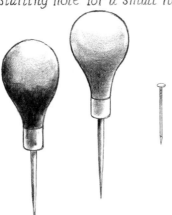

*using a scratch awl to make
starting hole for a small nail*

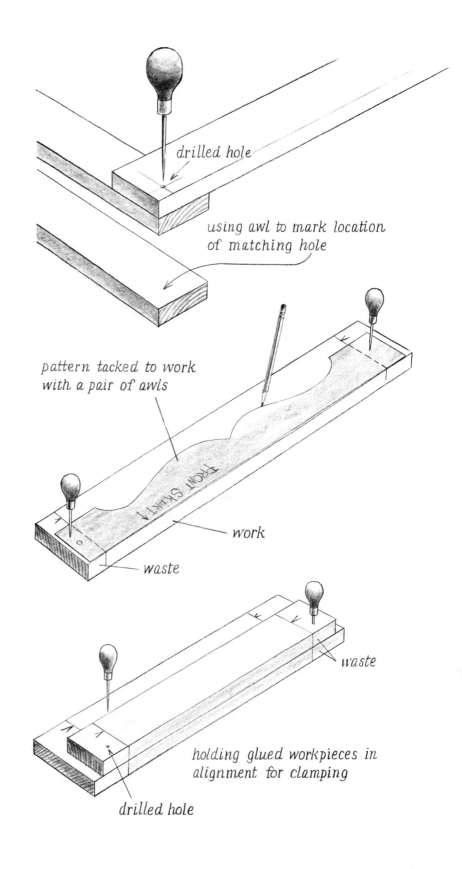

drilled hole

using awl to mark location
of matching hole

pattern tacked to work
with a pair of awls

work

waste

FRONT SKIRT

waste

holding glued workpieces in
alignment for clamping

drilled hole

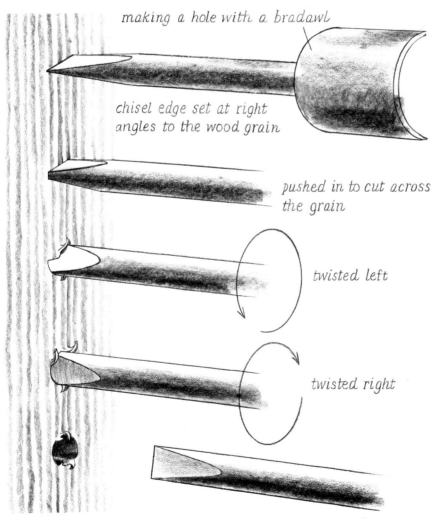

*making a hole with a bradawl*

*chisel edge set at right angles to the wood grain*

*pushed in to cut across the grain*

*twisted left*

*twisted right*

*makes a more ragged hole than a drill*

# 5

# Brace & Bits

This gentleman—plainly a chair-maker from another time—is holding a solid-wood brace, one of the chief tools of his trade used for boring holes. Fitted into the foot of the brace is a spoon bit, the part that did the cutting. And strapped to his chest is a breast bib to make it all work. This tool combination required considerable pressure to bore a hole. The head of the brace fitted into the cupped hollow of the bib, leaving both hands free to operate the brace. This brace did have a revolving head, or the work would have been even more difficult. By leaning on the bib, pressure was transmitted to the bit. Since the spoon bit was permanently fixed in the foot end of the brace, a man had a separate brace for each size of bit he customarily used.

## Mechanics of the Bit Brace

Boring a hole is a lot easier today. The modern brace is a sophisticated piece of equipment and one of the few tools that shows any noticeable improvement over its ancient counterpart. A first-class modern brace has a self-centering two-jaw chuck that takes bits of all sizes, and a box ratchet: a drive mechanism consisting of two pawls riding over a splined shaft. By turning the cam ring right or left, one pawl or the other is engaged with the splined shaft, allowing the brace to work either forward or in reverse; and with the cam ring in neutral,

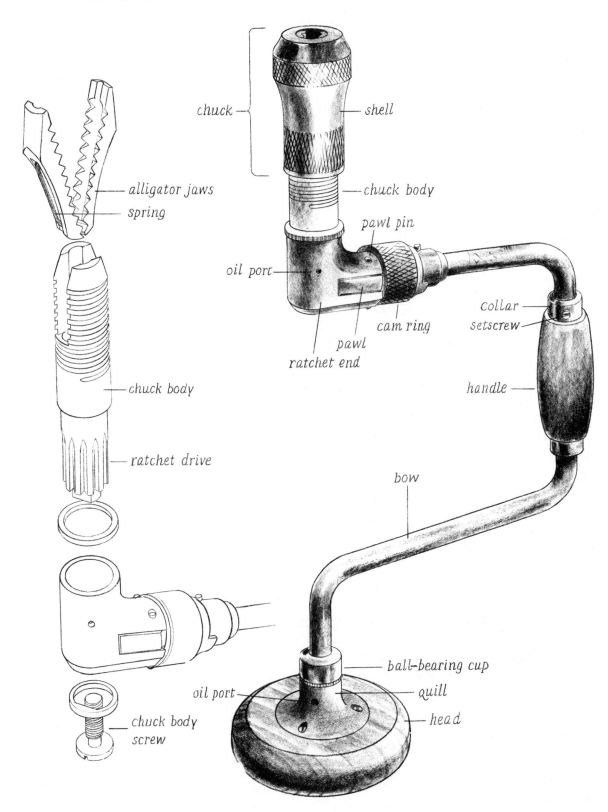

chuck

shell

alligator jaws

spring

chuck body

pawl pin

oil port

chuck body

cam ring

pawl

ratchet end

collar

setscrew

ratchet drive

handle

bow

ball-bearing cup

oil port

quill

chuck body
screw

head

*cutaway view showing operation of bit brace chuck*

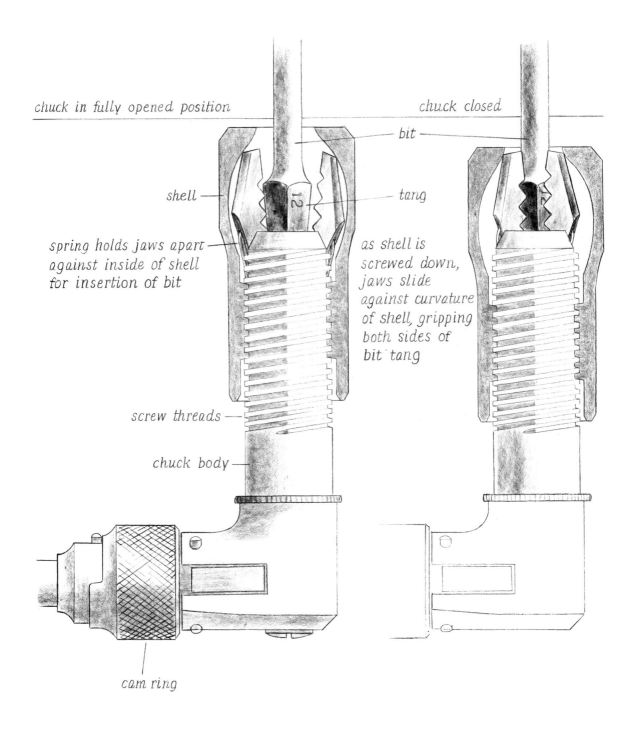

*chuck in fully opened position*

*chuck closed*

bit

shell

tang

*spring holds jaws apart against inside of shell for insertion of bit*

*as shell is screwed down, jaws slide against curvature of shell, gripping both sides of bit tang*

*screw threads*

*chuck body*

*cam ring*

*adjusting the cam ring*

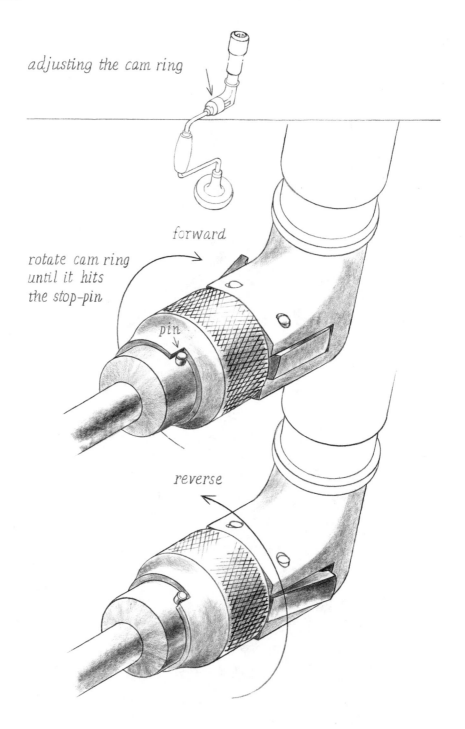

*forward*

*rotate cam ring
until it hits
the stop-pin*

*pin*

*reverse*

*schematic: mechanics of the ratchet drive*

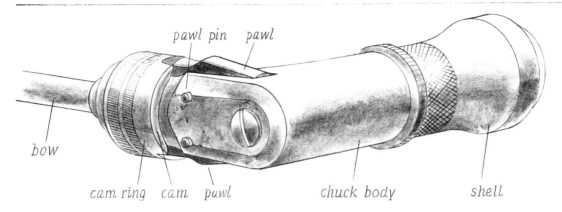

pawl pin   pawl

bow

cam ring   cam   pawl     chuck body          shell

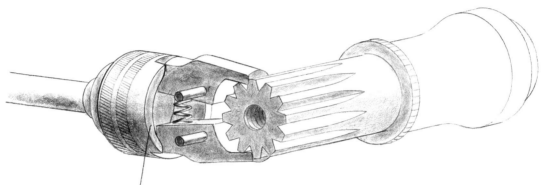

*cam ring in neutral position: both pawls are engaged, brace can be operated either forward or in reverse*

*cam ring rotated ¼ turn into reverse position,
the cam lifts and disengages the pawl, while the spring keeps the other
pawl driving the chuck in one direction only*

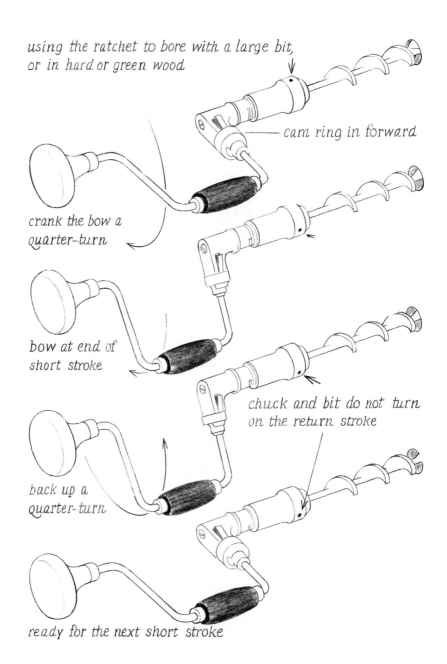

using the ratchet to bore with a large bit,
or in hard or green wood

cam ring in forward

crank the bow a
quarter-turn

bow at end of
short stroke

chuck and bit do not turn
on the return stroke

back up a
quarter-turn

ready for the next short stroke

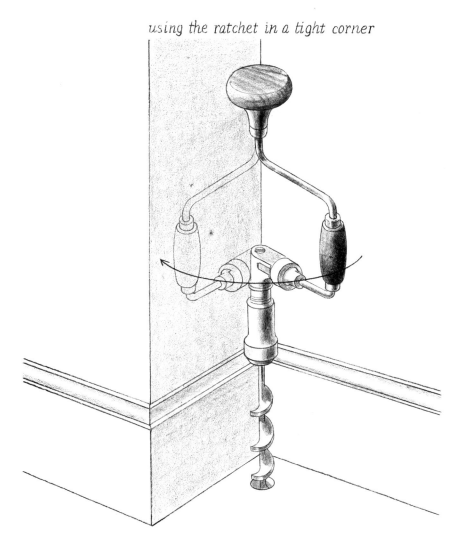

*using the ratchet in a tight corner*

the brace will turn in either direction independently of the ratchet. The beauty of the ratchet is that the bow can be swung a quarter-turn, backed up, then swung another quarter-turn, using only that part of its sweep that is convenient for an arm and hand position of maximum force: on the return stroke, the pawl clicks over the splined shaft without turning the bit. This avoids having to carry through a complete revolution of the bow, which often entails working the arm and hand in an awkward or ineffectual position. The ratchet is a great advantage in boring large holes, or boring in green and hardwood where greater force is needed. And it works in tight corners where a full sweep of the bow is impossible.

Other features include drop-forged steel construction, ball-bearing head, rotating wooden hand grip, oil ports, and provision for dismantling for cleaning and lubrication. Braces are made in several sizes, designated by the length of throw. A short 4-inch throw is fine for average light shopwork, but for boring thick stuff and in green or hardwood where more leverage is needed, a 5-inch or 6-inch throw is better. And of course the longer throw will handle either light or heavy work.

*the size of a brace is specified by the length of its throw*

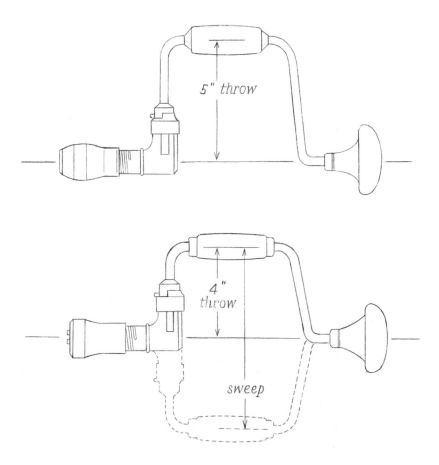

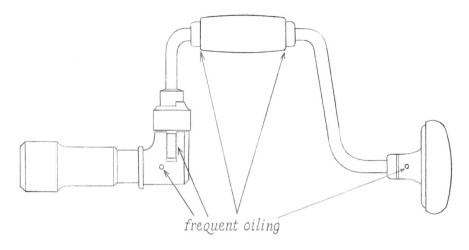

*frequent oiling*

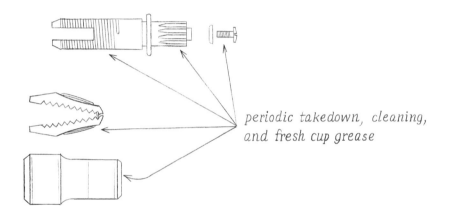

*periodic takedown, cleaning, and fresh cup grease*

# Maintenance

Periodically—at least twice a year—unscrew the shell, remove the jaws and clean out all sawdust, dirt, and old grease with a toothbrush and kerosene. Clean up the threads the same way. Then dry the parts with a clean cloth. Rinse out the cam ring assembly and bearings of the head by squirting kerosene from an oilcan into the available openings. Let drain and wipe dry.

Wipe a good grade of grease on all the chuck parts, and reassemble it. Oil the other moving parts with machine oil or light motor oil, rotating or working the parts so the oil penetrates thoroughly. Several times a year put a few drops of oil in the oil ports, especially the revolving head which gets the most wear.

Finally, wipe the excess oil and grease over the metal and wooden parts alike, then hang the brace on the rack. Any further drippings can be wiped off next time it's used.

*opening the chuck to insert a bit*

*inserting a bit*

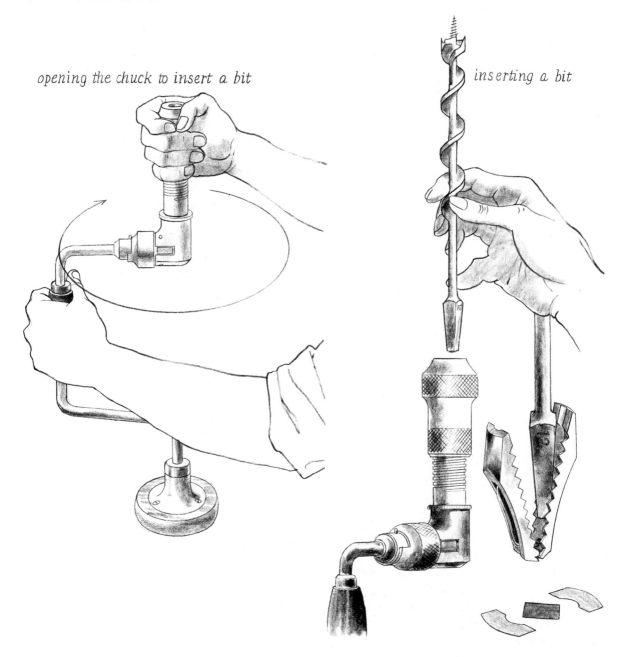

# Inserting a Bit in the Brace

Hold the brace by the chuck shell and with the other hand crank the bow round clockwise a few turns to open the jaws. Put the bit into the chuck, making sure that two opposing corners of the bit tang engage in the V grooves of the jaws. Turn the bow the other way to tighten the jaws. Then rotate the cam ring to the right, which locks the ratchet in forward position. Finally, give the chuck shell a hard twist to make sure the bit is good and tight. You're ready to bore a hole.

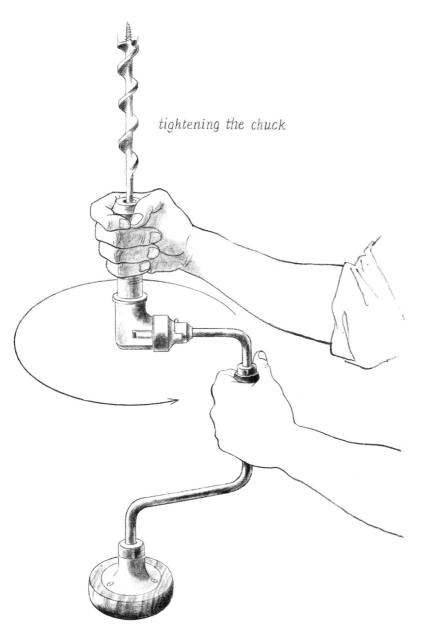

*tightening the chuck*

*how an auger bit works*

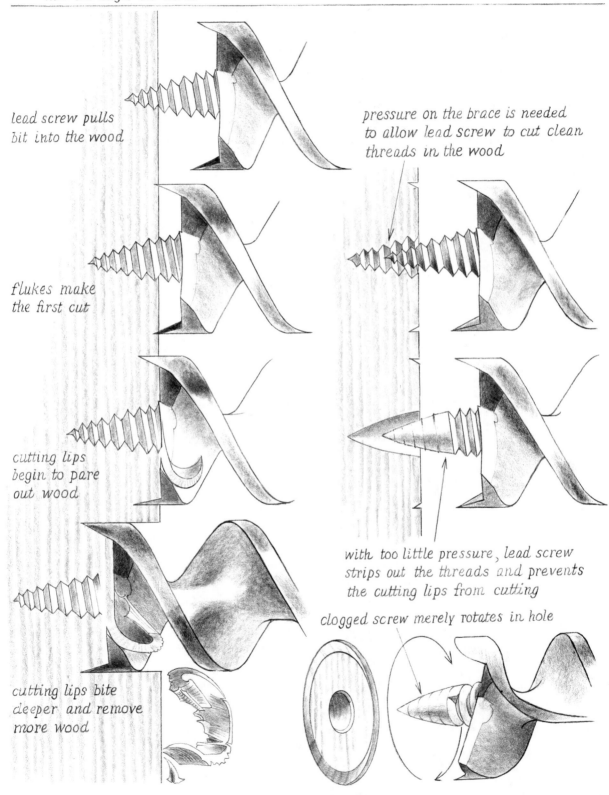

lead screw pulls
bit into the wood

pressure on the brace is needed
to allow lead screw to cut clean
threads in the wood

flukes make
the first cut

cutting lips
begin to pare
out wood

with too little pressure, lead screw
strips out the threads and prevents
the cutting lips from cutting

clogged screw merely rotates in hole

cutting lips bite
deeper and remove
more wood

# How a Bit Works

An auger bit has six working parts: a lead screw, two flukes, two cutting lips, and the twist. As the brace is turned, the lead screw pulls the bit into the wood, the flukes mark out (score) the wood to be removed, the cutting lips slice it loose, and the twist takes the wood out of the hole. They all work together; they must all be sharp; and for maximum efficiency must all be of the correct relative *lengths*.

These are the mechanical aspects of boring a hole. The rest is up to the operator: how the brace is held, how much pressure is applied, and the work methods that are used. The head of the brace is cupped in one hand, the bow cranked with the other. And force is applied by pushing against the forehead, chest, stomach, or thigh.

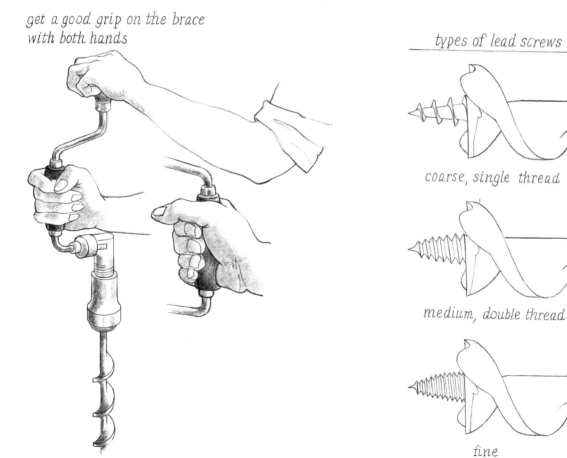

*get a good grip on the brace with both hands*

*types of lead screws*

*coarse, single thread*

*medium, double thread*

*fine*

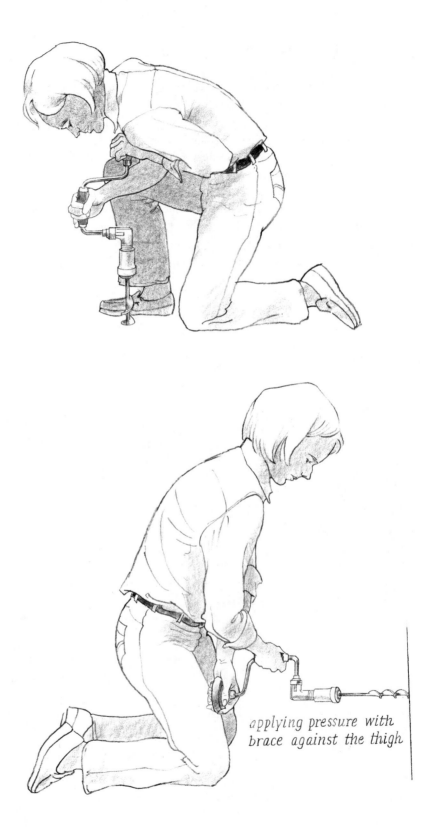

*applying pressure with
brace against the thigh*

*holding the brace against the abdomen for pressure*

*braced against the shoulder*

*single twist auger bit*

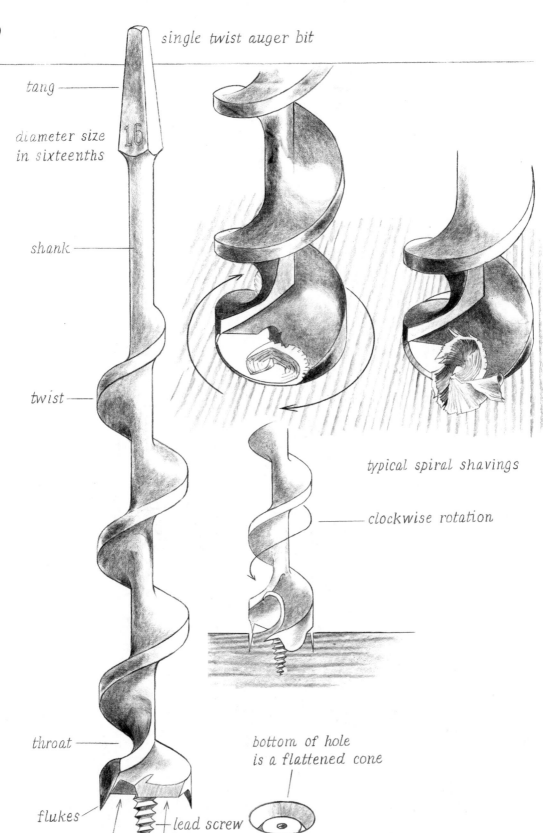

tang

diameter size
in sixteenths

16

shank

twist

*typical spiral shavings*

*clockwise rotation*

throat

bottom of hole
is a flattened cone

flukes

lead screw

cutting lips

When a bit is in good condition—sharp and not much worn—it will bore into softwood with very little pressure. It wants to cut. In hardwood, however, some extra pressure is needed. Held back by the resistance of the wood, the screw tends to strip the wood threads it has cut. The screw gets clogged and then merely rotates in a hole where there's nothing for it to take hold of. With the pulling action stopped, the flukes can't reach into new wood, and neither can the cutting lips. The larger the bit, the more pronounced this tendency: compared to a 3/8-inch bit a 1-inch bit cuts two and a half times as much wood with each turn and with a proportionate increase in resistance. Clogging is most common in end-grain boring, where the screw threads cut off the annual rings, which then pull loose. Putting extra pressure on the brace helps to keep the lead screw pulling and sometimes prevents stripping.

# Cleaning the Screw

When the screw does get clogged—as it will many times—it must be cleared before working it again. The thumbnail does the job fine, but if you don't like working that close to the sharp flukes, use a chip of wood or, better still, a modified spring clothespin. Set the clothespin jaws in the screw thread next to the cutting lips and flukes. Pinch the clothespin between thumb and finger, then turn the bit backward, or counterclockwise. This should strip out all the wood. Don't under any circumstances use a nail, knife, file, or anything metal—it will dull the screw threads.

*clearing a clogged lead screw*

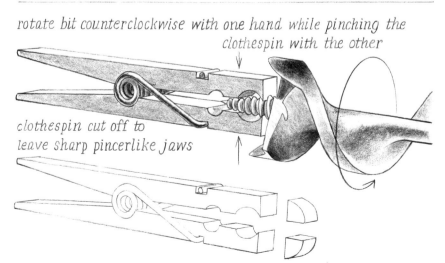

*rotate bit counterclockwise with one hand while pinching the clothespin with the other*

*clothespin cut off to leave sharp pincerlike jaws*

*method of boring a clean hole*

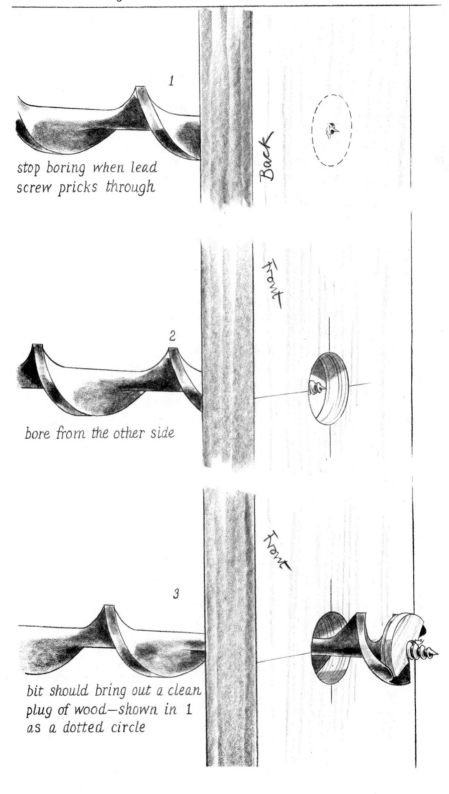

1

stop boring when lead
screw pricks through

Back

2

bore from the other side

Front

3

bit should bring out a clean
plug of wood—shown in 1
as a dotted circle

Front

boring clear through from one side invariably
splinters the other side of the work

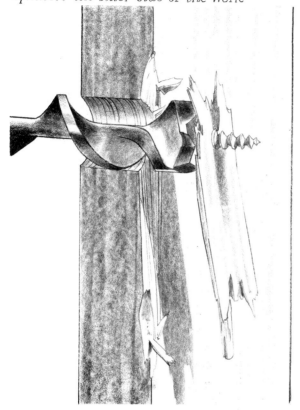

using a piece of scrap wood to get a clean
exit hole in the work

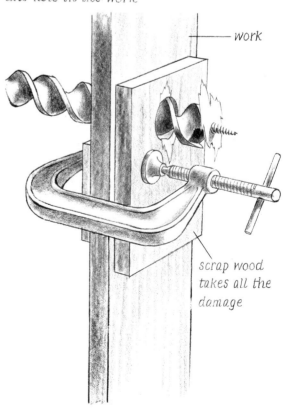

— work

scrap wood
takes all the
damage

*brad point drill*

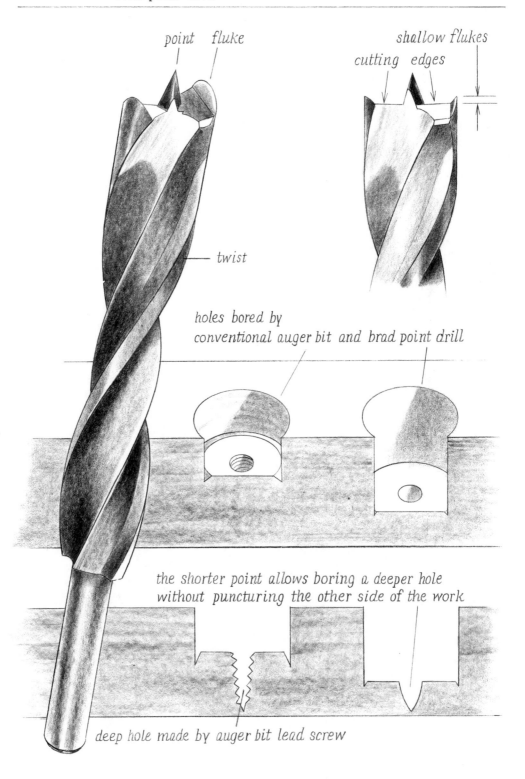

point   fluke

shallow flukes
cutting  edges

twist

holes bored by
conventional auger bit and brad point drill

the shorter point allows boring a deeper hole
without puncturing the other side of the work

deep hole made by auger bit lead screw

# Brad Point Drill

These drills are especially good for fine work where a nice sharp-edged hole is wanted with a comparatively flat bottom. They have round shanks and are made in a range of standard sizes. Instead of a lead screw, there is a sharp brad point which centers the drill, and the twist is similar to that of the conventional high-speed twist drill. Because the flukes are quite short the brad point drill should be started very slowly to prevent tearing up the wood on entry. Once the initial cut has been made, however, considerable pressure on the brace is needed, since this drill does not pull itself into the wood. Because of their shallow dimensions, these drills must be sharpened with extreme care.

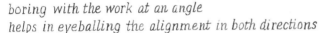

*boring with the work at an angle*
*helps in eyeballing the alignment in both directions*

# Boring Straight

Boring a straight hole—square or perpendicular to the work—is largely a matter of gauging by eye and instinct. There is no attachment for the brace that guarantees perfection. Boring straight is a freehand operation that must be learned by trial and error, much concentrated practice, and by observing the results of trials. And then more practice. There are several trial techniques that may be of some help in training the eye, but that's all they are—training aids.

MEASURED TRIALS    On a piece of scrap wood mark out the center point for a hole, and carry the marks over to the other side of the wood. Use a square and measure accurately to get both points in correspondingly identical locations. Start the bit on one center point, and bore until just the point of the lead screw pricks through the other side of the wood. The bore is perfect if the point hits the corresponding center mark. If it misses the mark, note the angle of error, then make another test boring, attempting to correct the error. For example, if several trials show that you're consistently to the left, on the next ones make exaggerated compensation by aiming too far to the right. Don't let the error become a habit. Although many repeated trials may be necessary, this is one of the best methods because it relies only on eye and instinct. When boring horizontally, it is further helpful to set the work in the vise at an angle rather than straight up and down, and eyeball the alignment in both directions at once.

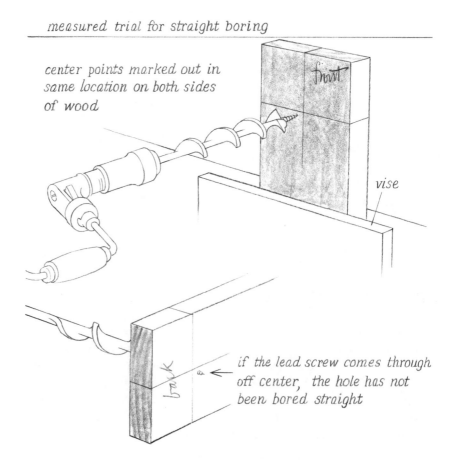

*measured trial for straight boring*

*center points marked out in same location on both sides of wood*

front

*vise*

back

*if the lead screw comes through off center, the hole has not been bored straight*

*an accurate and adjustable homemade depth gauge*

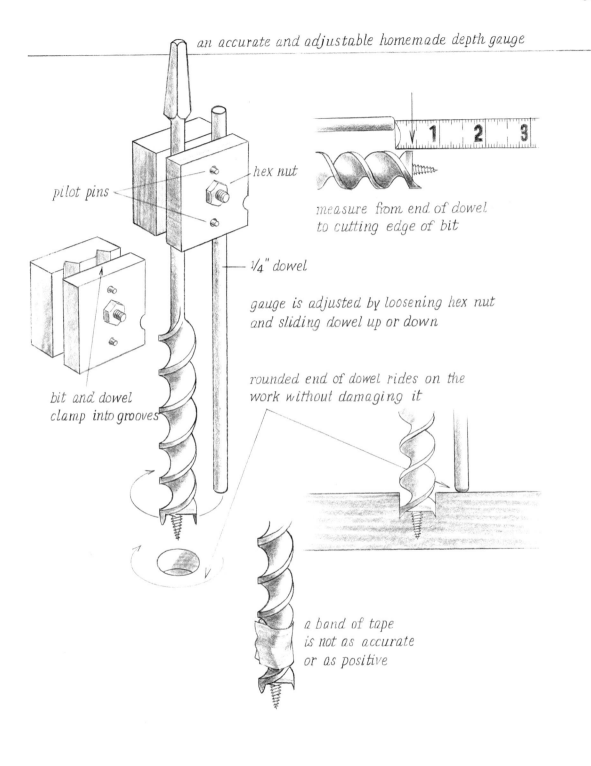

pilot pins

hex nut

¼" dowel

measure from end of dowel
to cutting edge of bit

gauge is adjusted by loosening hex nut
and sliding dowel up or down

bit and dowel
clamp into grooves

rounded end of dowel rides on the
work without damaging it

a band of tape
is not as accurate
or as positive

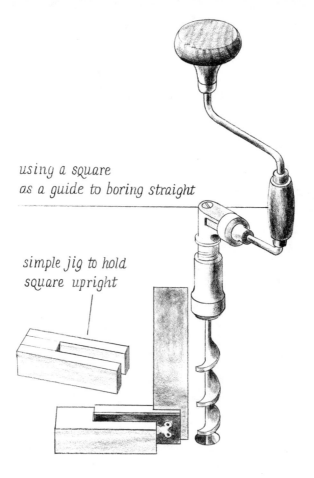

*using a square
as a guide to boring straight*

*simple jig to hold
square upright*

TRY SQUARE     To a certain extent the bit can be guided straight by using a try square or the head of a combination square. Start the bit and bore into the wood only two or three turns—just enough so the brace is supported. Set the square on the work next to the bit to see if the bit is parallel to the square. Now bore another couple of turns, making any necessary compensations, and check again with the square.

SHELF-AND-PEG     When boring horizontally with the work in the vise, this simple jig can assist the eye in keeping the bit straight. The bit lies on the shelf and the lines drawn on its top surface help keep the bit lined up straight. When the hole has been bored, insert a peg and check with the square.

BENT BIT     In softwood, it's possible to correct a bore that you see at the outset is going crooked, by shifting the position of the brace. Attempting this in hardwood, however, will bend the softer-tempered shank of the bit, causing it to wobble. Such a bend can usually be straightened by putting the tang end in a machinist's vise and putting a steady, two-hands' pulling pressure on the twist end.

Just exactly how you hold the brace—on the chest, stomach, or thigh—partially determines how straight it bores. After using whatever aids and practice prove helpful, and with increased experience, holding the brace in the most efficient position tends to become instinctive.

*shelf-and-peg trial for boring straight*

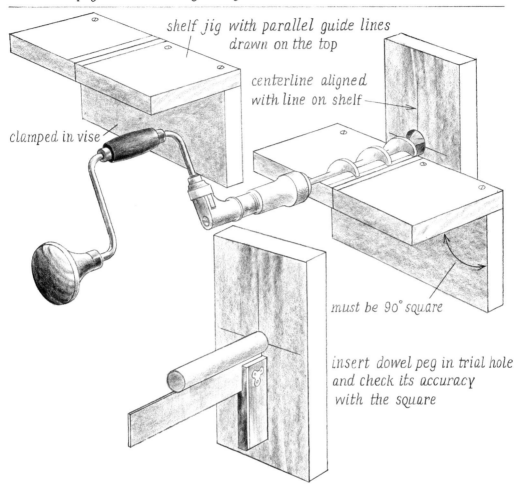

*shelf jig with parallel guide lines drawn on the top*

*centerline aligned with line on shelf*

*clamped in vise*

*must be 90° square*

*insert dowel peg in trial hole and check its accuracy with the square*

# Overheating of the Bit

The friction of boring holes always produces heat, a normal amount of which a bit is tempered to withstand. But in a very dense wood such as maple, it's a good practice to take the bit out every few turns to let it cool, avoiding the risk of drawing the temper and bending either the screw or the flukes—the thinnest and most vulnerable parts of a bit. This is especially important in very thick stuff where nonstop boring can easily make the bit too hot to touch. When the steel reaches that temperature, it doesn't take much to bend the flukes or break the lead screw.

*common types of damage to auger bits*

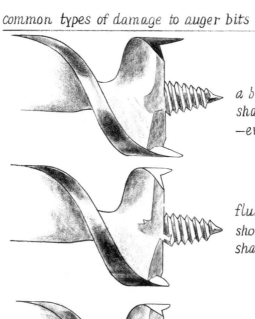

a brand new auger bit has a
sharp lead screw, long flukes
—everything in mint condition

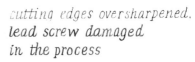

flukes have been drastically
shortened by excessive
sharpening

cutting edges oversharpened,
lead screw damaged
in the process

flukes too short, cutting edges
filed at a slant,    the bit
will work only with heavy
pressure

weakened by undercutting, the
lead screw has broken off

lead screw bent and broken,
flukes turned over

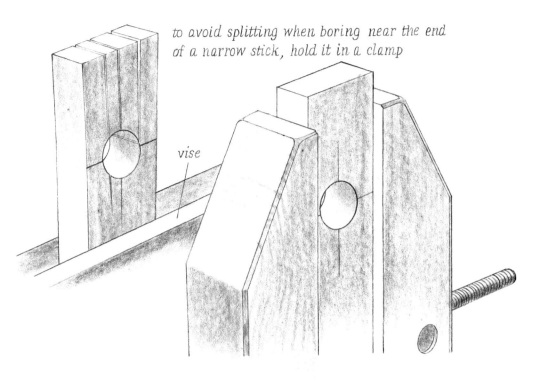

to avoid splitting when boring near the end
of a narrow stick, hold it in a clamp

*vise*

a jig for accurately boring at an angle

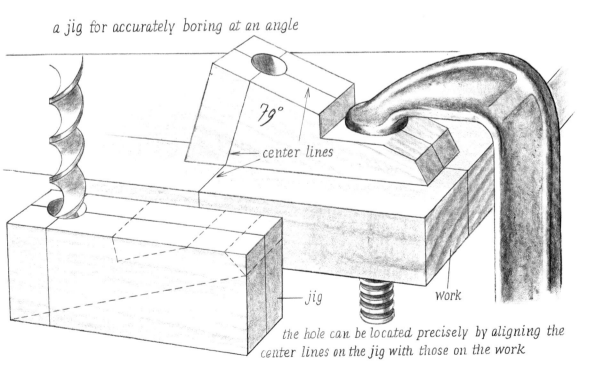

79°

center lines

jig

work

the hole can be located precisely by aligning the
center lines on the jig with those on the work

# Clearing Shavings

Ordinarily, the auger's twist does a good job of raking shavings out of the hole, even when boring in thick wood with the brace straight up. However, there are situations where shavings get jammed so tightly in the hole that the bit will hardly turn. If the wood is not completely dry, the bit will cut a rough-walled hole which readily snags and jams the shavings. And wood such as hemlock that has a stringy fiber will behave in the same way—dry or not—even if the bit is sharp.

To clear the hole, set the cam ring for reverse and back the bit out three or four turns or until the lead screw is free. Then return the cam to forward and turn the bow clockwise while at the same time pulling back on the brace to rotate the bit out of the hole, dragging the shavings with it. If any chips remain, they can usually be cleared by turning the work over and tapping it with a mallet.

# Expansive Bit

The expansive bit is used for making holes beyond the capacity of the standard auger bit, the largest of which is $1^1/_2$ inches in diameter. These bits are generally supplied with two interchangeable cutters capable of cutting holes from $7/_8$ inch to $1^1/_2$ inches, and from $1^1/_2$ inches to 3 inches.

Using an expansive bit requires considerable pressure on the brace, as well as firm control of the brace head to keep the bit aligned square to the work.

A standard auger bit has two cutters—one on each side of the bit and opposed to each other. The resistance is therefore evenly distributed to both sides of the bit, and the two cutters work in unison.

The expansive bit, on the other hand, is really a single cutter, despite its two cutting parts. Although the primary cutter starts the cut, it is the large secondary cutter that removes most of the wood. As this cutter is not balanced by an opposing one, it tends to lift out of the wood as it rotates, forcing the brace out of alignment; or to put it another way, putting the head of the brace into a wobbly orbit which makes the bit turn with difficulty without cutting much wood. This is especially true when boring in hardwood, where the normal resistance of removing so much wood with each turn of the bit is at least doubled by the density of the wood itself. Without heavy and steady pressure on the brace the screw cannot pull the bit into the wood.

*the workings of the expansive bit*

*the primary cutter bores a conventional hole which is enlarged by the secondary cutter paring off wood around the perimeter*

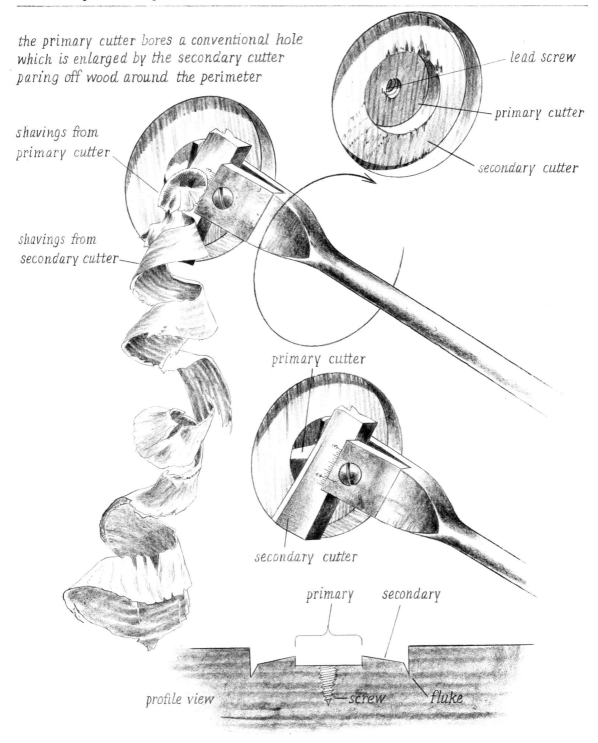

lead screw

primary cutter

secondary cutter

shavings from primary cutter

shavings from secondary cutter

primary cutter

secondary cutter

primary    secondary

*profile view*    screw    fluke

*setting and adjusting the expansive bit*

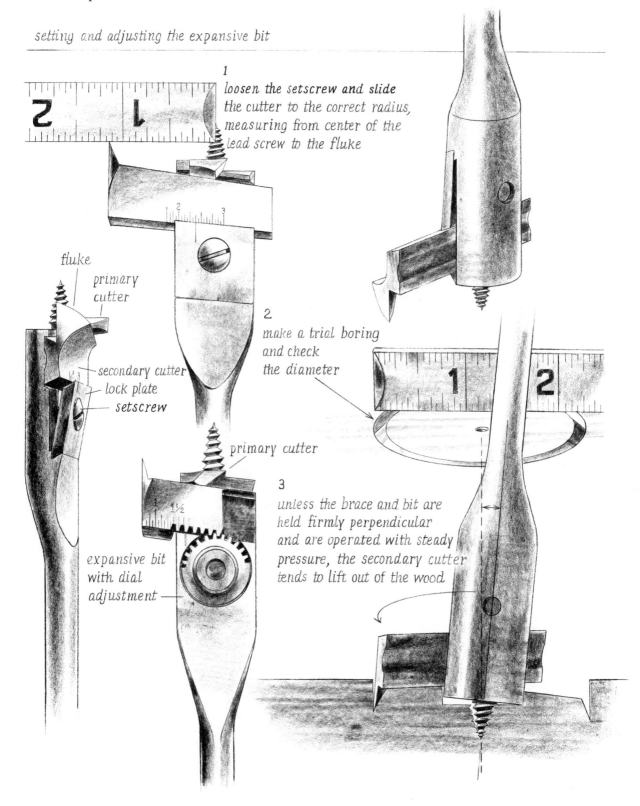

**1**
*loosen the setscrew and slide
the cutter to the correct radius,
measuring from center of the
lead screw to the fluke*

fluke

primary
cutter

secondary cutter
lock plate
*setscrew*

**2**
*make a trial boring
and check
the diameter*

primary cutter

expansive bit
with dial
adjustment

**3**
*unless the brace and bit are
held firmly perpendicular
and are operated with steady
pressure, the secondary cutter
tends to lift out of the wood*

To correct this problem, get a good hold on the brace head, and use the ratchet to make a series of short strokes—each one no more than an eighth of a revolution. Make a short stroke, cranking the brace in whatever part of its sweep gives the most forceful control. Then back up with the ratchet and make another short stroke, and so on. With this technique, the bit will remove wood uniformly round and round, and your elbow grease will be used to the best advantage.

ADJUSTING THE CUTTER    To set the cutter, loosen the setscrew and move the cutter in or out to the correct diameter setting. Most expansive bits have a calibrated scale etched on the cutter, and a gauge mark to which the cutter is set for the diameter. In one type, the cutter is moved in or out by turning a dial gear, while the other type is adjusted manually. In either case you must check the setting with a rule. However, neither the dial, the scale, nor the rule is accurate enough to simply set the cutter and start boring.

The diameter as set by the calibration on the bit probably won't match the measurement on the rule and most likely neither of them will correspond to the actual size of the bored hole. The only guarantee of accuracy is to set the cutter by the rule, measuring the radius *from fluke to screw point*. Then make a trial cut, checking and readjusting the bit as necessary. It may take three or four trials to get an accurate hole diameter. Then check to see that the setscrew is tight.

# Driving Screws

The brace and screwdriver bit has advantages over a hand screwdriver: more pressure can be exerted to hold the bit in the screw slot, and the bow gives far more leverage. Match the size of screwdriver bit to the size of the screw and its slot. Bits are made in several sizes for this purpose. The bit should fit well down into the slot to prevent its climbing out, slipping off the screw, and damaging the surface of the work. When this happens, the screw slot is usually damaged in the process as well, making it hard to get a good purchase, and more difficult to finish driving the screw.

Put the bit in the chuck, tighten it, and set the cam ring in forward. The ratchet allows not only good pressure and leverage in hardwood, but also drives screws in awkward corners where a hand screwdriver cannot be given sufficient pressure. It's advisable to first drill a pilot hole for the screw and tap the screw into it with a hammer to set it

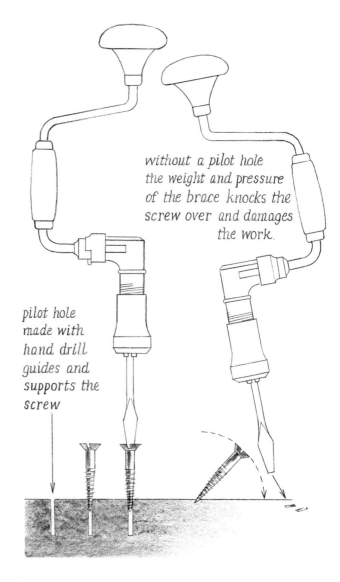

without a pilot hole
the weight and pressure
of the brace knocks the
screw over and damages
the work.

pilot hole
made with
hand drill
guides and
supports the
screw

screwdriver bits

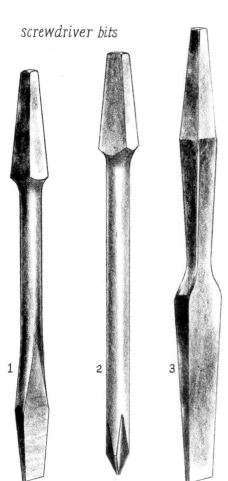

1  common flat blade

2  Phillips pattern

3  older types will work
   in a modern brace

*width and thickness of screwdriver bit should match the screw slot*

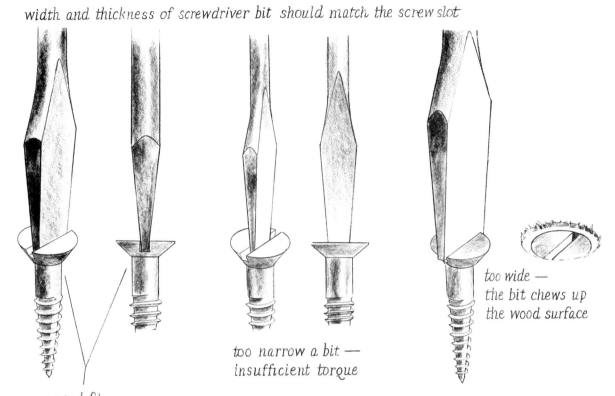

*too wide —*
*the bit chews up*
*the wood surface*

*too narrow a bit —*
*insufficient torque*

*a good fit —*
*blade fills the slot, maximum torque, minimal chance of jumping out*

straight. Otherwise, the weight of the brace will tilt the screw sideways. When driving screws in hardwood it is particularly important to make a pilot hole of the correct diameter and depth. Hardwood takes a vise grip on screws, and in a too-small pilot hole the tremendous crank leverage of the brace can easily overheat a screw and break it.

# Removing Screws

Screws are removed by setting the cam in reverse and cranking the bow counterclockwise. Just as much pressure is needed to remove a screw—sometimes more with a stubborn one—and just as much care to prevent the bit from jumping out of the slot. A hard-set screw can often be "started" by setting a hand screwdriver in the slot and giving the end of the handle a couple of smart whacks with a hammer. This jars loose the bond between wood and screw threads, in most cases enough so the screw will turn.

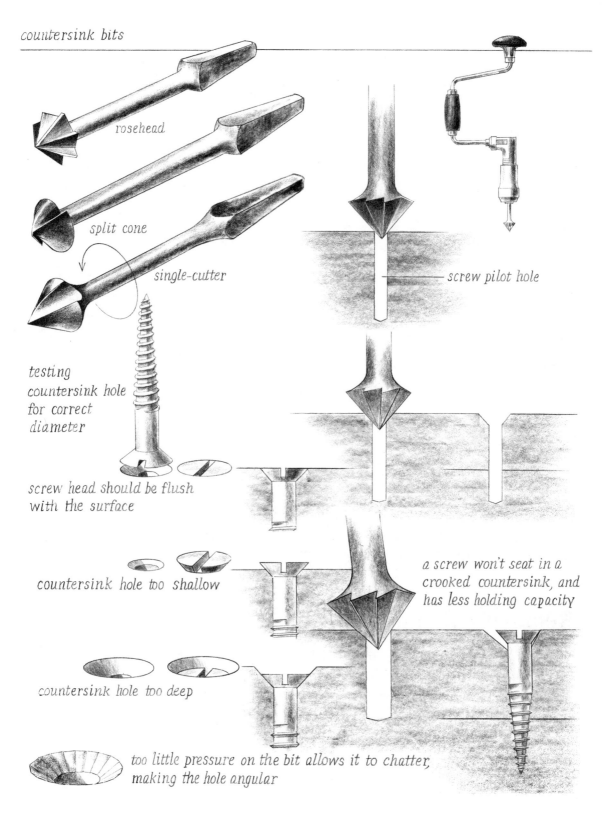

countersink bits

rosehead

split cone

single-cutter

screw pilot hole

testing
countersink hole
for correct
diameter

screw head should be flush
with the surface

countersink hole too shallow

a screw won't seat in a
crooked countersink, and
has less holding capacity

countersink hole too deep

too little pressure on the bit allows it to chatter,
making the hole angular

# Countersink

The countersink bit is designed to cut a beveled recess for a screw head, allowing it to lie flush with the surface. The most common countersink is the rosehead, whose multiple cutting edges tend to do the smoothest job. The bit should be sharp, especially for pine and other softwoods, otherwise the wood will be torn and left ragged. A fair amount of pressure is needed on the brace while keeping the bit perpendicular and turning the brace at a steady rate of speed. Too little pressure allows the bit to chatter—ride up and down—as it cuts across the wood grain, making the beveled hole rough and angular rather than smooth. Where a number of identical holes are to be made, counting the same number of revolutions of the brace will produce quite uniform results.

Usually the screw pilot hole is drilled first and the countersink last. However, this does not always produce a clean, round bevel. It is often better to do the countersinking first, drilling the screw hole afterward. Not all wood species behave uniformly well, so it is best to make a few trials on scrap wood.

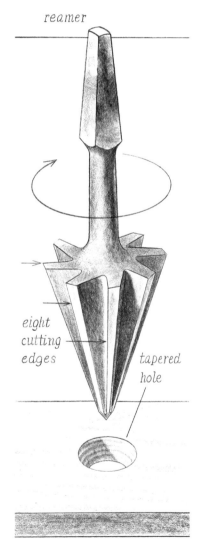

*reamer*

*eight cutting edges*

*tapered hole*

# Reamer

The reamer is a tapered cutting bit used for enlarging holes. With multiple cutting edges, it works on the same principle as the rosehead countersink, shaving off small amounts of material with each turn. Reams are made in various lengths and diameters, a common model having the capacity to enlarge a hole from $1/4$ inch to $1$-$1/8$ inches. A hole enlarged with a reamer will, of course, have a tapered diameter, which means that the reamer is most useful on thin gauge metals or where precision is not of prime importance. Used on wood, the reamer is limited to comparatively rough work where appearance and finish are of secondary importance.

*counterboring to conceal a screw under a wood plug*

A : *counterbore hole for plug*

   *make hole a stock size to match
   both dowel plug and auger bit —
   and big enough to accommodate
   the countersink bit*

B: *drill screw pilot hole*

C: *countersink pilot hole*

*countersink bit*

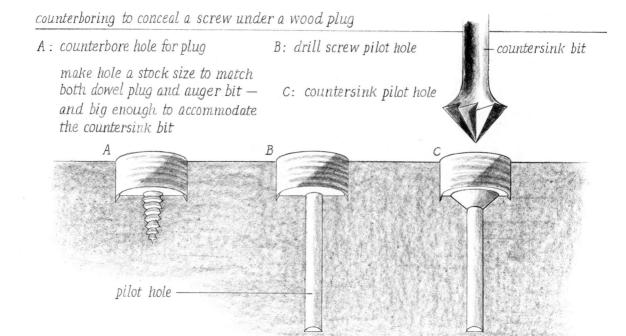

*pilot hole*

D: *turn the screw as tight as possible, glue and drive the plug*

E: *let glue dry thoroughly*

F: *trim plug flush with surface*

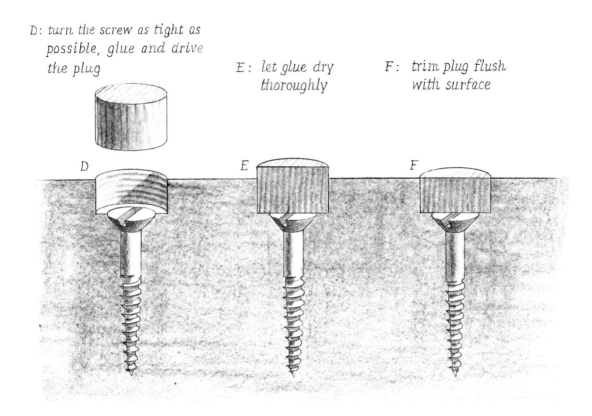

*wire, or scratch brushes*

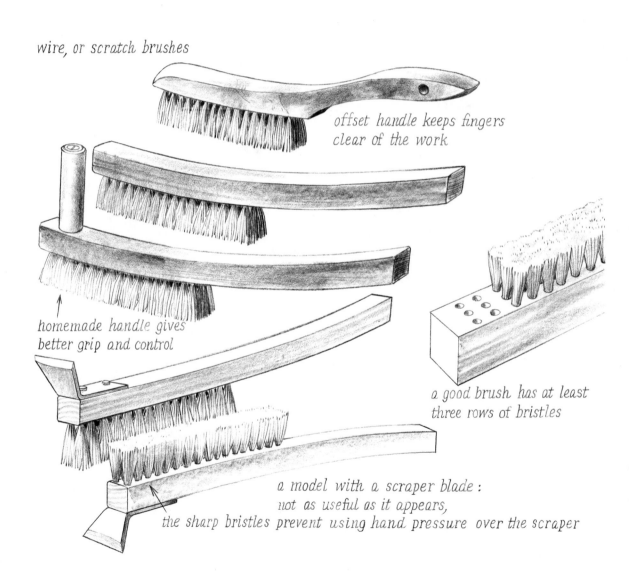

*offset handle keeps fingers
clear of the work*

*homemade handle gives
better grip and control*

*a good brush has at least
three rows of bristles*

*a model with a scraper blade:
not as useful as it appears,
the sharp bristles prevent using hand pressure over the scraper*

# 6

# Wire Brush

The wire brush is made to order for removing caked oil and rust, cleaning crud out of bolt and screw threads, cleaning the teeth of files and rasps, and removing old paint from metal. You can also use it to brighten metal for soldering, remove soot and dirt from brickwork, and do the same for blackened kitchen utensils. This is not a smoothing tool: don't use it on wood, as it cuts deeply into the grain.

They come in various lengths and handle shapes and are often called welder's or scratch brushes. A good one has three rows of springy steel wire tufts set closely together so that their ends form a solid wire surface with no gaps. Made this way, every tuft supports its neighbor and won't bend over. A handle that curves up at the end is better than a straight one, as the fingers are less likely to get barked. Some models have a scraper on the end but this is of little value: it gets in the way of the hand when scraping as well as when brushing.

Although it looks like a one-hand tool, you'll have better control over pressure and motion by holding it with both hands, the same as with a plane or file. And it's important to hold the work firmly in the vise, or clamp it down. Use a moderate pressure, and keep the bottom of the brush on a constant level as you "saw" the brush back and forth. Don't bear down with all your might, otherwise the bristles will splay out, bending the wires into a scraggly mass.

*as you work, rap brush on bench to dislodge any accumulation*

*cleaning rust, paint, and gum from tools and hardware*

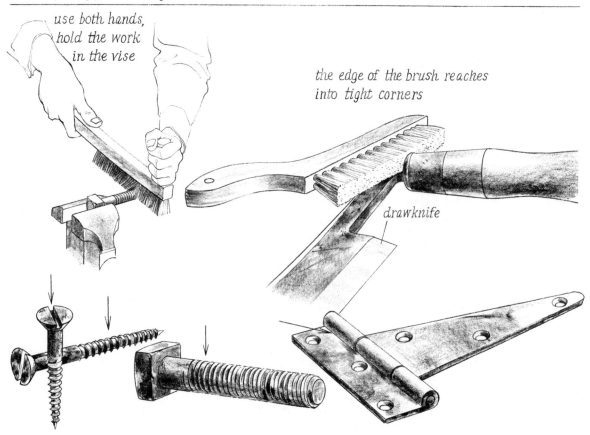

use both hands,
hold the work
in the vise

the edge of the brush reaches
into tight corners

drawknife

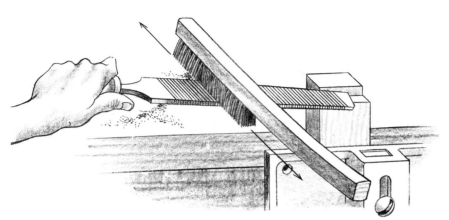

*run brush through file grooves to clean out caked sawdust*

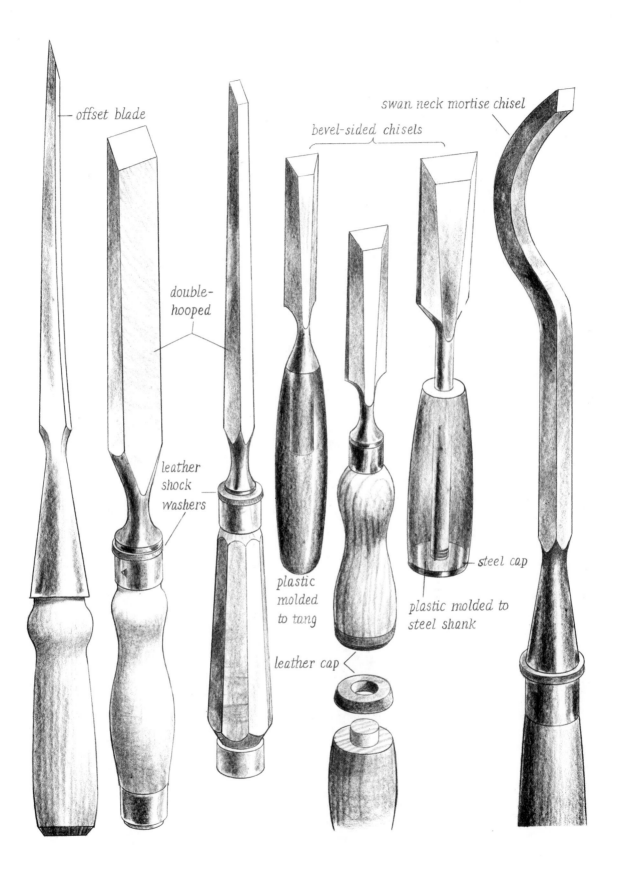

offset blade

double-
hooped

swan neck mortise chisel

bevel-sided chisels

leather
shock
washers

plastic
molded
to tang

leather cap

steel cap

plastic molded to
steel shank

# 7

# Chisels

Chisels are used for cutting joints, for shaping, and for trimming up the work done by saw, brace and bit, and plane. Depending on the particular job, you can hold the chisel with the bevel either up or down, use a mallet for heavy chopping, or just the hands for finer, more delicate paring. In any case, use both hands—one to control the point of the chisel, the other to push it or wield the mallet.

A chisel should not be used with the same abandon as a crowbar. Don't try to pry loose great chunks of wood, especially in hardwood. Tough as it is, a chisel may snap off close to the cutting edge where the steel is the most brittle, or its handle may break.

## Construction

Chisels are made in two types—one to be hand-pushed, the other to be struck with a mallet. Hand chisels are quite strong enough for anything your hands can do. Some of these lightweights are advertised as able to withstand "light mallet blows," but if the work needs a mallet at all, use a socket chisel that's made to take it. Otherwise, the handle may split or break away from the steel tang.

Within these two types are two variations of pattern. The straight-sided chisel is the strongest for heavy work, and of course will do light work as well. The bevel-sided pattern is made to work into tight-angled corners, but this is a negligible advantage. I prefer the straight-sided blade not just for its greater strength, but because a more positive purchase for thumb and fingers is possible when holding it up near the cutting end.

Chisel nomenclature has become needlessly confusing, as you can see by looking at the tool cataloges. In the main, however, the number of pattern variations comes down to: stubby blade (butt chisel), extra

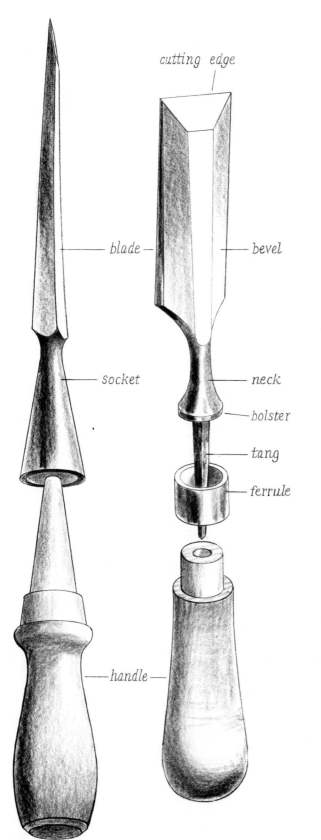

cutting edge

blade

bevel

socket

neck

bolster

tang

ferrule

handle

*using the shoulder muscles for pressure to pare and fit the end of a mortise*

long blade (patternmaker's), and intermediate length blade (firmer). It isn't essential to remember these names or to reconcile their conflicting meanings. The important thing is to understand the strengths and weaknesses of the main types, and to choose the one that will do the most work.

HANDLES     Handles are now made of plastic as well as wood. While polypropylene may be able to withstand hammer blows, so will a good ash or hickory handle, and a wooden handle can be replaced with a store-bought or homemade one. Because for strength the plastic must be molded around a core larger than a conventional chisel tang, replacing a broken handle—and they do shatter—is next to impossible. What remains cannot satisfactorily be fitted to a wooden handle. Handles are made in several different shapes: some round and smooth, others in various hand-grip shapes, and some octagon-shaped. While you may not always find the perfect handle on the chisel you want, try for a pattern that comfortably fits your hand and gives good control.

WHAT KIND AND HOW MANY     Chisels of every size are used so often on every imaginable job that a full set is almost essential. They are made in standard sizes designated by width of blade from $1/4$ inch to 2 inches. Four of the most commonly used sizes are $1/4$, $1/2$, $3/4$, and 1 inch. These match the standard sizes of other tools such as auger bits and the cutter irons of the grooving plane. Add another five sizes—

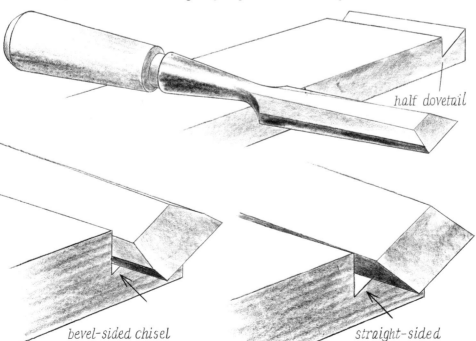

*bevel-sided chisel works only slightly farther into tight corners*

*half dovetail*

*bevel-sided chisel*

*straight-sided*

$^1/_8$, $^5/_{16}$, $^3/_8$, $^5/_8$, and $^7/_8$ inch—and you would be equipped for just about anything except cutting the joints in a barn frame. For this class of heavy work there are the socket slicks with blades from $2^3/_8$ inches to $3^3/_8$ inches wide. These giants have handles about 18 inches long and are meant to be held in both hands and braced against the shoulder when smoothing large surfaces and fitting joints.

All things considered, a good choice is the straight-sided, heavy-duty chisel with double-hooped wooden handle. These chisels are rugged enough to stand a lot of pounding, long enough to cut a deep mortise, and are comfortable for even fine paring. The straight-sided socket model is a close second, although it's doubtful that the leather-capped handle can take as much abuse. Still, replacing a socket handle is considerably easier. They both cost about the same, so any difference in price is secondary to getting the one you want.

*cutting flat in a straight line — close to the mark*

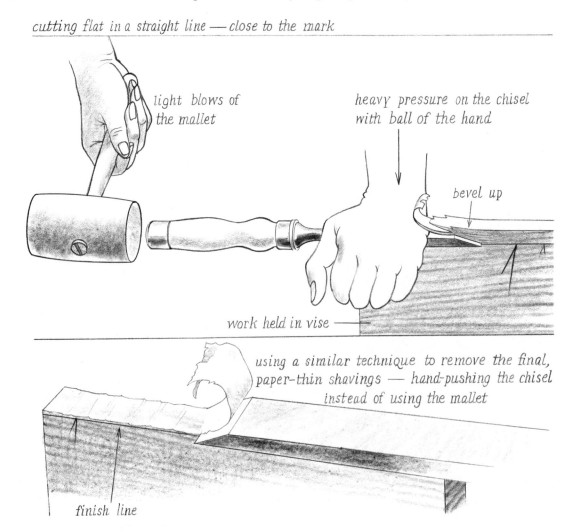

*light blows of the mallet*

*heavy pressure on the chisel with ball of the hand*

*bevel up*

*work held in vise*

*using a similar technique to remove the final, paper-thin shavings — hand-pushing the chisel instead of using the mallet*

*finish line*

working with the bevel down to smooth the inside of a recess

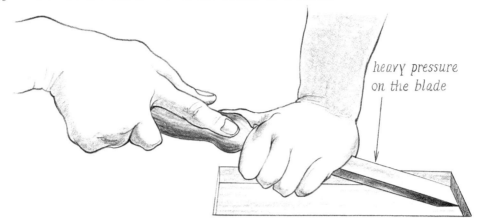

heavy pressure
on the blade

handgrip for heavy mallet work

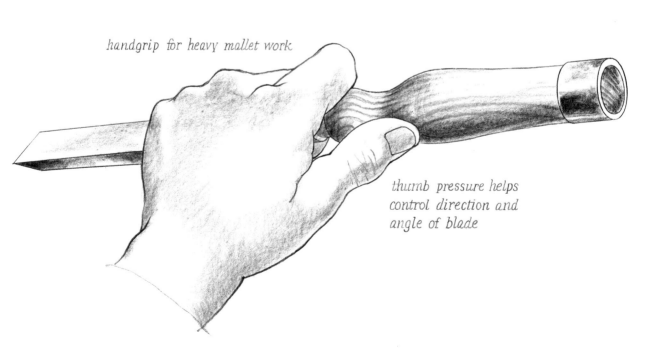

thumb pressure helps
control direction and
angle of blade

Grip a chisel firmly and strike the handle with a mallet; hold it lightly and push with the hands or swivel it side to side. This tool will work in ways similar to the drawknife, plane, and spokeshave. It will remove wood quickly in large splinters, take off paper-thin shavings, or slice across end grain—depending on how it is held and what type of force is used and how much. It outperforms all other edge tools in tight corners and in making joints.

Where the workpiece is small, a chisel will remove wood faster than a plane, and almost as smoothly. Work in the direction of the emerging grain and split off the bulk of the wood. The remaining wood can be taken off in one pass, working with the chisel bevel down. If the cut starts to go too deep, pushing the handle down will promptly direct it up again. Only a light stroke or two with the plane is needed to bring the cut even with the line.

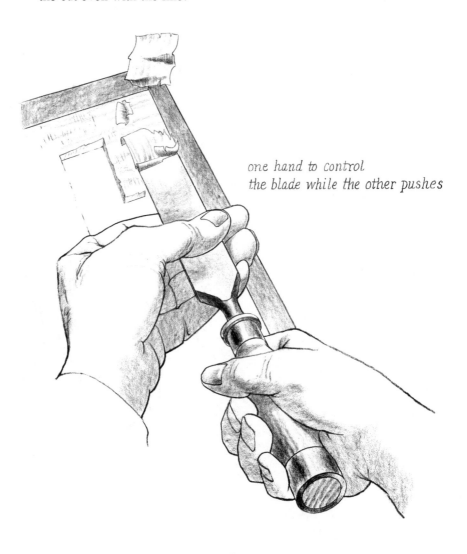

one hand to control
the blade while the other pushes

*chiseling to a line with the bevel down*

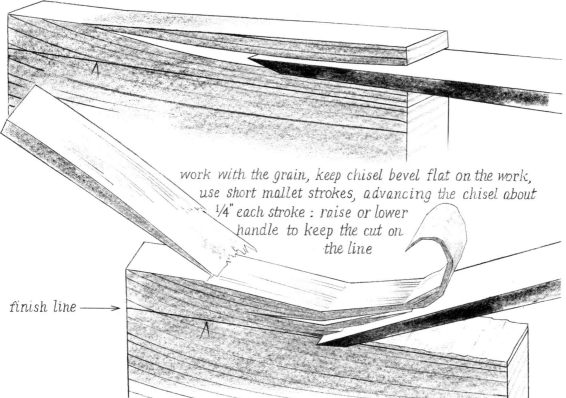

work with the grain, keep chisel bevel flat on the work,
use short mallet strokes, advancing the chisel about
¼" each stroke : raise or lower
handle to keep the cut on
the line

finish line ——→

COMPASS STROKE    This technique is very accurate, especially on end-grain work to remove slight amounts of wood in confined areas. Use the widest possible chisel, taking advantage of its flat expanse for maximum bearing on the work. The hands provide all the force—no mallet. Lay the chisel bevel up on the work, holding it flat on the work with good thumb pressure. With the other hand push the chisel against the wood, at the same time swivel it round compass fashion from one side to the other. Cut only with the trailing corner of the chisel. Work the chisel with one hand, hold it down with the other. Pull it back and make another stroke. Don't try to cut too much wood each time. It is more important to keep plenty of thumb pressure near the tip of the blade and make several light cuts, which produce the smoothest, most accurate surface.

*trimming to the line on end grain :*  A

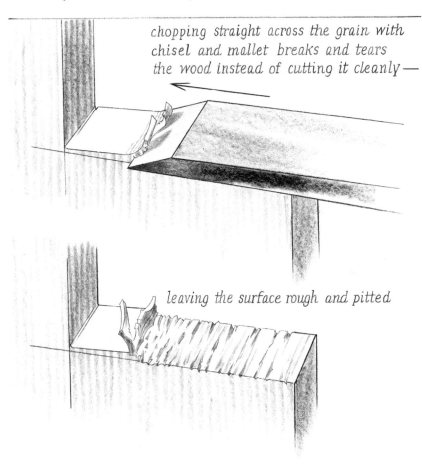

*chopping straight across the grain with chisel and mallet breaks and tears the wood instead of cutting it cleanly —*

*leaving the surface rough and pitted*

*trimming to the line on end grain :  B*

---

*the compass stroke does the job better, shearing the wood clean and smooth*

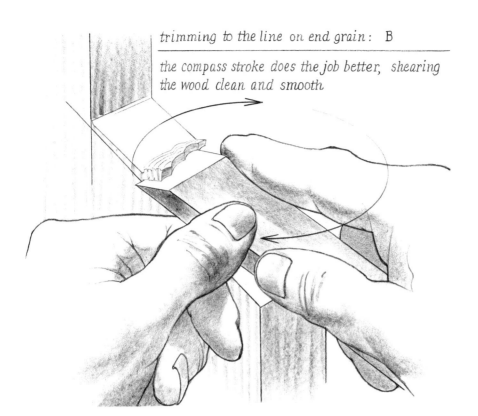

*trimming to the line on end grain :  C*

---

*swivel the hands and chisel compass fashion, cutting mainly with the trailing corner of the chisel*

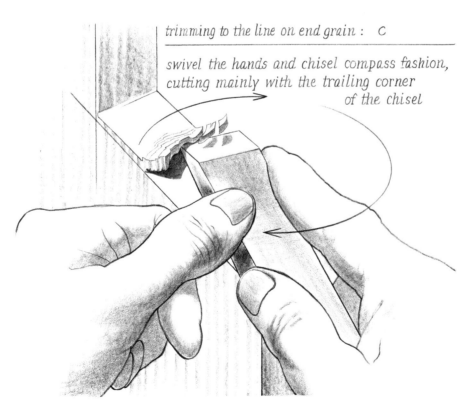

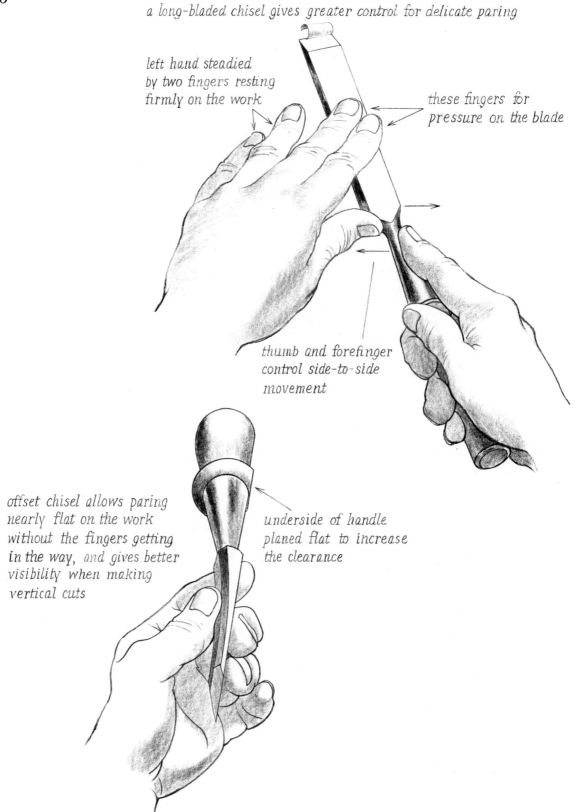

a long-bladed chisel gives greater control for delicate paring

left hand steadied
by two fingers resting
firmly on the work

these fingers for
pressure on the blade

thumb and forefinger
control side-to-side
movement

offset chisel allows paring
nearly flat on the work
without the fingers getting
in the way, and gives better
visibility when making
vertical cuts

underside of handle
planed flat to increase
the clearance

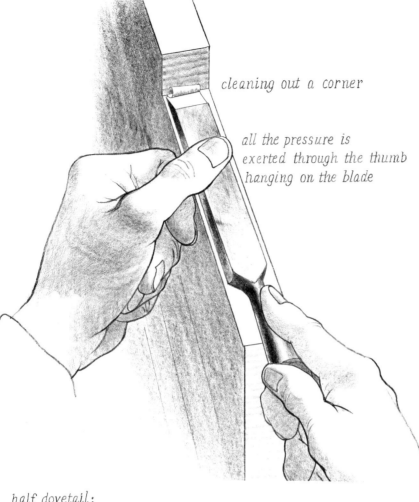

cleaning out a corner

all the pressure is
exerted through the thumb
hanging on the blade

half dovetail:
for a smooth, clean cut, chisel from the end — working with the grain

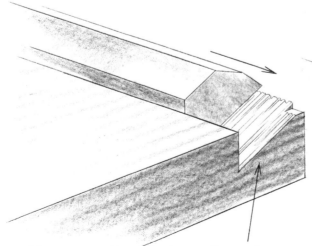

working across the grain leaves the surface
chipped and ragged

*cleaning out the inside corner of a rabbet*

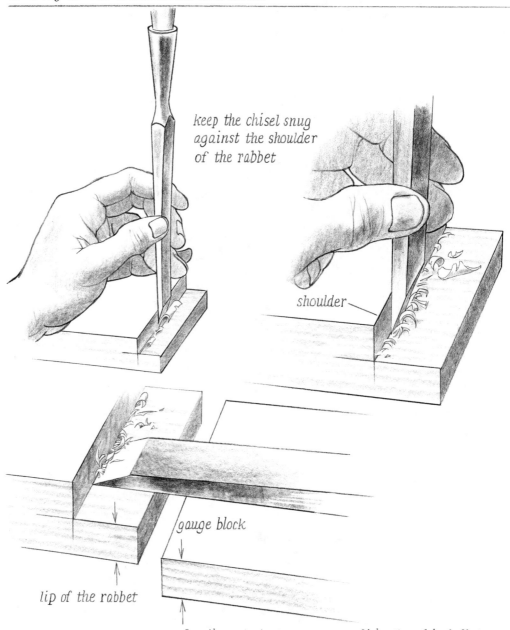

keep the chisel snug
against the shoulder
of the rabbet

shoulder

gauge block

lip of the rabbet

for the greatest accuracy, slide the chisel flat
over a gauge block of the same thickness as the finished rabbet lip

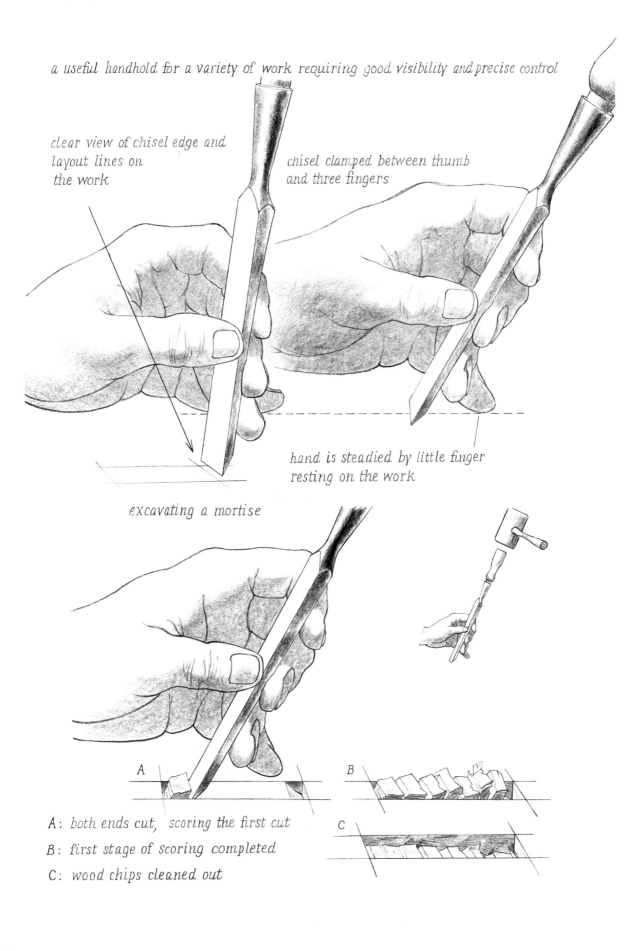

*a useful handhold for a variety of work requiring good visibility and precise control*

*clear view of chisel edge and layout lines on the work*

*chisel clamped between thumb and three fingers*

*hand is steadied by little finger resting on the work*

*excavating a mortise*

A: *both ends cut, scoring the first cut*

B: *first stage of scoring completed*

C: *wood chips cleaned out*

*correcting a saw cut in hardwood that has run off the mark*

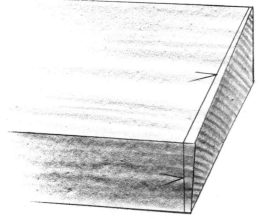

*hold chisel perpendicular, use solid mallet blows*

*don't use the full width of the chisel:
take narrow overlapping bites*

*don't chop clear through:
shave off the last 1/8" with
the work held end up in the vise,*

*using the chisel or block plane*

*cleaning out the waste wood in a cross-grained groove*

*hold chisel parallel with bottom of groove, use light mallet taps, work from both sides toward the middle*

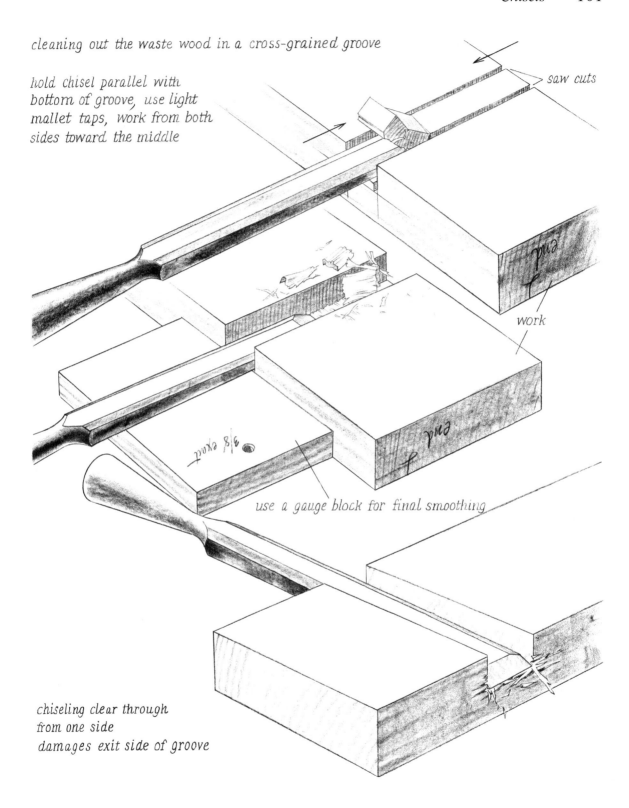

saw cuts

end

work

9/8 exact

*use a gauge block for final smoothing*

end

*chiseling clear through from one side damages exit side of groove*

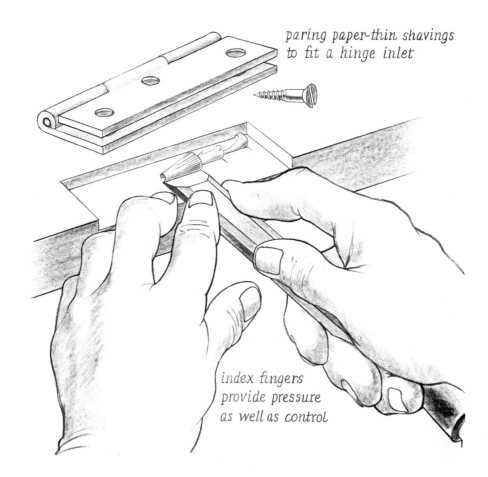

paring paper-thin shavings
to fit a hinge inlet

index fingers
provide pressure
as well as control

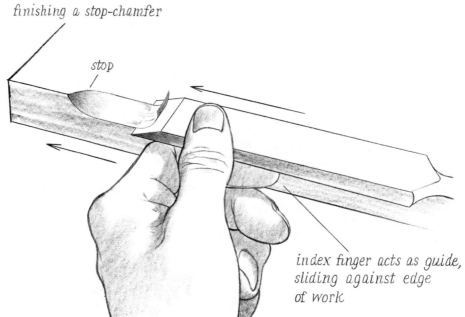

finishing a stop-chamfer

stop

index finger acts as guide,
sliding against edge
of work

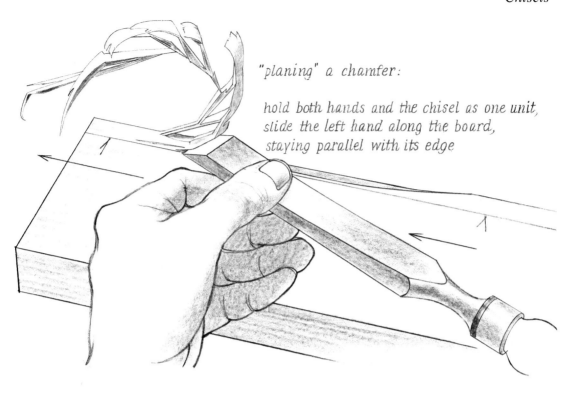

"planing" a chamfer:

hold both hands and the chisel as one unit,
slide the left hand along the board,
staying parallel with its edge

smoothing a sawn 45° miter cut

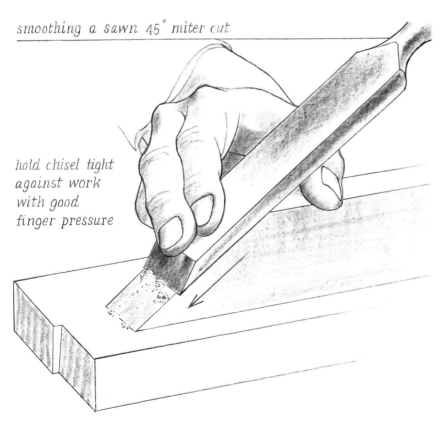

hold chisel tight
against work
with good
finger pressure

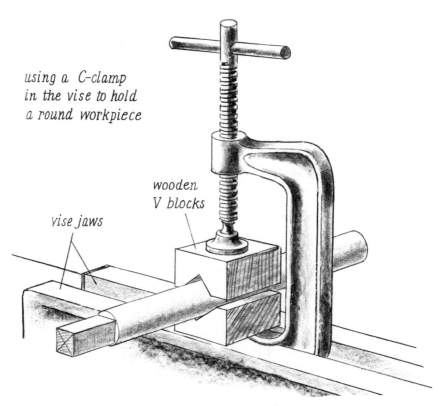

using a C-clamp
in the vise to hold
a round workpiece

vise jaws

wooden
V blocks

a long board clamped to a sawhorse in order to plane the end grain

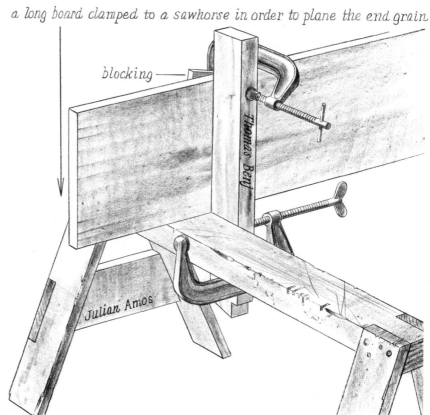

blocking

Thomas Berij

Julian Amos

# 8

# Clamps

You can't build much of anything without clamps—and the more you have the better. Once you own a half-dozen or so, you will marvel at how you got along without them. Clam, clamp, cramp—they sound like three different things, but these words share the same meaning as well as a common ancient ancestry. They all stem from related words with meanings and connotations rather alike: squeezed together, pinched, shut tight, compressed.

Clamps are essential for all gluing jobs and just as necessary for holding wood pieces together while you work with saw, plane, and chisel; while you bore properly aligned holes for bolts; to align pieces of wood and prevent them from slipping when driving nails and screws; and by the same token, when putting all the pieces together. Eight or 10 clamps will give you about the same advantage as four extra hands.

*ball-and-socket shoe*
*allows clamping of nonparallel workpieces*

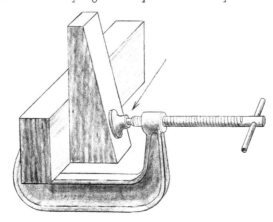

# Which Clamps?

There are about 40 types of clamps manufactured today, but two will see you through most of the usual woodworking procedures. Start with a pair each of 3-inch and 4-inch carriage clamps, and a pair each of 8-inch and 12-inch Jorgensen clamps, or handscrews, as they are sometimes called. Buy them in pairs: one clamp alone won't be of much use. More of the same, and other sizes—including some deep throat C-clamps—can be added as your particular work requires.

Experiment with your new clamps a bit. Run the screw in and out, practice opening and closing the jaws. You'll probably find that C-clamps have a lot of factory grease that comes off on your hands. This stuff will get transferred to the wood and stain it. With a clean rag and paint thinner, wipe off the excess grease, especially from the screw. After a lot of use, if the screw gets too dry to run easily, a drop or two of light machine oil will loosen it up.

*making uniform saw cuts to a precise depth*

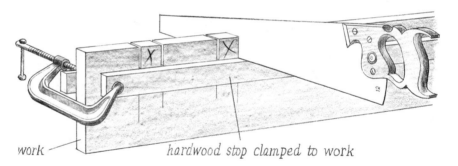

*work*                      *hardwood stop clamped to work*

# C-clamps

C-clamps are made in a variety of sizes and patterns for light, medium, and heavy-duty work. Clamps are sized by the maximum opening and the throat depth. For example, a $4'' \times 2^{1}/_{2}''$ clamp will open to a maximum of 4 inches and will reach $2^{1}/_{2}$ inches over the edge of the work. The style of C-clamp most common for general woodwork is the so-called carriage clamp, made with a malleable iron frame (bends before breaking), cold-drawn steel screw, and ball-and-socket shoe. For slightly heavier work there is another style: the body clamp, which has a deeper throat and a heftier frame. These clamps come with one of three types of handle: sliding tommy bar, fixed bar, or wing nut.

*typical iron or steel C-clamp*

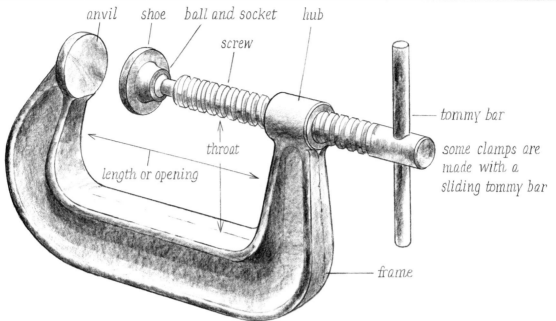

anvil    shoe    ball and socket    hub

screw

throat

length or opening

tommy bar

some clamps are made with a sliding tommy bar

frame

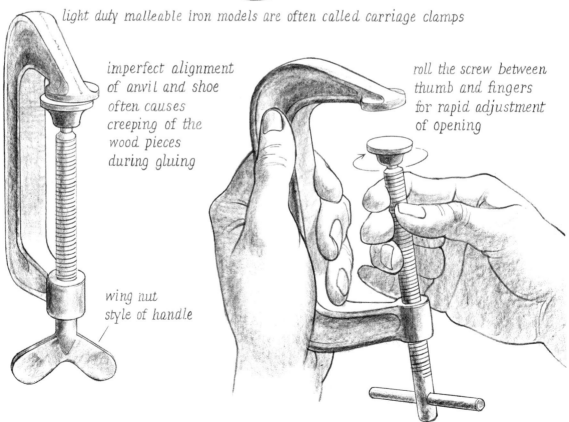

*light duty malleable iron models are often called carriage clamps*

imperfect alignment of anvil and shoe often causes creeping of the wood pieces during gluing

roll the screw between thumb and fingers for rapid adjustment of opening

wing nut style of handle

Don't buy inexpensive, pressed-steel clamps. They may be all right for handyman work, but they won't last and won't stand up to any heavy work. A set of malleable iron carriage clamps will do both, and you won't have wasted money on the cheap type.

Whether new or old, the anvil and screw of a clamp may not always align exactly on center. When putting clamps on, let the clamp "find its own seat." This helps prevent the creeping that comes from the screw pulling one way while the anvil sets in a different direction.

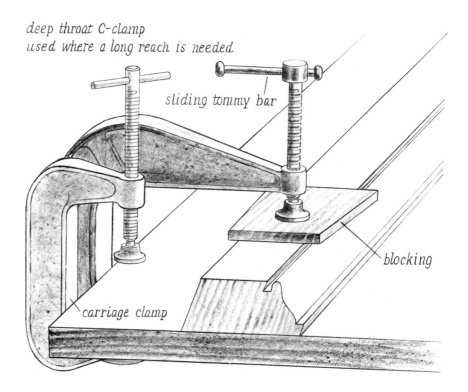

*deep throat C-clamp*
*used where a long reach is needed*

*sliding tommy bar*

*blocking*

*carriage clamp*

When tightened, the clamp will align where it wants—not where you think it should. The screw will pull the work with it as it is tightened, a tendency that is especially bothersome when clamping slippery pieces of glued wood.

MATCH THE CLAMP TO THE WORK    In general, the work should "fill" the clamp. A big clamp on small work puts considerable stress on the screw and the frame. Use a clamp with the smallest throat that the work allows: in other words, with the frame as close to the screw as possible. The deeper the throat, the more strain on the frame.

*use a clamp that fits the size of the work*

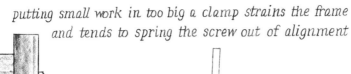

*putting small work in too big a clamp strains the frame
and tends to spring the screw out of alignment*

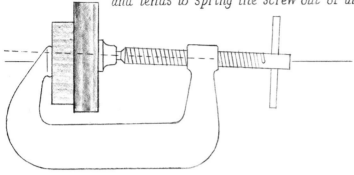

*if an oversize clamp must be used, fill it with thick
blocking so that most of the screw is
outside the hub*

*hub*

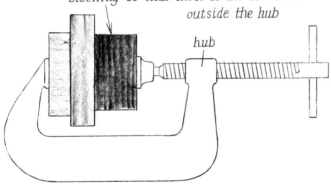

*the best solution — use a smaller clamp*

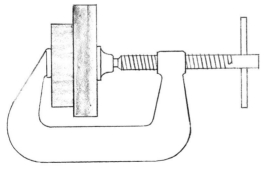

PRESSURE　　In terms of direct-transmitted pounds pressure, the C-clamp is one of the most powerful of clamps. A size $4'' \times 2\frac{1}{2}''$ carriage clamp can handle a load of up to 2,200 pounds—enough to crush a piece of white pine. You rarely need to tighten a clamp to its limit, not for holding pieces in alignment and certainly not for gluing, where excessive pressure should be avoided anyway.

Don't use a wrench or pliers to make it tighter! The wing nut or tommy bar is all you need. If the work calls for more pressure than your hand can give it, get a bigger clamp. Or gang up several clamps set close together. Uniformity of pressure is more important than crushing pressure, which is rarely called for. Four clamps tightened moderately do a better job than two which are wound up to full capacity. As one of the clamp manufacturers points out in his catalog: ''Any mechanic can wreck the best clamp made if he uses a wrench or a long enough bar!''

*for greatest accuracy, clamp the workpieces together to drill holes for bolts and screws or for nailing —— leave clamps on until all fastening is finished*

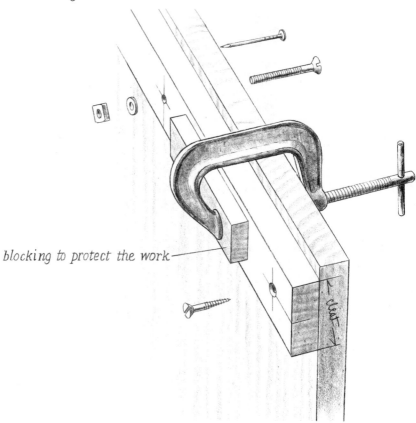

*blocking to protect the work*

*a 4" carriage clamp has the capacity to crush a piece of white pine*

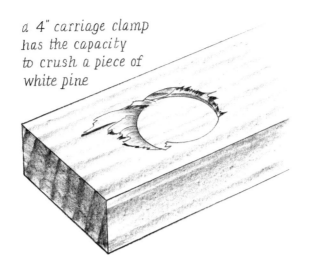

*a C-clamp used as an auxiliary vise to hold small work at a convenient height and position*

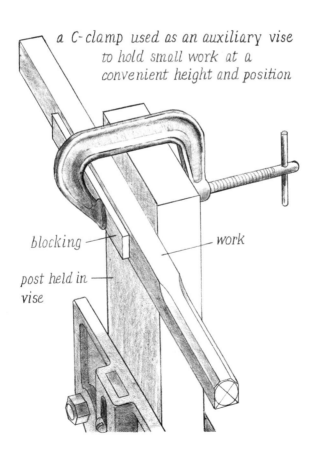

blocking

work

post held in vise

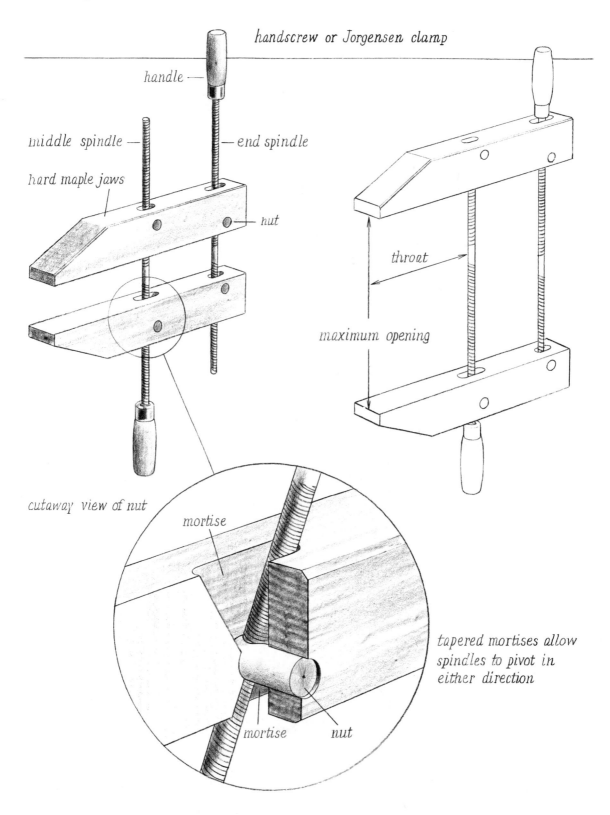

handscrew or Jorgensen clamp

handle

middle spindle

end spindle

hard maple jaws

nut

throat

maximum opening

cutaway view of nut

mortise

mortise    nut

tapered mortises allow
spindles to pivot in
either direction

# Jorgensen Handscrews

Jorgensen clamps are especially good for all kinds of gluing, and for assembling and repairing complex work such as furniture. The wide wooden jaws distribute pressure more evenly than iron clamps and hold the work without damaging it and without the need of using blocking. When clamping glued pieces, however, protect the jaws with waxed paper, and if glue does slop over onto the clamp, wipe it off immediately with a damp cloth. The double spindles allow holding nonparallel pieces with uniform pressure, and do not have the tendency of C-clamps to twist the workpieces or creep as they are tightened. The jaws can be cocked at an angle for awkward work without any loss of holding ability.

There is a trick to adjusting the opening of the jaws and tightening both screws to get uniform pressure. Hold the end spindle in the left hand, the middle one with the right. Crank both spindles away from you as though pedaling a bicycle. This opens the jaws rapidly and keeps them parallel. Crank backward to close them.

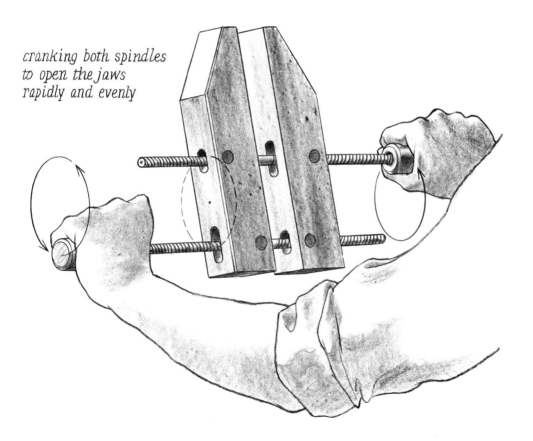

*cranking both spindles to open the jaws rapidly and evenly*

*jaws must be parallel
to get even pressure*

*all the pressure
concentrated at the
ends of the jaws*

*all the pressure
at the middle of
the clamp*

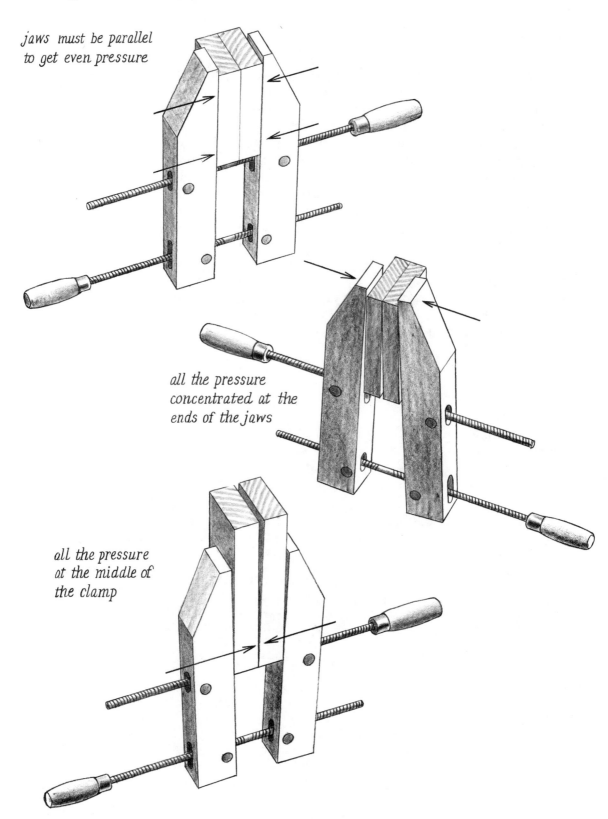

When the jaws are open approximately the right amount, slide the clamp over the work with the middle spindle as close to the work as possible, but not touching. Then turn both spindles simultaneously and in the same direction, to close the jaws on the work. Give them both another twist so the jaws are tight on the work. The middle spindle acts as a fulcrum, while the final pressure is applied with the end spindle.

Pressure should be uniform over the full length of the jaws, which simply means that when fully tightened the jaws should be parallel—the same distance apart at the ends as in the middle. To release the clamp, loosen the end spindle a quarter-turn, slide the clamp off, then turn the spindle back to its former position. This way, it is easy to keep the jaws in parallel relationship.

A good way to get your clamps "set" parallel is to crank the jaws to closed position so that both jaws are smack together. Then as you crank them open, there's a better chance they'll stay parallel.

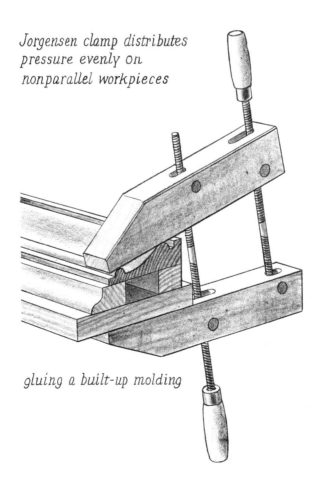

*Jorgensen clamp distributes pressure evenly on nonparallel workpieces*

*gluing a built-up molding*

clamp the work as close to the middle spindle
as possible

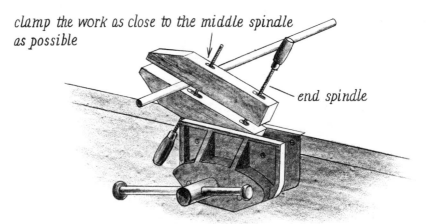

end spindle

by releasing the end spindle, the work can be removed from
the clamp without taking it out of the vise

# Other Types of Clamps

STEEL BAR CLAMPS    These long-reach models, sometimes called furniture clamps, are the only thing for making doors, bookcases, countertops, cabinets, and other wide or long pieces of work. They are made in sizes from $1\frac{1}{2}$ feet to 8 feet, are built with malleable iron castings, spring steel bars, cold-drawn screws, and a good margin of working pressure. A pair of 3-footers and another pair 4 feet long—in conjunction with your other clamps—will handle a considerable variety of work.

Various styles of tail stops are used, depending on the make and model. The older type of clamp—still manufactured—was made with a notched bar and a sliding tail stop that adjusts for length by engaging the appropriate notch. This kind of stop is released by tipping it out of the notch. Another style has a curved lever with teeth which grip the bar, a device which tends to slip when the teeth get worn down from extensive use. The newer type is fitted with a disc clutch—several hardened steel plates that grip the bar when pressure is applied.

CLAMP FIXTURES    A less expensive set of furniture clamps can be put together with a set of clamp fixtures—screw head and tail stop— to fit either standard iron pipes or wooden bars which you provide and cut to whatever length you want. The obvious advantage is that the

*spar clamps are easily made in various sizes*

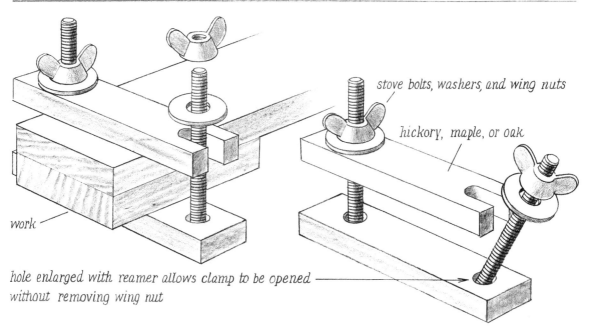

*stove bolts, washers, and wing nuts*

*hickory, maple, or oak*

*work*

*hole enlarged with reamer allows clamp to be opened without removing wing nut*

furniture, or bar clamps

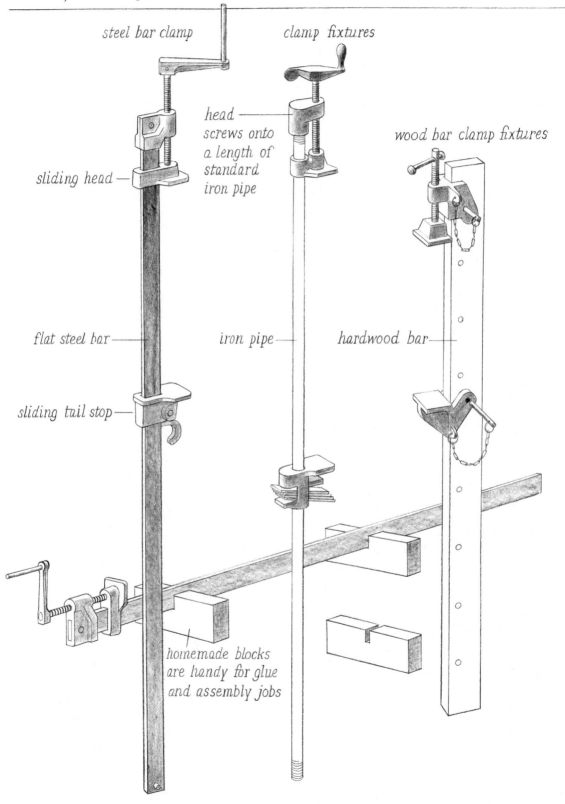

steel bar clamp

clamp fixtures

wood bar clamp fixtures

sliding head

head
screws onto
a length of
standard
iron pipe

flat steel bar

iron pipe

hardwood bar

sliding tail stop

homemade blocks
are handy for glue
and assembly jobs

fixtures can be used interchangeably with bars of several different lengths, and they're cheaper. But there are disadvantages: neither an iron pipe nor a wooden bar is as rigid as the flat spring steel bar. Both of these substitutes have a tendency to bend or twist, or both, and the longer the bar the more likely to do so. And again, with these big, tough clamps, blocking must be used to prevent crushing or otherwise damaging the work.

SPRING CLAMPS    These are of the clothespin type and meant only for small work where light pressure is needed. But they are very good. The hand opens the clamp, a heavy spring closes it and provides pressure. The spring is quite stiff, so you should try them out before buying: a dainty hand might have trouble with it. All the pressure is at the tips of the jaws, which makes it necessary to use blocking to protect the woodwork. The style with handles and jaws covered in polyvinyl takes care of this. And they are more comfortable to use.

*spring clamp*

*toolmaker's parallel clamp*

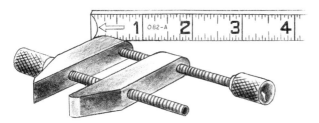

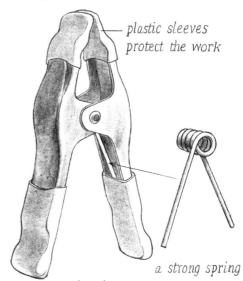

*plastic sleeves protect the work*

*works on the same principle as the Jorgensen clamp, good for pattern making, models, and other small work*

*a strong spring provides the necessary pressure, clamp is operated with one hand*

TOOLMAKER'S PARALLEL CLAMPS    These small clamps are used by machinists to hold metal pieces together for drilling and tapping, but are just as useful in the ordinary shop. The double spindle screws work the same as Jorgensen clamps, having tapered jaws to reach into tight places. They are excellent for gluing jobs in model work and, when held in a large vise, will hold small metal pieces for filing, shaping, and soldering.

CLAMP SUBSTITUTES    In certain situations perfectly acceptable glue work can be done without clamps. Properly set up, heavy weights do nicely and cost little or nothing. Find weights of the greatest possible density—your small bench anvil, a small slab of marble, cement blocks, bricks, even a heavy stone set in a shallow, homemade wooden tray to distribute the pressure. A stack of books or magazines works very well too. Paper is heavy and the amount of weight is easily adjusted.

# Blocking

Always use blocking with any iron or steel clamps used on finished pieces of wood. Otherwise, the clamps will damage the surfaces beyond repair. Blocking pieces are simply scraps of wood to lay over the finished work to protect against the clamp's crushing, and in the case of gluing to distribute the clamp's pressure. Without blocking, most of the pressure is confined to the area around the clamp's anvil and shoe— the pressure spreads very little.

The most useful wood for blocking—and the most practical—is hardwood such as maple, ash, or beech. These woods bend only imperceptibly, distribute the pressure, and will last a long time. Blocking pieces should be flat and smooth so they won't mar the work. Save cut-off scraps or prepare special blocking pieces from new stuff. Keep a good supply of them in a box—short pieces and long, narrow and wide. They can be used over and over many times. To make sure they don't get thrown away or burned for kindling, daub them with a spot of bright paint.

# How to Manage Without Six Hands

Glue two pieces of wood in alignment using two clamps, four pieces of blocking, and only two hands. How do you do it? When you tighten the clamps, the pieces of wood creep on the slippery glue. One end is in alignment but the other isn't. A piece of blocking drops to the floor. It takes patience, persistence, trial and error and, like every other aspect of using tools, a lot of practice.

Practice first with dry pieces of wood. When you get to the glue, tack the workpieces together with brads, provided of course the nail holes won't show. Start the brads before you spread glue. Let the glued surfaces set a few minutes before putting them together: the tackiness

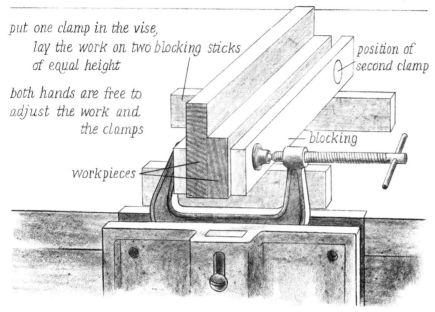

*keeping glued workpieces in correct alignment while clamping*

*put one clamp in the vise,
    lay the work on two blocking sticks
    of equal height*

*position of
second clamp*

*both hands are free to
adjust the work and
    the clamps*

*blocking*

*workpieces*

will help prevent slipping. Put one clamp in the vise so one hand is free to hold all the other stuff. Use long blocking to reach across both clamps. Try to simplify. But the main thing is to be persistent. Woodworkers have been juggling this kind of thing for centuries, and you can too.

Get everything ready before spreading any glue. Most modern adhesives set up fairly fast, leaving barely enough time to put on and tighten the clamps. Follow instructions on the adhesive container, especially as to temperature. If you use adhesives only occasionally, make a trial run with scraps of wood to learn the procedure for the particular adhesive.

Plan ahead as to how you'll proceed: holding one clamp in the vise often works well; other times it may be better to lock one of the workpieces in the vise, lay another glued piece on top of it, then apply clamps. Have enough blocking pieces laid out ready. Adjust the clamps to approximately the correct opening. Lay everything out on the bench within easy reach. If you'll need pieces of waxed paper, tear them off and have them ready too.

TIGHTENING THE CLAMPS    It doesn't take a lot of pressure for gluing, certainly not all that the clamp can exert. There should be a thin film of adhesive between pieces of wood to make a good bond. Winding up the clamps with all your might will squeeze out much of the glue and weaken the joint.

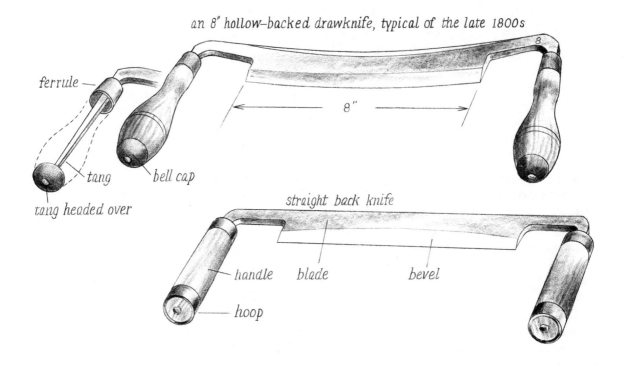

an 8" hollow-backed drawknife, typical of the late 1800s

ferrule

tang

tang headed over

bell cap

8"

straight back knife

handle

blade

bevel

hoop

# 9

# Drawknife

Whether called a wheeler's knife, mast shave, or chamfer knife, it is estimated that the drawknife dates back at least to A.D. 100 when it was used in shipbuilding and other woodworking trades. Since then, in an endless variety of shapes and sizes, it has been used by gunsmiths, coopers, wheelwrights, carpenters, mast and spar-makers, cabinetmakers, and furniture makers. If you were a wheelwright, this is the tool you'd have needed to shape a square stick into an oval, tapered spoke. It is a superb tool for rough shaping, and has always been much used for preparing pieces to go on the lathe.

But it is a more sophisticated tool than that. It will shave wood as smooth as glass, get into places where a plane won't fit, where a hatchet is too crude, and where a chisel is more difficult to control properly. It will indeed cut off great thick splinters the size of stove kindling, yet it can also cut shavings as thin as tissue paper. In practiced hands, the accuracy of a drawknife in hewing to a precise and finished line is impressive indeed. Skillfully manipulated, a drawknife will execute a chamfer to fully finished state needing no touching up or sanding.

Drawknives are made in several sizes from 5 inches to 14 inches—gauged by the length of the cutting edge. Pick a size that comfortably fits your particular hands-apart pulling attitude. Examine and choose a knife whose handles are attached in the strongest possible way. They should be cocked out a bit for a natural grip instead of coming off the blade at right angles. And fairly long, bulbous handles—typical of older knives—give the best grip for the hands. Many modern drawknives have handles that are too stubby and awkward to hang onto. You don't need the biggest drawknife even for heavy work.

On the other hand, a very small knife that forces the hands close together may prove inefficient if it constricts your natural arm-spread. It's more important that it fits you, and that it won't pull apart. Then, you can use it for all kinds of work—heavy as well as light.

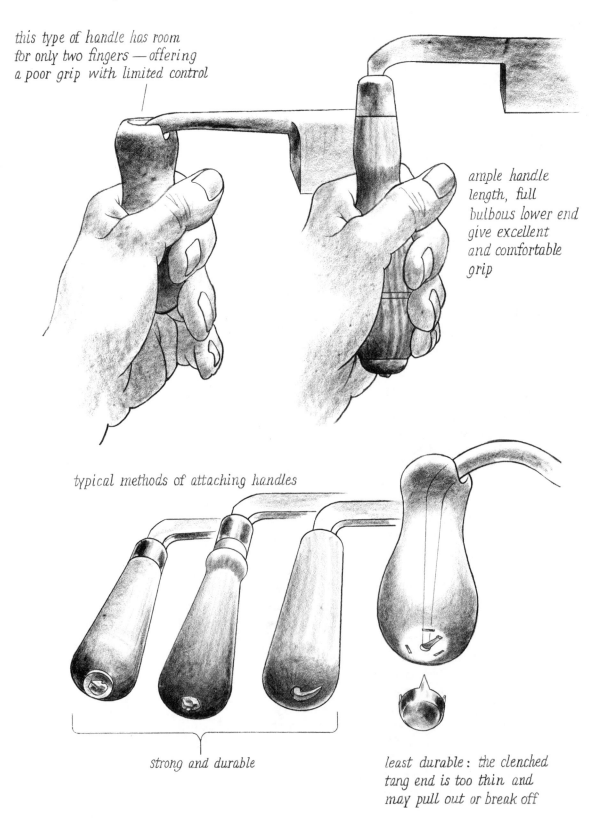

this type of handle has room
for only two fingers — offering
a poor grip with limited control

ample handle
length, full
bulbous lower end
give excellent
and comfortable
grip

typical methods of attaching handles

strong and durable

least durable: the clenched
tang end is too thin and
may pull out or break off

*a good handgrip for rough removal of wood*

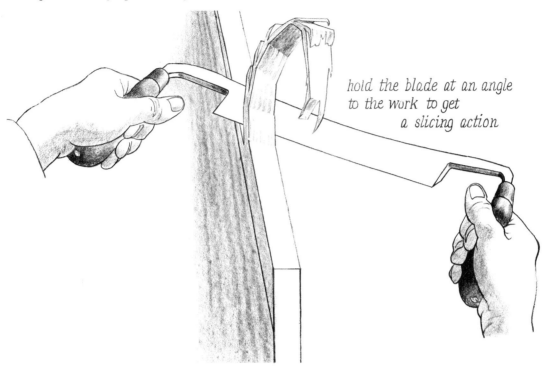

*hold the blade at an angle
to the work to get
a slicing action*

*this handgrip — with thumbs braced in the
corners of the blade — gives precise control
for very delicate paring*

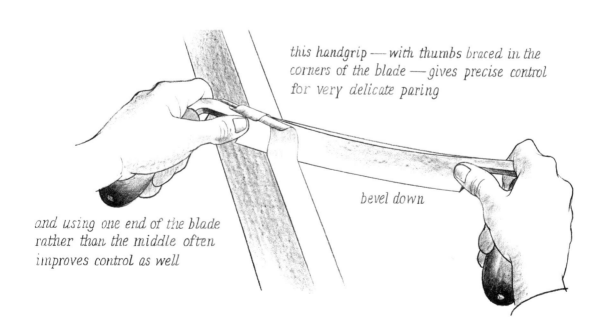

*bevel down*

*and using one end of the blade
rather than the middle often
improves control as well*

*basic technique for rough-cutting large amounts of wood*

*make a series of short, yanking strokes,*
*sliding the knife back after each one*
*to gain momentum for the next*

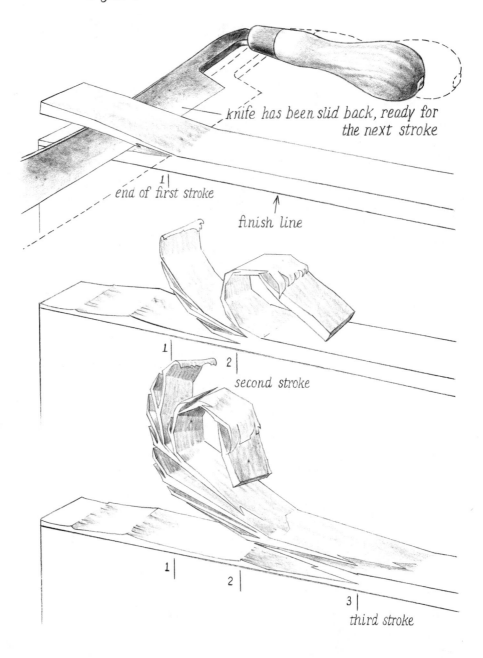

knife has been slid back, ready for
the next stroke

1
end of first stroke

↑
finish line

1    2
second stroke

1    2

3
third stroke

A hollow-backed knife with a curved blade is preferable to a straight one, since much of the drawknife's efficiency comes from a slicing action—greatly enhanced by the curved blade. Whether drawing or pushing the knife, working it at an angle to the wood is usually better than pulling straight, for a slicing knife always makes the cleanest cut. And the sliding, slicing strokes cut just as much wood as a straight pull, but with less effort and with more control.

You can draw the knife with the bevel up, keeping the flat of the blade on the work, but working with the bevel down gives more exact control. If the cut begins to go too deep, tip the handles up and the knife will come back to the line.

To remove a large amount of wood quickly, take a good grip on both handles. Hold the knife at an angle to the work—and pull. It takes considerable force, so brace your feet and use the power of arms, shoulders, and torso. Be sure to cut in the direction of the emerging grain of the wood, not against it. Don't try to shave the full length of the board. Use a series of short, heavy strokes. Make a cut, slide the knife back to gain some momentum, then yank the knife to the wood again. This also keeps the knife from running out of control and cutting where you don't want it to.

*tip the handles up*
*to bring the cut back toward the surface*

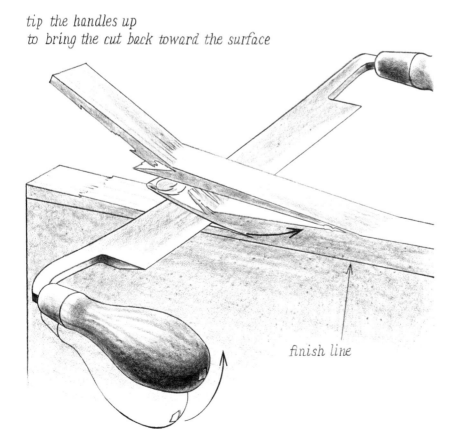

*finish line*

*the principle of the slicing stroke*

hold the knife at an angle,
pull it toward you
while at the same time sliding the blade
from one end to the other

this stroke takes less muscle
than pulling straight into the wood,
gives better control —
and cuts cleaner

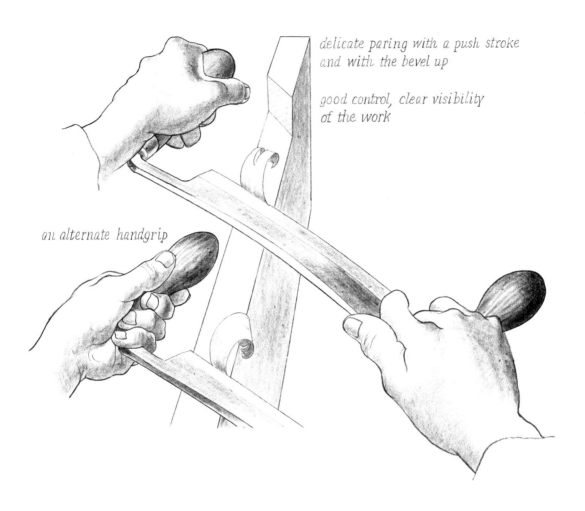

delicate paring with a push stroke
and with the bevel up

good control, clear visibility
of the work

an alternate handgrip

*cutting curved work with a drawknife*

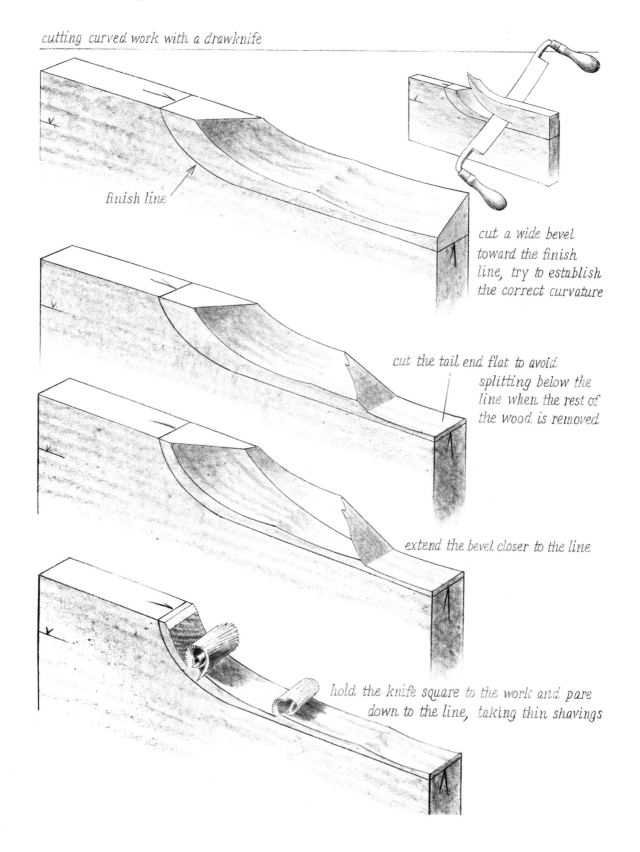

finish line

cut a wide bevel
toward the finish
line, try to establish
the correct curvature

cut the tail end flat to avoid
splitting below the
line when the rest of
the wood is removed

extend the bevel closer to the line

hold the knife square to the work and pare
down to the line, taking thin shavings

When cutting to a finished line, do it in two steps. First use the knife to make numerous scoring cuts close together. Hold the bevel side down and use slicing strokes. Cut down not quite to the line, starting at the near end of the board and working away from you. Then break loose the shavings with your hand. To finish the job—and have it flat and smooth—take longer but thinner parings, again holding the knife at an angle. With practice, the knife can be made to shave in the same precise fashion as a plane.

The drawknife is a two-handed tool, whatever the work you're doing, and whether it is pulled or pushed. Make it a rule always to pick it up with both hands: don't wave it around with one. If it's as sharp as it should be, it can easily slice a finger open. Don't lay it down on the bench! A drawknife is one of the most difficult tools to sharpen. Hang it up as soon as you're done with it.

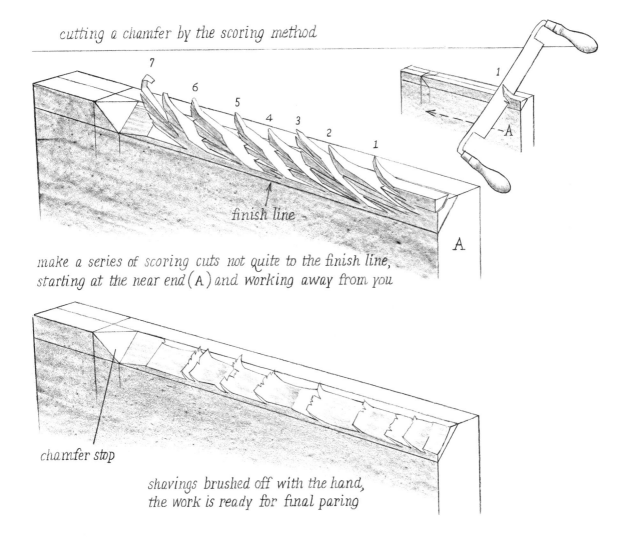

*cutting a chamfer by the scoring method*

*finish line*

*make a series of scoring cuts not quite to the finish line, starting at the near end (A) and working away from you*

*chamfer stop*

*shavings brushed off with the hand, the work is ready for final paring*

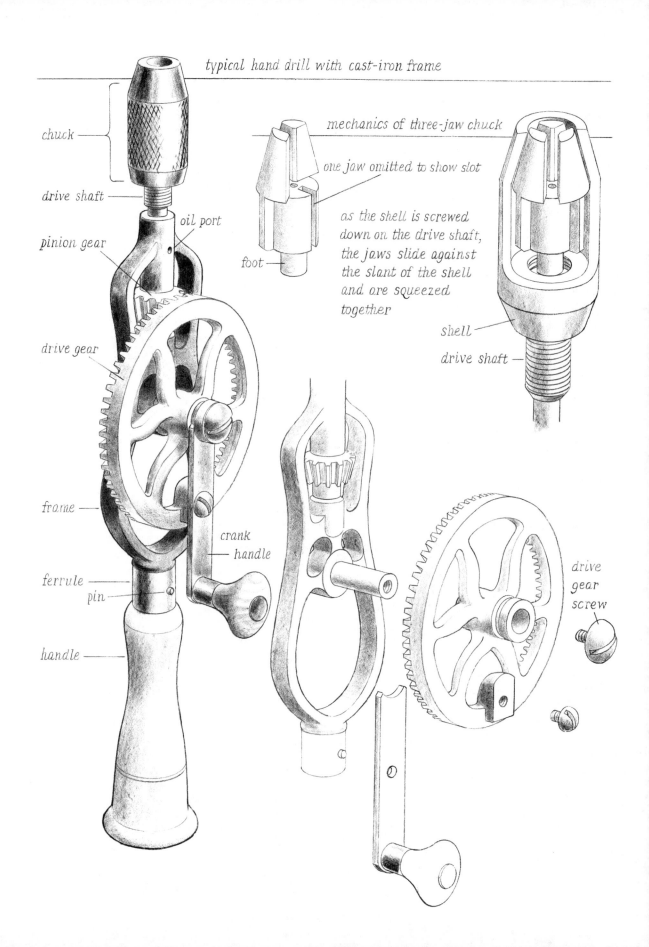

typical hand drill with cast-iron frame

chuck

drive shaft

pinion gear

oil port

drive gear

frame

ferrule

pin

handle

crank handle

mechanics of three-jaw chuck

one jaw omitted to show slot

foot

as the shell is screwed down on the drive shaft, the jaws slide against the slant of the shell and are squeezed together

shell

drive shaft

drive gear screw

# 10

# Hand Drill

A hand drill is essential for any job that requires small holes. Pilot holes should be drilled for nails and screws to avoid overheating and breaking them, and to prevent splitting the wood. And there are numerous other times when a drill is indispensable: for attaching hinges, angle irons and mending plates, and for making holes for small dowels and metal pins.

While the brace with its auger bits bores holes from $1/4$ inch in diameter on up to 3 inches, the hand drill is used to make holes from $1/4$ inch down to $1/16$ inch or less. It is built to use twist drills or points which can be bought individually or in sets in a complete range of sizes. A practical everyday set includes 13 drills from $1/16$ inch to $1/4$ inch in gradations of 64ths. The variety known as "high-speed twist drills" are made of a grade of steel that works in metal as well as wood.

A first-class drill should have a cast-iron frame, a three-jaw chuck, and gears with teeth that are machine-cut rather than cast. A top-quality drill has two pinion gears instead of one, and runs so easily that its noise is a barely audible whisper. The cheaper so-called handyman versions are likely to be missing one or all of these features and are a poor investment.

Simple as it is, a hand drill has several moving parts that need regular attention. The pinion gear and its drive shaft—since they turn at high speed—are subjected to considerable wear if they are run dry. Just as important is the free movement of the jaws. Because their opening and closing depends on a free sliding action, it is especially important that they be cleaned and lubricated frequently. These moving parts in the chuck can be flushed clean with kerosene and left to drip dry before oiling.

rapid adjustment of the drill chuck

roll the chuck
over the palm of the hand
to open or close the jaws

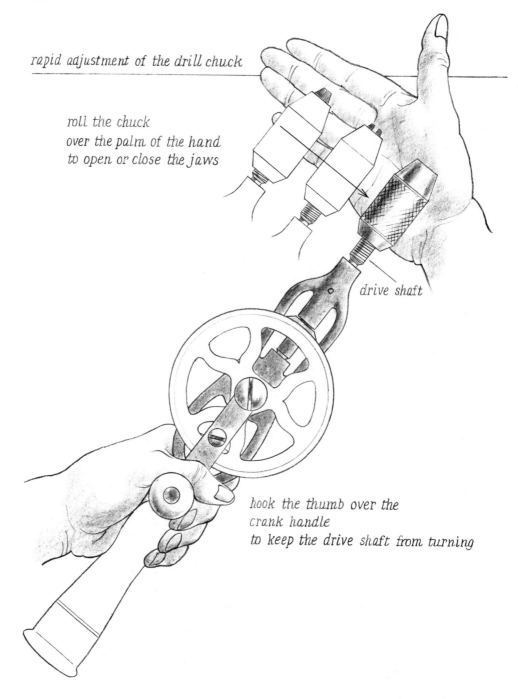

drive shaft

hook the thumb over the
crank handle
to keep the drive shaft from turning

# Operating the Drill

TO INSERT A TWIST DRILL    Open the jaws by turning the shell counterclockwise. The quickest way to do this is to hold the drill in one hand and roll the chuck shell against the palm of the other hand. Drop in the drill. Turn the shell the other way, keeping the drill in the center of the three jaws as they close on it. Then tighten the jaws: hook a thumb over the crank handle to hold the drive gear from turning and with the other hand twist the shell good and tight.

TO REMOVE A TWIST DRILL    Hold the drill with the drive gear on the side away from you and with a finger hooked over the crank handle to immobilize the drive gear. Then loosen the chuck. This grip also prevents getting the hand pinched in the gear.

VERTICAL OR HORIZONTAL    There are two main ways of drilling: in a vertical position with the work face up in the vise, or horizontally with the work upright in the vise. The horizontal method is the better of the two. Put the work upright in the vise and hold the drill level. Get a good grip on the handle and keep the elbow tight against

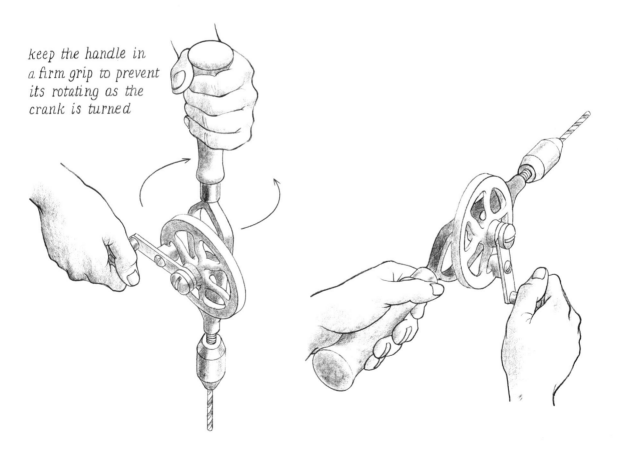

*keep the handle in a firm grip to prevent its rotating as the crank is turned*

*tightening a drill point in the chuck*

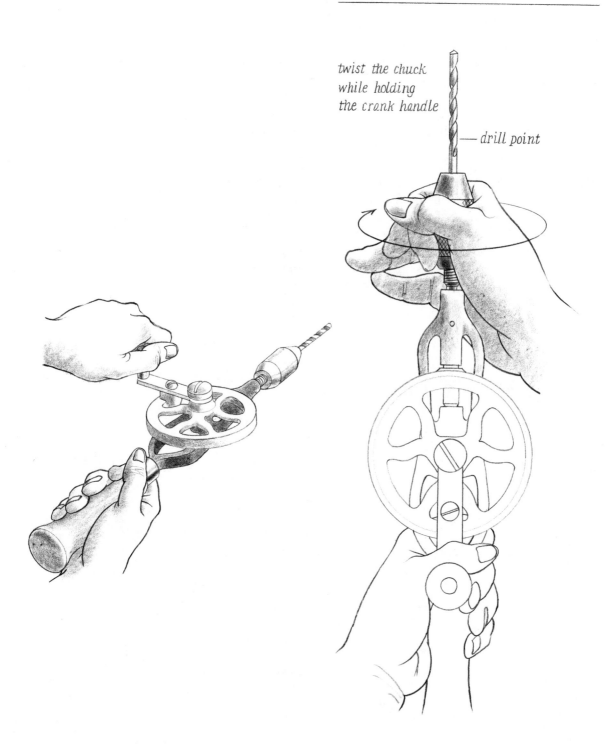

*twist the chuck
while holding
the crank handle*

— *drill point*

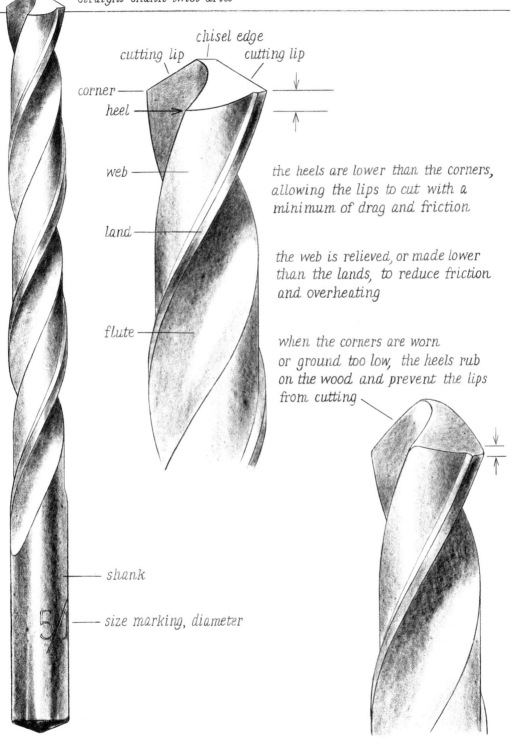

straight shank twist drill

chisel edge

cutting lip    cutting lip

corner

heel

web

land

flute

the heels are lower than the corners,
allowing the lips to cut with a
minimum of drag and friction

the web is relieved, or made lower
than the lands, to reduce friction
and overheating

when the corners are worn
or ground too low, the heels rub
on the wood and prevent the lips
from cutting

shank

size marking, diameter

your side. In this position the drill can be held steady and in better control while you crank with the other hand. And it will be easier to drill the hole straight and square to the work. If the work is too large or ungainly to go in the vise, clamp at least one section of it to the bench or to a sawhorse for support.

When drilling in a vertical position, it is more difficult to both hold the drill steady and keep it going straight. With nothing to lean against, the arm must do it alone. But the joints of the wrist, elbow, and shoulder cannot be held as rigid, and the drill wobbles from side to side under the pressure of turning the crank. Not only that, but this cranking motion also makes the drill rotate back and forth, which further reduces the degree of control.

SPEED AND PRESSURE    The cutting end of a twist drill is relatively flat and cannot gulp great quantities of wood. To make a clean hole, the drill must be turned fast but with only moderate pressure. Too much pressure punches the drill into the wood rather than cutting it. In general the larger the drill the faster it should turn. The drill should spin instead of laboriously chugging around. Something like 70 or 75 revolutions per minute is about right for a $1/16$-inch drill, but a $1/4$-inch size ought to run close to 120.

*avoid too much pressure on fine drill points, hold up on the handle so the drill "hangs" lightly*

*if the drill is not straight up and down, the drill point will bend and may break*

Small drills do not dissipate friction heat quickly, nor with their narrow flutes do they expel wood shavings as efficiently as the larger drills. They should be rested more often to cool off. While turning the crank forward, slowly pull the drill out of the hole and clean off the drill flutes with the fingers. This also clears the hole of shavings that tend to bind the drill.

High speed and light pressure help prevent a drill from sticking in hardwood or working loose in the drill chuck. When it does stick the drill may come out of the chuck completely. If so, open the jaws a bit and slide the chuck back over the drill. Then tighten the jaws again. To remove the drill from the wood, turn the crank slowly forward while at the same time pulling back on the drill handle.

GAUGING THE DEPTH    In cases of drilling numerous pilot holes all the same depth—for example, attaching hinges to cupboard doors—simple depth stops can be made from blocks of scrap wood. Drill a hole of the correct size in the block. Then cut it off so the drill protrudes to the depth of the hole. While this block will only work for one drill size and one depth, mark its size and keep it. You'll use it again, and eventually have enough stops for most situations.

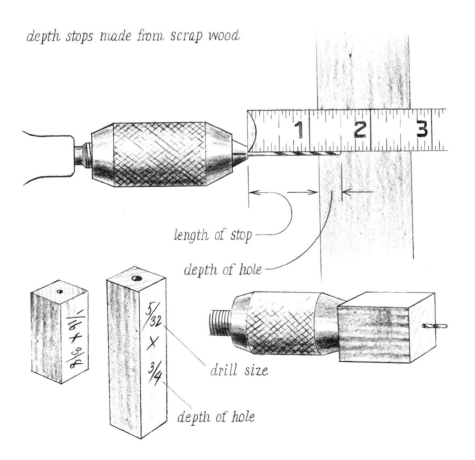

*depth stops made from scrap wood*

length of stop

depth of hole

¹/₈ × ³/₈

⁵/₃₂

X

³/₄

drill size

depth of hole

*file*

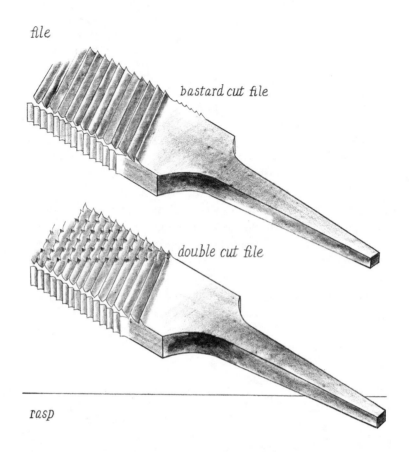

*bastard cut file*

*double cut file*

*rasp*

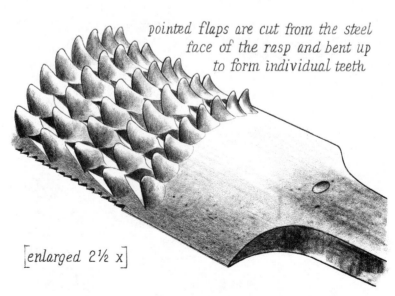

*pointed flaps are cut from the steel
face of the rasp and bent up
to form individual teeth*

[enlarged 2½ x]

# 11

# File & Rasp

point

— edge

— face

— heel

— tang

A file is often thought of primarily as a metalworking tool for smoothing, shaping, and for sharpening other tools. It is certainly all of that. But for generations woodworkers have used files for countless jobs where an extremely fine finish or a delicately fashioned curve or fit is wanted, especially on end grain or in hardwood. Files produce a crispness of finish that most other tools cannot match.

A rasp, on the other hand, while a close relative of the file, is used principally for the preliminary rough work of shaping wood which is to be finished with a plane, spokeshave, file, or sandpaper. Whereas a file *scrapes* off wood in minuscule particles, a rasp *chews* it off in quantity.

Files and rasps are simply bars of steel with teeth cut into their surfaces. They are cutting tools with several dozen miniature cutter irons arranged in closely spaced rows whose action is similar to that of a plane. They are tempered quite hard to give the teeth a long life,

*cutting notches, enlarging and shaping holes*

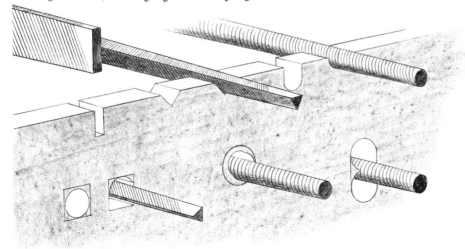

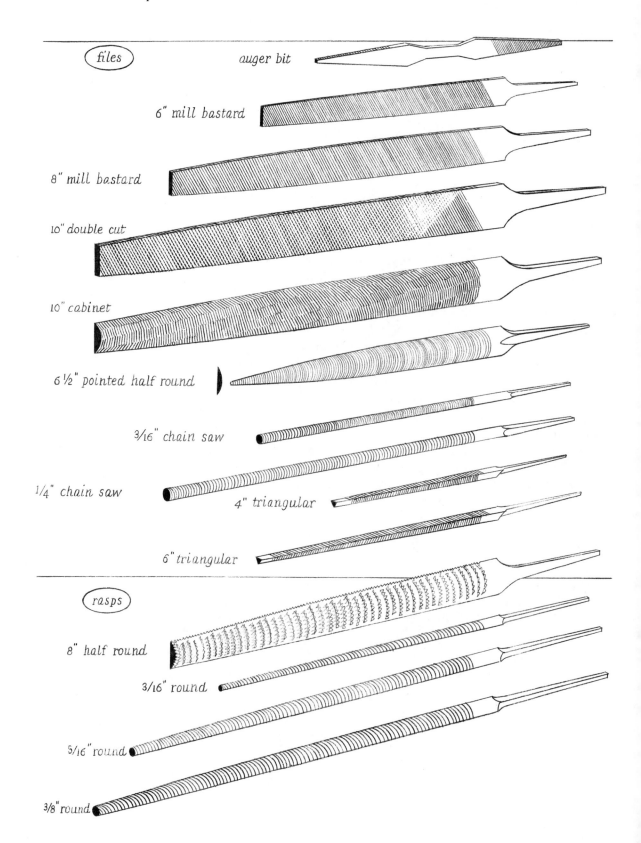

files

auger bit

6" mill bastard

8" mill bastard

10" double cut

10" cabinet

6 ½" pointed half round

3/16" chain saw

1/4" chain saw

4" triangular

6" triangular

rasps

8" half round

3/16" round

5/16" round

3/8" round

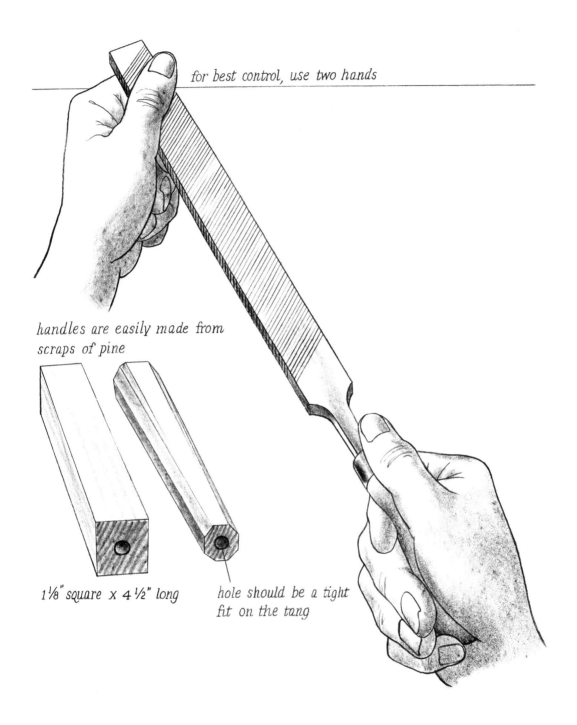

for best control, use two hands

handles are easily made from
scraps of pine

1⅛" square x 4½" long

hole should be a tight
fit on the tang

are very brittle, and easily broken. The teeth of the various models are shaped and arranged according to the work they are intended to do.

File teeth are cut the full width of the face, in rows set at an angle to produce a shearing cut. Depending on how closely the rows are spaced, files are classified as coarse, medium, fine, or extra fine. And the selection of a file is governed by the kind of wood and the degree of finish that is wanted. By contrast, rasps have individual teeth arranged in parallel rows across the face. Rasp teeth are comparatively coarse and the spaces between rows relatively large.

In either case—file or rasp—the spaces between teeth tend to fill up rapidly with wood or metal as the case may be, choking the cutting action and making the tool skid and skip over the work. They have to be cleaned frequently. With every few strokes, gently rap a file on a block of hardwood. This will dislodge most of the filings. Because of its larger teeth, a rasp is easier to clean: scrubbing a stiff nailbrush over the surface is often enough. For a more thorough cleaning use a wire brush, stroking it through the rows of teeth. A file that is clogged with metal filings would need the wire brush as well.

HANDLES    Files and rasps should be fitted with handles. Using a naked file with the tang sticking into your palm is painful, and hard to control as well. Since a file is a two-handed tool, something bulky is needed to hold onto for a good firm grip. Almost any kind of handle is better than none, even if it's no more than an old corncob punched over the tang. There are various plain and fancy file handles on the market, but a simple piece of scrap wood 4 or 5 inches long, with its sharp edges rounded a bit, works just as well and costs nothing to make.

# Using a File

CROSS FILING    Put the work in the vise or clamp it to something solid. Take the file in two hands—one hand on the point, the other holding the handle. File across the work at an angle, not straight across. And use good down pressure. Otherwise the teeth will catch on the grain of the wood, making the file chatter and leaving a rough surface. The chatter and the rough surface are caused by the teeth catching on the harder ridges of wood grain, then jumping up and skipping over to the softer wood between. Filing straight across on metal is even worse: the file sets the metal vibrating and produces a screeching noise fit to make a dog howl. Working at an angle is especially necessary with a rasp. Filing straight across will tear and break the wood, leaving the surface in ridges and the offside of the work ragged.

The teeth of files and rasps are designed to cut in only one direction—on the push stroke. Push the file for the cutting stroke, then lift it off the work to bring it back ready for the next stroke. Don't drag it back. Seesawing back and forth dulls the teeth and these tools cannot be sharpened.

DRAW FILING    This method cleans up the roughness of cross filing and leaves a smooth, scratch-free surface. Again hold the file in both hands, but in this case keep the file at right angles to the work. Push the file the full length of the work in one continuous stroke. Lift the file and come back for the next stroke.

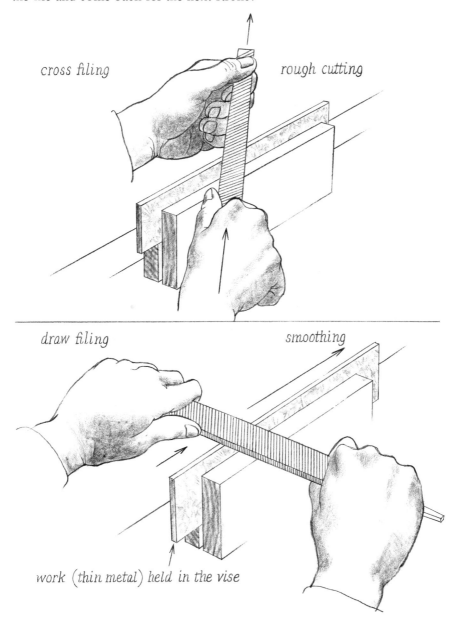

cross filing                    rough cutting

draw filing                    smoothing

work (thin metal) held in the vise

*tang bent up and fitted with a handle
for smoothing long flat surfaces*

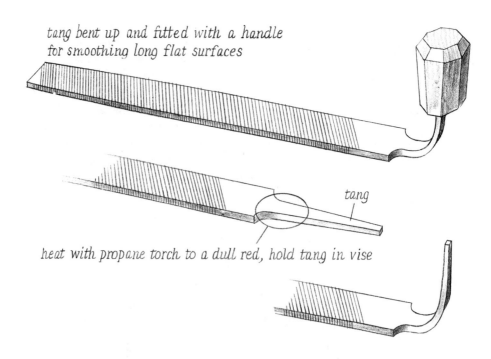

*tang*

*heat with propane torch to a dull red, hold tang in vise*

*smoothing end-grain work with a file*

*hold the file with plenty of pressure
to prevent its chattering and to
keep it flat on the work*

smoothing and adjusting
the width of a groove for the correct fit

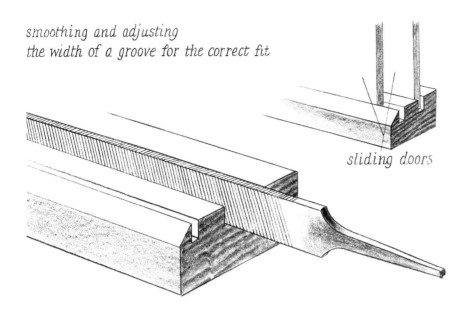

sliding doors

when filing thin metal or wood, clamp the
work close to the vise jaws to prevent
chattering of the file

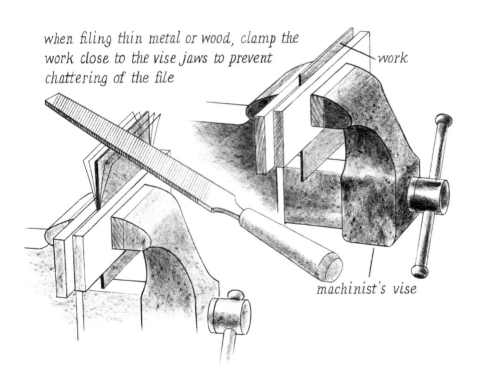

work

machinist's vise

*chair rung: reducing the diameter of round stock*

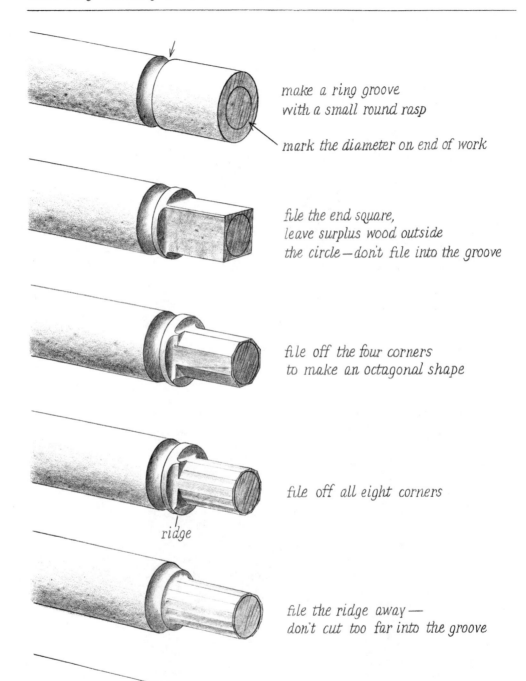

make a ring groove
with a small round rasp

mark the diameter on end of work

file the end square,
leave surplus wood outside
the circle—don't file into the groove

file off the four corners
to make an octagonal shape

file off all eight corners

ridge

file the ridge away—
don't cut too far into the groove

finish the rung to exact diameter,
using the round-and-round filing
technique,  clean up the shoulder with
a dowel wrapped in sandpaper

shoulder

*round-and-round* filing *to reduce the diameter of round stock*

1: *hold work tight in the jig with thumb*  2: *draw a gauge mark on top of the work*
3: *start filing next to this mark*  4: *rotate work slowly with one hand, use the other to*
*file with light, uniform strokes*  5: *file only when the work is turning—when your hand*
*hits the jig (bottom illustration), stop filing*  6: *take a new grip on the work and file*
*round another segment*  7: *run the file against the edge of the jig for control*
8: *keep the file level— don't try to wipe it around the work*

9: *remove only a slight amount of wood*
*with each turn*  10: *when the gauge mark comes*
*round to the top again, stop filing*

11: *before continuing, try the work in a*
*test block to check for roundness and correct diameter*

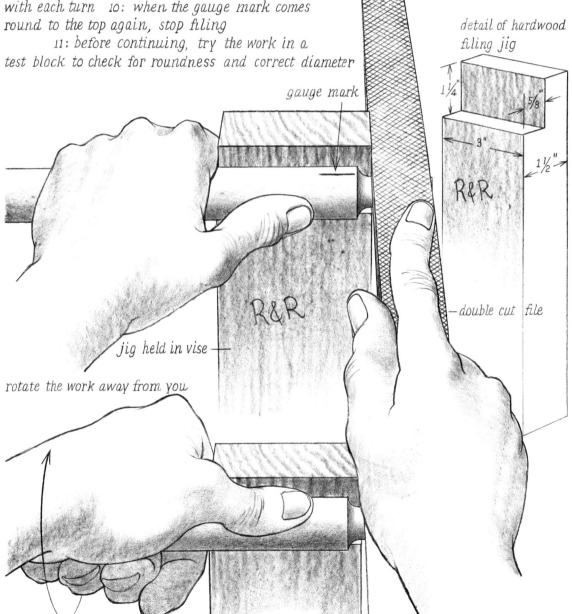

gauge mark

*detail of hardwood*
*filing jig*

1¼"

⅝"

3"

R&R

1½"

R&R

double cut file

jig held in vise

*rotate the work away from you*

*checking for roundness and correct diameter*

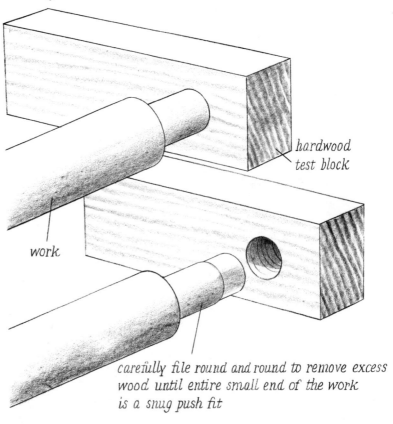

*hardwood test block*

*work*

*carefully file round and round to remove excess wood until entire small end of the work is a snug push fit*

*the round-and-round technique used for tapered work*

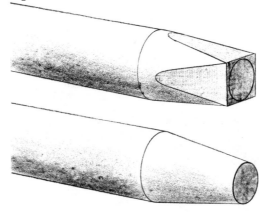

tang file-shaped and sharpened
for scraping grooves and moldings

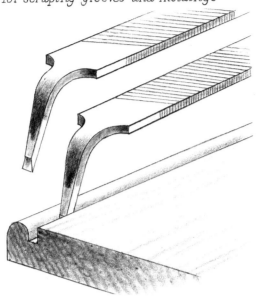

finishing the shaping of a saw handle with file and rasp

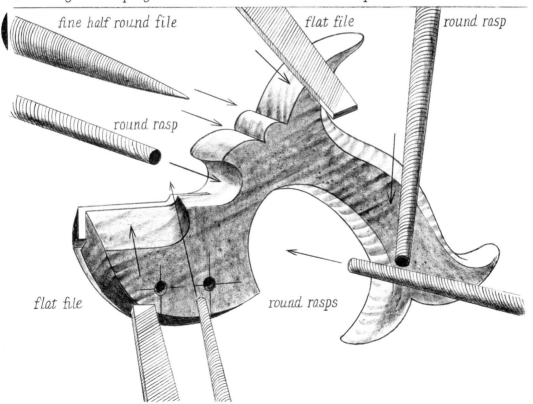

fine half round file

flat file

round rasp

round rasp

flat file

round rasps

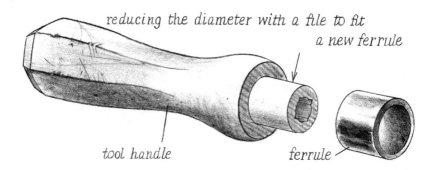

*reducing the diameter with a file to fit a new ferrule*

*tool handle*

*ferrule*

# Using a Rasp

FLAT RASPING     The tool is as good as its name: a rasp produces a pronounced grating sound and a vibration in the hands. It cuts crudely but rapidly, leaving it to some other tool to bring the surface to a clean finish.

Hold the rasp at an angle of about 40 degrees to the work. A rasp needs more down pressure and more push than a file to hold it on the work and prevent its chattering. As with other cutting tools, work with the grain, not against it. Don't rasp too close to the finish mark. If you do, smoothing up with one of the other tools will probably use up too much wood and go below the line.

CURVED WORK     Using a rasp on any roundwork calls on the close coordination of both hands. To smooth a curved section free of grooves and torn wood, it is important to think of the hands and the rasp as one unit moving over the wood in a motion that is more of a sweep than a series of short strokes. As this unit strokes over the curved surface, rotate the rasp backward without interrupting the forward motion of hands-holding-the-tool. This requires rolling the rasp by its point with one hand while at the same time rotating the handle with the other. This technique calls on two simultaneous actions: the one is a flat forward cutting, the other a rotary smoothing motion. There is a lot to think about and all at once. Keep the rasp square to the edge of the work, push it at an angle to the length of the work, and rotate the rasp backward at a steady rate. Perfecting this technique takes some practice, but when manipulated in this way the rasp will cut accurately and produce a surface that simply cannot be accomplished without back rotation. And since a curved section is difficult to clean up anyway, getting it as smooth as possible the first time around is the main objective.

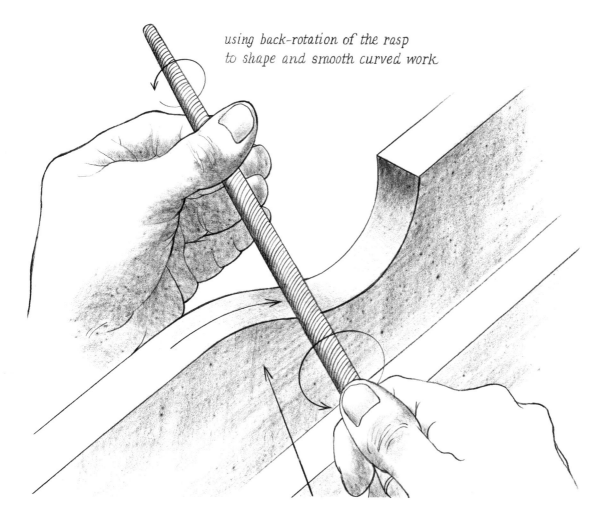

using back-rotation of the rasp
to shape and smooth curved work

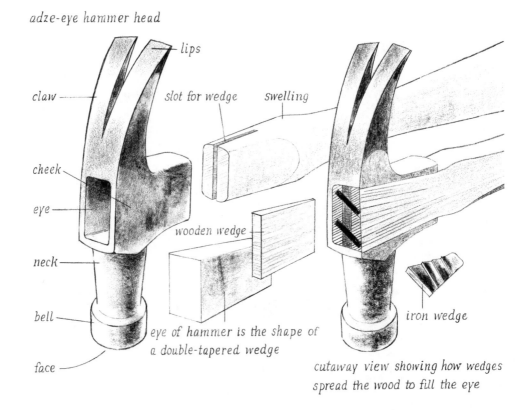

adze-eye hammer head

lips

claw

slot for wedge

swelling

cheek

eye

wooden wedge

neck

bell

face

eye of hammer is the shape of
a double-tapered wedge

iron wedge

cutaway view showing how wedges
spread the wood to fill the eye

# 12

# Hammer

Three things we can't do without: the wheel, the hammer, and the saw. Limited to a single function, the saw only cuts and the wheel merely turns. But the hammer combines two diametrically opposed principles—pounding and levering—with singular engineering simplicity. In pounding, the enormous stress of impact is absorbed almost entirely by the steel head whereas, in prying with the claws, it is the handle that takes most of the strain.

A number of factors influence the selection of the right hammer for the particular job: the weight and shape of the head, the length and material of the handle, and the curvature of the claws. In the annals of hammer design there are dozens of individual types; the woodworking trades alone account for at least 15 or 20. If you were a professional house framer, you would want something heftier than the light hammer used by a cabinetmaker. It's a good deal less exhausting to drive nails all day with a 28-ounce framing hammer—letting the heavy head do most of the work—than to use a 16-ounce model. If you are building scaffolds and concrete forms for a living—pulling nails as much as driving them—you'd be better off with a standard, curved-claw hammer that can do both.

## Wooden Handles

The common hammer has a foot-long hickory handle, secured through the eye of the head with a wooden wedge and a pair of iron ones. This hammer will do all the pounding, pulling, tapping, knocking, and prying likely to come up in a day's work. Since a hammer is no less an extension of the arm than any other tool, it is important to have one that is suited to your size and is comfortable to use. Wooden-handled styles are generally made either with an oval-turned shape or

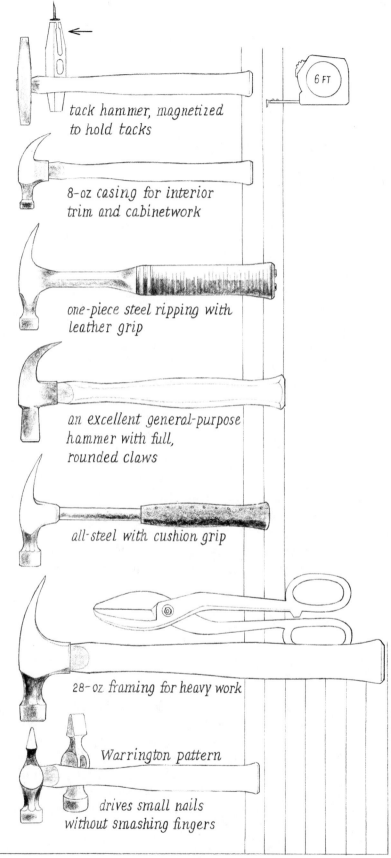

tack hammer, magnetized
to hold tacks

8-oz casing for interior
trim and cabinetwork

one-piece steel ripping with
leather grip

an excellent general-purpose
hammer with full,
rounded claws

all-steel with cushion grip

28-oz framing for heavy work

Warrington pattern

drives small nails
without smashing fingers

inches   11  12  13  14  15  16  17  18

an octagonal one. Of the two, the octagonal handle may have the edge in providing a more positive grip. Most wooden handles conform to a uniform design: the thinnest part is just back of the head, then it swells to a larger diameter, and tapers back to another swelling at the end, which keeps the hammer from slipping out of your hand.

Many woodworkers prefer a wooden handle to a steel one, partly because of the comfortable shape, partly because the tackiness of hand-on-wood provides better control, but also because the natural elasticity of wood absorbs more of the shock of pounding than steel. Despite its extreme hardness and strength, a hickory handle has surprising flexibility. Northern white ash is a close second, although its grain does not finish up or remain as smooth. Handles advertised simply as hardwood, although they may technically qualify as one of the hardwood species, will probably lack the necessary properties.

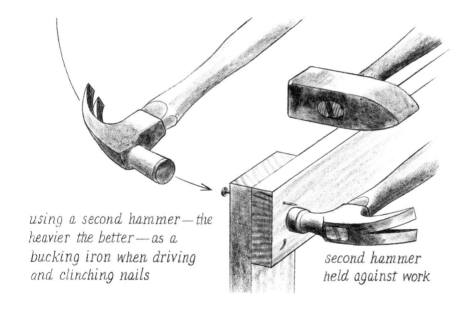

*using a second hammer—the heavier the better—as a bucking iron when driving and clinching nails*

*second hammer held against work*

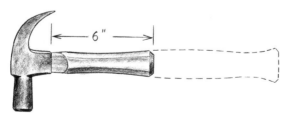

*an extra hammer with cutoff handle is excellent for working in cramped quarters*

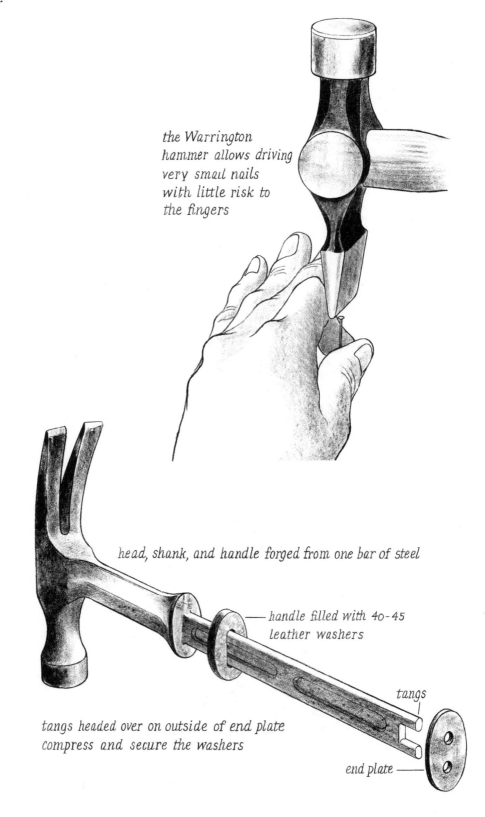

the Warrington hammer allows driving very small nails with little risk to the fingers

head, shank, and handle forged from one bar of steel

handle filled with 40-45 leather washers

tangs

tangs headed over on outside of end plate compress and secure the washers

end plate

# Warrington Pattern

This is an ideal bench hammer for general cabinetwork where nail pulling is not required. The thin, rounded cross peen drives quite a fine brad without the usual risk of hitting a finger. It is excellent for tapping wooden parts into alignment, for which purpose the face should be kept smooth and polished to avoid denting the work. As these hammers come from the factory, the peens may not all be uniformly shaped. An edge that is too pointed will glance off the nail, but a few strokes of the oilstone will give the peen a rounded shape.

# All Steel

Steel hammers are manufactured in several versions. One type is forged from a single bar of steel—head, shank, and handle all one piece, with a grip consisting of thick compressed leather washers. Of all the steel hammers, this one is the toughest. Another style is assembled from two separate pieces, a forged steel head bonded to a solid steel handle covered with a resilient sleeve. This version rates second place only because the bonding creates a joint and the possibility of a weak point. A third variety is pretty much the same except that the handle is of tubular steel. And, given enough stress, tubular steel can collapse. When it does, no more hammer.

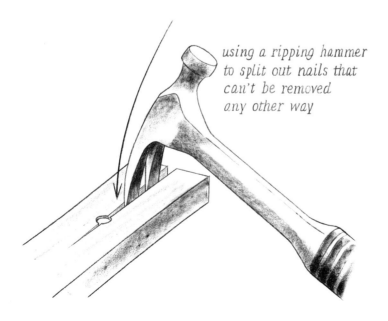

*using a ripping hammer to split out nails that can't be removed any other way*

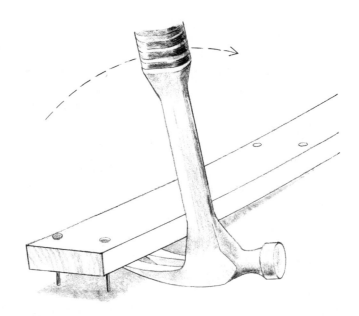

straight claw ripping hammer used for wrecking

claws chopped
behind the board
and pried out

pulling nail stumps

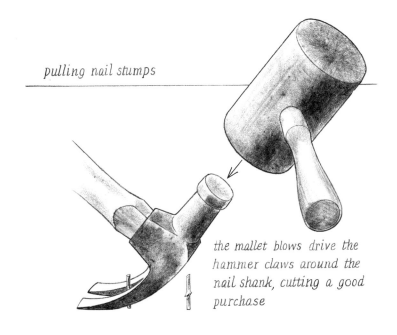

the mallet blows drive the
hammer claws around the
nail shank, cutting a good
purchase

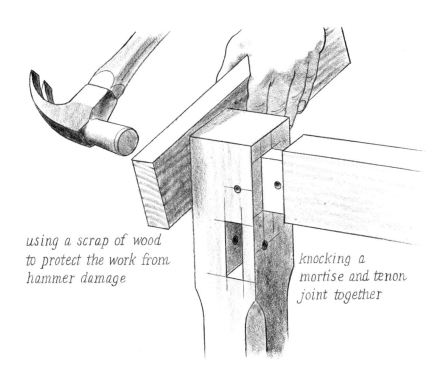

using a scrap of wood
to protect the work from
hammer damage

knocking a
mortise and tenon
joint together

*grip the handle about midway for light work*

*near the end for maximum driving force*

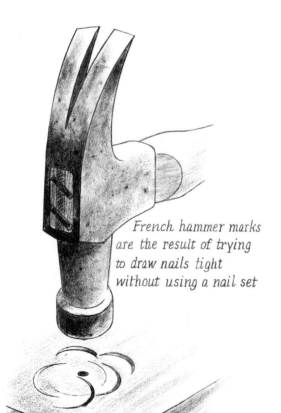

*French hammer marks are the result of trying to draw nails tight without using a nail set*

*thumb on top for more control*

The efficiency of the hammer depends to a large extent on where and how it is held, since this tool is an extension of the shoulder as well as the arm. Wrap the fingers around the handle in a natural grasp—good and firm but not so as to turn the knuckles white. In most hammer work there is little wrist action: locked onto the handle, the hand, wrist, and arm become one with it. Hold the hammer out near the end and you use its full mechanical advantage. Swinging from the elbow and shoulder delivers a tremendous force for driving spikes. For small nails, brads, and tacks, use the same grip but with a much lighter stroke, or slide the hand closer to the head, steadying the grip with a thumb laid on top of the handle. Somewhere between driving brads and pounding home a 20-penny nail is where the majority of work will fall.

On rough work requiring large nails, the blows are delivered with mounting force. The idea here is for the last and hardest blow to sink the nail head into the wood, drawing it up tight. Finish work, on the other hand, calls for a different approach. Use good steady blows, then ease up for the last two or three. The final blow should just kiss the wood. Where finish nails are used, drive the nail not quite flush with the wood. Leave the head projecting. Take up a nail set and hold the point firmly on the center of the nail. Finish nails are obligingly made with a slight depression in the center of the head. Hold the set perpendicular, then give the nail set a smart whack or two with the hammer to set the head $1/8$ inch or less below the surface. Despite its cupped end, the conventional nail set too often slips off the head of the nail and damages the work. Grinding a point on the set virtually eliminates any chance of this happening. A center punch can be used to set nails, but because of its thicker shank there is some danger of spreading the size of the nail hole.

Driving nails without battering the adjacent woodwork is not only a matter of good aim and plenty of practice but also of right thinking. In building a horse stall or some similar rough work, bruised wood is of small consequence, even if exasperating. But on finish work such as door and window trim, those French hammer marks will haunt the workman forever. Start the nail with a fair tap of the hammer, then slide the hand out near the end of the handle, ready for heavier strokes. Now apply the right thinking: (1) keep your eye on the nail—not on your hand or the hammer; (2) think of the hammer as part of your arm, swinging in an arc; (3) use decisive blows—not timid tapping; and (4) follow through, don't worry about bringing the stroke to a stop. The nail takes care of that.

Given the proper alignment of hammer and nail, powerful blows will drive nails without bending them, even in hardwood. It's all in the way you start. To make sure everything is lined up and ready, a carpenter will often give a starting nail a couple of tentative taps before drawing back for the heavy blows. Incidentally, the blacksmith uses the same trial tapping of hammer on anvil for the same reason: it gets him thinking straight blows and delivering straight blows.

Even with a well-aimed blow, a hammer will sometimes glance off the nail, bending it or denting the wood, or both. This is often because the face of the hammer has been polished by constant use. With this in mind, some hammers are made with a checkered face, but by scrubbing it on a stone or a cement block, an ordinary hammer face can be roughened sufficiently to prevent slipping.

The chief function of the curved claws is to pull nails, although they have other uses as well. Claw hammers are made in two patterns: the full-curved version and the straight ripping claw. A full, well-rounded claw excels at pulling nails. A ripping hammer can be used to pull nails that are neither very large nor deeply embedded, but it is particularly suited to ripping off wood and metal lath and shingles, and for tearing apart nailed or screw-fastened wooden pieces. In a good hammer the claws should be well beveled and come to clean, sharp inside edges for gripping nails—sharp enough to grab the smooth shank of a nail. The slot between the two claws should be wide enough to accommodate at least a 10-penny nail. Forcing the claws under the edge of a board for prying is easier if the lips are tapered and not too blunt. A little grinding with an oilstone will remedy this detail.

The most common trouble in pulling nails comes from trying to yank too big a nail from too hard a piece of wood. Remember—the thinnest part of a wooden handle is just back of the head, so designed to give the handle a shock-absorbing quality when pounding. When a hammer is used for pulling nails, however, that becomes its weakest point. A 10-penny nail can be drawn from soft pine with no risk to the hammer, but if embedded in solid oak it may well break the handle. The cure for this hazard is simple: put a block of wood under the claws to regain the full mechanical advantage and put the strain where it belongs. It might appear that the one-piece steel hammer is immune to these liabilities, yet this is not necessarily so. Everything has its limitations—even steel. A beefy carpenter using all his muscle on a 20-penny nail in a locust post can expect something to give. More than one such hammer has thus been bent. In a situation like that, reach for a wrecking bar—a tool that can really take it.

No matter how many hammers you decide to own, look them over carefully and pick them to match the work they'll be asked to do. Within each of the basic hammer types there are several variations, and although they all will drive nails and some will also pull nails, among the lot there is bound to be one that suits you. When you can reach out and pick a familiar hammer off the bench without looking at it, you'll know you have one that fits.

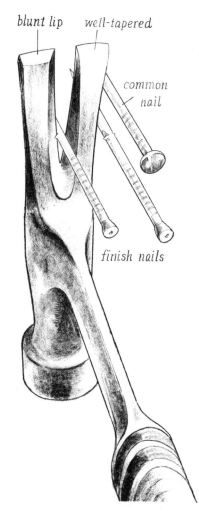

*blunt lip*    *well-tapered*

*common nail*

*finish nails*

*put a block of wood under the claws*
*to relieve the strain on the handle*

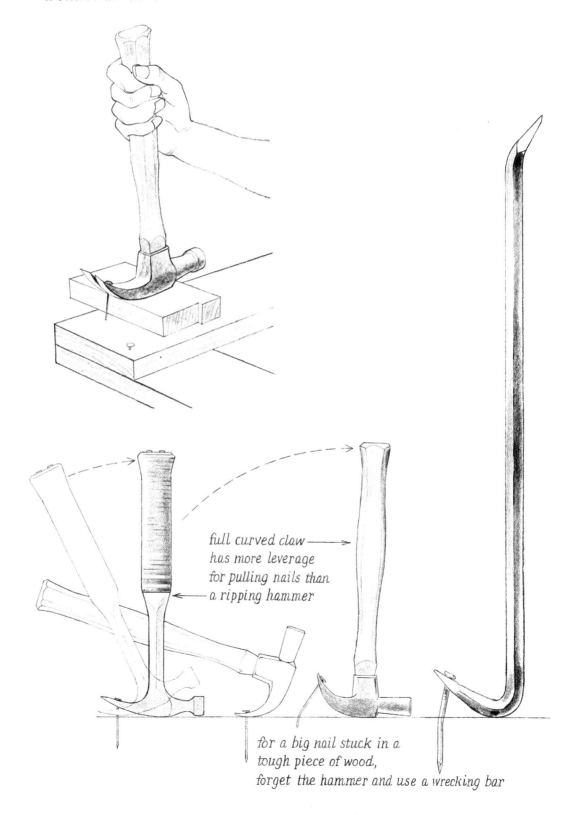

*full curved claw*
*has more leverage*
*for pulling nails than*
*a ripping hammer*

*for a big nail stuck in a*
*tough piece of wood,*
*forget the hammer and use a wrecking bar*

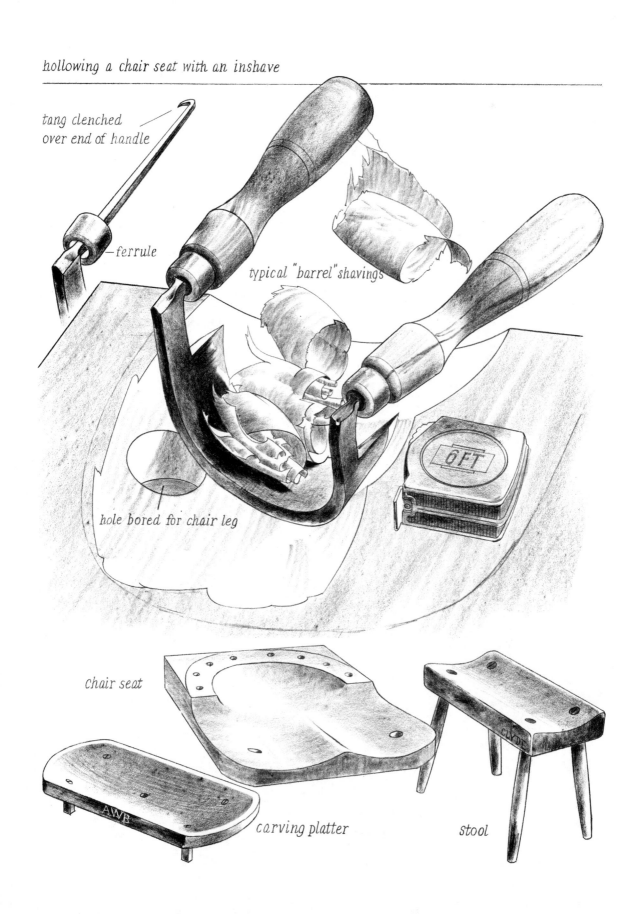

tang clenched
over end of handle

ferrule

typical "barrel" shavings

hole bored for chair leg

6FT

chair seat

carving platter

stool

AWB

# 13

# Inshave

This is the tool for hollowing a chair seat, bowl, trencher, or carving platter. It is built tough to accommodate the necessary heavy pulling of the shoulder and back muscles. Although hollow work can be done with chisels, mallet, and scraper, this "crooked drawknife" does the work directly to bring the wood surface to a nice finish with far less clean-up work.

Most of the work techniques used with a drawknife apply to the inshave as well. Set your feet apart, one a little ahead of the other to brace and establish your balance. Get a good grip on the handles, then lean back while holding your arms in a fixed position. Good control comes from using not just the hands and arms but the whole body. Let your legs, hips, and back provide the force.

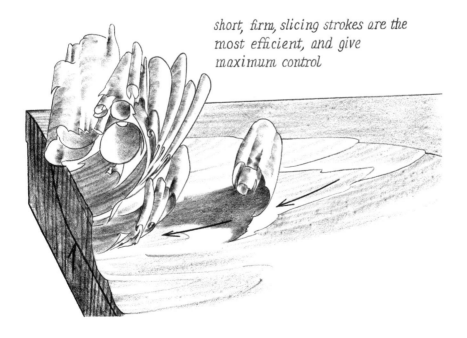

*short, firm, slicing strokes are the most efficient, and give maximum control*

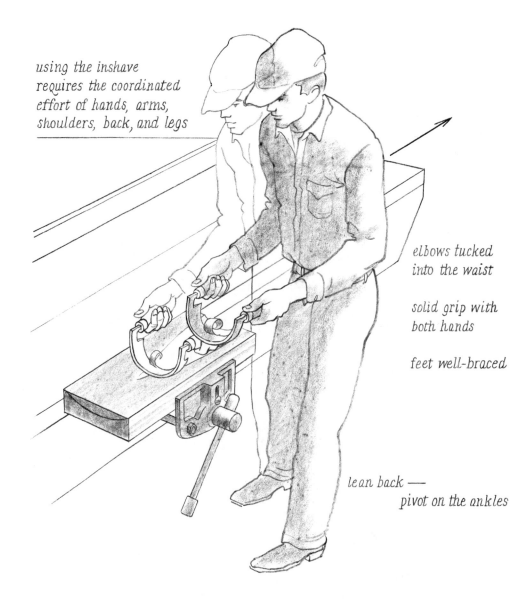

using the inshave
requires the coordinated
effort of hands, arms,
shoulders, back, and legs

elbows tucked
into the waist

solid grip with
both hands

feet well-braced

lean back —
pivot on the ankles

Draw the blade at an angle to the work for easier cutting. This slicing gives the most control not only for heavy cutting but also for removing wood in thin peels. Use short firm strokes. They produce better results than attempting long, continuous ones. With this way of working, the blade is less likely to dig too deeply or to yank out of the wood and send you off balance.

Cut in the direction of the emerging grain, the same as with any cutting tool. Working into a hollow with an inshave means cutting down toward the center from all four sides, calculating the strokes to meet evenly in the bottom. A sharp inshave will do this, and will slice cleanly across the grain at an angle, but it won't work at all well unless it has a really keen edge.

Because this oddly shaped tool requires such painstaking work to sharpen, it is worth a good deal of trouble to keep the cutting edge in good condition. A simple wooden blade guard that can be made in one evening will protect it and at the same time provide a safe way to store it on a shelf. The Appendix gives directions for making a blade guard.

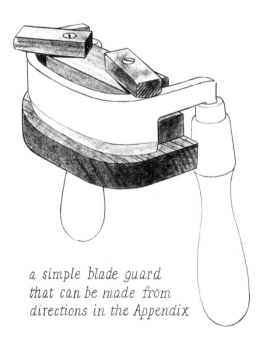

*a simple blade guard*
*that can be made from*
*directions in the Appendix*

*a knife is more accurate than a pencil for marking out, leaving a sharp, clean line for the saw to follow*

*enlarged view of mark scored by knife*

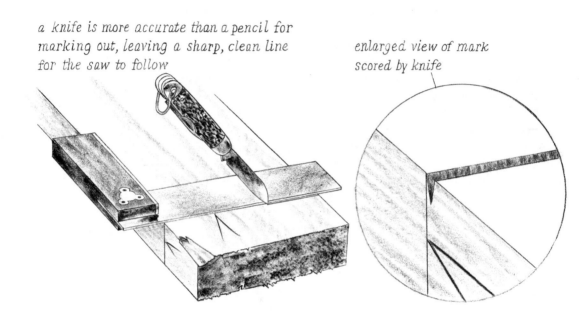

*quick and easy way to keep pencils sharp*

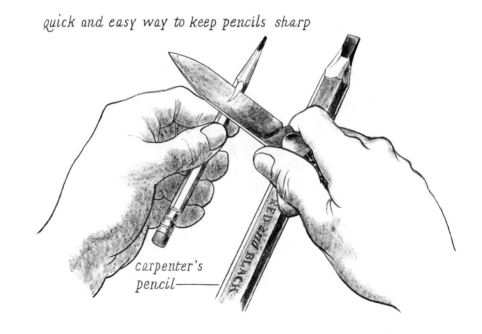

carpenter's pencil—

# 14

# Jackknife

A jackknife has a lot of everyday uses in the shop. A knife is the most accurate tool for laying off lines on wood to be sawn, planed, or otherwise accurately fitted. The line scored by a sharp knife is thin, clean, and definite: there's no mistaking where the mark is, and it won't rub off.

A simple knife with one or two blades is better than any of the types with a can opener, corkscrew, and screwdriver. They are too clumsy and the extra blades are of no value in the shop. But get a jackknife—not a pocket or penknife, both of which are too thin and flexible. And pay enough to get a good brand name that will hold an edge. A knife with a ring in one end is the easiest to hang up and keep track of.

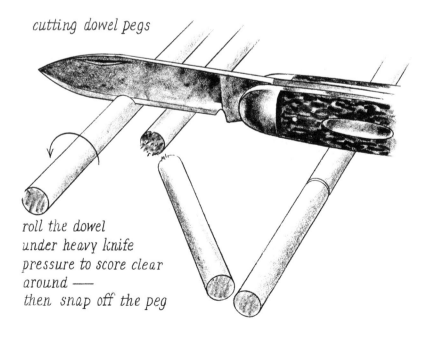

*cutting dowel pegs*

*roll the dowel under heavy knife pressure to score clear around —*
*then snap off the peg*

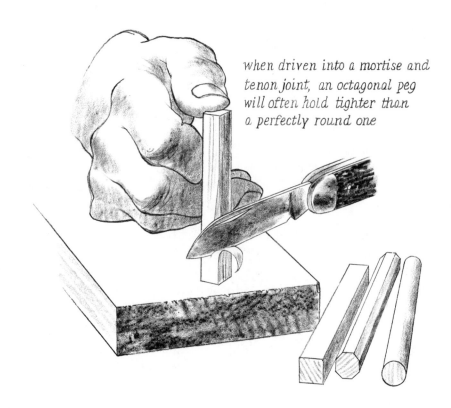

when driven into a mortise and
tenon joint, an octagonal peg
will often hold tighter than
a perfectly round one

splitting out joinery pegs
from a block of scrap wood

use light blows of
a rawhide or
wooden mallet

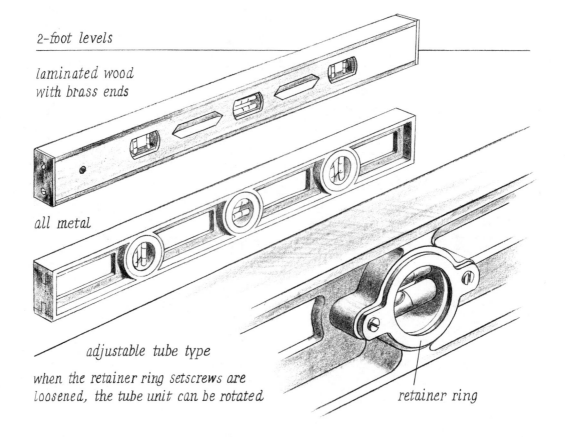

2-foot levels

laminated wood
with brass ends

all metal

adjustable tube type

when the retainer ring setscrews are
loosened, the tube unit can be rotated

retainer ring

# 15

# Level

The carpenter's level is a testing tool to check if your work is horizontally level and vertically plumb. It is an essential tool for framing a house, erecting partitions, installing windows, doors, staircases, and all the other permanent structural parts, as well as for remodeling and cabinetwork.

Levels are made of wood or metal. Laminated wood levels are more durable than the one-piece wooden style because they are less likely to warp or twist. They will generally take more abuse than a metal one because of the shock-absorbing qualities of wood. The metal models are virtually warp-proof and more weather-resistant, but the shock of mishandling is more directly transmitted to the glass tubes.

Although levels are made as long as $6^1/_2$ feet, the more common version is the 2-foot carpenter's level fitted with three sets of liquid-filled tubes. Note that there are two lines marked on each tube and that there is an air bubble trapped in each. The air bubble is calculated to the same length as the distance between the two lines. This is the whole works of a level. Absolute level is indicated when the bubble rests exactly between the two lines. The tubes in the center give horizontal level readings while the end tubes are used to check the plumb of vertical work. With one exception, the level must always be set against the work on edge, whether leveling or plumbing. Marking a plumb line on the wall for hanging wallpaper is an example of the one exception. In this instance, the level is laid flat on the wall, the plumb reading being taken as usual from the end tubes as though the level were on edge against a doorframe.

Whether made of wood or metal, a level is a sensitive instrument and should be treated as such. Dropping it on anything hard—floor, concrete, or pavement—is very likely to jar the tubes out of adjustment. And while for this reason some levels are made with adjustable tubes, recalibrating them is a touchy job.

*used vertically to test for plumb*

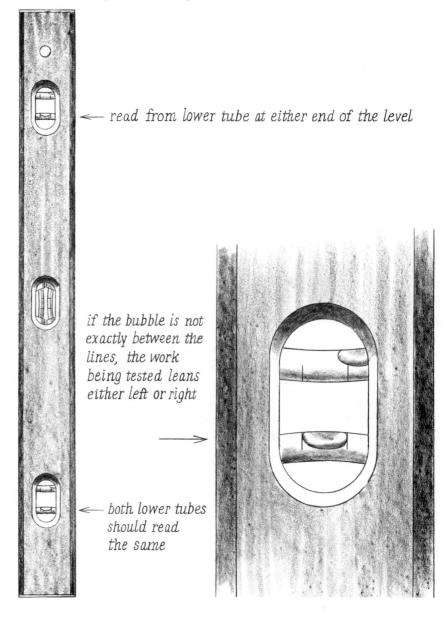

← read from lower tube at either end of the level

*if the bubble is not exactly between the lines, the work being tested leans either left or right*

← both lower tubes should read the same

*used horizontally to test for level*

*read lower tube*

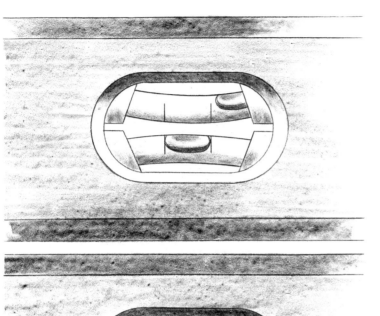

*always read only from the lower tube —— when the bubble rests exactly between the lines, it indicates level*

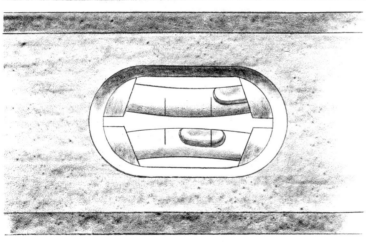

*not level — low on the left*

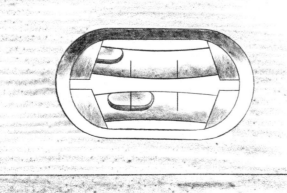

*not level — low on the right*

# Using the Level

Here is a typical situation—the installation of a 6-foot bookcase along a wall and 8 inches from a doorway in order to stay clear of a light switch. The bookcase is finished except for putting on the skirt board, which will rest on the floor.

Make a pencil mark on the wall near the switch and 8 inches out from the doorframe. Stand the bookcase against the wall, then shuck it one way or another until it touches the mark. At first glance it is obvious that something is wrong: the bookcase tilts away from the doorframe. There's nothing the matter with the bookcase—it was built square. The door could be at fault, but it's plain to see that it's the floor. In old houses—and sometimes in new ones—it is quite common to find floors that are not level and walls that are out of plumb. This is usually because the timbers have dried out, allowing the floor beams to sag and settle. In newer houses, however, these defects more often point to the use of inferior lumber and poor construction. These are the conditions, too, that make doors stick or prevent their shutting.

CHECKING THE FLOOR FOR LEVEL    Simply laying the 2-foot level on the floor will not give an accurate measure of its levelness, since it will only test a distance equal to its own length. Even a $6^1/_2$-foot mason's level would not be much more accurate here. What's needed is a long straightedge—some way to extend the length of the level clear across the room. Find a 5-inch or 6-inch board that will span the whole floor or the best part of it. Sight along an edge to make sure it is straight, then mark the center of the board with a pencil line. Stand the board on edge and hold the level on top of it, centered over the pencil mark. Look at the set of tubes in the middle of the level. Take a reading from the lower one. Put shims of scrap wood under the low end of the board until you get a true level reading. This shows by how much the entire floor is out of level, but since the slope may be wavy rather than perfectly even, the bookcase itself must be leveled right where it stands.

CHECKING THE BOOKCASE FOR LEVEL    Lay the level on one shelf and take a reading. If the air bubble is off center—not at rest exactly between the two lines—the floor under the bookcase is also out of level. Get some wooden shims. The thin ends of tapered wooden shingles are ideal. Slide a shim under the low end of the level and take a new reading. Add shims until the bubble comes to rest between the

a typical situation: installing a bookcase to make it level on a sloping floor

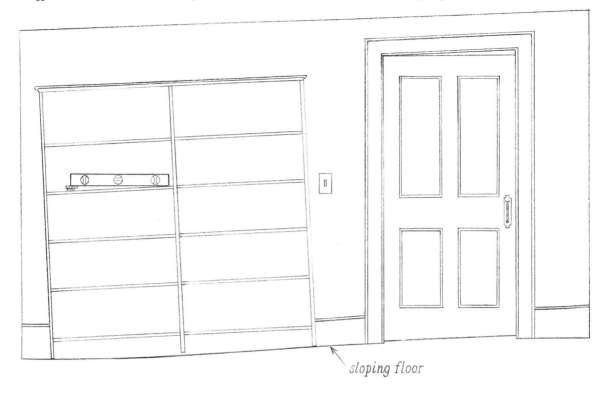

sloping floor

using a long straightedge to determine how much a floor is out of level

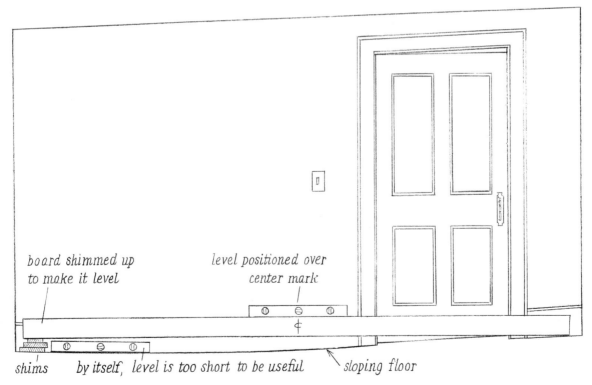

board shimmed up
to make it level

level positioned over
center mark

shims    by itself, level is too short to be useful    sloping floor

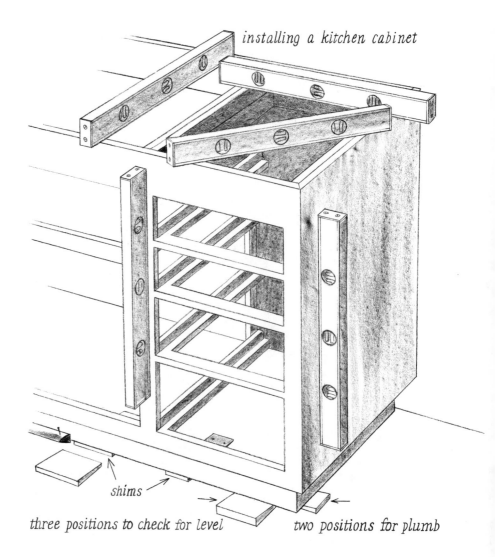

*installing a kitchen cabinet*

*shims*

*three positions to check for level*

*two positions for plumb*

lines, then measure the total thickness of the shims. Assume that it is $1/4$ inch. Since the level is 2 feet long, the bookcase is out of level $1/4$ inch in every 2 feet; and as the bookcase is 6 feet long, the low end has to be raised $3/4$ inch:

$$\frac{6 \text{ ft.}}{2 \text{ ft.}} = 3 \times 1/4'' = 3/4''$$

If the process of lifting and putting shims under the bookcase has shifted it away from the 8-inch mark on the wall, carefully inch it back, then make a final check with the level, trying it at both ends of the shelf and in the middle.

Now make a permanent shim $3/4$ inch thick and slide it in place. Lift the bookcase with a pry bar to avoid shucking it out of position. Now check the other direction. Does the bookcase tilt out from the wall? Lay the level on top of the bookcase, sticking straight out from the wall. Hold it down with one hand. Check the lower tube again, and go through the same procedure to see how much shimming is needed under the front edge of the bookcase. Make the shims and put them in place. Then check your work one more time with the level. If everything reads level, tack the shims to the floor with brads, scribe and cut the skirt board to fit the sloping floor, and nail it on.

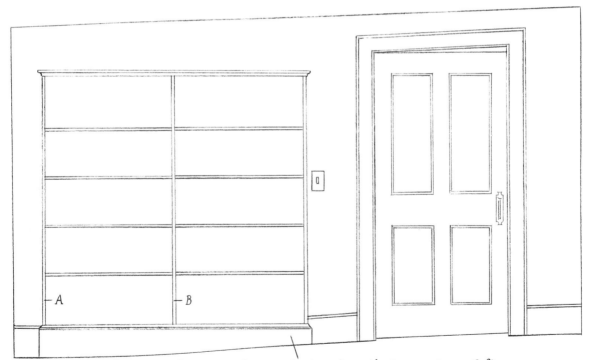

*shims nailed in place under legs A and B, skirt board scribed to contour of floor and nailed in place*

A similar problem comes up when situating a table on an uneven floor. Three of the table legs will be too short but each to a different degree. Putting shims under table legs is a somewhat shiftless solution, even if you don't intend moving it. A much neater way is to add wood to the short legs, having first determined the correct length for each by using the same shim-and-level method. Bore holes in the ends of the short legs and insert dowels that are a bit smaller in diameter. Don't glue them in. Instead, glue a narrow band of paper around the hidden end of the dowel, enough to make a tight push-fit. Then trim off the dowels to bring the tabletop level. These short stumps will be unobtrusive and can easily be removed without damaging the table.

TESTING FOR PLUMB    Hold the level vertically against the work. In checking the same bookcase, hold it against one end. Take readings from the lower tube at both ends of the level—the ones that arch up. If the bookcase was built square and you have leveled it carefully, the level should now show a plumb reading with the lower bubbles in both end tubes exactly the same.

DOUBLE CHECKING    To check your accuracy, switch the level end-for-end and side-for-side as well as diagonally, where it's practical. All the readings should check out. If not, the tubes may be out of adjustment. They can be corrected, provided the level is one with adjustable tubes and the manufacturer's instructions are followed. But there's not much to be done for a level with permanently fixed tubes.

*situating a table on an uneven floor*

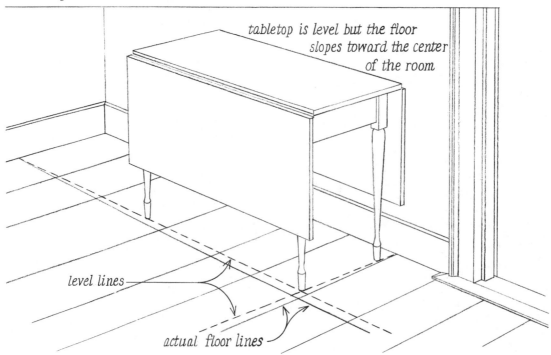

tabletop is level but the floor slopes toward the center of the room

level lines

actual floor lines

*adding wood to the short legs*

*find the center and bore a hole 1" deep*

cut off to length

band of paper
glued to
dowel

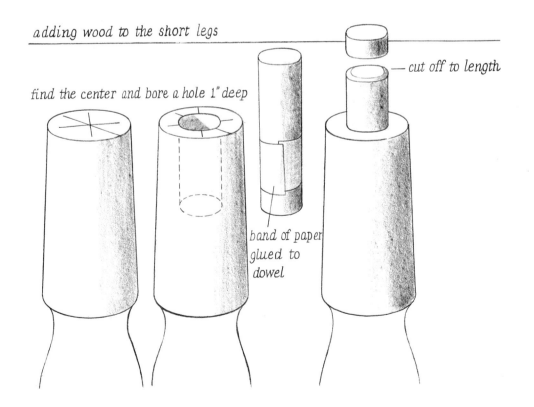

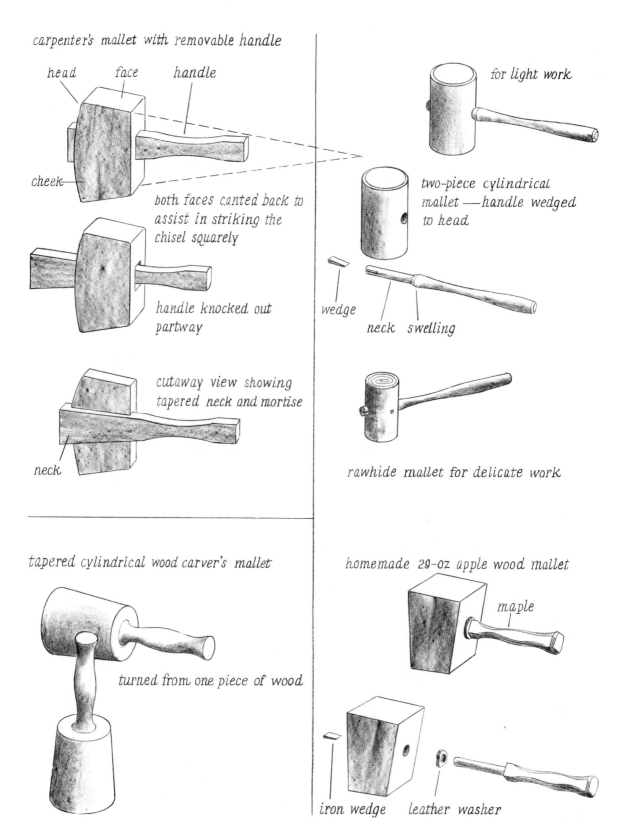

carpenter's mallet with removable handle

head    face    handle

cheek

for light work

both faces canted back to assist in striking the chisel squarely

handle knocked out partway

two-piece cylindrical mallet — handle wedged to head

wedge

neck    swelling

cutaway view showing tapered neck and mortise

neck

rawhide mallet for delicate work

tapered cylindrical wood carver's mallet

turned from one piece of wood

homemade 29-oz apple wood mallet

maple

iron wedge    leather washer

# 16

# Mallet

The wooden mallet is designed primarily for one job—to drive chisels without mushrooming or splitting their handles. Although some handles are reinforced with steel hoops or made of high-impact plastic, supposedly able to withstand the pounding of a hammer, the wooden mallet is still the best tool for the job. Its larger face gives a mallet a clear advantage over a hammer. The face of a hammer is no bigger than the end of a chisel handle, which puts upon the workman the difficult obligation to strike always with infallible aim just when he should be watching the cutting end of the chisel instead. And with its polished face, the hammer too often glances off, bruising a hand, or missing the chisel entirely, often with irreparable damage to the work.

On the other hand, it is difficult to miss with a mallet whose face area is close to $7^1/_2$ square inches. And the wooden mallet "sticks" to the end of a chisel handle better than a hammer, which is likely to bounce back.

Mallets are built very much the way they have always been, hardly more than a chunk of wood with a handle stuck into one side. Mallet heads are made of close-grained, shock-resistant hardwoods such as maple, hickory, beech, cherry and other fruitwoods, and the tropical lignum vitae which is extremely dense, although in our drier climate it is susceptible to end checking.

Of the three types—cylindrical, carpenter's, and wood carver's—the first is more of a tapping mallet for light chisel work or for gently knocking pieces of finished wood together during assembly. The much heavier carpenter's and carver's mallets have short handles which in itself contributes to delivering more forceful blows. Where a chisel must remove large amounts of wood, a heavy mallet head combined with a choked grip on its handle do the job more easily. With the hand snug against the head there is more efficient control than when using the kind of wide arc swing typical of driving spikes with a hammer, as well as a feel for directing the blows more accurately. The mallet should heft and work in the manner of a doubled-up fist pounding on the chisel.

Picking a handle that fits your particular hand has a strong bearing on how well it will perform. It should be large enough in circumference so that your fingers don't dig into your palm when they close around the handle. One reason the cylindrical mallet is not suited to heavy pounding is that the fingers cannot get a firm enough grip on its slender handle.

In these respects a 24-ounce carpenter's mallet is an exceptionally handy choice. Because both faces of this type are canted back toward the end of the handle, striking it squarely on a chisel comes much more naturally, and with less fatigue. If you think about holding a weight attached to the end of a stick, it's plainly easier to support it when the hand is close to the weight. Swinging a long-handled mallet would soon cramp the wrist and waste energy that could be better used for pounding.

If a mallet is used for nothing but striking wood-handled chisels it will last a good long time. But when substituted for a hammer to drive nails, bolts, or a nail set, the smooth face so necessary for reliable chisel work is soon mutilated beyond repair.

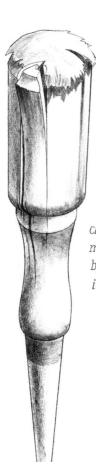

*chisel handle mushroomed and split by the use of a hammer instead of a mallet*

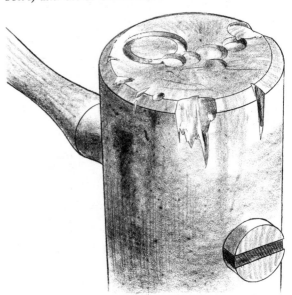

*mallet face damaged by pounding nails, bolts, and other hardware*

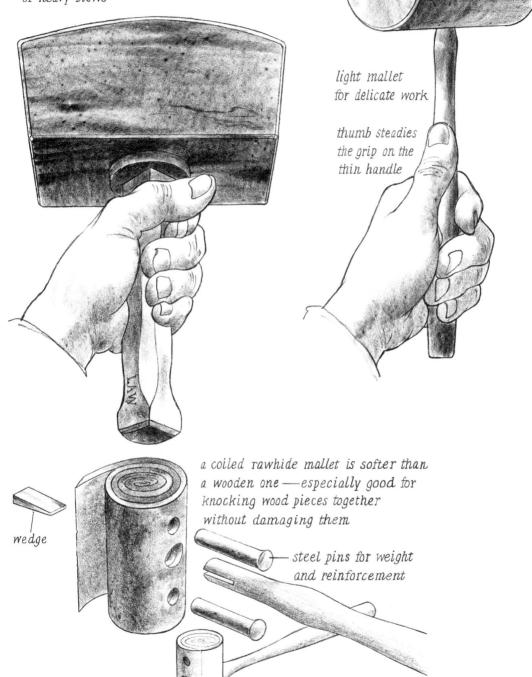

a choked grip on a large circumference handle gives good control of heavy blows

light mallet for delicate work

thumb steadies the grip on the thin handle

wedge

a coiled rawhide mallet is softer than a wooden one — especially good for knocking wood pieces together without damaging them

steel pins for weight and reinforcement

*hardwood marking gauge with brass fittings*

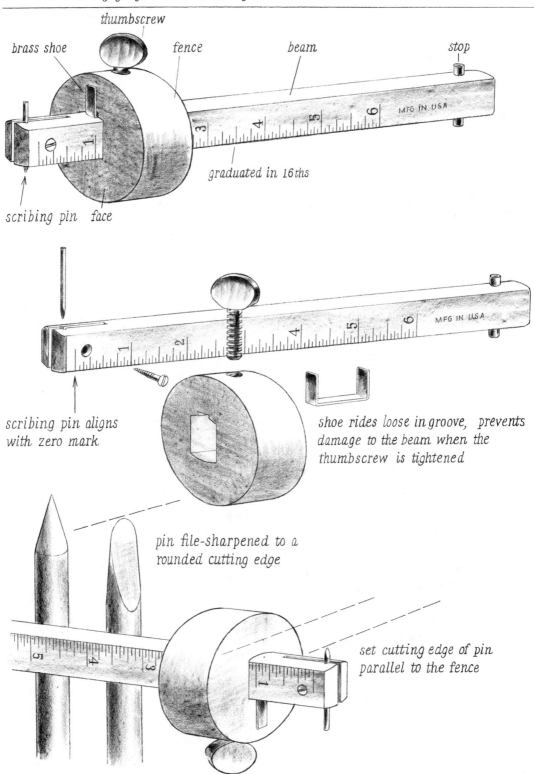

thumbscrew

brass shoe    fence    beam    stop

scribing pin    face

graduated in 16ths

scribing pin aligns
with zero mark

shoe rides loose in groove, prevents
damage to the beam when the
thumbscrew is tightened

pin file-sharpened to a
rounded cutting edge

set cutting edge of pin
parallel to the fence

MFG IN USA

# 17

# Marking Gauge

This is a marking tool for laying off lines to guide the work to be done with the saw, plane, chisel, or brace and bit, especially where precision is required as in a mortise and tenon joint. In principle it is a "notched stick with an adjustable notch." And it is a great time-saver when laying out identical repeat operations.

Absolutely simple in construction, it consists of a fence that slides on a beam and is held at any setting by a thumbscrew. There are numerous plain and fancy gauges on the market, some made of exotic woods and fitted with inlaid brass wear plates, some with beams graduated in 16ths, and others with no scale at all.

No matter how elaborate and expensive, they all work in the same way. To set the gauge, loosen the thumbscrew and slide the fence along the beam to the measurement you want and tighten the thumbscrew—a little. Only a slight pressure on the screw is needed to hold the fence. Whether or not your gauge has a scale, the setting should now be checked with a rule. Set the rule on edge, resting on the point of the scribing pin and butted against the fence. If necessary, readjust

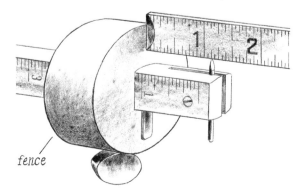

*check the setting with the rule butted against the fence and resting on the scribing pin*

*fence*

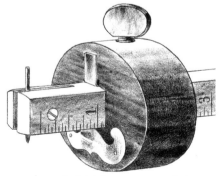

*some gauges have inlaid brass wear plates to protect the face of the wooden fence*

the fence, then run off a trial marking on a scrap of wood. Check the trial with the rule. Setting the fence by the scale alone is not as accurate as making trials until the precise setting is obtained. In this respect, therefore, the scale on the beam is primarily useful in getting an approximate setting.

Some gauges have a simple pointed pin that makes a relatively ragged mark very much like that of a scratch awl. I prefer to flatten the point on the anvil and then sharpen it so that it scores a clean line with no fuzzy edges. And such a point marks just as neatly across the grain as it does the long way.

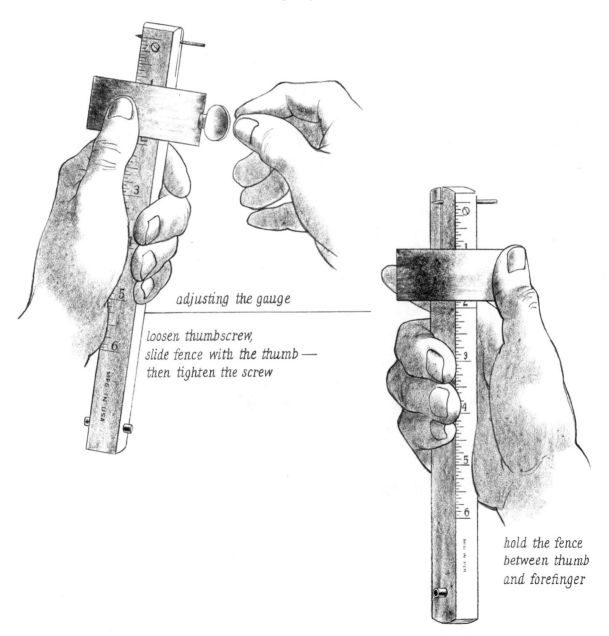

*adjusting the gauge*

*loosen thumbscrew,*
*slide fence with the thumb —*
*then tighten the screw*

*hold the fence*
*between thumb*
*and forefinger*

*scribing a line with the marking gauge*

*start the gauge a distance in from the end of the board — tip gauge away from you so the point of the scribing pin drags at an angle*

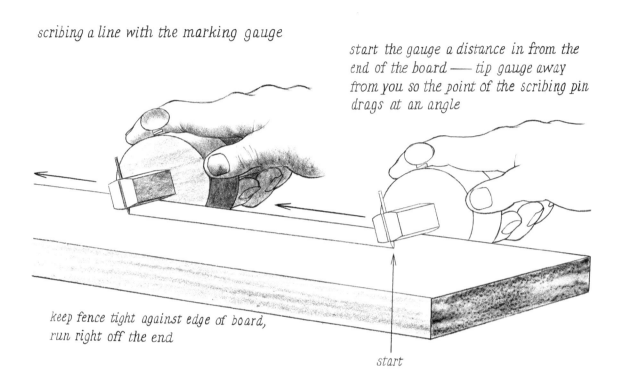

*keep fence tight against edge of board, run right off the end*

*start*

*tip the gauge toward you and draw it back and off the end of the board*

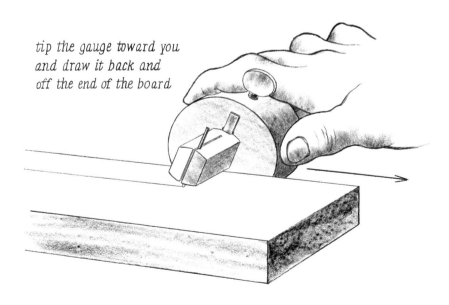

*laying out joints*

rabbet

mortise

the gauge marks a
line that is precise
and that will not
rub off or get blurred

tenon

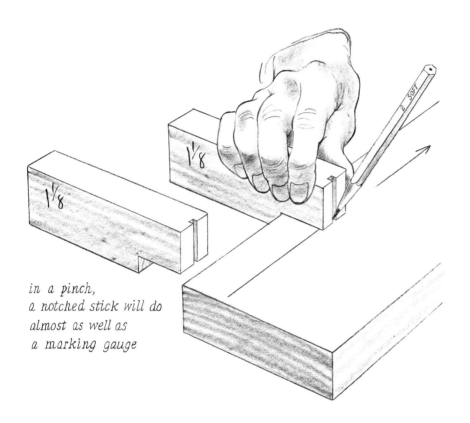

*in a pinch,*
*a notched stick will do*
*almost as well as*
*a marking gauge*

mitered corners used in finished interior woodwork

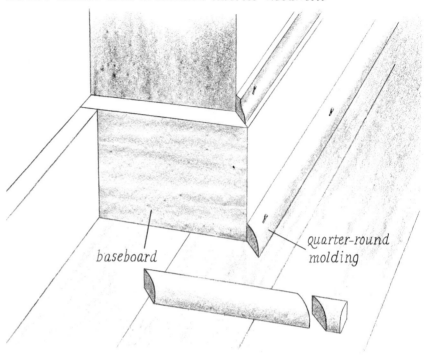

quarter-round molding

baseboard

corner made with a butt joint

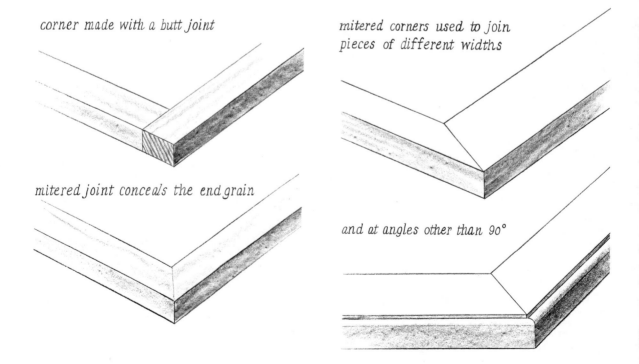

mitered joint conceals the end grain

mitered corners used to join pieces of different widths

and at angles other than 90°

# 18

# Mitering Tools

The most common mitered joint is one in which the ends of two sticks are cut at 45-degree angles in order to go together and make a 90-degree square corner. Typically, this joint is used when fitting moldings around corners, making cupboard door frames, and for any work where neat appearance requires covering the end grain of wood.

The difficult part of making a mitered joint is not in marking it out but in sawing it accurately and then planing it true. The work can be laid out easily enough with a combination square or by using the halved-square method. The problem comes in sawing accurately in two planes at the same time: 45 degrees in one plane and 90 degrees in the other. And there is the same difficulty in later smoothing up the saw cut with a plane or chisel.

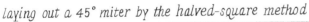

*laying out a 45° miter by the halved-square method*

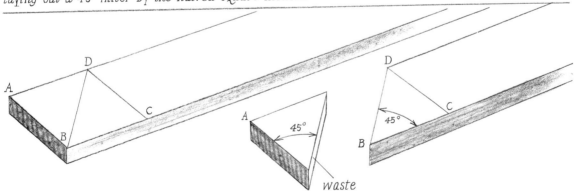

*square the end of the board and measure its width A B*

*mark off the same dimension along edge of board, from B to C*

*using a square, draw a line from C to D*

*draw a diagonal line from D to B*

To facilitate this work there are a number of simple jigs and devices designed to guide the cutting tool: saw, plane, or chisel as the case may be. The common miter box and miter block are for cutting 45-degree and 90-degree angles, usually with a fine-toothed backsaw. For the work of cleaning up after the saw the shooting board and donkey's ear are used in conjunction with a plane, and the miter template with a chisel.

There are a half-dozen types of miter boxes and guides on the market, differing widely in price and quality, from $5 to $350, some made entirely of wood, some all steel, and others a combination of the two. The cheap $5 box will most likely be quite inaccurate, and even one of the $50 models that was tested required much tinkering with shims before it would cut an accurate 45-degree angle.

With the exception of the expensive professional models whose critical parts are made of machined steel, no miter box produces cuts that are absolutely precise, perfectly smooth, and ready to be joined. There is always some plane or chisel work to be done.

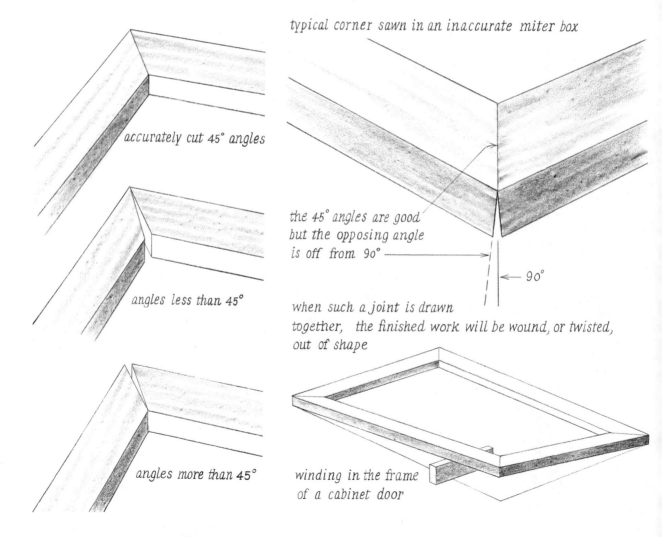

*typical corner sawn in an inaccurate miter box*

*accurately cut 45° angles*

*angles less than 45°*

*angles more than 45°*

*the 45° angles are good but the opposing angle is off from 90°* ⟶

⟵ 90°

*when such a joint is drawn together, the finished work will be wound, or twisted, out of shape*

*winding in the frame of a cabinet door*

plain wooden miter box

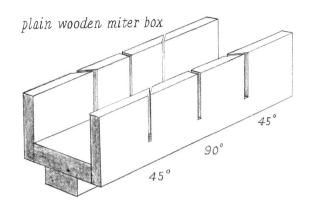

45°
90°
45°

a similar box with braces to reduce
inaccuracies due to warping
of the sides

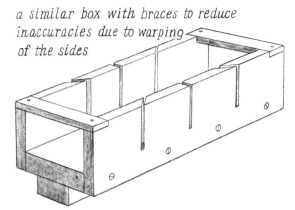

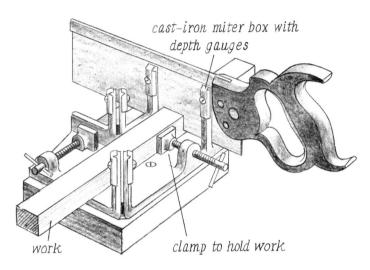

cast-iron miter box with
depth gauges

work

clamp to hold work

cutting a miter on a wide board
with a guide strip clamped to the work

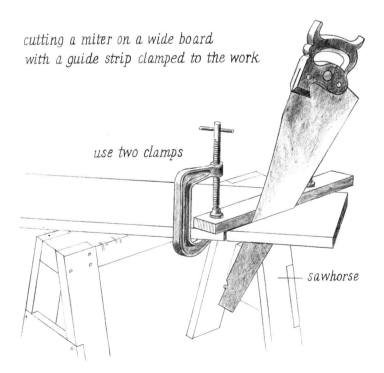

use two clamps

sawhorse

The most reliable way to make clean and accurate miters is to use either a miter block or a miter box in combination with a shooting board. In this two-step method the angle is first cut in the miter block with a fine backsaw and then shaved smooth with a plane on the shooting board.

One approach to acquiring these tools is to buy the best miter box you can afford, and make your own shooting board. However, since the procedures necessary to make one are the same as to make the other—and can be carried out with ordinary hand tools and a vise—both can be homemade at very little cost other than time and patience. I have found that a reliable miter block is simpler to build than a miter box and does excellent work every bit as precise as that done in a miter box. Detailed directions for making these tools are included in the Appendix.

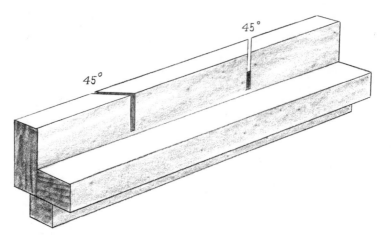

# Using the Miter Block

Clamp the miter block in the vise. It must be solid and secure, something against which to hold the work with one hand while you saw with the other. Lay the work on top of a piece of protective scrap wood in the miter block, then put the saw into the slot. *It is important to use the same saw that cut the slot in the block.* If you made the block with a 12-point backsaw and now use a 10-point crosscut to cut the miters, the thicker kerf of the 10-point will immediately destroy the accuracy of the miter block.

Gently lower the saw into the slot as you slide the work up to the mark. Saw outside the mark. When everything is lined up, squeeze the work against the block with one hand so it won't move while you saw clear through and into the scrap wood.

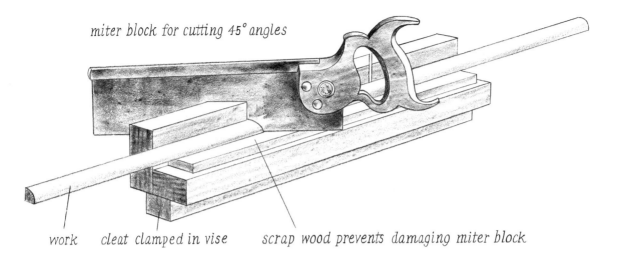

*miter block for cutting 45° angles*

*work*   *cleat clamped in vise*   *scrap wood prevents damaging miter block*

# Using the Shooting Board

The technical jack plane was designed especially for this work. Both its sides are machined square to the bottom, and the wider flare of its sides gives more bearing on the platform of the shooting board. However, any plane that tests similarly square will work just as well.

Set the plane for a very fine cut, making sure that the cutting edge is parallel with the bottom of the plane. Then lay it on its side on the shooting board. Put the workpiece on the shooting board against the stop and clamp it there with one hand. Ease the workpiece out into the path of the plane, at the same time sliding the plane forward and back along the shooting board. When the plane begins to cut wood, hold the workpiece tight so it can't move. Keep the plane tight against the stop and flat on the platform.

*shooting board for truing up sawn angles on small workpieces*

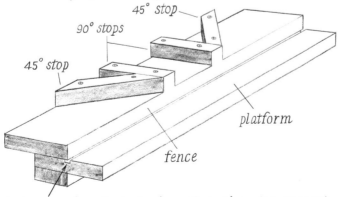

*45° stop*

*90° stops*

*45° stop*

*platform*

*fence*

*dust groove to collect shavings that otherwise prevent the plane from running tight up against the fence*

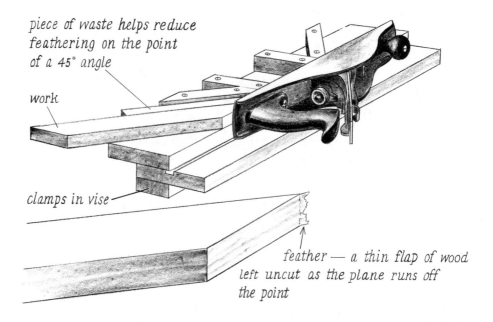

piece of waste helps reduce
feathering on the point
of a 45° angle

work

clamps in vise

feather — a thin flap of wood
left uncut as the plane runs off
the point

Shave off the least amount of wood possible. Four or five passes of the plane are normally enough to clean up the cut. However, if rough wood still shows on the angle and the plane has ceased cutting, push the work a whisker more into the plane's path and make two or three more passes.

The thin point of the mitered stick may "feather" as the saw drags wood past the corner. This can be avoided by laying a piece of waste wood in back of the work. The miter is finished when its entire area shows a uniformly clean, smooth-planed surface. Finally, use the combination square to check the accuracy of the work.

donkey's ear—
a shooting board for planing 45° angles on small workpieces

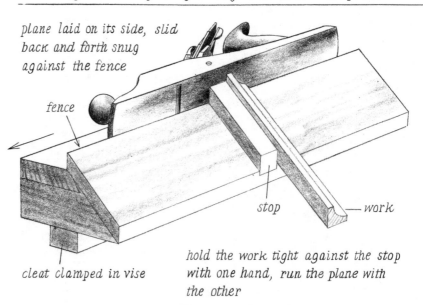

plane laid on its side, slid
back and forth snug
against the fence

fence

stop

work

cleat clamped in vise

hold the work tight against the stop
with one hand, run the plane with
the other

any plane whose sides are square to
the sole can be used with a
shooting board or donkey's ear

using a miter template and chisel to fit a 45° joint in a doorframe

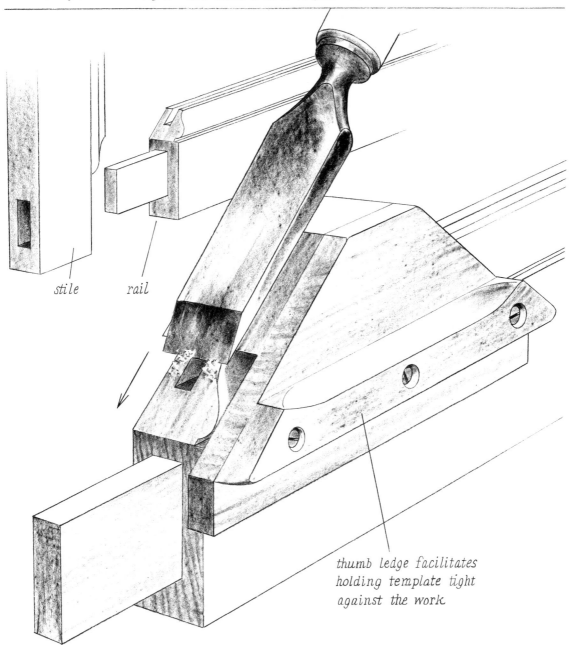

stile

rail

thumb ledge facilitates
holding template tight
against the work

hold the nail set perpendicular
and pressed firmly against the nail

nail set ground to a point

# 19

# Nail Set

This is a companion tool to the hammer used almost exclusively in interior woodwork which is fastened with finish nails: window and door trim, baseboards, staircases, paneling, or any other place where the nailing must be concealed and the wood surface left unmarred.

Used in the manner of a punch, it is held on the nail head and then given two or three smart hammer blows to drive or set the head about $1/8$ inch below the surface. These holes are then filled with putty which, when it has dried, are sanded flush with the woodwork, leaving the nails concealed.

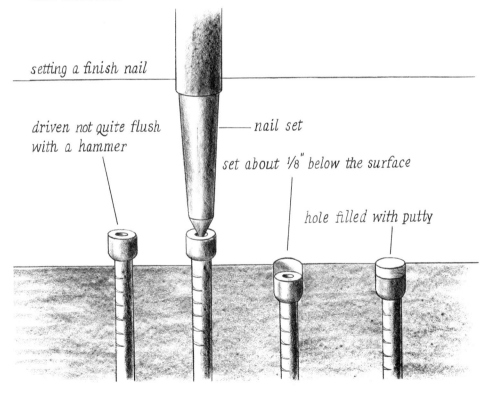

*setting a finish nail*

*driven not quite flush with a hammer*

*nail set*

*set about $1/8''$ below the surface*

*hole filled with putty*

In addition to this routine work, a nail set—or nail punch as it is often called—is useful for driving nails in close quarters where the hammer might strike the nearby wood, such as when nailing down molding next to a finished baseboard. It is safe enough to start a nail and drive it partway, but with the hammer striking so close to good wood, using a nail set eliminates the chance of denting it.

For either of these situations, the shape and size of the set are important. The tapered shank should be smaller in diameter than the driven nail, otherwise the set will spread the nail hole. Just as important is the shape of the point. One style of set has a simple, flat point, which is likely to slip off the nail head and punch holes in the surrounding wood. Another has a cupped point and works somewhat better, but both of them tend too much to skid off the nail and cause damage.

*nail set with*
*simple flat point*

*this handhold gives good visibility*
*when using a nail set in close quarters*

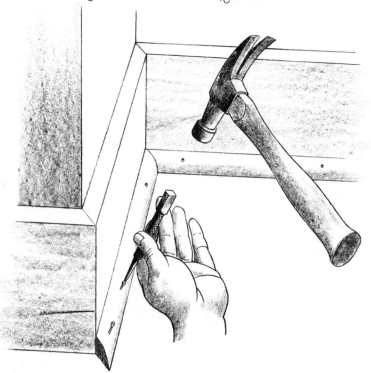

Most nails have a residue of manufacturing oil which makes them too slippery for either of these sets to hold onto reliably.

The best one I've used has a tip ground to a beveled point that fits neatly into the depression manufactured into the head of a finish nail. With the first hammer blow, this point punches a small crater in the nail head, and as long as the set is held in plumb alignment with the nail, it is virtually slip-proof. This type of set will also work on nails with perfectly smooth heads.

Common nails with large heads are rarely set because they are normally not used for finish work. But when you want to go round and tighten common nails, particularly old ones in long-dried lumber, a large punch draws the nail tighter into the wood and may actually sink the head below the surface.

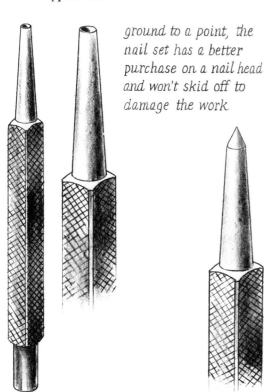

*conventional nail set with cupped end*

*ground to a point, the nail set has a better purchase on a nail head and won't skid off to damage the work*

*the nail set with cupped end is intended to cut a nonskid ring in the nail head and thus prevent the set from slipping off and damaging the woodwork ——*

*nail set ——*

*finish nail—*

*but this works only when the set is in perfect condition, and in perfect alignment and contact with the nail*

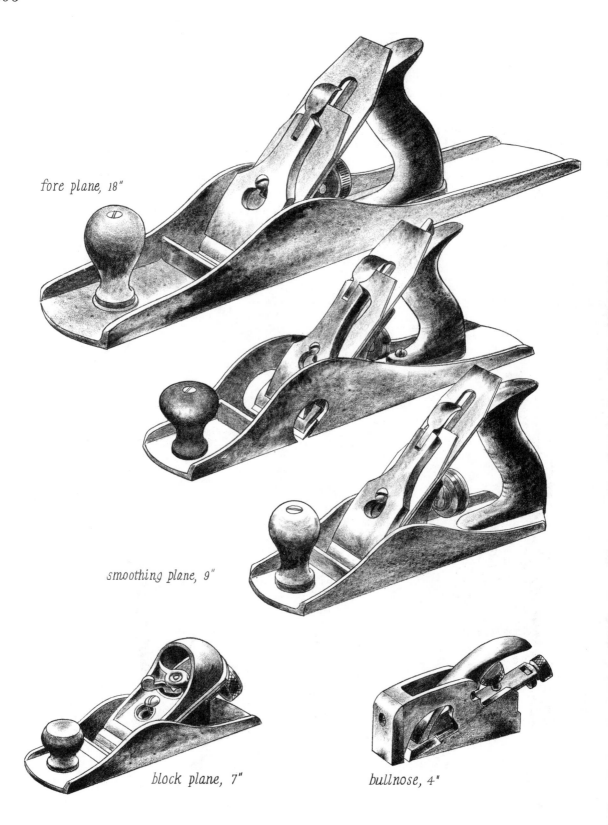

*fore plane, 18"*

*smoothing plane, 9"*

*block plane, 7"*

*bullnose, 4"*

# 20

# Planes

No matter how simple a thing of wood, it is scarcely possible to put two sticks together decently without using a plane. Wood must be smoothed, squared up, and made to fit—the three main jobs of a plane. It has always been so. The earliest known plane was a flat-bottomed tool for smoothing wood and nothing more. But by the late 1800s a multitude of variations had been developed—one plane for one job—to do a great variety of work, including chamfers, grooves, moldings, rabbets, scraping, and slitting. These special planes were more properly shaping tools designed to cut wood in particular ways, shapes, sizes, and contours, although like all planes they left the cut surface so smooth as to require little or no sanding.

Planes perform a range of work that can be grouped in thirteen categories: (1) jointing or making edges true; (2) smoothing the sides of boards; (3) sizing or planing to a uniform width; (4) end-grain work; (5) final fitting and clean-up; (6) rabbets; (7) grooves; (8) moldings; (9) bevels, chamfers, and angles; (10) round, oval, and tapered work; (11) planing thin stock; (12) dressing rough-sawn lumber; and (13) planing to reduce thickness.

## Design and Construction

The best way to see the workings of a plane is to take it apart and put it together again. A screwdriver is the only tool you need for this. All modern planes are nearly identical in construction and can be taken apart according to the sequence shown in the illustrations.

With all the main parts removed—it isn't necessary to take off the wooden handles—turn the adjusting wheel to right and left and watch the action of the adjusting lever dog which fits into the rectangular hole in the cap iron and controls the depth of cut.

cap lock

lever cap

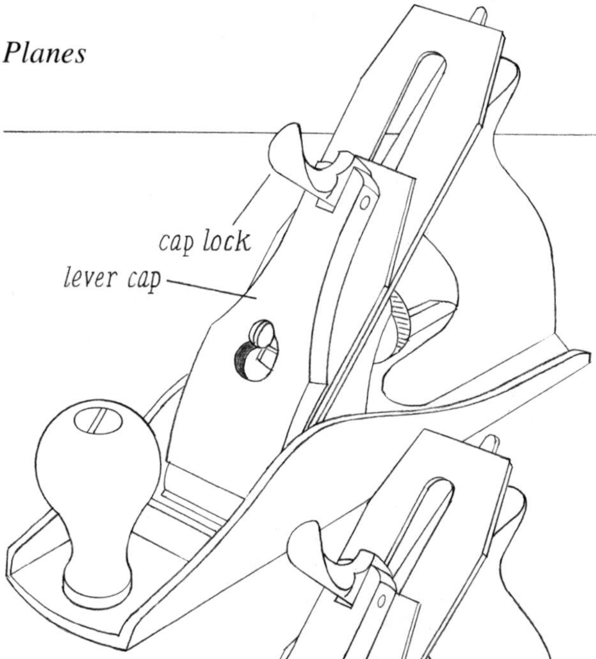

1
*lift cap lock, releasing pressure*

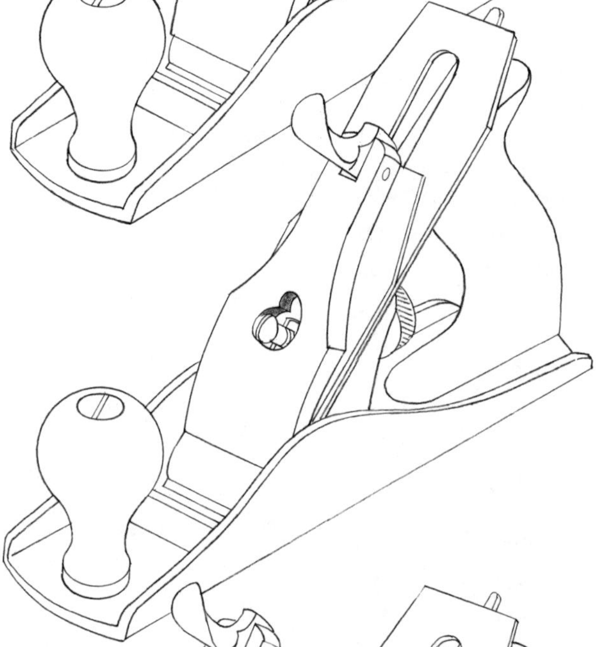

2
*slide lever cap up so that screw head*
*will pass through large end of hole*

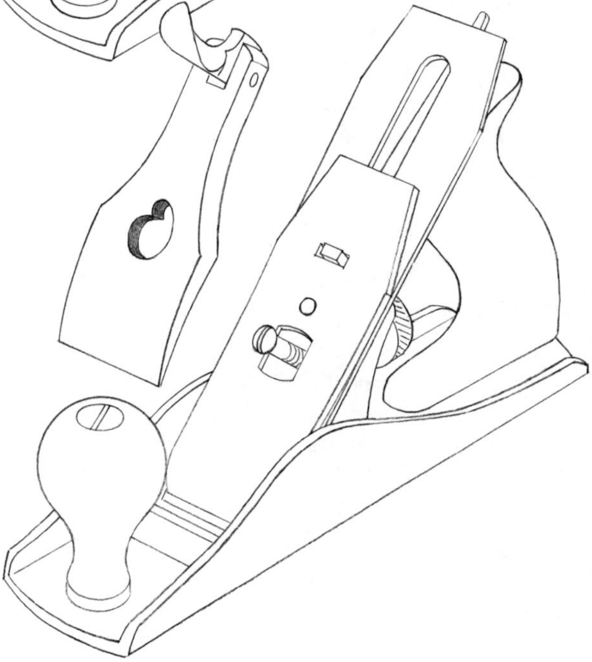

3
*lift out the lever cap*

*taking a plane apart,* continued

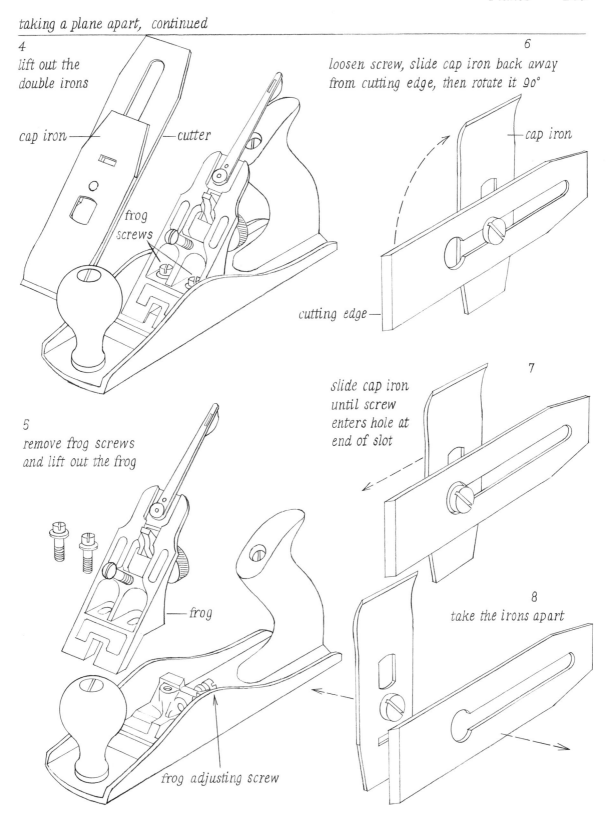

4
lift out the
double irons

cap iron —          — cutter

frog
screws

5
remove frog screws
and lift out the frog

— frog

frog adjusting screw

6
loosen screw, slide cap iron back away
from cutting edge, then rotate it 90°

— cap iron

cutting edge —

7
slide cap iron
until screw
enters hole at
end of slot

8
take the irons apart

*parts of a typical plane and* LUBRICATION POINTS (OIL)

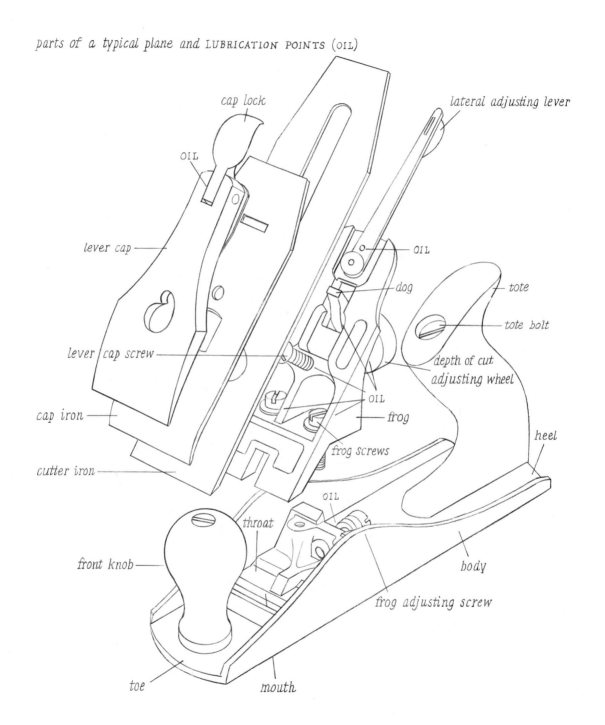

Move the lateral lever side to side. The wheel on its lower end engages in the long slot of the cutter iron and shifts it one way or the other to align it square with the mouth of the plane. This can also be seen when the plane is assembled.

Some planes have an adjustment to vary the size of the mouth, which must be open enough for shavings to pass through into the throat without clogging. The adjustment is made with the plane dismantled. Loosen the frog screws about a quarter-turn, releasing the frog to slide forward or back. Turn the frog adjusting screw to the right to close the mouth, and to the left to open it. After adjusting the mouth, tighten the frog screws again. A narrow mouth will pass fine shavings and can be used for planing hardwood, while a wider one is necessary for coarse cuts

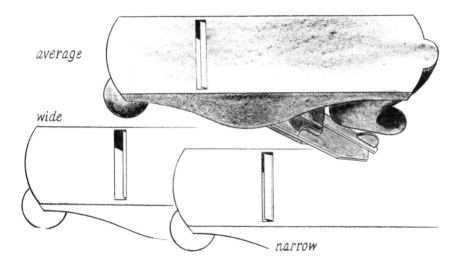

*average*

*wide*

*narrow*

in softwood and especially when planing rough-sawn lumber. As a general rule, however, an average mouth opening will accommodate most planework, and once it has been set seldom needs further adjustment except on special occasions.

To reassemble the plane, start with the double irons shown at the end of the take-apart sequence (8), and follow the eight steps in reverse. When you reach step (4), adjust the irons with a gap of $1/16$ inch between the edges of the cap iron and the cutter iron. Then tighten the screw. Lay the double irons into the plane, making sure the rectangular hole drops over the adjusting lever dog. Wiggle the lateral lever to see that it's engaged in the cutter iron and moves it to the right and left. Next, turn the plane bottom up to be sure the cutter is square with the mouth. Then replace the lever cap, slide it down as far as it will go and snap the lock down against the irons as it was in the beginning.

# Adjustments

A plane has five adjustments, the first four of which require day-to-day watching: (1) gap between the ends of the cap iron and the cutter iron; (2) depth of cut; (3) lateral adjustment; (4) tightness of lever cap screw; and (5) size of the mouth, already mentioned above. Whenever making any adjustments, verify their accuracy by trying the plane on a piece of scrap lumber before starting to work on good stuff. This is especially important when you reassemble the cap iron and the cutter after sharpening.

GAP BETWEEN CAP IRON AND CUTTER IRON    These double irons work together—the cutter iron slices wood shavings, and the cap iron breaks them away and starts them up through the plane's throat. Without a cap iron, the shavings would tend to drive back and jam against

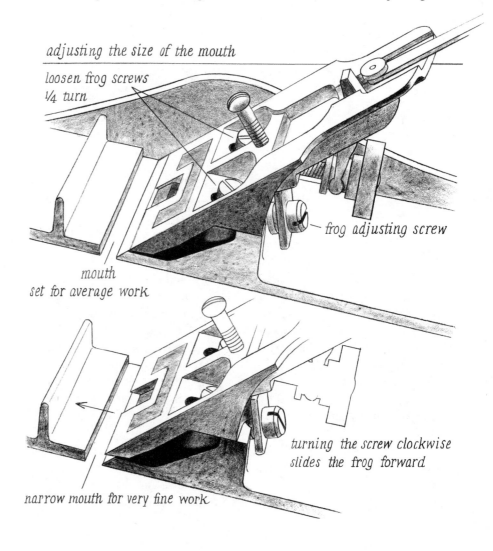

adjusting the size of the mouth

loosen frog screws ¼ turn

frog adjusting screw

mouth set for average work

turning the screw clockwise slides the frog forward

narrow mouth for very fine work

the cutter iron, a fact that was observed about 1760 when the cap iron first made its appearance. The amount of gap between the two irons should be adjusted according to how thick a slice of wood is taken, whether the wood is soft or hard, and to the degree of finish that is wanted. The thicker the slice or the deeper the cut, the wider the gap must be: a thick slice will break instead of curling. Soft wood curls out more readily than hardwood. This is a fine adjustment. Leaving a gap as big as ¹/₄ inch, for example, would throw the cutter iron well below the plane's bottom, and the adjusting wheel simply hasn't enough turns to bring it back up to working level.

The cap iron serves another important purpose. In a single-iron plane having no cap iron there is a tendency for the cutter as it meets resistance, especially in hardwood or when cutting end grain, to jump off the wood and then clap down on it again, producing what is known as

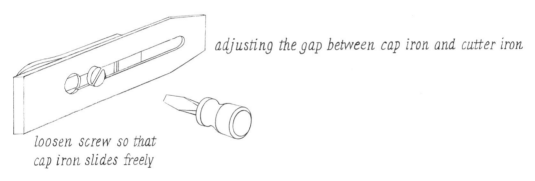

adjusting the gap between cap iron and cutter iron

loosen screw so that
cap iron slides freely

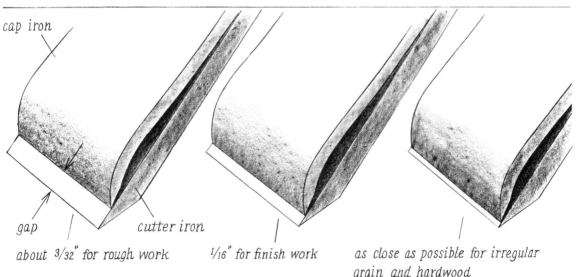

cap iron

gap   cutter iron

about ³/₃₂" for rough work          ¹/₁₆" for finish work          as close as possible for irregular
grain and hardwood

*chatter eliminated by tension and pressure*

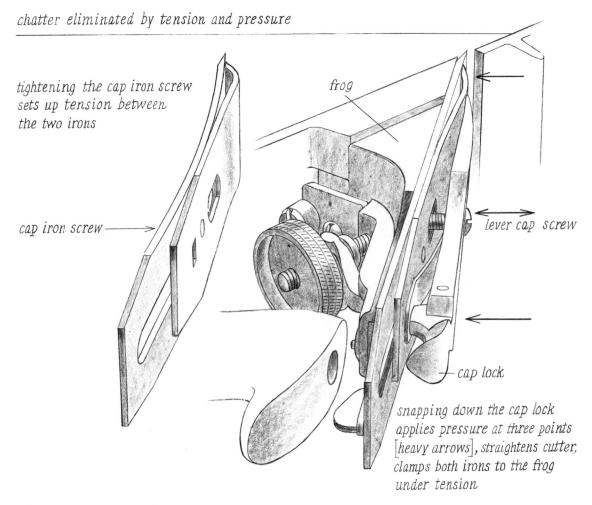

*tightening the cap iron screw
sets up tension between
the two irons*

frog

cap iron screw

lever cap screw

cap lock

*snapping down the cap lock
applies pressure at three points
[heavy arrows], straightens cutter,
clamps both irons to the frog
under tension*

*importance of correctly shaped and fitted cap iron*

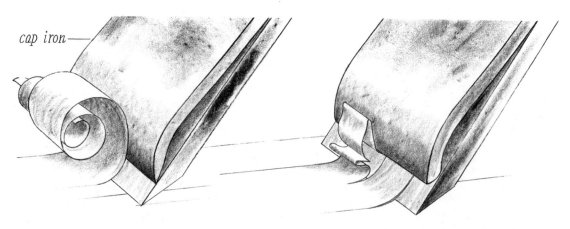

cap iron

*the cap iron should fit tight against
the cutter iron in order to curl the
shavings up and out of the throat*

*a faulty cap iron causes shavings to
get pinched and folded —
and the plane to stop cutting*

chatter. The principle of chatter can be simply demonstrated. Hold the end of a long pencil tight between thumb and one finger. Set it straight up and down on a piece of paper, then push it across the paper. Instead of drawing a continuous line the pencil tends to skip over the paper in a series of dots and blips. It chatters. By the simple remedy of steadying the pencil point with the other hand it is easy to make a continuous line. The cap iron does the same for the cutter iron: clamped to the cutter iron and held there under tension by the lever cap, the whole assembly is held rigid.

DEPTH OF CUT     On most planes the depth of cut is governed by an adjusting wheel—turn it to the right for a heavier cut, to the left for a lighter one. There is some natural slack in this wheel adjustment, and there is more slack where the dog of the lever engages the hole of the cap iron. This combined slack may be considerable, and must be taken up before starting work, especially when adjusting from a coarse to a fine cut. Simply backing off the wheel isn't enough. After making the adjustment, turn the wheel to the right again until resistance is felt. This prevents the iron from working back into an even finer cut, as it will under the pressure of planing.

*depth of cut adjustment*

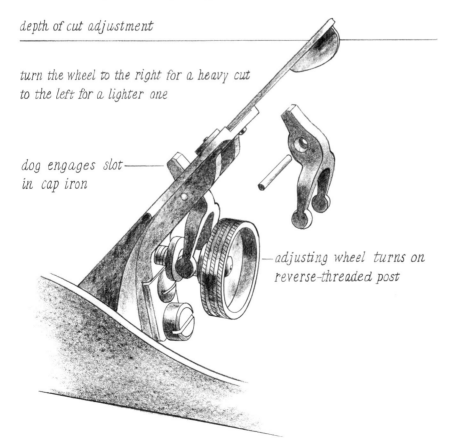

*turn the wheel to the right for a heavy cut to the left for a lighter one*

*dog engages slot in cap iron*

*adjusting wheel turns on reverse-threaded post*

To adjust for a fine cut, put a piece of scrap wood in the vise. Retract the plane's cutter iron until it cuts nothing. Then turn the wheel to the right a quarter-turn and run the plane over the wood. Continue advancing the wheel and trying the plane on the wood after each advance until a tissue-thin shaving is produced.

LATERAL ADJUSTMENT     For all routine work, the cutter should be kept square with the plane's bottom. Prolonged planing, especially in hardwood, may push the cutter iron sideways and out of proper alignment with the plane bottom. When this happens, one corner of the iron will leave gouging marks on the work. The lateral adjusting lever is a simple device for realigning the cutter. If the cutter persistently gets out of alignment, it is probably because the cap iron screw is not tight enough.

To take full advantage of the lateral adjustment, make sure that the sharp edge of the cutter is ground square to its sides. Then, when the cutter is locked in place, it is a simple matter to maintain proper alignment by shifting the lever to one side or the other. However, aligning a cutter that is ground at a cockeyed angle will use up all the slack in the lever, leaving no chance for further adjustment as work progresses.

*lateral adjustment*

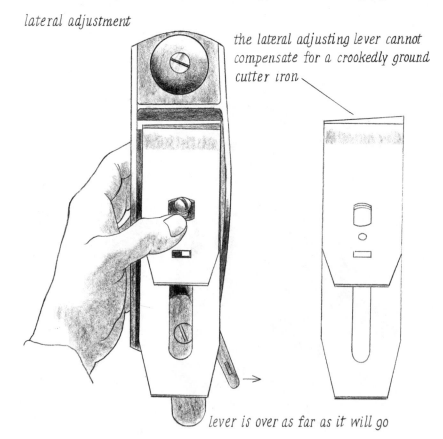

*the lateral adjusting lever cannot compensate for a crookedly ground cutter iron*

*lever is over as far as it will go*

*sighting along sole of plane to check lateral adjustment of cutter iron*

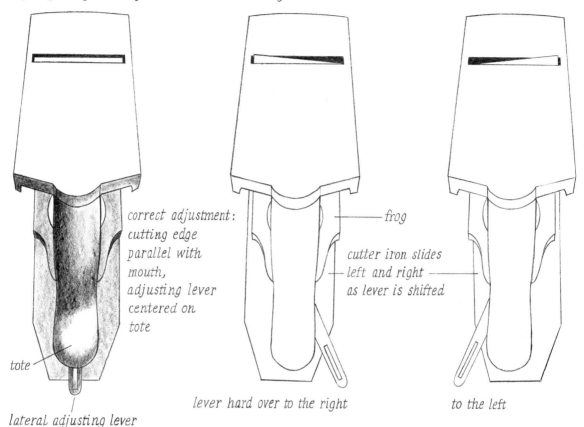

*correct adjustment: cutting edge parallel with mouth, adjusting lever centered on tote*

*frog*

*cutter iron slides left and right as lever is shifted*

tote

*lateral adjusting lever*

*lever hard over to the right*

*to the left*

TIGHTNESS OF LEVER CAP SCREW    The lever cap screw should be just tight enough to keep the cutter from working out of adjustment. Remember: the cutter iron must be free to slide up or down to adjust the depth of cut, and to swing from side to side. If the cap iron is too tight it will be difficult to make these adjustments. On the other hand, if it's too loose, the cutter will work out of adjustment simply from the force of planing. To get the correct pressure, loosen the cap screw, then place the lever cap over it and snap the lock down. Tighten the screw fairly tight. Then loosen it a little at a time until the lock can be lifted with relative ease.

Sight and sound tell something of how a plane is working. When sharp and properly adjusted, a plane turns out nicely curled shavings of uniform character, to the tune of an even pitch. Each kind of wood produces its own vibrations. Listen for them. Keep an eye on the shavings as they come out of the throat, and keep your hands alert to the feel of the plane.

# Sharp Cutter Irons

A dull plane is hard to push, difficult to control, and does very poor work no matter how much you adjust it. And as you continue working with it the edge rapidly worsens to a condition requiring a major grinding instead of a simple sharpening.

The best system is to keep the cutter iron from getting dull in the first place. If you work pretty constantly in the shop that might mean a light honing once every day or two, depending on whether you are planing hardwood or softwood. Naturally, the ideal is to have a spare

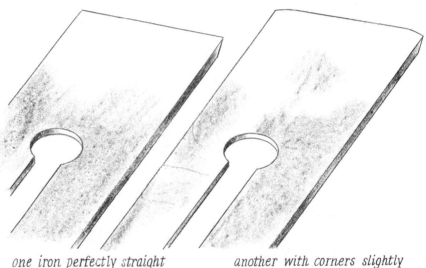

*one iron perfectly straight and square for jointing*

*another with corners slightly rounded for surface planing*

iron for each plane and do your sharpening during off-hours. Replacement irons for most planes can be bought from mail-order dealers and some retail stores for about 10 percent of the plane's cost. However, factory-new cutter irons have relatively crude edges and must be sharpened before using them. To take this idea a step further, it is an advantage to have more than one spare iron, each ground for a different kind of work: for example, one perfectly straight for jointing, another with corners slightly rounded for surface planing to avoid gouge marks.

# Grip and Stance

Planes are meant to be operated with both hands, one on the front knob and the other gripping the rear tote. Together they control the attitude of the plane and provide the necessary pressure. This is true of the block plane as well, for while there are situations where a one-hand grip is the only one possible, better results come from using two hands.

The main thing is to get both hands into a firm but relaxed hold. The tote of a smoothing plane will accommodate all the fingers of a small hand, but a large hand simply won't fit. Since the index finger is the one that usually gets crowded out, it is laid alongside the plane.

*the tote of a smoothing plane will accommodate all four fingers of a small hand*

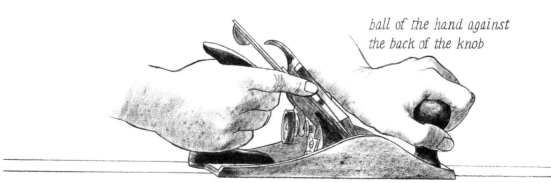

*the index finger of a large hand is usually laid alongside the double irons*

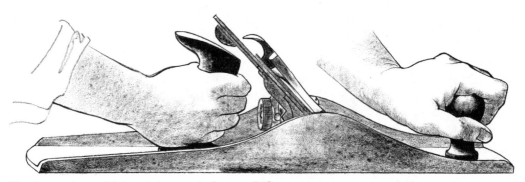

*the big planes have higher totes and plenty of finger space*

This is the standard grip for all but the big jointer planes which have higher rear totes with ample finger space.

While all the different handholds on the front knob are natural and comfortable, resting the ball of the hand solidly against the back of the knob provides the most pressure and the best control.

# Pressure

It takes fairly heavy and sustained down pressure to do good planing. What is pressure? Try this: put a short board on edge in the vise. Set the plane for a fine cut and rest it on the board. Then take hold of the rear tote with one hand—keep the other one in your pocket. Push the plane. Nothing much happens: the plane indeed moves but it skids to one side, cuts a bit here and skips some more there. Now take hold with both hands and push. There is an immediate improvement, and the difference is pressure. Without it, the cutter cannot maintain contact with the wood, hence it cuts erratically and out of control. At the end of a stroke, lift the plane off the work to bring it back. Dragging it back over the wood dulls the cutter iron.

The height of the workbench has an important influence on pressure. As stated earlier, the top should come about to the wrist as you stand with arms hanging straight down. The plane performs best when the work is at the right height in relation to your anatomy, and you'll find most other benchwork a lot less tiring too.

HOLD THE WORK SECURELY    Because of the pressure and body force necessary to operate a plane, it is imperative to hold the work securely, either in the vise, with clamps, or by some other holding device.

PLANE WITH THE GRAIN    Make it a rule always to plane with the grain, which simply means plane in the same direction in which the grain emerges at the surface. Usually a glance at one side and one edge of a board will plainly show which way the grain runs. When a plane is run against the grain, the wood fibers are broken off rather than sliced; the surface is left rough, the shavings are more likely to jam between cutter and cap iron, and it takes more effort to push the plane.

There are times, of course, when the grain wanders to the surface in one direction and then suddenly dives below again in the other. When this happens, plane in one direction until the grain shifts, then turn the board around and work the other way. Where this switching back and forth is impractical, try holding the plane at an angle to the work so that the plane cuts with a shearing action. Or turn the plane around and pull it instead of pushing.

# Maintenance

Now and then put a drop or two of light machine oil on the adjusting wheel shaft, the pivot of the lateral adjusting lever, and the hinged joint of the lever cap. Once a year, or oftener if necessary, take the plane completely apart for a general cleaning. Remove any rust with steel wool or extra fine emery paper wet with kerosene. Stay away from the cutting edge of the iron. Remove the caked sawdust and dried oil. Use a toothbrush and kerosene or liquid wrench to scrub the whole frame clean, including the threaded shaft of the adjusting wheel. Dry everything thoroughly with a clean cloth. Finger-wipe the cutter iron and cap iron with oil, then put the plane together, making sure that the frog is in its original position. Put a drop or two of oil on the moving parts as you go. Finally, check all the adjustments.

*jack rabbet and block plane*

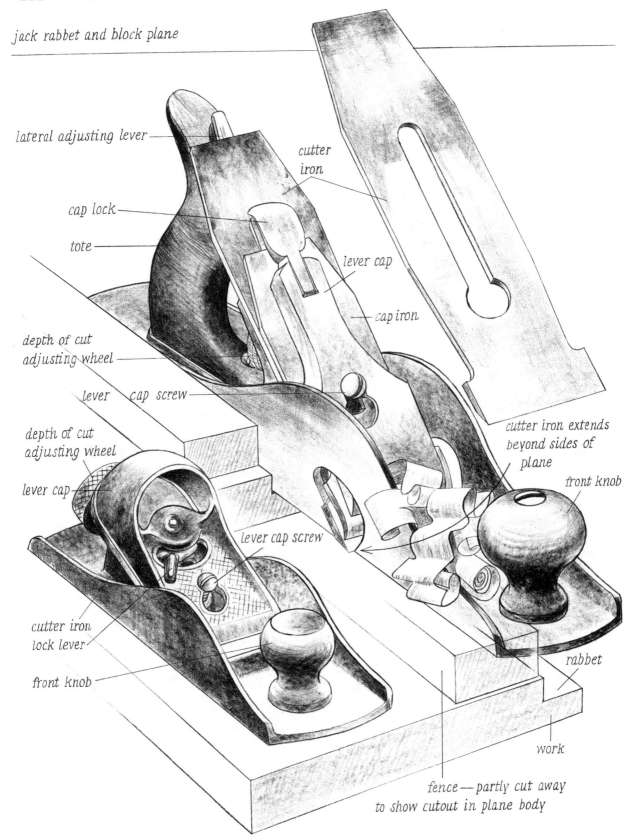

lateral adjusting lever

cutter iron

cap lock

lever cap

tote

cap iron

depth of cut adjusting wheel

lever    cap screw

depth of cut adjusting wheel

cutter iron extends beyond sides of plane

lever cap

front knob

lever cap screw

cutter iron lock lever

front knob

rabbet

work

fence — partly cut away to show cutout in plane body

# Jack Rabbet & Block Plane

In a shop equipped to do the full range of handwork it would be normal to find at least 9 or 10 different planes, and perhaps more, to accommodate every job from dressing rough-sawn lumber to the making of custom moldings. At today's prices this collection represents a very substantial investment—unless it can be justified by a good volume of work for hire. The practical alternative for the hand woodworker with limited means is to buy a couple of planes that will handle the basic work, and add other planes as the variety of work expands and finances permit.

Such a pair is the jack rabbet and the block plane. Together they will do a large proportion of plane work: jointing, smoothing, sizing, end-grain work, fitting and clean-up, rabbets, bevels and chamfers, round and tapered work, planing thin stock, dressing rough-sawn lumber, and planing to reduce thickness.


# Jack Rabbet Plane

This plane performs for jointing, smoothing the sides of boards, sizing boards to width, planing bevels and chamfers, and for cutting rabbets. At 51 ounces (3.19 pounds) it is heavy enough to stay down on the work, yet noticeably lighter than the special jointer planes which weigh upward of 110 ounces (6.97 pounds). A very comfortable plane to handle.

LUMBER NEEDS FURTHER PREPARATION    Before taking up the specific tasks of the jack rabbet, something must be said about the wood itself. Although most lumber today is kiln-dried and dressed—or planed—four sides, it is not ready to use. The edges of boards are often far from straight, as a squint along an edge will show: there are hollows and high spots. And the sides have a washboard pattern of cross-grain scallops left by the knives of the rotary planing machine. Such lumber straight from the yard is all right for rough storage shelves, but for something like a living room bookcase where accuracy and nice finish are wanted, the boards should first be jointed and smoothed.

These operations are not as laborious as they may sound, especially when compared to the preparation of lumber that the old-time cabinetmaker was obliged to carry out. His stuff came from the sawmill with tufted rough surfaces, often with bark on the edges, and frequently with wandering thickness. Every stick had to be planed to thickness and smoothed by hand, resawn to width, and jointed. Then, at last, it was ready to use.

JOINTING    Jointing means planing the edge of a board straight, square, and true and is usually done first with the board held in the vise, followed by smoothing with the board laid flat on the bench. This order of work exposes a board to less bruising from the vise jaws. The first step is to locate the hollows and high spots, which must be planed off before starting to plane the full length of the board. For example, an edge knot makes quite a bulge. If full-length passes are begun without these preliminaries, the plane will ride up and over the knot,

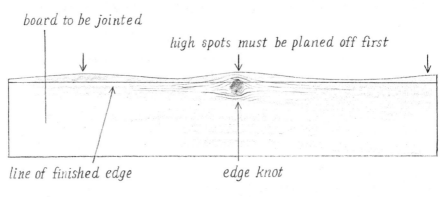

*board to be jointed*

*high spots must be planed off first*

*line of finished edge*          *edge knot*

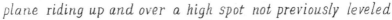

*plane riding up and over a high spot not previously leveled*

*line of finished edge*

*marking high spots to be planed off before jointing*

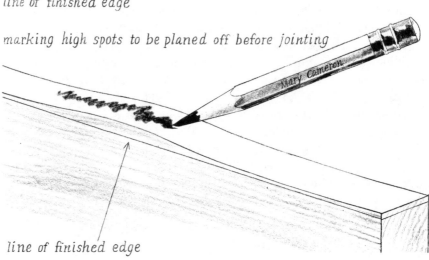

*line of finished edge*

removing more wood on either side of it than from the knot itself—in effect making the bulge larger. You could plane away in this fashion for half an hour without making much progress.

Use the jack rabbet for jointing. Set the iron for a very light cut. Its long body reaches from one high spot on a board to the next, enabling the plane to shave them off level rather than ride up and over them, as a short plane will do. To find the high spots, set one end of the board on the bench, holding the other end up at eye level. Sight along the edge: at this flat angle, any irregularities show up immediately, the eye being extremely sensitive to the slightest deviation from a straight line.

Once sighted, mark each high spot with scumbled marks of a pencil. Then plane off the pencil marks, nothing more. Take another sighting. If necessary make new marks and repeat the spot planing. When the edge appears to be generally straight, begin making full-length passes with the jack rabbet. Don't rush at it. Throughout the entire stroke the plane bottom should run flat and true to what the finished surface will be. If your mind wanders, the plane will probably take more wood off the ends than in the middle, or will tip to one side and plane on the slant instead of square. Start the first stroke with just the toe of the plane resting on the work, elbow in close to the body. The wrists,

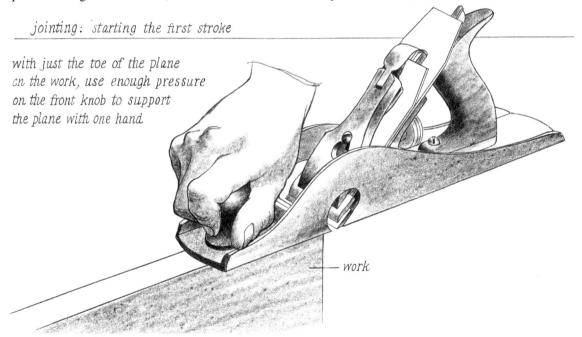

*jointing: starting the first stroke*

*with just the toe of the plane on the work, use enough pressure on the front knob to support the plane with one hand*

— *work*

forearm, and plane should all line up with the board. Put enough pressure on the front knob to support the plane without using the other hand. Keep the pressure, then push the plane with the other hand. The first pass will take off very little wood. The plane shaves off only the

*at the end of the stroke,*
*ease up on the front knob*
*and put all the pressure on the heel*

tops of the high spots, taking a bit here and a little there. Don't set the cutter deep to speed things up: the wood will be torn instead of sliced. Each successive pass will take more and more wood, until finally the plane turns out one long, unbroken shaving the full length of the board. If a sighting shows a clean sharp edge as straight as a die, it's finished—jointed. This is the working edge. Mark it with an X for future reference. As work proceeds, all measurements and squared lines should be taken from this true edge.

The other edge has to be jointed as well, but before doing so, check the board's width at both ends and a couple of points in between. The entire board has to be planed down to the width at its narrowest point. Find this point and mark the same dimension at both ends and at one or two intermediate points. First plane off the sections that are too wide, treating these wide places the same as high spots. Then joint the edge as before.

# Smoothing

Ordinarily, a 9-inch smoothing plane might be used for this job, but the jack rabbet works very nicely. With the board secured flat on the bench, set the cutter for a very light cut. It must be sharp. Paper-thin cuts are slower than coarse ones but will leave the better surface. After adjusting the iron, run a trial pass on a scrap of wood to make sure the plane produces a shaving the full width of the blade. Start planing at the far end of the board and work back toward the near end. Plane off patches rather than attempting long swaths. This is more practical because using the full width of the cutter iron takes a lot more muscle than jointing. Watch for scored marks made by a corner of the iron gouging the wood. If this happens, it means that the cutter is not set square with the plane bottom. Shifting the lateral adjustment lever a whisker should correct the problem. Again—plane off the high spots first. On a cupped board, the areas along the edges have to be planed first, and on the reverse side the center of the board is planed first. It is always a matter of bringing the high places down to the same level as the lowest ones.

To test for flatness, stand the square or a straightedge across the board and look for any light showing under it. An equally good method if you have a sensitive touch, is to run the fingertips over the board. Make pencil marks where you feel high spots, then plane them off. Repeat the process until it feels flat, when it should also pass the straightedge test.

A warped board can be salvaged by planing only one side flat, provided the bad side will be hidden. This is useful when a particularly wide and nicely colored board is at hand.

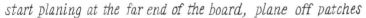

*start planing at the far end of the board, plane off patches*

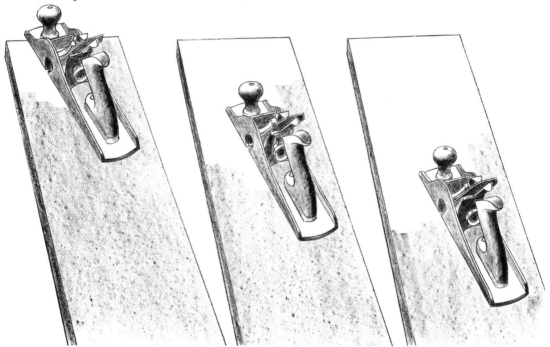

watch for scored marks
made by a corner of the cutter iron
gouging the wood

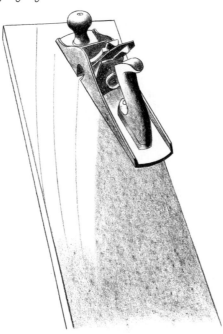

planing a cupped board flat on both sides

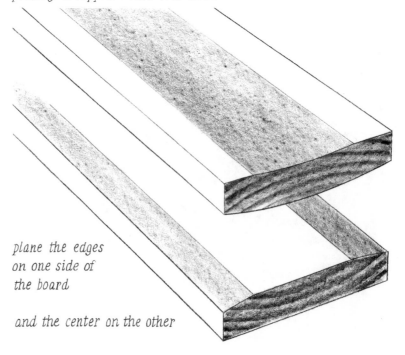

plane the edges
on one side of
the board

and the center on the other

*using the light test for flatness*

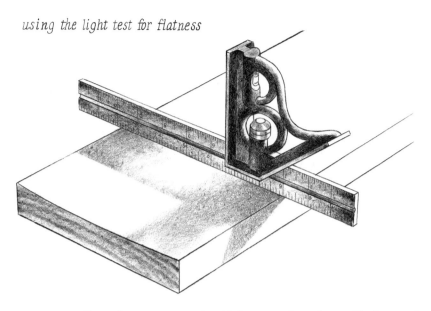

*make pencil marks where you feel high spots, then plane off the marks*

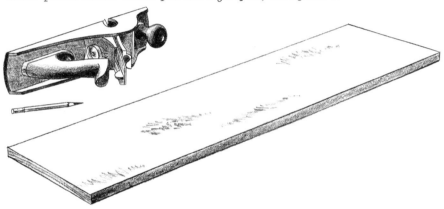

# Sizing to Width

Rarely does a piece of stock-width lumber exactly fit the work at hand. In almost every instance a board has to be sized, or trimmed down to your specifications. This usually means cutting off the waste with a ripsaw and jointing the rough edge as before. However, when only $^1/_8$ inch or so must be taken off, it is more efficient to use the jack rabbet than to attempt sawing a sliver that thin.

The procedure is to first joint the better edge, marking it as the working edge. At both ends of the board, mark the width you want and connect the marks with a line drawn against a straightedge. Joint the edge down to a point a little wide of the line. Then check the dimension at both ends of the board with a rule. Make any additional passes with the plane one at a time, checking with the rule, until both ends of the board and the middle show the same measurement. This is more accurate than planing right down to the pencil line.

# Cutting Rabbets

A rabbet, or rebate as it is sometimes called, is a recess or channel cut along the edge of a board to make a joint with another. Rabbet construction has been used in furniture-making since the sixteenth century, and is still extensively used in many branches of woodworking. The jack rabbet plane is ideal for this work. The cutter is wider than the plane bottom, which allows working a clean, square rabbet with a sharp inside corner. Since the two cutter spurs extend through side cutouts in the body of the plane, it works from either side, right or left-handed. It will cut rabbets up to 2 inches wide and to any depth. However, since this plane has neither a depth gauge nor a fence to control the width of cut, the usual practice is to nail or clamp a straight length of wood to the work, acting as a guide fence for the plane to run against. With this done, set the toe of the plane on the edge of the work with the side of the plane snug against the fence. Slide the plane

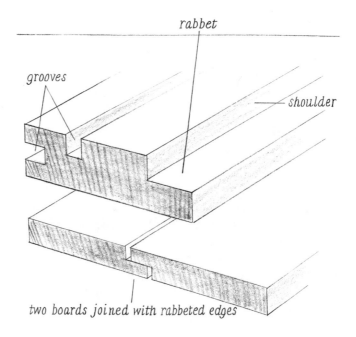

*rabbet*

*grooves*

*shoulder*

*two boards joined with rabbeted edges*

*plane must be held square to the work when shooting a rabbet*

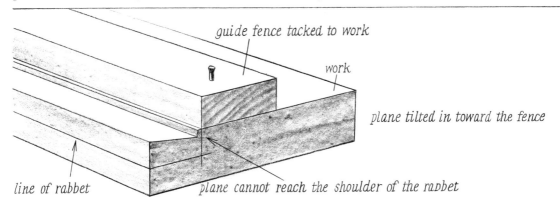

*guide fence tacked to work*

*work*

*plane tilted in toward the fence*

*line of rabbet*

*plane cannot reach the shoulder of the rabbet*

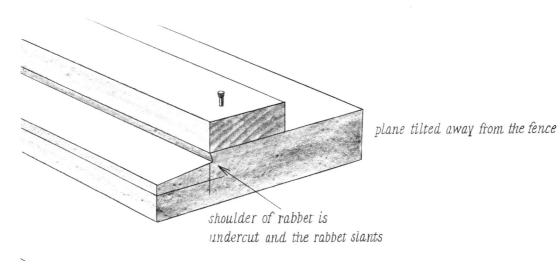

*plane tilted away from the fence*

*shoulder of rabbet is
undercut and the rabbet slants*

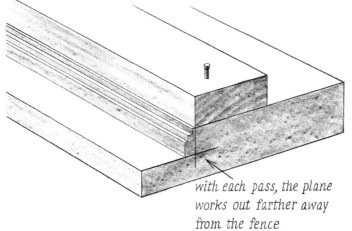

*not enough pressure of the plane
against the fence*

*with each pass, the plane
works out farther away
from the fence*

until you feel the cutter iron catch on the wood. Don't worry about the plane—it will cut all right. Concentrate on keeping the plane flat with the work, and tight against the fence. The plane must always run hard up against the fence, from the first pass until the last. On long work-pieces, the proportionately longer fence must be wide enough to withstand the side pressure of the plane without bending. The depth must be marked on the work and constantly checked as you go. Yet if uniform pressure is used on each pass, the plane cuts depth with remarkable uniformity.

Concentration is essential when making the starting passes with the plane. It should be held square to the work. If it tilts, the rabbet will start and end up crooked. Cutting a rabbet takes quite some side pressure, so brace your feet and lean into it. Otherwise the plane is likely to pull away from the fence, causing the first pass to run off the mark. So will all the others, working out farther and farther and making a very poor rabbet with a ragged shoulder.

An alternate method is to first make a cut the length of the work with a ripsaw, again using a fence. Saw down not quite to the bottom of the rabbet. With one hand riding the back of the saw blade about in its middle, and doing most of the cutting with the heel of the saw, this is not as hard as it sounds. Leave the fence in place. Then clean out the rabbet with the plane, using full-length passes and checking the depth frequently. With this method there is a bit more chance to correct any slope in the cut, because the saw kerf provides some leeway in which to tilt the plane.

*starting a rabbet with a ripsaw cut*

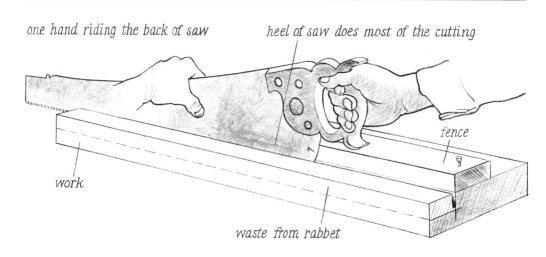

one hand riding the back of saw

heel of saw does most of the cutting

fence

work

waste from rabbet

*rabbets used in door trim*

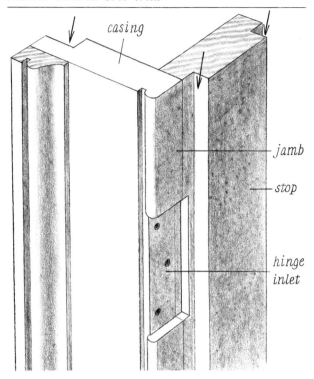

casing

jamb

stop

hinge
inlet

*typical block plane*

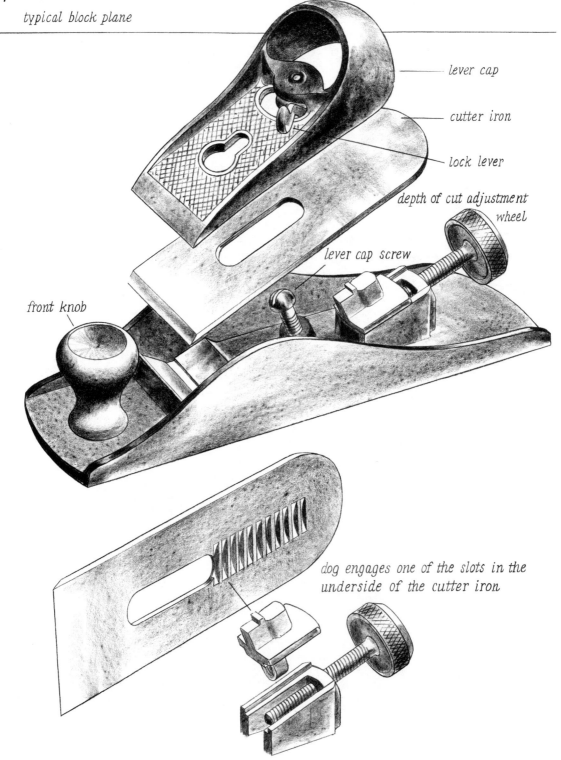

*lever cap*

*cutter iron*

*lock lever*

*depth of cut adjustment wheel*

*lever cap screw*

*front knob*

*dog engages one of the slots in the underside of the cutter iron*

# Block Plane

The block plane is a true extension of the hand. It can be pushed or pulled, used with both hands or only one, operated up or down in a vertical position, and worked in awkward places where longer, heavier planes are cumbersome. It is especially efficient for end-grain work, for these reasons: the plane is small and compact, fitting easily into one hand; because the blade is set low rather than poking into the air, it does not interfere with this cupped-hand grip; all the thrust of the arm and hand is transmitted through the ball of the hand to the cutter and almost exactly in line with it. This last reason is important since it is the secure grip and firm pressure that prevents the plane from chattering—the root of most trouble when planing end grain.

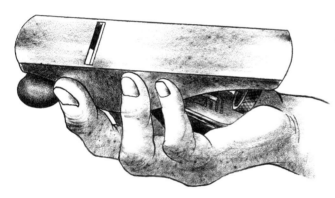

*block plane fits easily into one hand, the back of the lever cap cupped against the ball of the hand*

*one-handed grip with the index finger controlling the front of the plane*

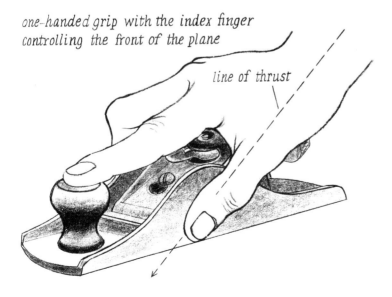

*line of thrust*

*block plane operated with one hand*

*one-handed grip for light work—two fingers on edges of plane body*

tap one edge of the cutter iron or the other to make fine adjustment of alignment between the cutting edge and bottom of plane

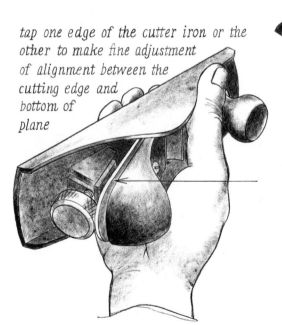

PRESSURE     When planing end grain, pressure should be applied by the whole body—hands, arms, shoulders, torso, and not the least by the action of the feet. Standing casually at the bench planing with the arms alone isn't enough. Running a block plane with only one hand is fine for small work where little pressure is needed or where space is cramped. You can reach a block plane to the top of a door with one hand and trim off enough wood to make it shut. That's one of the plane's virtues. But two hands are always better, one hand for pushing and the other for pressure and control.

*planing a chamfer on the end grain*

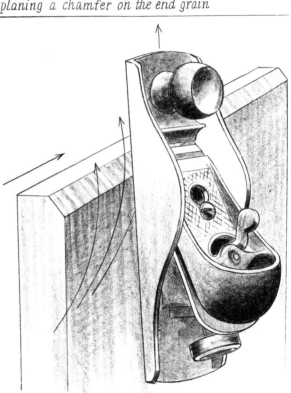

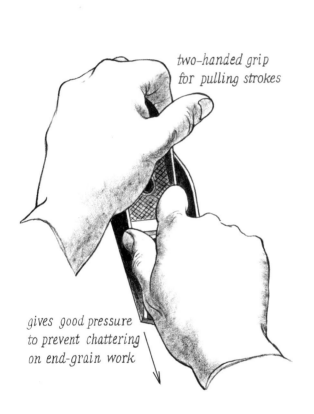

*two-handed grip for pulling strokes*

*gives good pressure to prevent chattering on end-grain work*

*swinging, slicing strokes make a cleaner job than planing straight across parallel to the edge*

PLANING END GRAIN LEVEL AND SQUARE     Important as it is to maintain good pressure, it is just as essential to keep the plane bottom level and square with the work. This is more difficult on end grain than it is on the edge of a board, because the work itself is short, and the reference line of flatness is more imagined than real. Concentration here is of the essence. Start the first pass of the plane with just its toe resting on the work. Bear down on the front knob and slide the plane until you feel the cutter iron catch against the edge of the wood. Give it enough pressure so the plane is supported flat on the work and hanging in midair without using the other hand at all. Hold the plane down with one hand while pushing with the other hand. The iron should be set for a very fine cut. Several fine cuts do a neater job than a single coarse one, and with less elbow grease.

As the plane moves, its heel will probably tend to drop. Don't let it. Plane from both edges of the board toward the center. This avoids splintering the corners, which happens when the plane is run off the

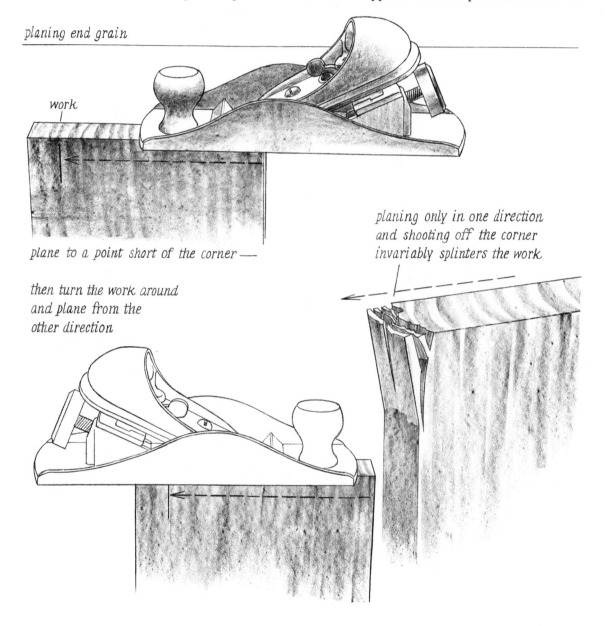

*planing end grain*

*work*

*plane to a point short of the corner —*

*then turn the work around and plane from the other direction*

*planing only in one direction and shooting off the corner invariably splinters the work using pencil marks to gauge the squareness of end-grain planing*

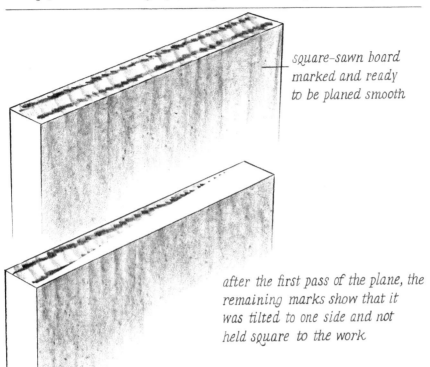

*square-sawn board marked and ready to be planed smooth*

*after the first pass of the plane, the remaining marks show that it was tilted to one side and not held square to the work*

far corner. Check the work with the square every couple of passes, and tilt the plane right or left to maintain a square cut.

While constant practice will eventually make end-grain planing as routine as any other, there is a useful trick that may help in getting the hang of it. Make pencil marks on the end grain along both edges before using the plane. If the plane is cutting square to the board, both pencil marks will be shaved off clean. If not, the remaining marks will show which side is in error. Planing two workpieces at the same time also simplifies this problem, since the working surface is twice as wide. On a single workpiece, the same advantage can be gained by clamping a piece of waste wood flush with the end grain of the work. Both these methods provide a wide surface that is easier to plane, and one that can be more accurately checked with the square.

SHEAR-CUTTING    Planing straight against end grain breaks the wood fibers rather than slicing them clean. This leaves a rough, pitted surface that is impossible to fix, no matter how much sanding is done. This can be avoided by shifting the plane a little sideways and running it at an angle. The cutter iron will then shear the grain smooth, rarely needing any sandpaper at all. Since this slicing action takes less push, the plane will be easier to control, and the results will be much better. And the iron will hold a sharp edge longer as well.

*waste wood clamped to the workpiece provides a longer bearing surface for more accurate end-grain planing*

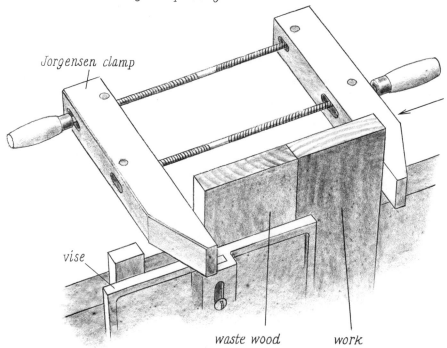

*Jorgensen clamp*

*vise*

*waste wood*          *work*

# Final Fitting and Cleanup

Not infrequently there is some final plane work after the job has been put together. Hand-cut joints are not always absolutely perfect—even those made by experienced woodworkers. A slight discrepancy in the thickness of two joined pieces; a fractional measuring error no greater than the thickness of a pencil line; a bit of warp or twist on a rainy day—any of these may create minor imperfections.

Then, too, many woodworkers deliberately leave excess wood on some joints, preferring to clean them up at the time of assembly. Mitered corners, mortise and tenon joints, dovetailing, and rabbeted joints are typical instances where this method proves useful. The block plane does this work admirably.

Some of this cleanup may have to be done with a chisel, a flat file, or a sandpaper block. Before indiscriminately sanding everything, however, keep in mind what the overall finish will look like. Wood surfaces finished only with a plane have a different kind of smoothness than sandpapered ones—a glazed sheen. Sandpaper often leaves the surface softer looking and almost fuzzy. When it comes to waxing, sealing, or staining, each type of surface takes the finish in its own way, and may not look identical to adjacent pieces.

*final fitting and cleanup with a block plane*

*mitered corner*

*mortise and tenon*

*dovetail*

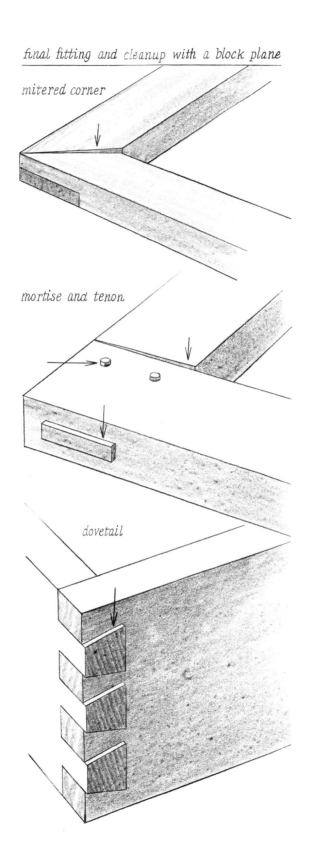

planing bevels and chamfers

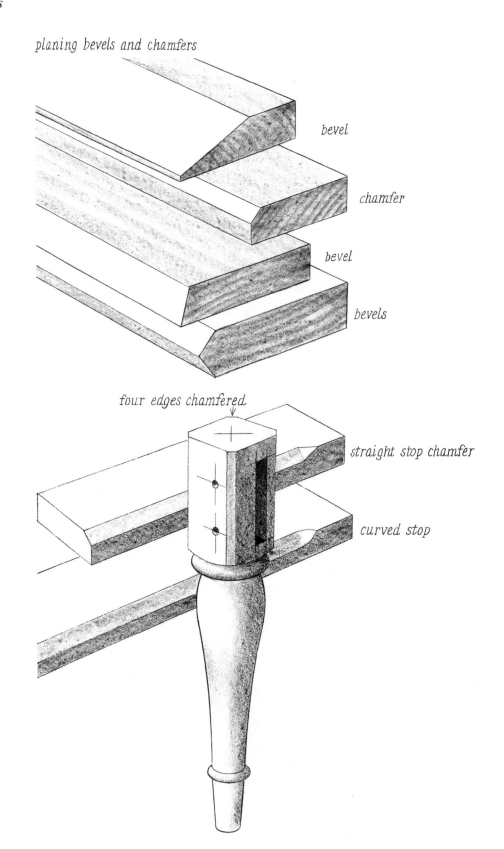

bevel

chamfer

bevel

bevels

four edges chamfered

straight stop chamfer

curved stop

# Planing Bevels and Chamfers

As far as simply removing wood with the plane is concerned, a bevel and a chamfer are the same although by proper definition a bevel is any slanting surface, while chamfer generally refers to a narrow slant cut only on the edge of a piece.

The jack rabbet and the block plane perform about equally well for bevels, chamfers, and roundwork, the choice depending on the length of the workpiece and the width of the bevel. Broadly speaking, the block plane is used for small stuff and the jack rabbet for longer pieces. In the case of a very wide bevel where much wood is to be removed, the jack rabbet's two hefty handles and heavier, longer body make it the better tool for this job, as it holds to the angle of bevel with more accuracy than a block plane.

The block plane is easier to manage for small or short pieces of work, where the sheer bulk of the jack rabbet would prevent clearly seeing what you're doing. Beveling or chamfering is very much a free-hand type of work that must be watched closely at each stroke of the plane.

Bevels or chamfers should be accurately marked out on two sides of the work and on both ends. Make marks that are easily seen, since these are the reference points to which you'll work with the plane and other tools. Because this work is done strictly by eye—without fences or jigs—it helps to make a few practice runs on scrap wood before starting the final work in order to get the feel of the angle you want.

The first two or three passes with the plane are the most vital. The aim is to establish the correct angle at the outset. What commonly happens is that the bevel is wider at the start than at the finish. This is only too obvious from looking at the marked-out lines. Correct this at once: if you wait to do it later, there may not be enough wood left! Tilt the plane a whisker and make a short pass with the plane over the section that's too narrow. Then follow up with a full-length pass or two to fair it up. Once you have the correct angle, concentrate on holding the plane bottom in a consistent attitude. It is really a matter of visualizing the bottom of the plane steadily cutting lower into the wood, and eventually coming to a stop when both sides of the plane iron touch both layout lines simultaneously.

The so-called through-chamfer, for example, as worked on a bed-post, is relatively simple to do, the chamfer running straight off both ends. The stop-chamfer with curved or straight stops is a more difficult version—often used on furniture. Where the run between stops is long, a block plane can be used for the straight section, and the stops worked with chisel, rasp, drawknife—or all three—and then finished with a file or sandpaper.

The block plane also works well for jointing short pieces of work where a longer model would tend to "dip." Dipping simply means taking more wood off both ends of a run than in the middle—a condition that steadily worsens unless care is taken. This plane is excellent for smoothing small work, and on large boards it can be used effectively to plane isolated hollows that a long-bodied plane won't fit into.

*planing a chamfer*

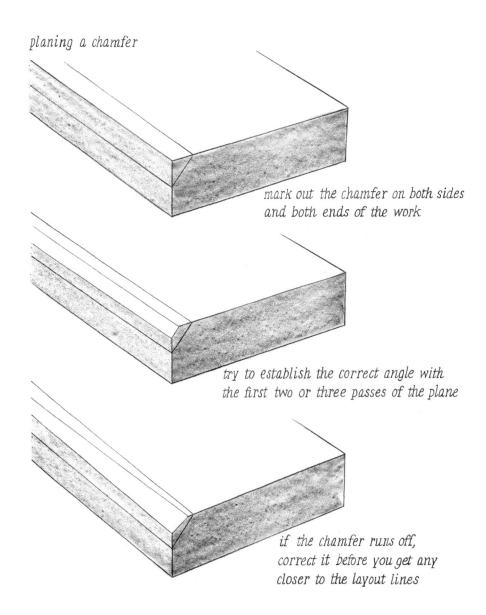

*mark out the chamfer on both sides and both ends of the work*

*try to establish the correct angle with the first two or three passes of the plane*

*if the chamfer runs off, correct it before you get any closer to the layout lines*

# Nine-Inch Smoothing Plane

This a fine tool for the one-plane shop, or as an item to add to a growing collection. The smoothing plane is outstanding for surface planing of boards, its short body getting into low spots more effectively than a longer plane. And except for very small work, it will plane end grain as well as bevels, chamfers, and roundwork. However, it is too short for satisfactory jointing where the length of the plane body really counts.

As a general rule, the cutter iron should be set very fine to do good smoothing. On narrow stuff—boards less than 6 inches wide—the planing-mill corrugations can easily be cleaned off by running the plane the length of the board. Wide boards are more likely to have uneven surfaces, in which case planing in swaths and a bit across the grain not only allows the plane to follow the irregularities but also increases the shear-cutting effect.

SWIPE AND LIFT    The swipe-and-lift stroke is another useful technique for wide stuff where stubborn low places tend to get skipped in ordinary planing. To practice this stroke, mark a pencil X on a scrap

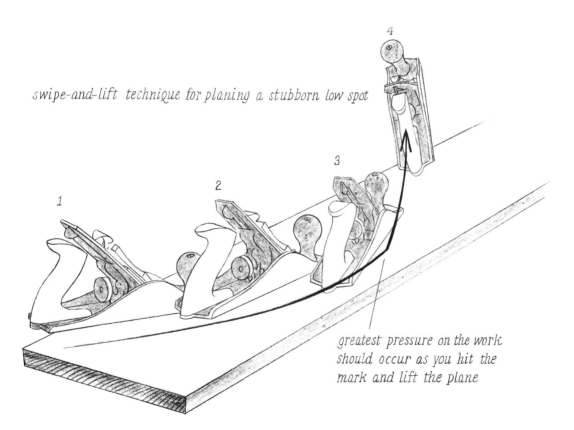

*swipe-and-lift technique for planing a stubborn low spot*

*greatest pressure on the work should occur as you hit the mark and lift the plane*

board, then take a swipe with the plane, aiming to shave off the X and no more. Slide the plane in a curve over the board, lifting it clear as you hit the mark. More pressure comes from this swipe action, helping force the plane into the low area.

PLANING TO REDUCE THICKNESS    Planing cross grain and in swaths is especially efficient when the object is to remove wood in a hurry, for example, to reduce the thickness of a $^3/_4$-inch board to $^5/_8$-inch. Start planing at the near end of the board. Plane across it at an angle, taking a swath only about an inch wide, or half the width of the iron. Let each new swath overlap the last one. With this technique, the iron can be set quite coarse without the job becoming exhausting. Of

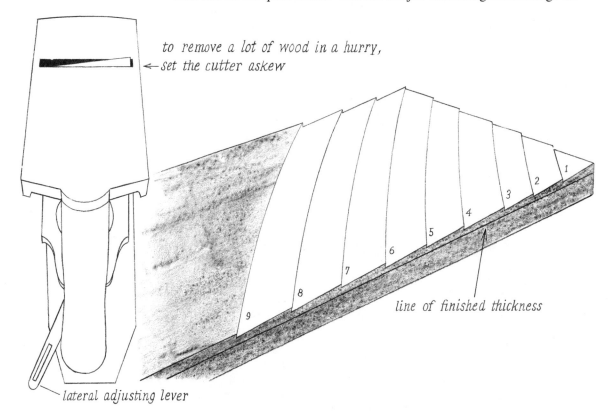

*to remove a lot of wood in a hurry,*
← *set the cutter askew*

*line of finished thickness*

*lateral adjusting lever*

course, the work should first be marked out on both edges of the board, and on both ends. Plane a bit wide of the marks, then set the cutter for a finer cut and shoot the finishing passes lengthwise of the board.

DRESSING ROUGH-SAWN LUMBER    Dressing rough-sawn lumber requires the same method: the plane set for a coarse cut, planing at a cross angle, and working in swaths. As it comes from the sawmill, this type of wood has a very rough surface replete with tufts, splinters, and ridges left by the big saw—just the sort of material that quickly chokes

*planing across the grain to reduce the thickness or to dress rough-sawn lumber*

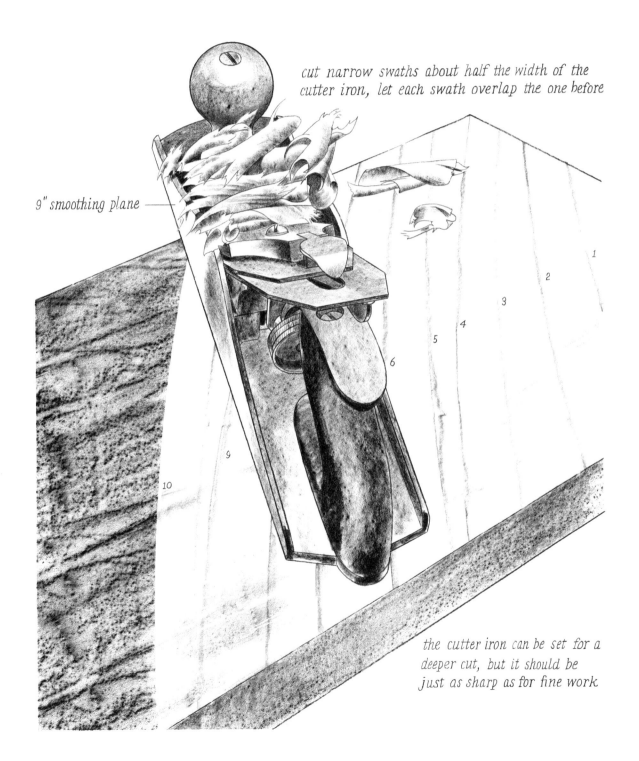

*cut narrow swaths about half the width of the cutter iron, let each swath overlap the one before*

9" smoothing plane

*the cutter iron can be set for a deeper cut, but it should be just as sharp as for fine work*

the plane. This is one instance where it is advisable to readjust the plane mouth so that it is open wide enough to let all this clutter pass through.

Despite the apparent crudity of this kind of planing, the cutter must be sharp. To avoid unnecessary dulling of the edge, before touching plane to rough lumber, scrub the surface with a stiff brush to clean off as much grit, dirt, and whiskers as possible. This takes a lot less time than sharpening an iron.

A further advantage can often be had by setting the cutter askew so that one side cuts deeper than the other. This leaves the board with a ridged surface which has to be gone over, but it takes off wood quickly.

PLANING OLD LUMBER    When working with secondhand or salvaged boards—and they are often of much better grade than new stuff—they'll need planing to eliminate dents and scars, and to true them up. First remove any old paint, a process that will reveal any tacks, nails, or screws. They must be painstakingly extracted—all of them! Certainly don't remove paint with the plane. Use a scraper. Paint remover does the job but it wets the wood and raises the grain, and a plane works miserably on wet wood. Let the wood dry thoroughly before using the plane on it.

PLUCKED GRAIN    Under ideal conditions—a clear straight piece of wood with no knots—planing is a pleasure. But that kind of stuff is increasingly hard to find and going up in price. Run-of-the-mill lumber eventually shows you every imaginable flaw, erratic grain being one of the most annoying. The plane may run along fine, then without warning hit a spot where the grain seems to erupt from the surface in three directions at once. Too late, the plane runs over the place, not cutting the wood fibers but *yanking* at them—what is termed "plucking up." Sometimes you can coax these weird areas by planing in both directions, but another remedy is generally more effective. Use a freshly sharpened iron, set it for a very light cut, and push the plane slowly and with good pressure. Hold the plane at an extreme angle and, as it passes over the plucked area, swivel the plane to get as much shearing as possible.

# Grooving Plane

The addition of this tool—which is also known as a plow plane—considerably expands the diversity of work that is possible in a hand tool shop. The simple groove, worked in a variety of sizes on the sides and edges of boards, is basic to joints and construction whose strength, utility, and attractiveness have made them traditional with cabinetmak-

*parts of a typical grooving plane*

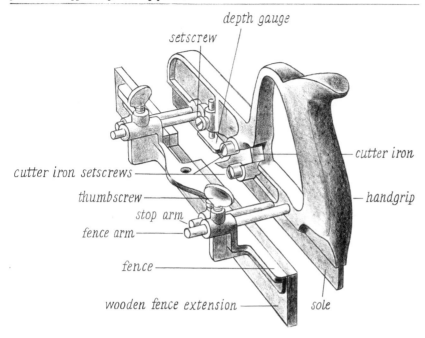

ers since at least the mid-seventeenth century. The solid firmness of a chest, its neatly built drawers, the substantial ruggedness of paneled doors, benches, and wainscoting, and the trim, quiet, sliding doors in a modern house—all owe their existence to the groove and a plane with which to cut it.

Not only is the groove a simple concept, in its own way as rudimentary and logical as the neat round holes made by the brace and bit, but it is also comparatively easy to make, provided of course that you have the right tool. Further, the groove is compatible with the nature of wood: it lends itself to being worked with the lengthwise grain of a board.

Stanley once manufactured the excellent No. 248, designed to cut grooves and nothing more. It has a depth gauge, six cutter irons of different widths ($\frac{1}{8}$, $\frac{5}{32}$, $\frac{3}{16}$, $\frac{7}{32}$, $\frac{1}{4}$, $\frac{5}{16}$, and $\frac{3}{8}$ inch), and an adjustable fence mounted on two arms which screw into either side of the frame. Two arms provide much greater accuracy than the single one found on some of the newer models. The modern combination planes do a fine job of grooving, but because they have several attachments to do several other jobs as well, they are quite expensive.

# Adjustments

TIGHTEN FENCE ARMS    Since the fence controls the location of the groove, make sure both arms are tightly screwed into the frame and that the thumbscrews are also tight.

ADJUST SIDE FENCE    Loosen the thumbscrews so the fence will slide. Turn the plane bottom up, slide the fence in or out to make the adjustment. To set the distance from the edge of the work to the edge of the groove, lay a rule *under* the sharp edge of the cutter iron, the end of the rule touching the fence. Tighten the thumbscrews—just barely. Check the measurement again. Next, make sure the fence is parallel with the plane sole. The measurement from fence to sole must be identical at both ends. Then go back and check the distance to the cutter. If it's still on the mark, tighten the thumbscrews. If not, loosen the thumbscrews again and correct the adjustment until you have a parallel fence and the correct measurement from edge of board to edge of groove. Last, loosen the setscrews over both stop-arms, push them until they touch the plane frame, then tighten them. This allows returning the fence to the same setting in the event that it works out of adjustment or is taken off.

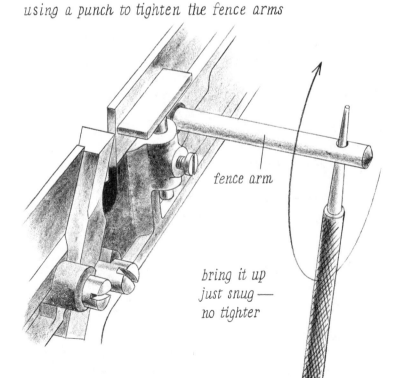

using a punch to tighten the fence arms

fence arm

bring it up
just snug —
no tighter

*adjusting the fence: distance from edge of work to edge of groove*

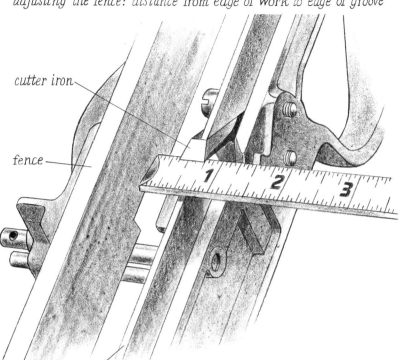

cutter iron

fence

sole

DEPTH GAUGE    This determines the depth of the groove. Turn the plane on its side and loosen the depth gauge setscrew. Lay the rule flat on the fence and butt it against the depth gauge foot. Let the edge of the rule touch the cutting edge of the iron. That's the place to take a reading. Move the depth gauge to the setting you want, then tighten the setscrew. Check the measurement again with the rule.

DEPTH OF CUT    Loosen the two cutter iron setscrews, releasing the cutter iron. Note that on the plane illustrated, these screws are flanged to overlap both sides of the cutter and hold it in adjustment. Turn the plane bottom up and sight along the sole. Slide the cutter up or down and set it for a fine cut, showing as a thin dark edge projecting above the sole. Tighten the setscrews lightly, first one, then the other. Then go back and finish tightening them, in the same order so that the cutter iron is evenly seated. Run a trial groove on scrap wood to verify the adjustments. A grooving plane works best with a very light cut—paper-thin shavings that curl out through the throat. A common error is to set the cutter too deep, which invariably jams the throat with heavy shavings.

*adjusting the depth gauge*

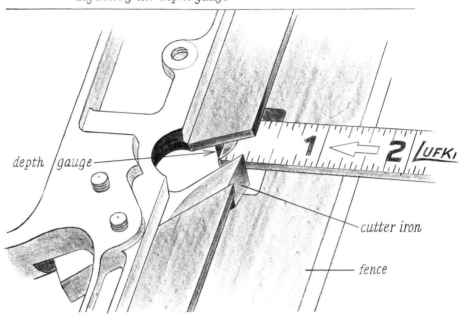

depth gauge

cutter iron

fence

*sighting along the sole to adjust the depth of cut*

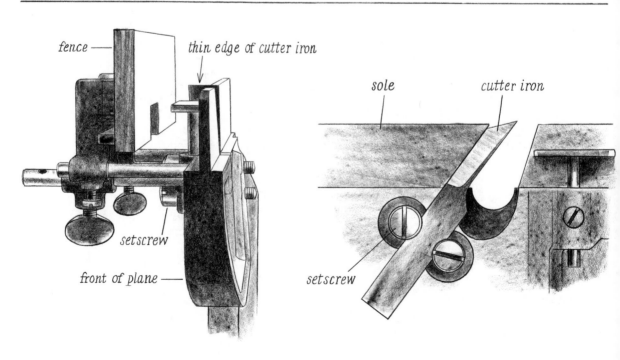

fence

thin edge of cutter iron

setscrew

front of plane

sole

cutter iron

setscrew

For grooving work use the best grade of lumber you can afford, preferably free of knots and with a grain that is straight on the surface as well as when seen on the edges. This applies to the other fence planes as well—rabbet, tongue and groove, combination, the multiplane, and the Stanley 45 and 55. Although these planes can be made to work on inferior stuff, the final job will lack the crisp, sharp edges and neatness of appearance which are characteristic of the work they were designed to produce. Apart from this, running through knots and erratic grain raises hob with the cutting edges. And sharpening a $1/8$-inch grooving iron is a tedious chore that no one wants to repeat any oftener than necessary.

Where to start the groove, on the near or the far end of the board? Doing good work with this type of plane depends on the fence running snug against the work with as much of its length as possible in contact

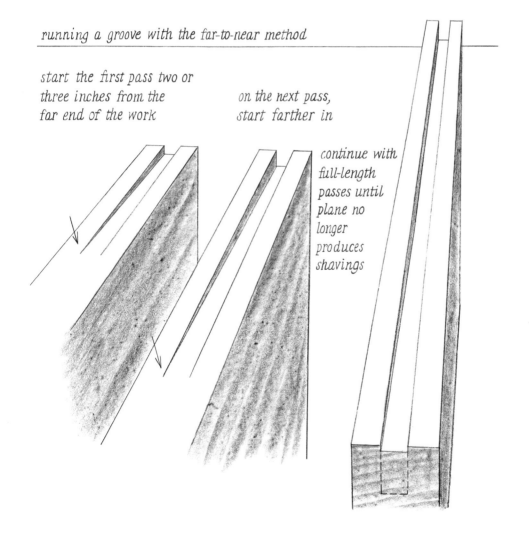

*running a groove with the far-to-near method*

*start the first pass two or three inches from the far end of the work*

*on the next pass, start farther in*

*continue with full-length passes until plane no longer produces shavings*

with the work. If you start the cut at the near end, only an inch or two of the fence will touch the edge of the board, which is too little for accurate work. By starting at the far end, the entire fence lies against the work, enabling the plane to cut accurately right from the first pass and with the least effort.

For maximum control, get a good grip on the plane with both hands. Use one hand to hold the fence tight against the work, the other to push the plane. Since the first pass establishes the correct location of the groove and makes the initial cut which subsequent passes will follow, concentrate on keeping the fence tight against the work. The first shaving out of the plane will show if the cutter iron is removing wood evenly across its full width.

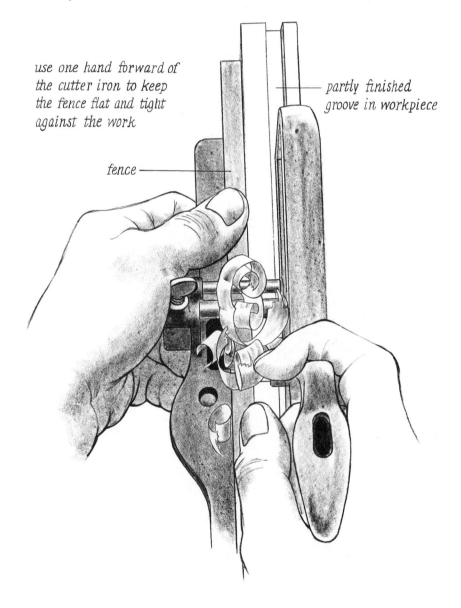

use one hand forward of the cutter iron to keep the fence flat and tight against the work

partly finished groove in workpiece

fence

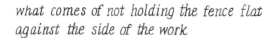

*what comes of not holding the fence flat against the side of the work*

*a crooked groove that never can be made right*

# Tongue and Groove Plane

As an adjunct to the basic collection of planes, a tongue and groove plane multiplies the work capacity of a hand tool shop to an impressive extent. The tongue and groove joint provides the means of making up wide sections of solid wood from two or more boards, and is used in the construction of tabletops, chests, countertops, cabinets, and other furniture as well as for flooring. The groove on the edge of one board locks with the tongue on the matching one, and when glued makes a tight joint that for all practical purposes is just as strong as a single piece of wood.

The success of a tongue and groove joint depends on beginning with properly jointed boards and on the accuracy of the plane. It must cut tongues and grooves that exactly match in size, that are centered on the edges of the boards to be joined, and that are the correct depth so that the two halves of the joint will ''match'' without any gap showing. In the bygone time of wooden-bodied planes, this type of work was done with two separate handmade planes, the cutter irons for which necessarily had to be ground with exceptional care, the groove of one

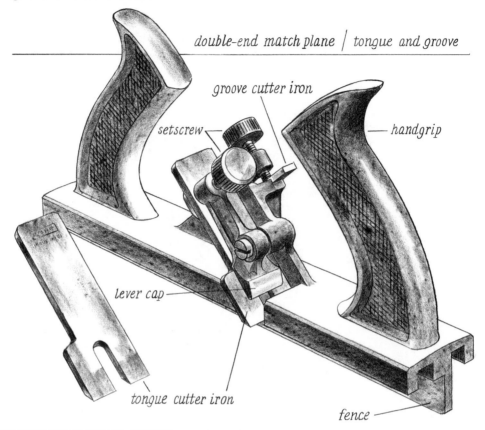

double-end match plane / tongue and groove

groove cutter iron

setscrew

handgrip

lever cap

tongue cutter iron

fence

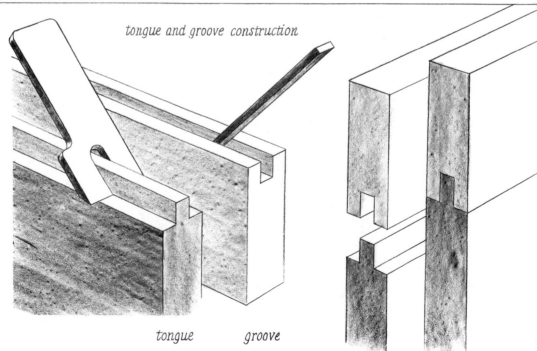

tongue and groove construction

tongue    groove

good tongue and groove joints depend on properly prepared boards —
jointed, edges squared, and sized to uniform thickness

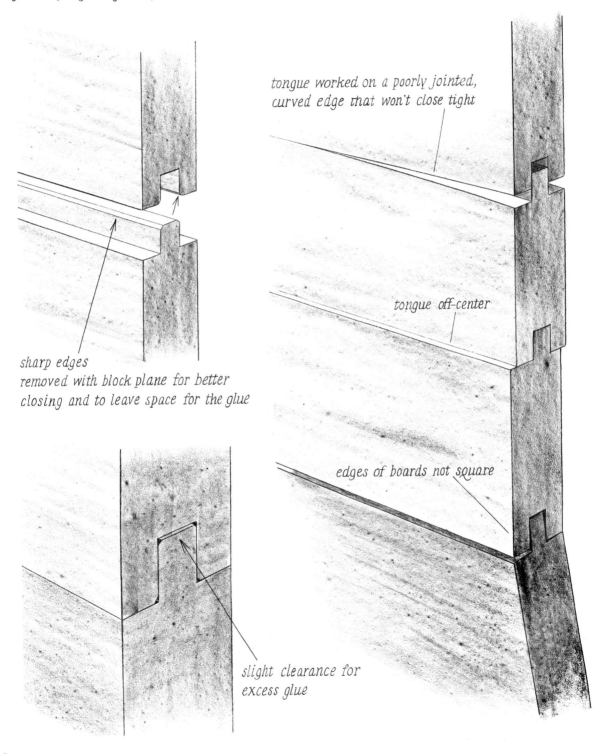

tongue worked on a poorly jointed,
curved edge that won't close tight

tongue off-center

sharp edges
removed with block plane for better
closing and to leave space for the glue

edges of boards not square

slight clearance for
excess glue

to match the tongue of the other. Hence the term "match planes." As a consequence these planes were sold as pairs, since the tongue of one pair would not fit the groove of another.

In 1900 when to a large extent steel had replaced wood, there were manufactured several sizes of what was called the double-end match plane which was in effect two planes in one: a tongue cutter on one side and a groove cutter on the other. Pushed in one direction, the plane cut a groove centered on the edge of one board; when the plane was turned end-for-end the other cutter made a matching tongue on a second board. Each size was made to fit boards of only one particular thickness. For example, the Stanley No. 148–$^{7}/_{8}$ worked only on stuff that was $^{7}/_{8}$-inch thick, and their No. 147–$^{5}/_{8}$ was limited to boards $^{5}/_{8}$-inch thick, the reason for this being that the fence was cast as part of the tool and so offered no adjustment. The correct depth of groove and length of tongue were automatically determined by the plane.

As far as I know these planes have been discontinued, but there are secondhand ones in circulation and they are well worth the effort to locate. For this work they are simpler to operate than the modern combination and multiplanes and do excellent work, especially with the addition of an auxiliary wooden fence that you can make yourself. A handy size is the $^{7}/_{8}$-inch model. It will work on our common $^{3}/_{4}$-inch lumber by designing the auxiliary fence to center the cutters, or it can be used as is. In the latter case, however, take care to work both tongue and groove *from corresponding sides of both boards,* since both will be slightly off center.

Working from far to near, along with the other general rules and work methods outlined for the grooving plane, apply as well to the tongue and groove plane, the multiplane, and the combination plane.

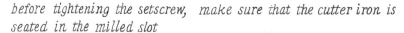

*before tightening the setscrew, make sure that the cutter iron is seated in the milled slot*

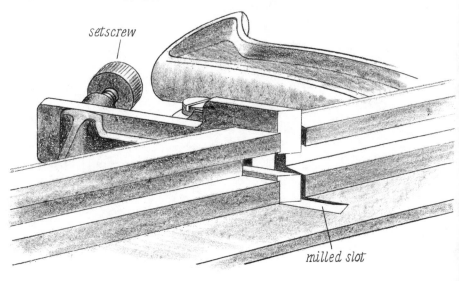

*setscrew*

*milled slot*

# Combination and Multiplanes

These are complex tools manufactured to replace Stanley's discontinued model 45 and the 55, which was described in the 1909 catalog in this fashion: "The regular equipment sent with this plane comprises 52 cutters. . . . A further line of 41 special cutters are regularly made. With the complete line of cutters there is practically no end to the variety of work which can be done with this plane. . . ."

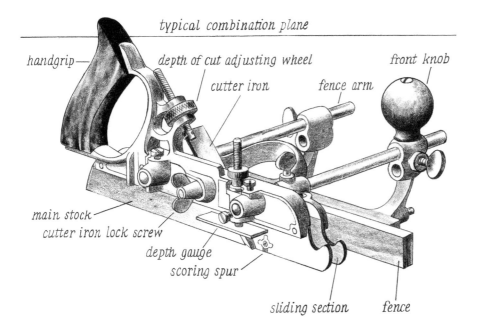

*typical combination plane*

*handgrip* — *depth of cut adjusting wheel* — *front knob*

*cutter iron* — *fence arm*

*main stock*
*cutter iron lock screw*
*depth gauge*
*scoring spur*
*sliding section* — *fence*

They will cut not only excellent tongue and groove joints but also rabbets, dadoes, beads, and numerous moldings. However, their success depends on several precise and time-consuming adjustments and then prooving their accuracy with trial runs on scrap wood. And making them perform the sharp work of which they are capable demands particularly close attention to holding the fence snug and square against the edge of the work. Otherwise, careless operation is quite likely to produce disappointing results.

The intricacies of setting up, adjusting, and operating these tools are fully explained in the manufacturer's instruction booklet that comes with the plane. To get the most out of these planes, it is a good idea to experiment with the various attachments and cutter irons, using the booklet as a guide.

*the long, heavy planes are superior for jointing*

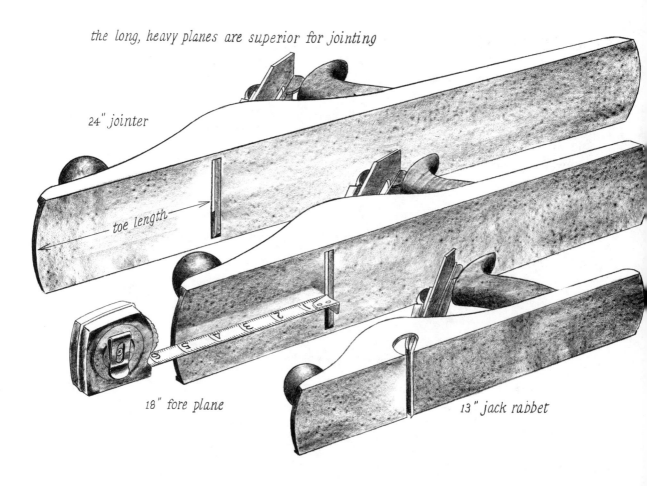

24" jointer

toe length

18" fore plane

13" jack rabbet

*a long-bodied jointer spans several low spots
and seeks to make the edge straight, flat, and level*

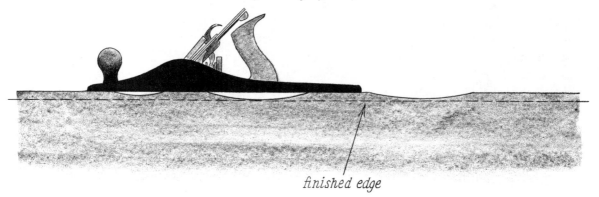

finished edge

# Fore and Jointer Planes

Long, wide, and heavy, these planes were designed specifically for jointing and smoothing, and are recommended for the most professional results or where the daily routine involves a considerable amount of this work.

They are built with the same features as other bench planes and are fitted with large, well-placed front knobs and rear totes. The increased amount of toe length—distance from the toe of the plane to the mouth—is a decided advantage in good control at the start of a jointing pass. And the weight is of notable assistance in holding the plane down on the work, as it generates a degree of momentum to carry the plane through a smooth, continuous pass.

JOINTING    The long body makes it possible to level off irregularities quickly and accurately: the plane spans a considerable portion of a board's length. The average fore plane measures 18 inches and the jointer is made in 22-inch and 24-inch versions. It should be pointed out, however, that the extra long body—even the 24-inch model—does not eliminate the need for preliminary sighting of a board and planing off the high spots.

WALKING A BOARD    Good jointing requires making each stroke as one nonstop pass. This is simple enough on short pieces of wood, for the normal arm-reach allows pushing the plane from one end of a board to the other without changing the position of the feet. But jointing boards as long as 4 or 5 feet requires shifting the feet in order to follow the plane through. You can run the plane the length of an arm's reach, take a step forward, then make another similar pass. However, "walking a board" from one end to the other produces better work and is no more difficult than the stop-and-go method, once the technique has been practiced.

With the cutter iron adjusted for a fine cut, set the plane on the near end of the board. Look at the far end to gauge how long a walk you have. Hold the plane in both hands as though planing a short board, then move ahead with arms and shoulders, and begin the pass. Keep your eye on the far end of the board. Once your hips, arms, and shoulders are in position, hold them there and walk the plane to the end of the board. Keep pressure on the plane; keep it centered on the board; keep it moving until the cutter iron runs off the far end.

SMOOTHING    A plane of this type might seem ungainly for smoothing, yet, properly sharpened and adjusted, it will do a superior job of removing tissue-thin shavings. Here again, its weight and length contribute to a natural ease of producing a flat surface, and if long passes are worked in swaths from one edge of a board to the other, only minor sanding will be necessary. Shoot the first pass with the cutter overhanging the edge of the board. The second pass should overlap the first, and so on. Work these swaths clear to the other edge of the board. Forget any untouched low places until you've worked clear across the board. Then go back and begin a second series of swaths, which on good lumber should be sufficient to produce a nice surface.

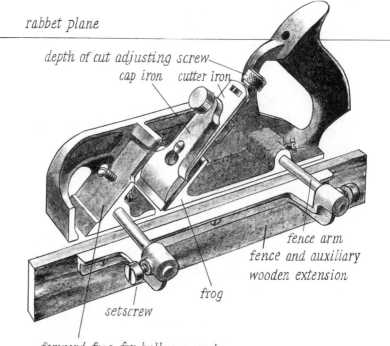

*rabbet plane*

*depth of cut adjusting screw*
*cap iron*    *cutter iron*
*fence arm*
*fence and auxiliary*
*wooden extension*
*frog*
*setscrew*
*forward frog for bullnose work*

# Rabbet Plane

This tool has features which facilitate the cutting of precise rabbets with a minimum of guesswork: adjustable fence, depth gauge, and cutting spur. It will cut a rabbet up to $1\frac{1}{2}$ inches wide and to a maximum depth of $\frac{3}{4}$ inch with the depth gauge attached. Remove the gauge and unlimited depth is possible, for example, when working with stuff 2 inches or more in thickness. The long fence slides on two arms, providing accurate parallel alignment with the plane body. By attaching an auxiliary wooden fence, holding the plane square against the work is made easier and its accuracy is substantially increased.

The cutting spur is designed primarily for working across the grain. Its intended purpose is to score a clean line just ahead of the cutter iron so that as the cutter removes wood in its wake, the shoulder edge of

depth gauge

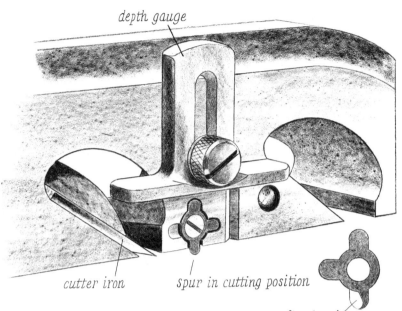

cutter iron     spur in cutting position

inside of leading edge should be sharpened on a flat bevel

a very fine ribbon shaving
cut across the grain
with a good sharp rabbet plane

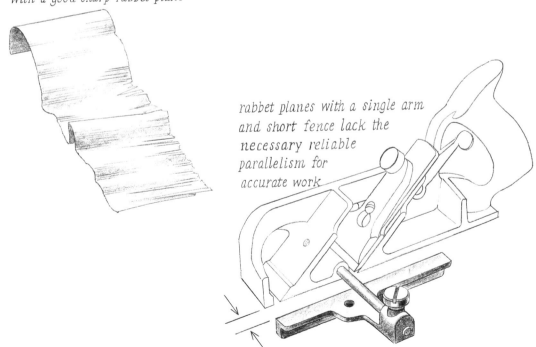

rabbet planes with a single arm
and short fence lack the
necessary reliable
parallelism for
accurate work

the rabbet will be clean and not ragged. The difficulty is that the spur doesn't always cut that well. The steel is too soft to hold the kind of edge necessary to make a clean cut in wood as soft as pine.

A sharper rabbet can be made by first scoring the wood with a utility knife and then using the rabbet plane with the spur. By this method, the spur leaves a terminal furrow on the inside corner of the rabbet, although this is not serious when the ends of the rabbet are to be hidden. For the most professional job, tack or clamp a wooden guide strip to the work, and with a backsaw cut down to a point just short of the bottom of the rabbet. Then clean out the waste with the rabbet plane without the spur. The inside corner of the rabbet can be shaved clean, using the plane laid on its side against the shoulder of the rabbet.

The plane will cut through small knots, but don't expect a clean, crisp rabbet. The grain surrounding a knot runs and turns every which way, consequently much of this wood will be torn rather than sliced.

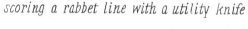

*scoring a rabbet line with a utility knife*

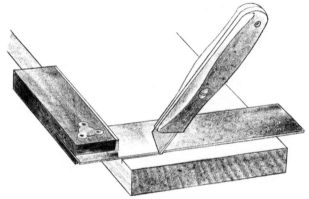

*the spur leaves a furrow on the inside corner of the rabbet*

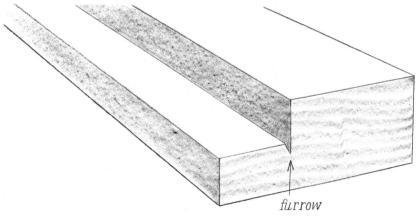

*furrow*

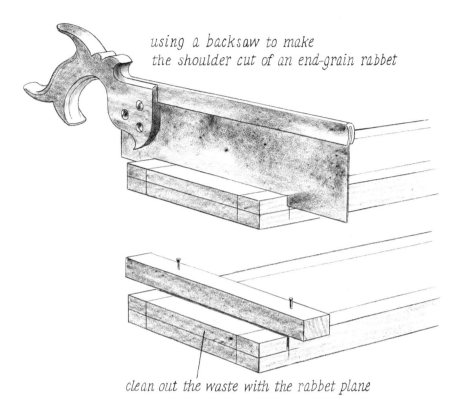

*using a backsaw to make
the shoulder cut of an end-grain rabbet*

*clean out the waste with the rabbet plane*

*to avoid this ragged look, use only clear straight lumber, or lay out
the work to miss the knots*

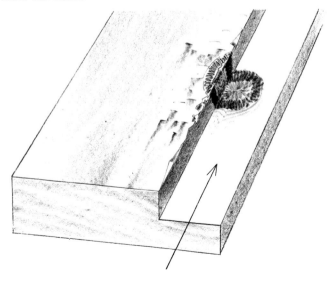

Generally the spur is not needed when working parallel to the grain. The cutter will make a clean edge right from the start unless the grain is irregular. In that case, it is a good precaution to use the spur for the first couple of passes to score a nice edge, after which it can be dispensed with. But don't remove the spur! It is tiny, easy to lose, and difficult to replace. Set it in the idle position by loosening the setscrew and rotating the spur a quarter-turn. Make sure the recess is clear of shavings before tightening the screw, otherwise the spur may stick out and gouge the shoulder of the rabbet.

When running wide rabbets make sure the cutter is sharp and adjusted for a fine cut, because using the full cutter width takes considerable physical force. Each pass with the plane should be nonstop. Try it out on a scrap first. Then plant your feet farther back from the work and away from the bench, so that you can really lean on it.

Adjustments of the fence and depth gauge, as well as the technique of planing—particularly in the use of the far-to-near method—are the same as for the grooving plane.

HOLDING THE WORK     Rabbeting work has to be held securely. Where the rabbet is to be cut on the flat of a board rather than its edge, the board must be clamped flat over the edge of the bench. And it must

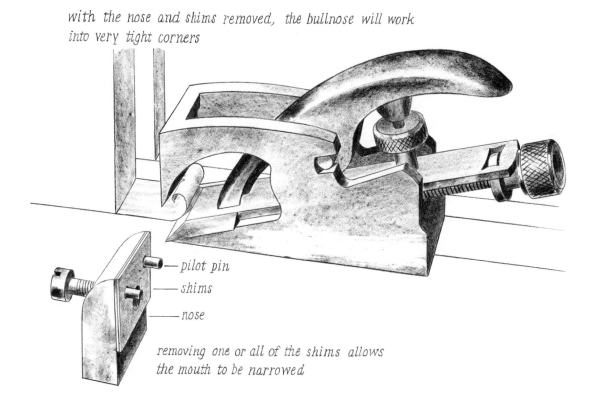

*with the nose and shims removed, the bullnose will work into very tight corners*

—*pilot pin*

—*shims*

—*nose*

*removing one or all of the shims allows the mouth to be narrowed*

be extra wide to allow room for the hold-down clamps without their getting in the way of the plane. The fence of a rabbet plane must hang down over the edge of the workpiece and be able to slide along it. Putting the work flat in the vise doesn't work simply because the vise completely obstructs the operation of the plane.

Therefore, but especially when the rabbeted pieces are narrow, such as the frames for a paneled cupboard door, start with a wide board and use this method: (1) joint one edge of the wide board to provide a smooth track for the plane to run against; (2) clamp it to the bench and run a rabbet; (3) rip off the workpiece to rough width—which now leaves the wide board with a rough edge to be jointed. Then repeat the process. Joint a new edge on the board, clamp it to the bench and run the second rabbet, then rip this piece to rough width. With this method there is always enough extra width in the board to accommodate the clamps, and the rabbeted pieces can be put in the vise to joint their other edges.

# Bullnose Plane

This is a nice little plane and very useful for all manner of delicate shaving, paring, and trimming, especially in quarters too cramped for a large model. The removable nose allows cutting into corners, for this purpose doing the work of a chisel but possibly with more finesse and control. Laid on its side, the bullnose can be used to trim the shoulder of a rabbet. For its size it is surprisingly solid and will stay down flat on the work surface.

To remove the cutter, loosen the lock screw until the whole cap iron disengages from the notches and will slide back. There is very little spare room in which to take out the cutter, so it must be canted at an angle. Then slide it out carefully to avoid damaging the cutting edge against the plane body. To replace the cutter, reverse these steps. Tip the cutter at an angle, ease it into the plane bevel side up, and lay it on the slanting bed. Be sure the slot in the end of the cutter drops over the top of the adjusting ring. This is what moves the cutter up and down. Align the cutter with the sides of the plane with thumb and fingers and hold it there while you replace the cap iron. Then tighten the lock screw a bit to hold things in place.

To set the depth of cut, turn the cutter adjusting screw, then try the plane on a scrap of wood. When a fine cut has been obtained, tighten the cap iron lock screw and it's ready to go. The depth of cut cannot be changed unless the lock screw is loosened a little. See that the pins don't slip out of the notches.

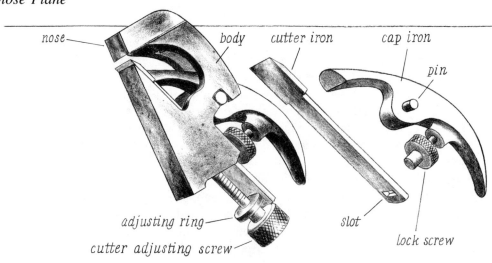

nose — body   cutter iron   cap iron   pin

adjusting ring —

cutter adjusting screw —   slot   lock screw

shims

hold edges of cutter in
alignment with sides of plane
while tightening the lock screw

# Round and Tapered Work

In work where square stock is to be made round, an edge rounded, or a round piece is to be tapered, the critical thing is to maintain roundness every step of the way. Start with square stock. First find and mark the center on the end of the work by drawing diagonal lines. Set a compass on the point where the lines cross and scribe a circle. Draw four lines just outside the circle to make an octagon. Then carry lines over to the sides of the work to serve as chamfer guides. Set the plane

*planing square stock round*

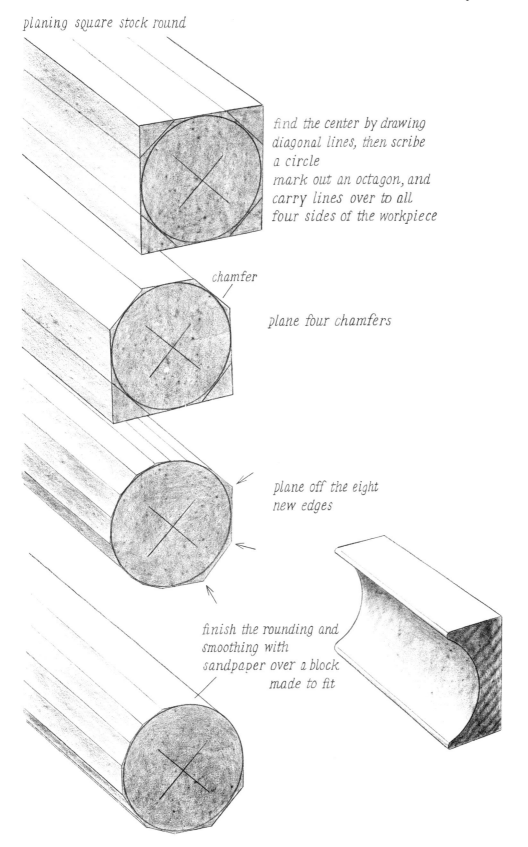

find the center by drawing
diagonal lines, then scribe
a circle
mark out an octagon, and
carry lines over to all
four sides of the workpiece

*chamfer*

*plane four chamfers*

*plane off the eight
new edges*

*finish the rounding and
smoothing with
sandpaper over a block
made to fit*

for a fine cut and plane these four chamfers down to the lines but leave them showing. The final sizing should be done with file or sandpaper.

Once you have an octagon, plane off each of the eight new edges. The final step is to plane off all the edges again—sixteen this time. Any plane with a flat bottom will do this job, but exactly which one depends on the thickness and length of the work. To repeat, the object is to maintain roundness every step of the way. To keep this under control, leave the cutter iron set for a light cut throughout the whole process, and remove wood evenly from end to end, from the first pass until the last. This is much simpler than trying to correct a lopsided oval.

Finish the rounding with a sandpaper block, running it lengthwise with the grain, and rotating the work a bit after each stroke, again removing wood uniformly.

This principle is especially important when making a tapered dowel or chair rung. After the taper end has been shaped to an octagon, make a pencil mark on the side of the work for a reference point. Holding the work in one hand, start the first plane stroke next to the pencil mark. Then rotate the work a whisker, stop and make another plane

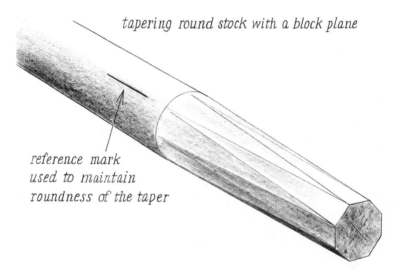

*tapering round stock with a block plane*

*reference mark used to maintain roundness of the taper*

stroke. Rotate the work again, make another stroke, and so on. Turn the work evenly—the same amount each time. When you come round to the pencil mark again, you know you've completed one revolution. This system helps maintain roundness.

Follow the same technique for smoothing with file or sandpaper. After some practice, you will discover that rotating the work continuously while sanding continuously produces a taper or round that is geometrically very uniform.

*table leg worked with plane, chisel, rasp, and file*

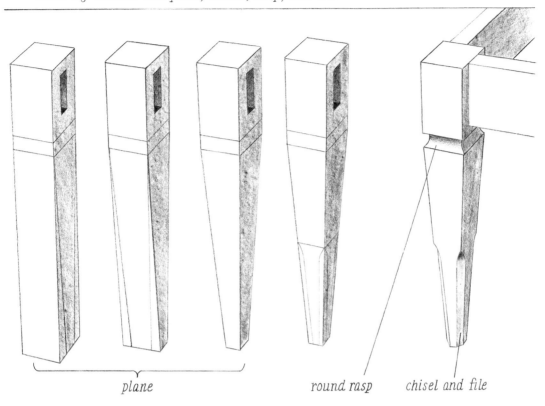

plane          round rasp     chisel and file

# Testing for Uniform Diameter

Having made a square piece round, how do you tell if the diameter is the same over its entire length? Make a test block by boring a hole of the correct diameter in a short piece of wood. Remember, the scribed circle should still be visible on the end of the work when the plane work is done. With a flat file, round off one end for the first couple of inches, until it will fit snugly into the hole in the test block. Now make a pencil mark on the work alongside the test block, and remove the work. Then file round for another inch or so, filing away the pencil mark. Fit the work into the test block again. It should go farther in this time. Make another pencil mark, and file round some more. The important thing is to file gingerly—don't take off too much wood.

*use a test block to try the uniformity of a rounded edge*

*saw through the block
below the center*

# Planing Thin Stock

In ordinary plane work, it's the wood that is held secure so the plane can run over it. However, this is impractical where thin stuff is concerned. Wooden stops nailed flat on the bench must of course be thinner than the work, and often they either don't hold, or there is the risk of nicking the plane iron on the nails. When thin stuff is clamped in the vise only a fraction of wood can be left above the vise jaws, which again may damage the plane iron. And with only the top surface of the work in sight, planing it true is too much a matter of guesswork.

There is a simple way to plane the thinnest piece of wood. Clamp a plane bottom side up in the vise—the longer the plane the better—and run the piece of thin stuff over the bottom of the plane. Make a notched stick with which to push the work through.

The cutter iron must be sharp and set for a very fine cut. Lay the work on the toe of the plane and set the notched stick on top, the notch caught on one end of the work. Bear down on the stick and slide it until the work catches the edge of the cutter iron. Keeping plenty of pressure on the stick, push the work through. Lift the work and the stick at the end of each pass and repeat the sequence.

With thin pieces of hardwood, more deliberate control can be had by tapping the back end of the notched stick with a mallet instead of pushing with the hand. Either way, pieces as thin as $3/16$ inch can be planed easily, accurately, and with no danger of cutting a finger. A long jointer plane works best because the greater toe length makes it easier to start the work through flat.

So long as good pressure is maintained, and the work is pushed slowly, quite long strips can be handled in a similar fashion. Lay one end of the work strip on the plane, and hold the other end with one hand. With the other hand, hold a flat block of wood on top of the work to keep it flat on the plane bottom, then push the strip through. Strips that are exceptionally thin and flexible may tend to buckle. If so, bowing up the pushed end a little usually puts enough tension in the strip to make it feed through flat.

*using an 18" plane and a notched stick to plane thin stuff*

*keep all the pressure over the work*

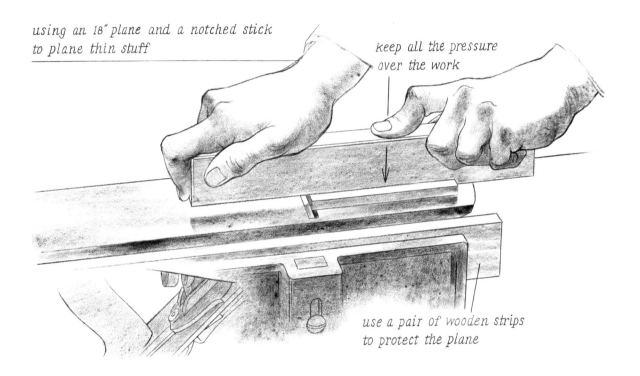

*use a pair of wooden strips to protect the plane*

*notched planing stick*

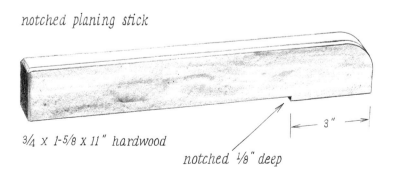

*3/4 x 1-5/8 x 11" hardwood*

*notched 1/8" deep*

*3"*

*needle-nose pliers*

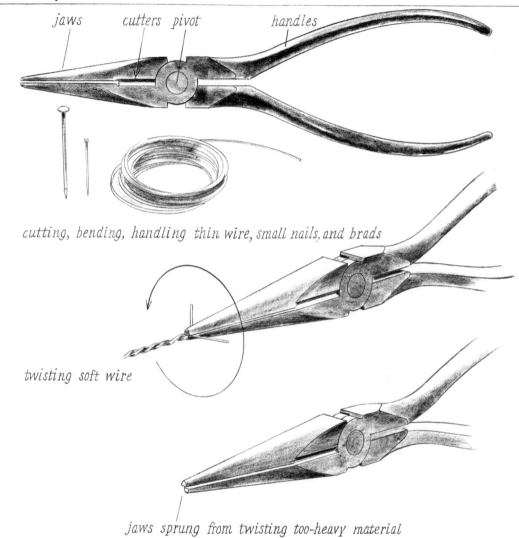

jaws  cutters  pivot  handles

*cutting, bending, handling thin wire, small nails, and brads*

*twisting soft wire*

*jaws sprung from twisting too-heavy material*

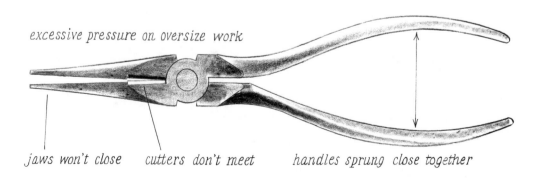

*excessive pressure on oversize work*

*jaws won't close*  *cutters don't meet*  *handles sprung close together*

# 21

# Pliers

Three pairs of pliers are useful in a woodworking shop for cutting and bending wire, pulling small nails, holding metal pieces that are to be filed or hammered, and as an occasional substitute for a wrench.

Pliers are designed primarily as single-handed tools, although in some situations the heavy lineman's pliers often need two hands. The clamping pressure is exerted by thumb and fingers in a squeezing action, and because the size of the hand determines how much pressure can be applied to the pliers, choose a pair that fits. The hand uses its squeezing pressure most efficiently when half closed. If you have to open it wide in order to clamp the pliers on the work, they are too large for you and much of their potential leverage will be lost.

*working pliers with one hand*

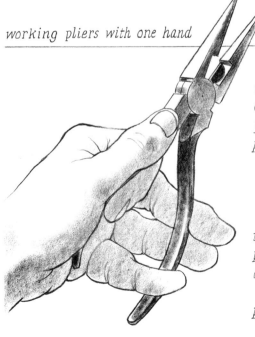

*this handgrip allows both opening and closing the pliers without shifting position of fingers*

*two middle fingers squeeze pliers shut and apply pressure*

*pinky opens pliers*

Although pliers are made of tough malleable steel, they should never be pounded with a hammer or otherwise forced to work beyond their capacity, as this kind of treatment will either spring the jaws or chip the tempered cutting edges which are difficult to sharpen. If the heft of the job in any way suggests the use of a hammer, then use it on some tool other than pliers.

# Needle-Nose Pliers

These pliers are made for cutting and bending thin wire, small nails, or brads. Their slender jaws are easily sprung out of alignment, so they should not be used for anything but the lightest kind of work. However, just because of their size, needle-nose pliers are particularly handy for reaching into confined spaces to retrieve small objects and to hold fine brads for driving with a hammer.

# Diagonal Cutting Pliers

Sometimes called wire cutters, this type has scooped jaws which makes them ideal for extracting small nails. By working the points of the jaws under a nail head and then prying the pliers over a small stick of wood, a nail can be removed with a minimum of damage to the surrounding wood.

# Lineman's Pliers

Sometimes called engineer's pliers, these are the heaviest of the three and will easily cut through a 10-penny nail, twist heavy gauge fence wire, or bend sheet metal. In a woodworking shop, however, their most useful function is to act as a maneuverable vise in which to hold nails, wire, rivets, and other objects that are to be worked in conjunction with a hammer or file.

Of the three types, the lineman's are the only ones that should be used in place of a wrench. Their wide, heavy, checkered jaws and long handles provide the leverage and nonslip hold necessary to turn the head of a bolt, the nut, or a stubborn screw whose slot is too chewed up to be removed with a screwdriver.

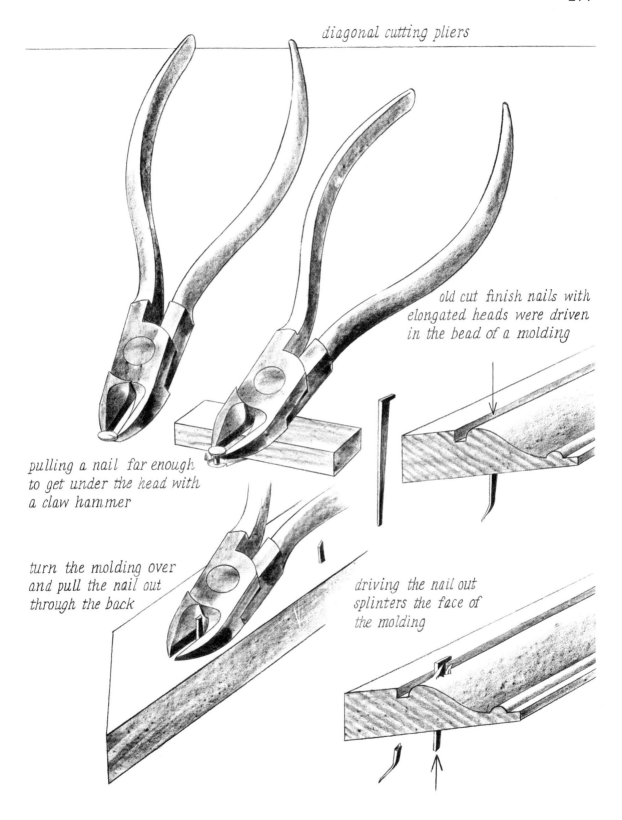

old cut finish nails with
elongated heads were driven
in the bead of a molding

pulling a nail far enough
to get under the head with
a claw hammer

turn the molding over
and pull the nail out
through the back

driving the nail out
splinters the face of
the molding

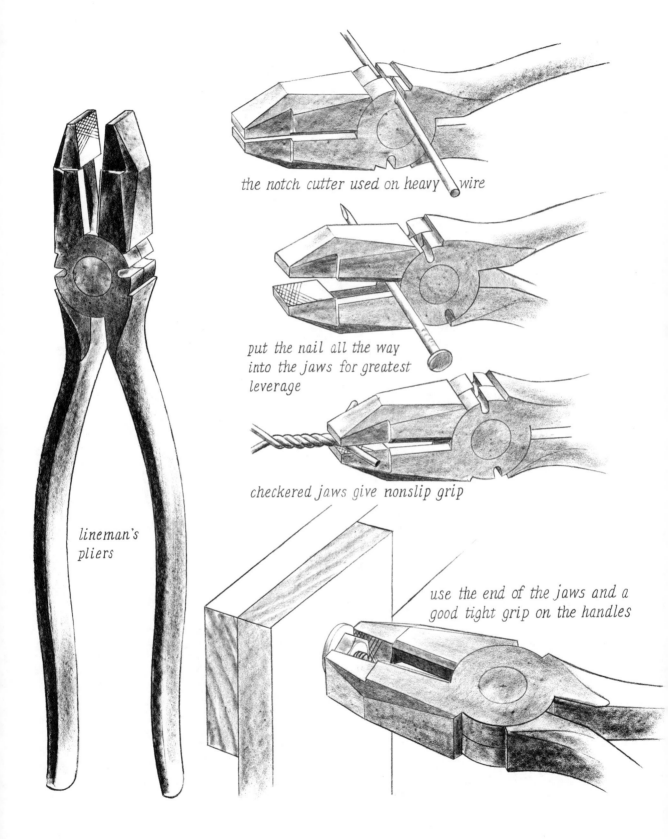

*the notch cutter used on heavy wire*

*put the nail all the way into the jaws for greatest leverage*

*checkered jaws give nonslip grip*

*lineman's pliers*

*use the end of the jaws and a good tight grip on the handles*

# 22

# Pry Bar

A superior pry bar for woodworking can be made from an automobile spring leaf from the junkyard with only an hour's time spent in refining its shape. For those jobs where wood pieces must be carefully removed or dismantled and the same pieces used again, this is an ideal tool. The thin flat point can be forced between two pieces of wood, either by hand pressure or hammer tapping, without chewing up the wood. The curved shape provides a natural rocker for exerting controlled pressure, and the leaf is thick and thin in just the right places: thin at the point and thick at the heel where most of the force is applied.

Find a leaf about 36 inches long with a curvature similar to the one shown in the illustration. Have it cut in two. The rest you can do yourself. The most important thing is the shape of the pointed end. Grind or file it a bit rounded and thin down both sides as shown. The simplest way to get the edge right—neither too sharp nor too blunt—

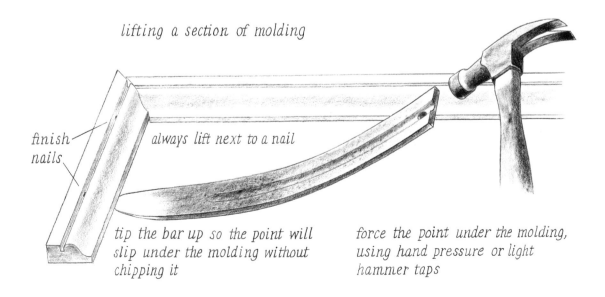

*lifting a section of molding*

*finish nails*

*always lift next to a nail*

*tip the bar up so the point will slip under the molding without chipping it*

*force the point under the molding, using hand pressure or light hammer taps*

*pry bar made from half a spring leaf*

*hole for center bolt*

*point*

*heel*

*5"*

*18"*

*as you find it, the point is thick, blunt, and very rough*

*after shaping the point, smooth and polish both flat surfaces as bright as possible*

*profile of the finished point*

is to first sharpen it to a cutting edge and then dull it with a file and emery paper. Polish the entire tapered end with emery paper, as well as both sides, so that the blade will slip against the compression of joined pieces of wood.

These leaves are made of tough spring steel and will stand almost any kind of abuse. This bar can be used with little danger of denting or crushing the work, since the wide, flat blade distributes pressure quite evenly. In such situations as removing a delicate molding from a wall, where other tools would crush or crack the plaster or splinter the wood, a spring leaf pry bar is usually quite safe.

One advantage of this homemade tool is its flexibility. Under heavy pressure it will give, and if the wood piece shows no sign of coming loose, the springing of the tool reminds you to stop before you snap the wood in two, which can easily happen.

*using two pry bars together:*

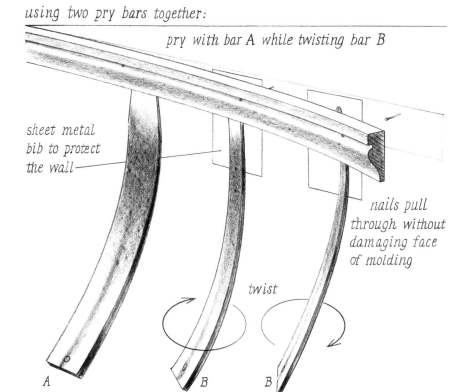

*pry with bar A while twisting bar B*

sheet metal
bib to protect
the wall

nails pull
through without
damaging face
of molding

twist

A          B        B

*checking the depth of a rabbet*

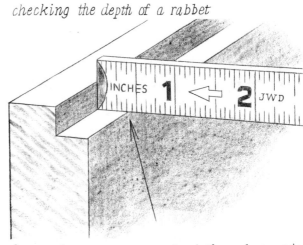

*for maximum accuracy, stand the rule on edge*

*a rule graduated only in 16ths would be workable but tiresome to use*

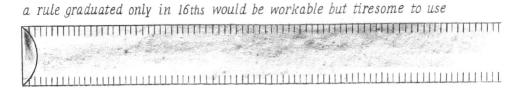

*the addition of 1" and ½" marks is a considerable improvement*

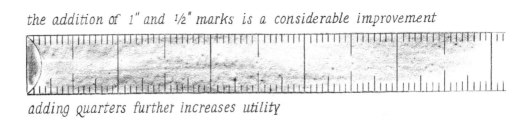

*adding quarters further increases utility*

*standard graduations: 16ths, 8ths, quarters, halves, and inches*

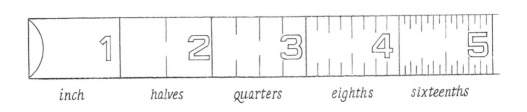

inch      halves      quarters      eighths      sixteenths

# 23

# Rules

Here is where it all begins. It is a fine thing to be able to plane square and saw straight but these skills are lost on work that is measured and laid out incorrectly. While "measure twice and cut once" is always pithy advice, it is more important to measure *accurately* and to know that you have.

The rule has three functions: (1) to measure the size of a board; (2) to mark off on it where cuts are to be made; and (3) to check the finished work to make sure it is correct. In any case there must be the ability to take a reading from the rule, to transpose the measurement into written numbers and fractions, and to find a specified dimension on the rule and mark it on the work.

On a standard rule the inch is divided into 16 parts, or 16ths. The better quality tape rules also have the first 6 inches calibrated in 32nds, which provides ample precision for most woodwork. In theory, that's all you need: a rule with nothing but 16ths would be workable, albeit very tiresome in counting off lines to find the particular mark. And there would be the strong probability of losing track and making an error.

To make it easier to read, the rule is further divided into units of 8ths ($^2/_{16}$), quarters ($^4/_{16}$), and halves ($^8/_{16}$). For quick identification, the lines that mark these divisions are of graduated lengths, the 16ths being the shortest, 8ths next, and so on up to the inch mark which runs clear across the rule.

For particularly exacting work it is advisable to use the same rule throughout the job, since any two apparently identical rules may disagree by as much as $^1/_{32}$nd of an inch in one foot. Switching from an extension rule to a tape to a square and back again may create errors that at the end of the job cannot be traced.

When taking a measurement, if the thing being measured does not line up exactly with a mark on the rule—and this happens quite often—the dimension can be written as either "plus" or "minus." For example, the width of a board that is slightly more than $4^1/_2$ inches can be expressed as $4^1/_2+$ or $4^9/_{16}-$. It doesn't matter which, but in order to avoid confusion and mistakes it is safest to adopt one plan or the other and stick to it.

# Folding Extension Rule

The wooden folding extension rule is still the reliable standby. When extended, it is rigid enough to measure a fair distance without drooping, and when folded shut, fits easily into a pocket without disappearing out of your grasp. The best ones are made of select hardwood and fitted with brass swivel joints that lock open automatically to minimize end-play inaccuracy. One version has a sliding brass extension in the first arm for taking inside measurements. While they are made in lengths up to 25 feet, the 6-footer is a convenient size for benchwork.

A wooden rule is easily damaged, especially when fully extended. Opening it only to the length you need—and then folding it up when you're through—may save it from getting stepped on or broken by a falling hammer or a length of wood. If the joints dry out and get tight from constant use, a drop of sewing machine oil will usually restore them to good working order.

*typical 6-foot folding extension rule*

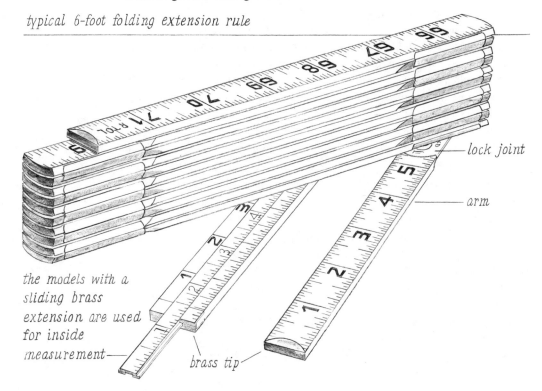

lock joint

arm

*the models with a sliding brass extension are used for inside measurement*

brass tip

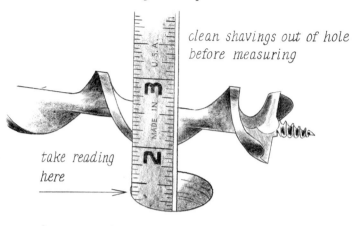

clean shavings out of hole
before measuring

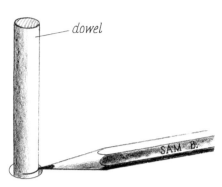

dowel

*take reading
here*

*keep edge of rule against side of hole*

*use a dowel to measure depth
of a small diameter hole*

*using the rule to divide a board into equal parts*

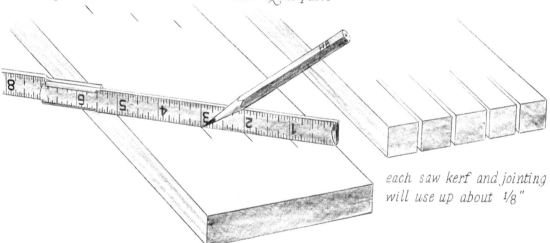

*each saw kerf and jointing
will use up about 1/8"*

*using the extension to take an inside measurement*

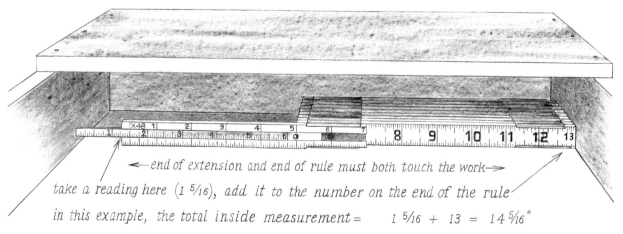

←*end of extension and end of rule must both touch the work*→

*take a reading here (1 5/16), add it to the number on the end of the rule*

*in this example, the total inside measurement =* $1\,5/16 + 13 = 14\,5/16\,"$

*a fast marking method that is satisfactory for rough work*

*crease the pad of a finger over the edge of the work — hold the pencil rigid*

*draw your hand along the board toward you*

*using the thumbnail as a sliding stop makes for more accurate measuring than sighting down over the rule*

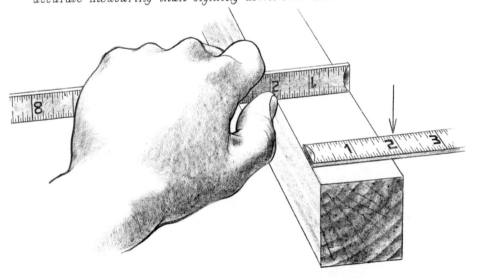

# Tape Rule

This version consists of a ribbon of spring steel wound into a case on a spring-loaded spool. A hook on the end of the tape makes it easy to catch the edge of a board and draw the tape out against the tension of the spring. The ribbon is slightly concave in its width so that it will stay straight and rigid when pulled out. The tape is locked open simply by pushing a slide button; it rewinds automatically when the button is released. In some models the tape is removable for use as a straight rule.

Constant flexing and the friction of repeatedly winding the tape in and out tend to weaken the steel and wear off the numbers and calibrations. If this happens the worn tape can simply be taken out and replaced with a refill.

*typical tape rule with lock and spring rewind*

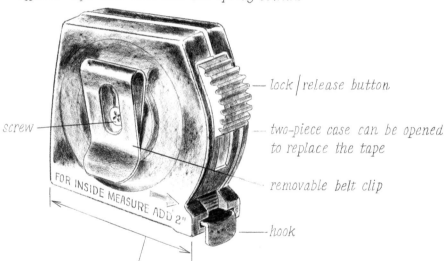

*— lock / release button*

*screw —*

*— two-piece case can be opened
to replace the tape*

*FOR INSIDE MEASURE ADD 2"*

*removable belt clip*

*hook*

*for inside measure, add the length of the case to the tape reading*

# Other Ways of Measuring

Rules are not the only accurate devices for measuring. When a dimension falls between two marks on a rule and the plus or minus system is too inexact, transfer the dimension to a slip of paper or a thin slat of wood and use that instead. Notched sticks are also useful as well as accurate, particularly when the same measurement is to be

*with the hook caught over the edge, draw the tape out and take a measurement*

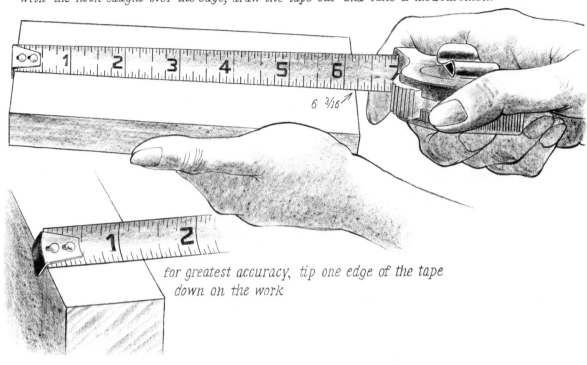

6 3/16

*for greatest accuracy, tip one edge of the tape down on the work*

*tape rule with one half of case removed*

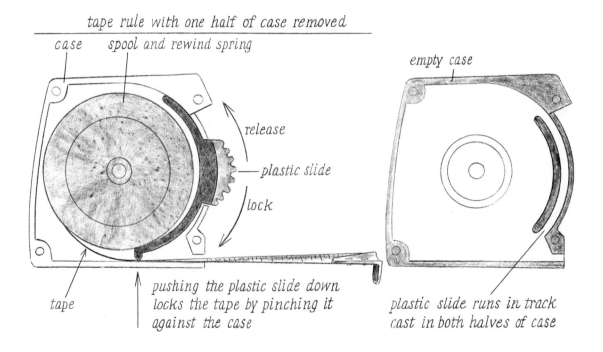

case    spool and rewind spring

release

plastic slide

lock

tape

*pushing the plastic slide down locks the tape by pinching it against the case*

empty case

*plastic slide runs in track cast in both halves of case*

repeated again and again. The English chair bodger who turned chair legs and rungs on his pole lathe in the forest used a *dotter* to mark the points where holes were to be bored. Once the dotter or notched stick has been made just so, it works with more reliable uniformity than marking the same dimension over and over again with a rule.

If you feel at all uncomfortable about using a rule, take time out to brush up on its workings. Collect a dozen pieces of wood at random and measure the width, length, and thickness of each one. Write the three measurements on the wood, then ask someone to check your work. Follow this with another approach. On a sheet of paper mark off with the rule this series of inched dimensions: $2^1/_2$, $3^5/_{16}$, $9/_{16}$, $3^1/_8$, $1^7/_{16}$, $4^5/_8$, $7/_8$, $5^1/_{16}$, $3/_{16}$, $3^1/_4$, $3/_8$, $1^1/_2$, $3^3/_4$, $1^{15}/_{16}$, $3^{13}/_{16}$, and $2^{11}/_{16}$. Write each dimension beside the marks and again have someone check the work. In other words, practice. Practice until you feel at ease with the rule and can take off measurements, write them down, and transfer them to wood with confidence. Then you might try some practice work in reading the rule upside down, as this is a handy skill in certain situations.

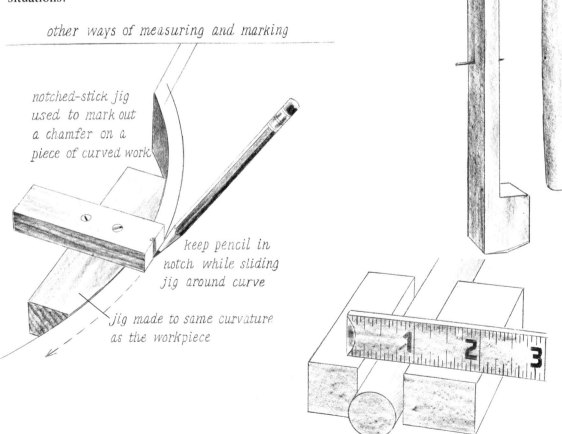

*dotter used by English chair bodger*

*chair leg*

*other ways of measuring and marking*

*notched-stick jig used to mark out a chamfer on a piece of curved work*

*keep pencil in notch while sliding jig around curve*

*jig made to same curvature as the workpiece*

*an accurate method for finding the diameter of roundwork*

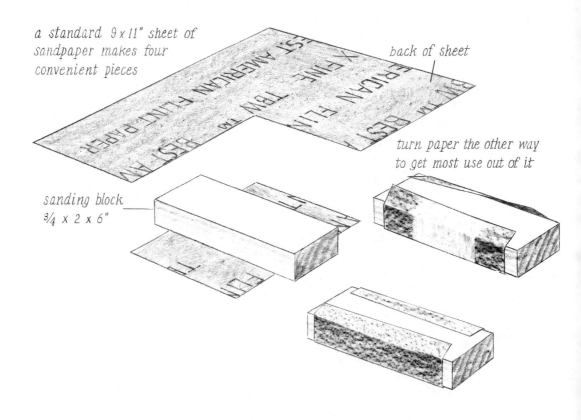

a standard 9 x 11" sheet of
sandpaper makes four
convenient pieces

back of sheet

sanding block
¾ x 2 x 6"

turn paper the other way
to get most use out of it

# 24

# Sandpaper

Sandpaper is a generic term referring to any of the abrasive sheets and is used primarily for the final smoothing of wood. Whatever the type—flint, garnet, emery, or silicon carbide—they all work on the same principle. Hard, sharp, angular particles are bonded with an adhesive to paper or cloth, the grade or grit determined by the size of the particles and how closely together they are arranged. Rubbed over a wood surface, the particles cut and grind off fragments of wood in the form of powdery sawdust.

Sanding smooths the wood by cutting the ridges and high spots down to a uniform level. But it has its limitations. Don't expect sandpaper to accomplish what you should have done with the plane. A properly fitted piece of wood ought not to need more than a moderate sanding to finish it.

Flint paper is the cheapest everyday sandpaper but is less durable than garnet, emery, and silicon carbide. All abrasive sheets can be had in various grits from coarse to extra fine. Cloth-backed sheets usually last longer and are therefore a better buy. There is no hard and fast rule as to which types or grits are the best to use. Buy a sheet of each and learn how they behave. Try them on different scraps of wood, hard and soft, side grain and end grain, dark and light. For the same grade of paper may not necessarily produce the same results on every kind of wood.

Cut the sheets into small pieces. A standard $9'' \times 11''$ sheet is too large for most work, but when quartered will make four convenient pieces. Cut straight, using a pair of old scissors or tearing it against a steel straightedge. Cut pieces as you need them. Now and then you may need a full sheet for a special purpose.

Use sandpaper wrapped around a block of wood, a rectangular block for flat work, a dowel for rounds, and various other shapes contoured to match the work at hand. You can buy fancy sanding blocks with patented clamping devices designed to hold the paper, but it is much

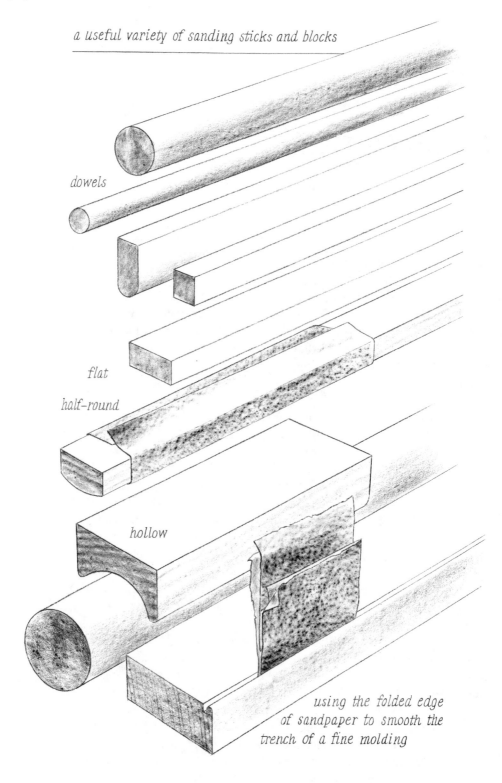

*a useful variety of sanding sticks and blocks*

*dowels*

*flat*

*half-round*

*hollow*

*using the folded edge
of sandpaper to smooth the
trench of a fine molding*

simpler just to pinch a loose piece over the block. This allows replacing the paper quickly or turning it the other way to get the most use out of it.

Take time to make decent blocks. Make sure they are flat. Smooth up the ends and sand off the sharp edges to make the paper last longer. One precaution: these blocks are easily mistaken for pieces of wood that are ''just right for that small job.'' To avoid having to make new blocks every time, daub them with a spot of bright paint.

Whenever possible hold the work securely when sanding—vise, clamps, bench dogs, or hold-downs. This practice leaves both hands free to manipulate and control the sanding block. Always sand with the grain. Going across or at an angle to it indeed cuts wood faster but it also scores grooves that are next to impossible to get rid of, espe-

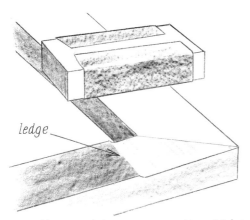

*sanding straight across a mitered joint leaves scoring marks, and may also cut a ledge*

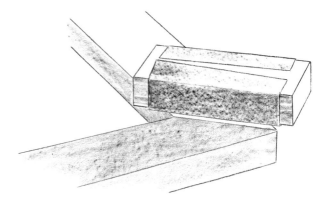

*hold sanding block at a 45° angle and sand only up to the miter line*

cially in hardwood. And these marks will show up all the more clearly when the varnish or other finish is applied. When sanding end-grain work, follow the long dimension of the workpiece. On flat surfaces, hold the sanding block flat and use a fair amount of pressure, much as you would a plane. Use two hands. Keep an even pressure. Don't let the block tip this way and that or dip off the ends of the work. Don't let sawdust and abrasive particles build up under the paper. They form a layer that interferes with the paper sliding in full contact with the wood. Brush off the work and clean out the sandpaper after making several strokes. Take the paper off the block and rap it smartly face down over the edge of the bench to knock loose the caked particles.

*when sanding end grain,*
*use plenty of pressure to keep sanding block flat on the work*

*don't run clear off the*
*corners—keep most*
*of the block on the work*

*work held in vise*

Scrub the sanding block back and forth, working over the full length of the work and lapping the strokes in order to ensure removing wood uniformly over the whole area. Above all, avoid a casual side-to-side or circular motion, which is guaranteed to leave the surface replete with scratches. For a really smooth job, put a worn piece of paper under the good one for padding. This allows the paper to better follow any unevenness in the surface.

Prolonged heavy sanding, particularly with the coarser grades of paper, moves things into the realm of shaping. For example, a piece of garnet paper wrapped around a dowel and used in the manner of a rasp can be used to shape tight or elaborate curves, and leaves the work with possibly a smoother finish. In other words, shaping with sandpaper may often be faster in the end than with a rasp.

In this connection, good lighting is important, especially when refining free-form shapes. This kind of contour shaping is best done in a strong light, whether from the sun or an artificial source. Striking across the work at an angle, the light instantly reveals the most subtle irregularities as well as indicating when the shadows have been smoothed out.

Sandpaper that is used on a painted or varnished surface rapidly clogs and builds up a burned-in glaze that no amount of rapping on the bench will dislodge, and the finer the grit the more quickly this happens. Using a lighter pressure may help some as it generates less friction heat, but where much paint has to be removed, it is more efficient to use a scraper for the preliminary work and then sandpaper to finish the job.

STORAGE OF SANDPAPER    Abrasive sheets, especially the paper-backed type, have a way of curling into a tight roll in reaction to changes in temperature and humidity. Because paper absorbs moisture rapidly, the backing expands at a faster rate than the abrasive side, which is sealed by the adhesive material. Curled sheets are exasperating to work with, but what is worse, when they get too damp the abrasive particles soften or come loose.

When you buy sandpaper, immediately stack the sheets together under a flat board and hold them down with a brick or some other weight. The pressure will help exclude moisture and air and keep the paper in better working condition.

*to avoid rounding the corner,*
*use a long block and good pressure on the back end*

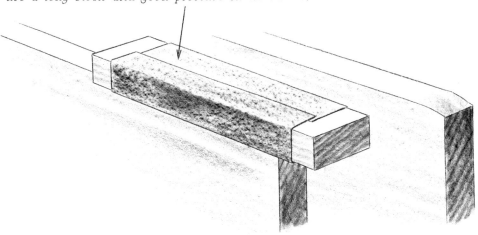

*when the block starts to shoot off the end —— stop*

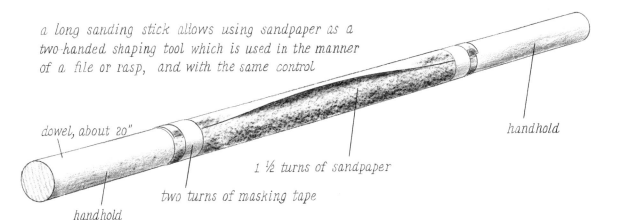

*a long sanding stick allows using sandpaper as a*
*two-handed shaping tool which is used in the manner*
*of a file or rasp, and with the same control*

*dowel, about 20"*

*handhold*

*handhold*

*two turns of masking tape*

*1 ½ turns of sandpaper*

schematic: cutting action of crosscut and ripsaw

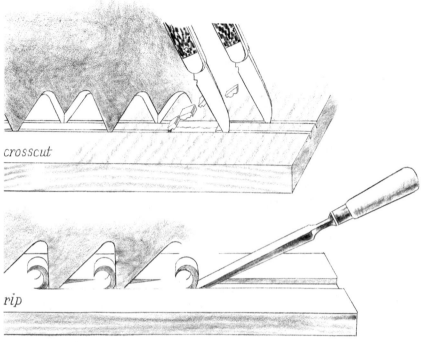

crosscut

rip

measuring the size of a saw

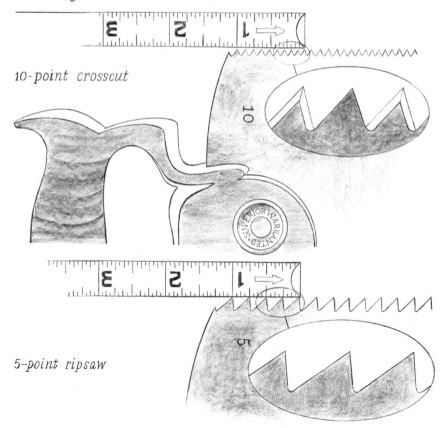

10-point crosscut

5-point ripsaw

# 25

# Saws

There are two kinds of saws—crosscut and rip. The one is for cutting at right angles to the wood grain, the other for cutting parallel with it. To put it another way, the crosscut makes a board shorter and the ripsaw makes it narrower. Regardless of type, size, or special function, all saws fall into one category or the other, made either with crosscut or rip teeth.

The teeth of a crosscut are shaped like knife points and slice across the wood grain in two parallel lines, cutting loose small particles of wood that drop out as sawdust. Ripsaw teeth are more like chisels. Set in a long row, each tooth pares out a curled chip of wood along the grain. Since it is easier to chisel with the grain than across it, rip teeth are relatively large and coarse to take bigger bites of wood than a crosscut. A ripsaw leaves a ragged cut which needs more finishing with a plane or some other tool, and for this reason rip cuts should be made wider of the mark to allow extra wood for the purpose.

Saw Size     In saw parlance, the size of a saw is gauged by how coarse or fine a cut it makes and is specified in terms of the number of tooth points to the inch—*points*, not teeth. Length and width of blade are of secondary significance. This point system applies to all handsaws and characterizes the size and quality of their cuts. For example, whereas an 8-point saw cuts fast and ragged, a 12-point makes a fine, clean cut, but saws rather slowly.

Crosscut and ripsaws are both made in a full range of point sizes. Crosscuts are available in 6, 7, 8, 9, 10, and 12. At one time they were also made in 14-point, a superior saw for precision cabinetwork but difficult to find now except as a secondhand item. Ripsaws can be had in point sizes of $4^1/_2$, 5, $5^1/_2$, 7, 8, 10, and 12.

Kerf and Set     The slot or cut made by a saw is called the kerf. The width of the kerf is determined not only by the thickness of the saw blade itself but also by the amount of set in the teeth. From heel to toe along the cutting edge, alternate teeth of a saw are bent out

*schematic: kerf and set*

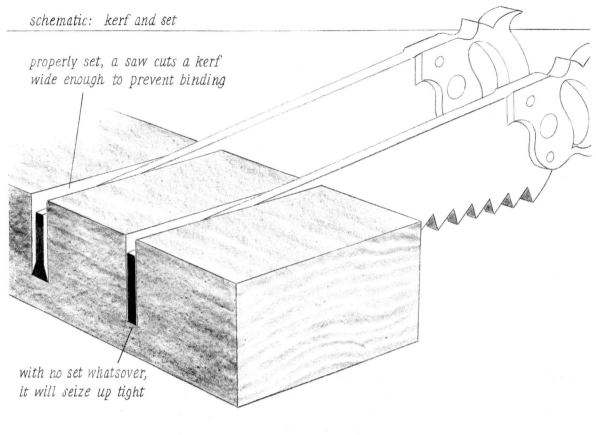

properly set, a saw cuts a kerf
wide enough to prevent binding

with no set whatsover,
it will seize up tight

crosscut teeth
before and after
setting

thickness of blade

kerf

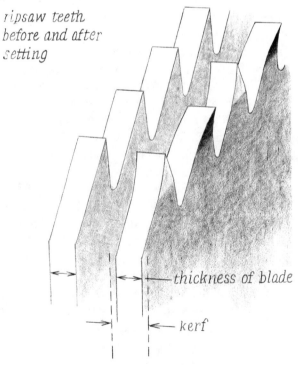

ripsaw teeth
before and after
setting

thickness of blade

kerf

slightly so that the saw cuts a kerf wider than the thickness of the blade, giving it room in which to run freely. The amount of set varies according to the point size of the saw and the kind of work it is to do. Wood that is soft, green, or wet generally requires a coarse-toothed saw with considerable set, whereas a fine-toothed one with less set is used for thoroughly dry stuff, especially hardwood.

Even though freshly sharpened, a saw with no set at all cuts a kerf only as wide as the blade is thick. Friction from the wood squeezing against both sides of the blade causes it to stick or bind. After sawing only an inch or two, and as more of the blade is pinched, the saw will seize up tight.

Since setting a saw is a time-consuming job, usually done only when it must be sharpened, it is impractical to change the amount of set to suit each kind of work. If you are sawing rough, half-dry lumber one day and bone-dry stuff the next, you would have two different saws.

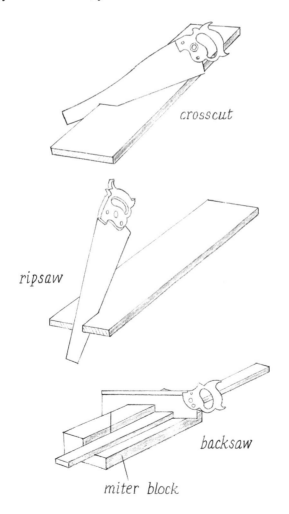

*crosscut*

*ripsaw*

*backsaw*

*miter block*

to tighten a saw handle
loosened by shrinkage
of the wood

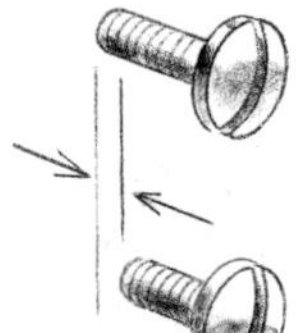

shorten the bolts by
filing 1/16" off their ends

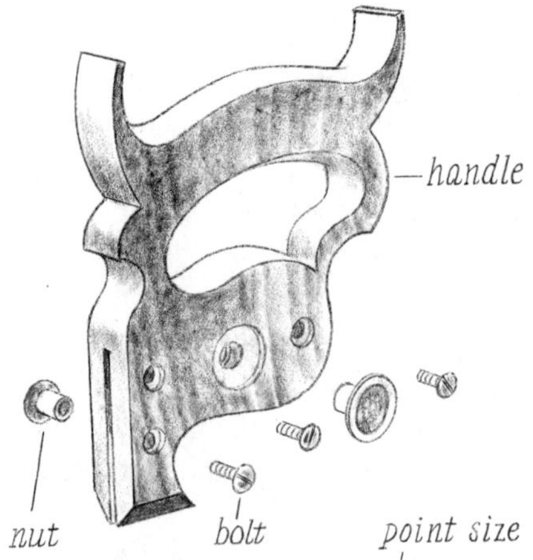

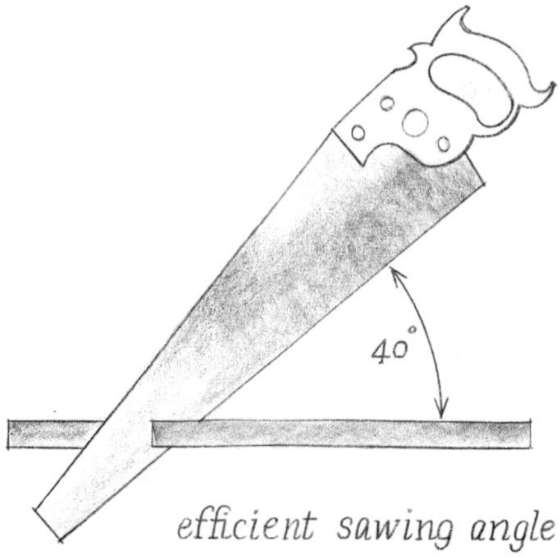

handle

nut

bolt

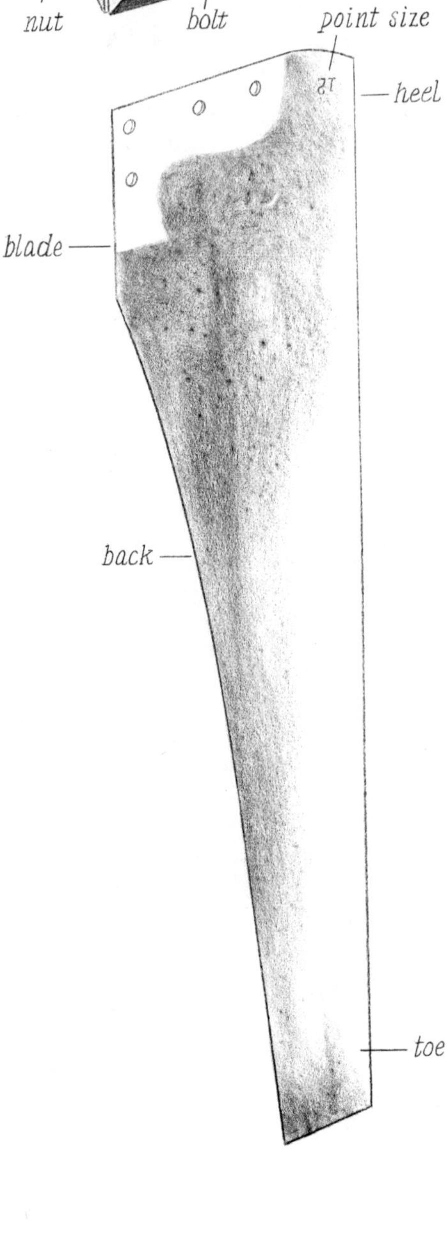

point size

heel

blade

back

toe

40°

efficient sawing angle

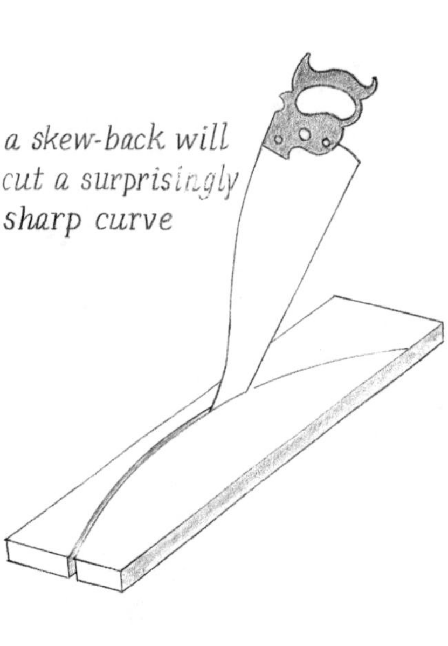

a skew-back will
cut a surprisingly
sharp curve

TAPER-GROUND OR FLAT-GROUND    In a high-quality saw the back edge of the blade is thinner than the cutting edge. And the gauge is also tapered thick to thin from heel to toe. These features, along with the amount of set, prevent the blade from binding in the cut and make the saw run more easily. A flat-ground blade is the same thickness throughout and is typical of cheap saws that are not a good investment.

STRAIGHT OR SKEW-BACK    These terms refer to the profile of the back or top edge of a saw. In a straight-back saw—whether crosscut or rip—the top line from handle to toe is straight, giving the blade some added stiffness which is often an advantage when sawing rough or green lumber. The top of a skew-back is curved, or hollow, and usually has a narrower toe. A skew-back is slightly lighter in weight, but its chief advantage lies in its ability to twist and follow moderate curves, especially when ripping.

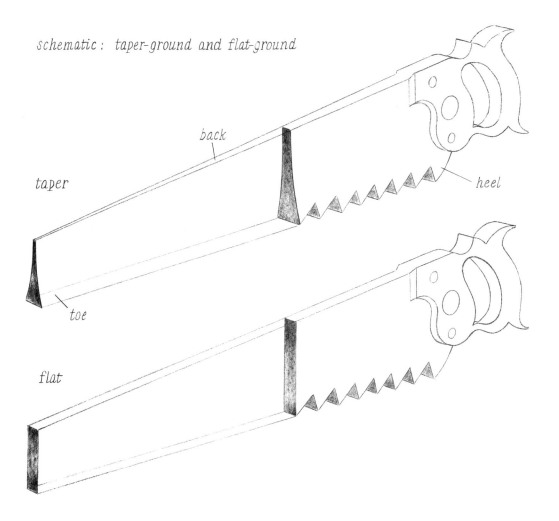

*schematic : taper-ground and flat-ground*

back

taper

heel

toe

flat

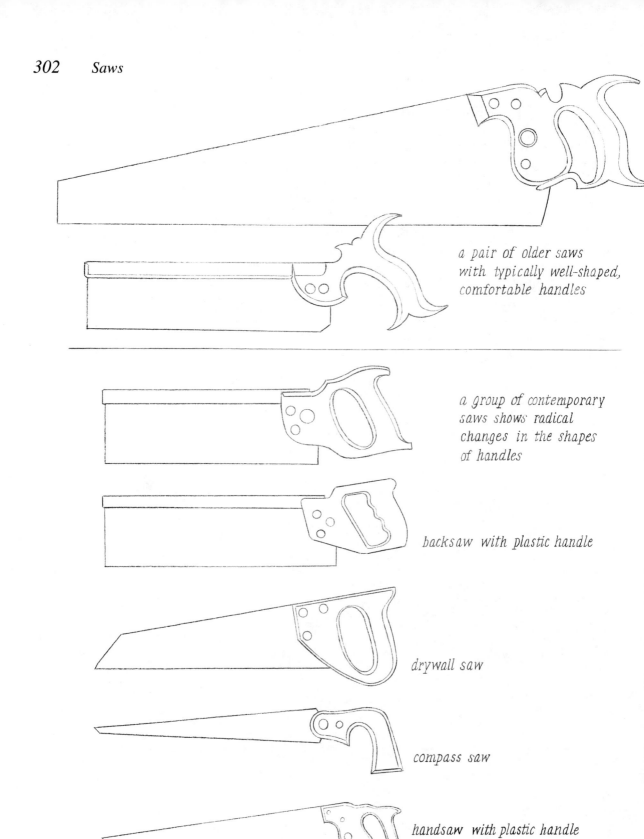

a pair of older saws
with typically well-shaped,
comfortable handles

a group of contemporary
saws shows radical
changes in the shapes
of handles

backsaw with plastic handle

drywall saw

compass saw

handsaw with plastic handle

A COMFORTABLE HANDLE    Points per inch, length of blade, straight or skew-back, taper-ground or flat—you may have considered all these factors and made your choice. But did you look at the handle, take hold of it to see if it fits? A tool that's used as constantly for every imaginable woodworking job as the saw ought to have a handle designed for maximum comfort. Unfortunately, this is not always the case. You can select the blade you want but you are pretty much stuck with the handle that comes with it. After something like 4,500 years of saw-making, and ignoring the very comfortable handles so common in the 1800s, manufacturers today fit their saws with handles that appear to have been designed primarily to accommodate the limitations of the machines that make them, rather than the hand that does the work. An ill-fitting wooden handle can often be somewhat improved by patient work with rasp, file, and sandpaper. But probably the better solution is to make your own. And while fashioning a saw handle does indeed take time, when you're done you will work with less effort and fewer blisters.

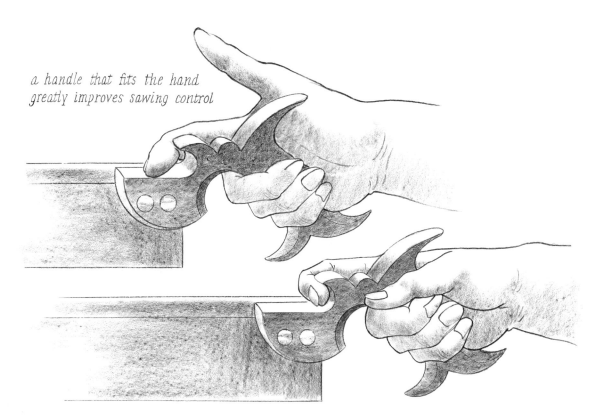

*a handle that fits the hand greatly improves sawing control*

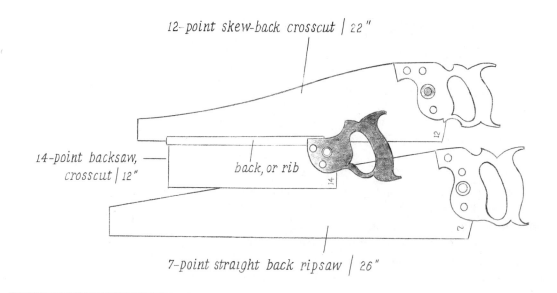

12-point skew-back crosscut | 22"

14-point backsaw, crosscut | 12"

back, or rib

7-point straight back ripsaw | 26"

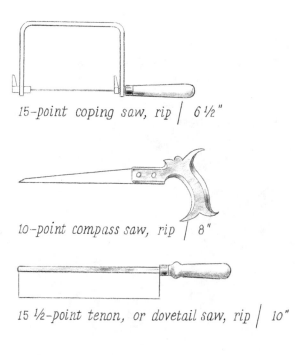

15-point coping saw, rip | 6½"

10-point compass saw, rip | 8"

15½-point tenon, or dovetail saw, rip | 10"

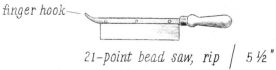

finger hook

21-point bead saw, rip | 5½"

# Which Saws and How Many

A crosscut, rip, backsaw, and a coping saw will do most general work as well as some of the more exacting cabinetmaking operations. Start with these four and add others as the particular job requires.

# Crosscut and Ripsaw

Get a 12-point crosscut and a 7-point ripsaw. Both of these saws cut a bit more slowly than coarser-toothed models but at the same time they leave a cleaner cut, requiring far less clean-up work. Don't be misled that one saw will do the work of two. You can in a pinch rip a board with a crosscut, but there is no such turnabout with a ripsaw. It is no good for crosscut work. If you're doing rough framing you will probably need a second crosscut such as an 8-point, which cuts much faster.

ARM-THROW    Crosscut saws are made in blade lengths of 16, 20, 22, 24, and 26 inches; ripsaws in 20, 24, and 26. For comfortable work, the length of a saw should be in accord with that of your natural arm-throw, which is easily determined. Stand facing a wall. Make a fist with your sawing hand, then extend it straight in front of you as far as it will comfortably go. Move toward the wall until your fist just touches it. With the other hand, butt a yardstick against the wall and hold it there. Draw your sawing arm back until the fist is about in line with your shoulder. The distance from fist to wall is your arm-throw. Add another $2^1/_2$ inches to find the saw length. This surplus leaves enough extra length to prevent the saw handle from striking the work on the forward stroke and the blade from jumping out of the cut on the return stroke.

# Using a Saw

HOLD THE WORK SECURELY    Put it in the vise, use clamps, or kneel it down on a sawhorse. And there are times when the best way is to put the work on a box and hold it there with one foot. If no better means is at hand, have someone sit on the work while you concentrate on sawing. House carpenters often hold a board braced against a knee, but this kind of sawing is only satisfactory for rough work.

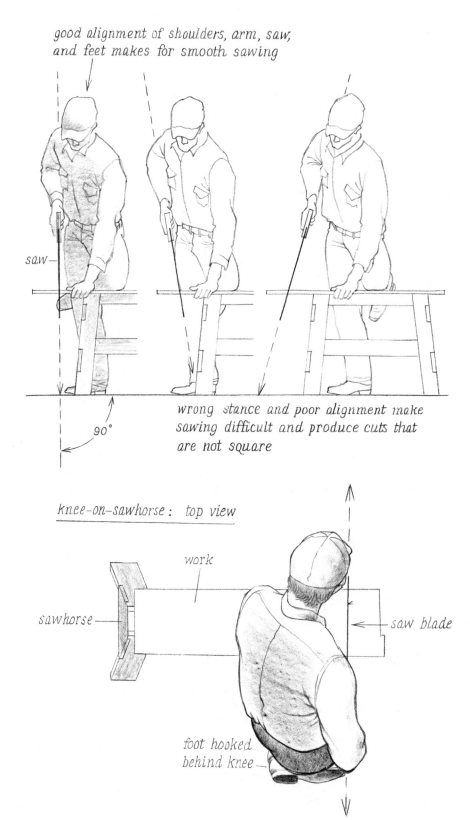

good alignment of shoulders, arm, saw, and feet makes for smooth sawing

saw

90°

wrong stance and poor alignment make sawing difficult and produce cuts that are not square

knee-on-sawhorse : top view

work

sawhorse

saw blade

foot hooked behind knee

SAWING ON A HORSE     For large boards the knee-on-sawhorse method is probably the best. This not only holds the board tight, but it also puts your shoulder and sawing arm in the best position to cut straight and square. This stance also leaves one hand free to support the cutoff waste as you finish the cut. The height of the sawhorse is important here. When you kneel on it, most of your weight should shift automatically to the knee that's holding the work. A sawhorse that comes to the kneecap is about right, but before cutting off its legs, try it out and be sure. If you're building your own sawhorse, first try kneeling on a box, chair, or bench—with a board laid on it, of course. When you find something that feels right, make the sawhorse the same height.

STANCE     Putting your feet in the right place is just as important. Saw, hand, elbow, and shoulder should be on a line that is plumb or perpendicular to the work. Similarly: chin, foot, and the hand holding the board should be on a plumb line.

A sharp saw cuts its own way with little effort. There is no side pressure, no sticking or jamming, and the sound tells you so. By contrast, when your stance is wrong, more force is needed to overcome the resistance of the blade curving through the cut. A good test is to saw with a loose, relaxed grip, merely pushing with the ball of the hand while the fingers are crooked just enough to pull the saw back.

Chattering of the saw blade is a common complaint. On the return stroke as the blade whips back through the cut, the toe end may vibrate violently from side to side to the accompaniment of a severe racket. If this happens it probably means that you are standing out of line with the cut to one side or the other.

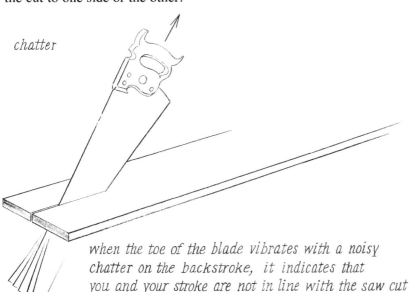

*chatter*

*when the toe of the blade vibrates with a noisy*
*chatter on the backstroke, it indicates that*
*you and your stroke are not in line with the saw cut*

*holding small workpieces in the vise*

*hold the work with the other hand to prevent its vibrating*

*cutting joints*

*this is a poor way to cut off a board*

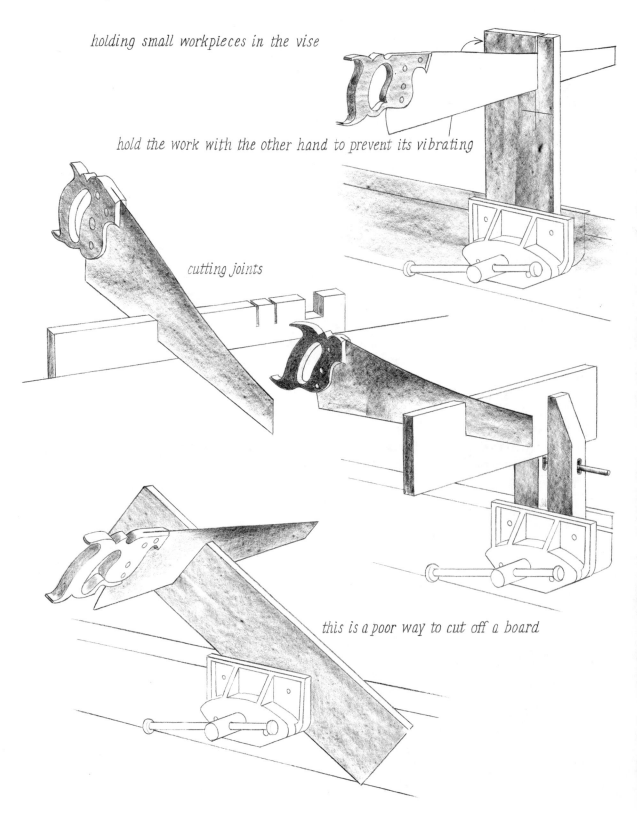

Practice makes perfect. Make a dozen or so trial cuts on scrap wood or sacrifice a whole new board if necessary. Practice is not a substitute for experience but it helps immeasurably. Be sure to mark a line with the square for each cut. As you start the cut, try to discover the stance that makes the saw run the smoothest. If you feel it binding or chattering, stop and find out what is wrong. Move your feet, get everything realigned, and start again.

SAWING AT THE VISE    As a means of holding saw work the vise is mainly useful when cutting joints or sawing pieces that are too small to manage on a sawhorse. Start the cut with the heel of the saw tipped down to avoid splintering the wood on the back side of the board, then level off and continue. Almost no pressure is needed, as the weight of the saw is enough to make it cut its own way. Normally, small stuff should be cut off in a miter box, but lacking that the vise will hold the work rigid, leaving both hands free to concentrate on sawing with care. When cutting a board clear through, however, this is not a good method. The board must then be cocked up at an angle to keep the saw clear of the bench, and in this position the end of the board tends to vibrate and jam the saw. Running the saw smoothly is further obstructed by the fact that the natural arm motion is out of sync with the canted position of the work.

SAW WIDE OF THE MARK    Except for rough construction where surface finish is less important, always saw a bit wide of the mark. No matter how fine-toothed, none of these long saws produces a surface that can be considered highly finished. It has to be cleaned up with a plane.

Saw on the waste side of the mark and leave the mark showing. You need the extra wood for planing exactly to the mark. How far wide of the mark? For a crosscut saw $1/16$ inch should be enough, but because a ripsaw makes a more ragged cut to begin with, it is safer to allow at least $3/32$ inch.

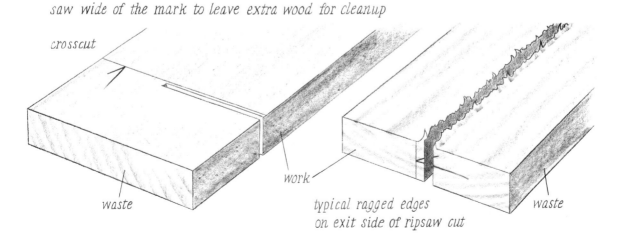

*saw wide of the mark to leave extra wood for cleanup*

*crosscut*

*waste*

*work*

*typical ragged edges on exit side of ripsaw cut*

*waste*

STARTING THE CUT    Using a square, mark a line across the board for the saw cut. Take your stance. With the saw in one hand, hold the board with the other. Use the thumbnail of this hand to guide the saw blade exactly to the mark. Set the saw on the edge of the board, then draw it back a few inches to cut a starting notch. The notch helps prevent the saw from jumping off the mark.

The first 2 inches of cut are the most important. Use short strokes at first until you have established a straight cut following the line. Then use longer strokes. Keep your eye on the line. The minute the saw begins to wander off, twist the blade a little and use the toe end to bring it back to the line.

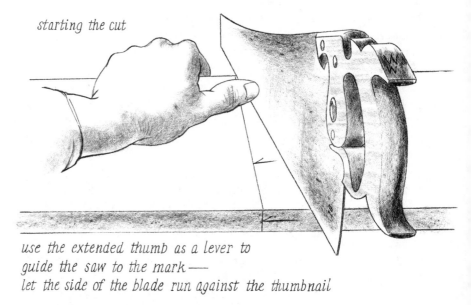

*starting the cut*

*use the extended thumb as a lever to guide the saw to the mark —*
*let the side of the blade run against the thumbnail*

Imagine that the saw is a mechanical device running smoothly back and forth along a straight line, and that your hand is merely riding on the handle. Saw with long strokes. Imagine, too, that the saw is longer than its actual length. When you push, reach ahead so the teeth back near the handle must cut. And on the return stroke pull the saw way back. Make it cut to within a couple of inches of the toe. In other words, use all of your arm-throw and all of the saw.

Get into an even rhythm—back and forth, back and forth, like the slow swinging of a long pendulum. Short jabbing strokes waste energy and get in the way of sawing straight, as well as putting more wear on the middle teeth than the others.

FINISHING THE CUT    When the board is almost cut off, slow down. Reach over the saw with the free hand and take hold of the waste piece. Then make short, light strokes to cut off the last wood.

Otherwise, as the waste is cut off and falls away it may break into the good part of the board.

If you are sawing a long board in half, support one half of its length on two sawhorses, and either have someone hold up the other end or put a box under it. And again—reach over and hold up the cutoff section as you finish the cut.

REVERSE SAWING     When cutting out a small piece to precise dimensions, turn the saw around and cut away from you. This allows you to see exactly where the saw is going and eliminates the chance of cutting beyond the mark. Also, supporting the waste piece is much easier this way.

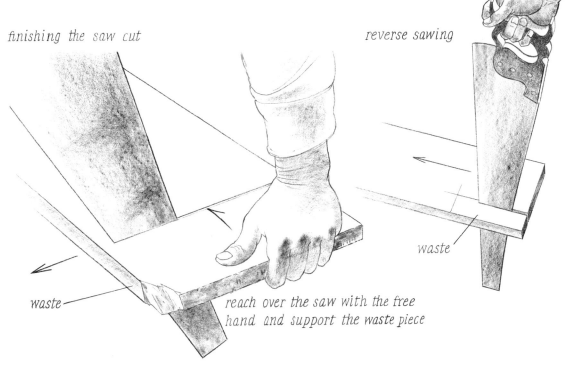

*finishing the saw cut*

*reverse sawing*

*waste*

*waste*

*reach over the saw with the free hand and support the waste piece*

# Backsaw

So called for the heavy rib crimped over its back edge, this short crosscut is essential for making nice clean joints. The rib holds the blade absolutely straight and rigid. A model with 14-point teeth will make clean, smooth cuts that need only a minimum of clean-up with a plane, chisel, or sandpaper. But for this kind of precise work it should be used with a miter box or a miter block, both of which are shown in the section on *Mitering Tools*.

Hold the work tight against the miter box fence with one hand. If the work slips during the first saw strokes the edge of the cut will not come out sharp and clean. Use short strokes of the saw and light pressure, letting it cut its own way.

While the backsaw is primarily for crosscut work, it does a creditable job of ripping short sections such as tenons and dovetails, although you may have to withdraw the blade occasionally to clear out the sawdust.

When used in a miter box the backsaw is a one-handed tool simply because you must hold the work with the other hand. If the work is held in the vise, however, then it is a good practice to use both hands on the saw to maintain better control.

Take good care of this tool. File-sharpening any saw finer than 12 points is a ticklish job that requires a magnifying glass, a good light, and a much finer file than you will find in most hardware stores.

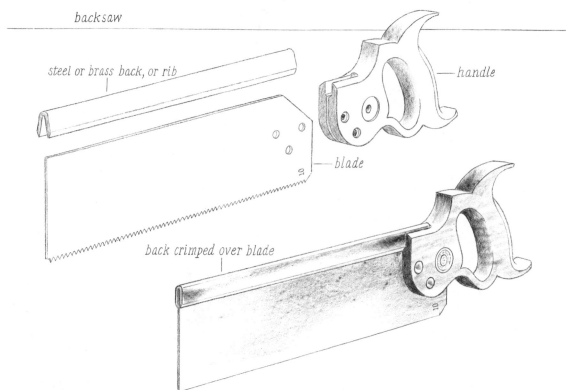

*backsaw*

*steel or brass back, or rib*

*handle*

*blade*

*back crimped over blade*

*mortise and tenon joint as used in the construction of a paneled door*

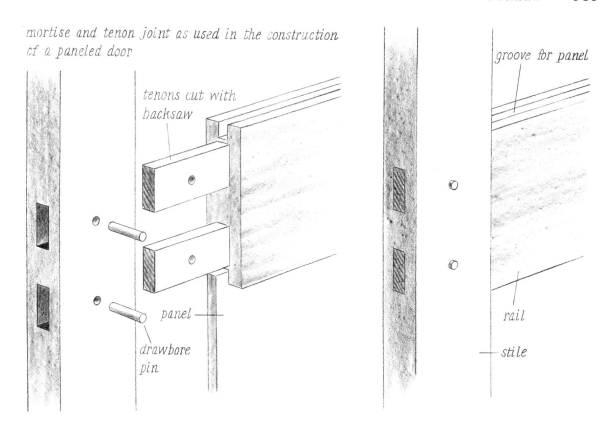

tenons cut with backsaw

groove for panel

panel

drawbore pin

rail

stile

*dovetail joint used in drawer and chest construction*

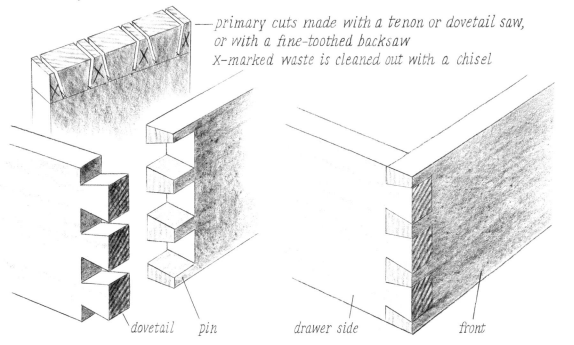

primary cuts made with a tenon or dovetail saw, or with a fine-toothed backsaw
X-marked waste is cleaned out with a chisel

dovetail    pin

drawer side    front

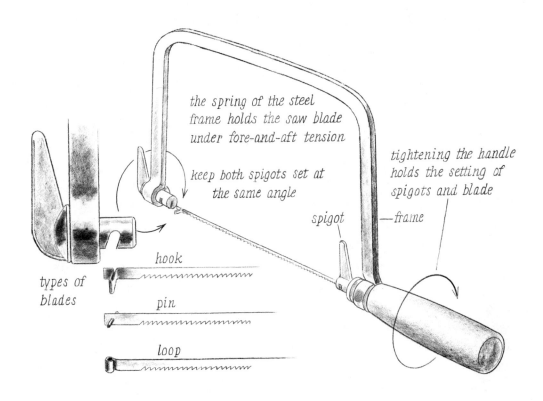

the spring of the steel
frame holds the saw blade
under fore-and-aft tension

keep both spigots set at
the same angle

tightening the handle
holds the setting of
spigots and blade

spigot

—frame

types of
blades

hook

pin

loop

# Coping Saw

This saw is designed for scrollwork, intricate curves, and trapped cutout shapes. It takes a very slender blade that will cut to a very small radius. Although coping saw blades have rip teeth, they are so fine that they make a clean, smooth cut in crosscut as well as ripping work. These blades are easily damaged. Constant furious sawing heats the steel, making it more liable to twisting and breaking. A bent or bowed blade won't cut straight and it can't be straightened. Neither can it be sharpened, a fact of small concern since these blades rarely last long enough to get dull and are inexpensively replaced.

The blade is held taut by the tension of the saw frame. To remove or replace a blade, hold the end of the handle against your thigh with one hand. Set the end of the frame against the side of the bench and push, using your body pressure to compress the frame. Then lift out the blade with the other hand.

Put a new blade in with the teeth raked away from the handle in position to use the saw as a push tool. With the blade in the other way you can also pull this saw, but in my estimation this is efficient only when sawing very thin stuff on a saw table used to raise the work to comfortable working height.

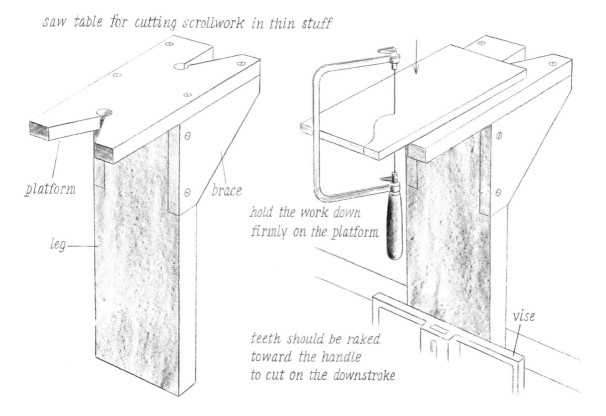

*saw table for cutting scrollwork in thin stuff*

platform

brace

leg

*hold the work down
firmly on the platform*

*teeth should be raked
toward the handle
to cut on the downstroke*

vise

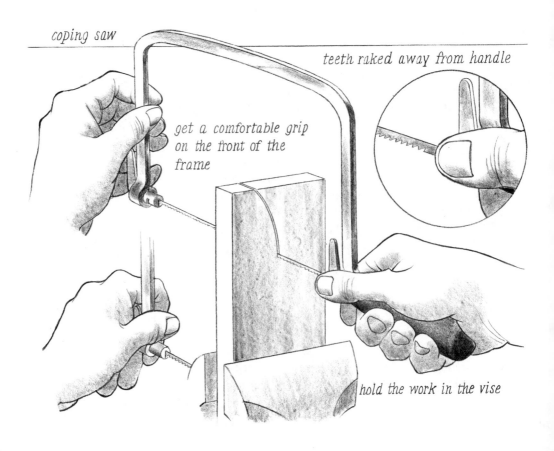

coping saw

get a comfortable grip
on the front of the
frame

teeth raked away from handle

hold the work in the vise

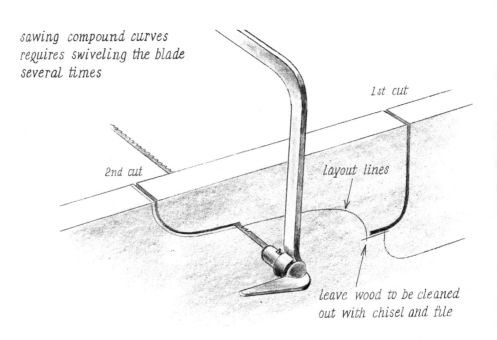

sawing compound curves
requires swiveling the blade
several times

1st cut

2nd cut

layout lines

leave wood to be cleaned
out with chisel and file

Use both hands in the same way you manipulate a rasp. Saw with fairly slow strokes and a steady rhythm. Think about keeping the blade square and level with the work. Use a light pressure. Bearing down heavily will bend the blade, the more so when it heats up. Stop every now and then to let it cool off. When you want to cut as accurately to the line as possible, use the 2 inches of blade next to the handle where it is the most rigid.

To make cuts in trapped areas, first bore a hole in the work. Remove the blade from the coping saw, put it through the hole, then replace the blade in the saw frame. As you saw into a curve, look ahead of the blade to anticipate how much turn of the saw will be needed. This helps to make the curves fair and smooth.

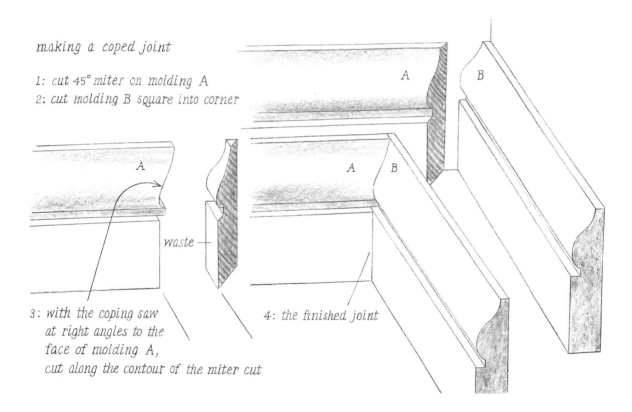

*making a coped joint*

*1: cut 45° miter on molding A*
*2: cut molding B square into corner*

*A*

*waste*

*3: with the coping saw*
*   at right angles to the*
*   face of molding A,*
*cut along the contour of the miter cut*

*A*    *B*

*4: the finished joint*

*A*    *B*

# Compass Saw

In the work it does—cutting curves, circles, and trapped cutouts—this ripsaw is a heavy-duty version of the coping saw. It cuts much faster because the blade is thick and the teeth relatively coarse. But it cuts a wide kerf and leaves ragged edges that must be worked smooth with a spokeshave, rasp, plane, or sandpaper. For this reason the cut should be quite wide of the mark to allow for cleanup.

Compass saws are made in 7, 7½, 8, and 10-points. A good size for general work is the 10-point which cuts more slowly than the others but does a cleaner job. Because the blade tapers to a slender point in order to saw around curves, the outer end is not stiff enough to withstand much pushing pressure without buckling. Therefore, do the heavy work with the heel of the blade, and when sawing with the tip end use lighter, shorter, more gentle strokes. A kinked blade can be straightened but it will tend to kink the next time in the same place.

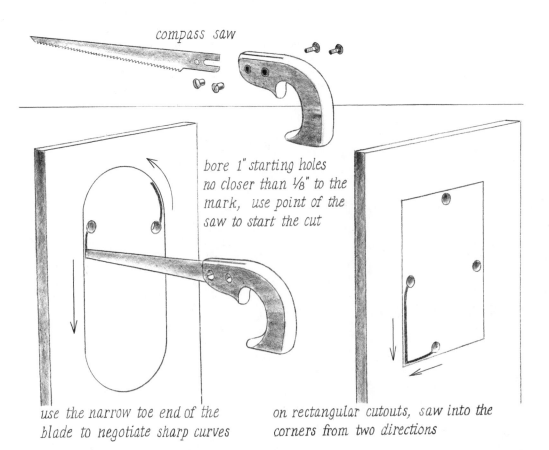

compass saw

bore 1" starting holes no closer than ⅛" to the mark, use point of the saw to start the cut

use the narrow toe end of the blade to negotiate sharp curves

on rectangular cutouts, saw into the corners from two directions

# Tenon, Dovetail, and Bead Saws

Although these saws may look like miniature backsaws, all three have rip teeth and are intended for extremely fine end-grain work, such as the cutting of tenons and dovetails. They are made in several sizes ranging from $15^{1}/_{2}$ to 38-points, which is too fine to be file-sharpened. Nevertheless, these saws will last a long time if treated with care and used only for this type of work.

The smallest is the bead saw with a blade about $5^{1}/_{2}$ inches long. This midget, like the other two, will cut only so deep before the back rib strikes against the work. Despite the appearance the straight handle gives that it is for one-handed operation, these saws are more efficient when worked in the same fashion as a file, with one hand grasping the handle and the other laid on the back rib or pinching it between two fingers for good control.

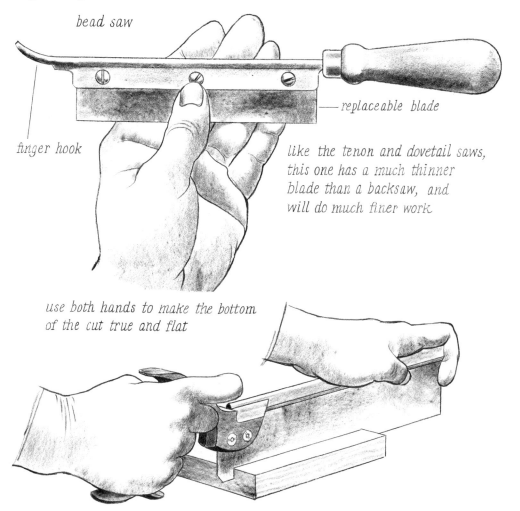

bead saw

finger hook

replaceable blade

like the tenon and dovetail saws, this one has a much thinner blade than a backsaw, and will do much finer work

use both hands to make the bottom of the cut true and flat

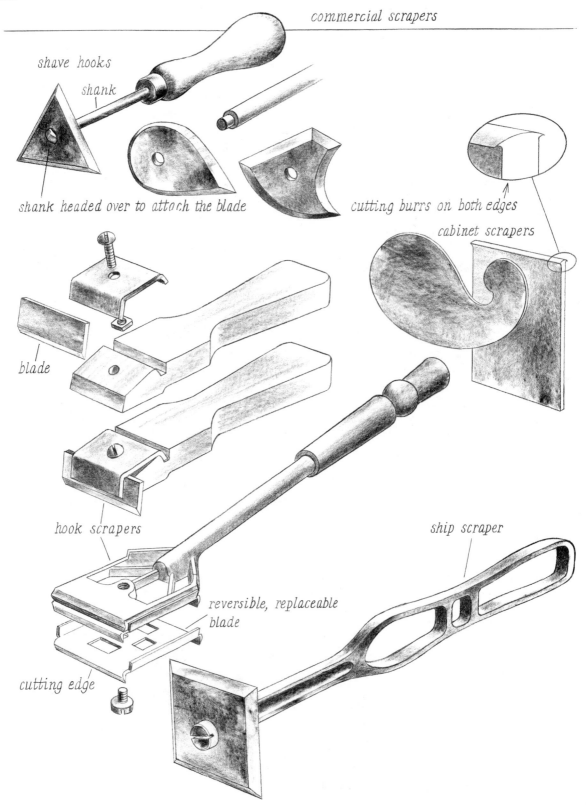

*shave hooks*

*shank*

*shank headed over to attach the blade*

*cutting burrs on both edges*

*cabinet scrapers*

*blade*

*hook scrapers*

*reversible, replaceable blade*

*cutting edge*

*ship scraper*

# 26

# Scrapers

For the final finish on a piece of wood—to make it finer than sand-paper, finer than fine—a scraper imparts a unique sheen and polish. Scraping is not a substitute for sanding but simply a different technique for producing a smooth surface. One is not better than the other: both methods make wood smooth. The difference between them is one of character rather than degree. When seen under a high-powered lens, a sanded surface has a somewhat fuzzy texture, softer, and with fewer highlights. By contrast, a scraper glazes and burnishes the surface to a completely individual smoothness. The residue reflects this difference, too. Sandpaper leaves behind a fine, powdered dust quite unlike the tailings from a scraper, which more closely resemble shavings from a microscopically small plane. A scraped finish also takes oil, stain, and varnish in a different way than a sanded one, naturally varying according to the kind of wood.

The best way to see and appreciate what can be done with a scraper is to experiment on scrap wood, trying the various strokes, angles, and pressures. In the past, cabinetmakers used lumber obtained as rough-sawn stuff and were obliged to plane every stick of it by hand. Hand-planing left a board generally flat, to be sure, though not in the sense of having a mechanical, milled perfection. The scraper was well suited to smoothing such stuff, as it followed the minor irregularities with ease.

Their cabinet scrapers were simple, flat plates of steel, ground with straight or curved edges as required, and then sharpened. This same type of scraper is available today, along with other models having handles and replaceable blades. Scrapers are fairly simple to make. For example, good ones can be fashioned from mower sections—the individual teeth that are riveted to the cutter bar of a mowing machine. Farm implement dealers sell sections to fit the various makes of machines, but as long as they are not serrated, it doesn't matter which make you get. They are all made of steel that is soft enough to be file-shaped to any contour you want.

*new mower section*

*one side ground to a curve*

*filed to match
a bead molding*

*new or used
piston rings are
good for scraping
scoops and hollows*

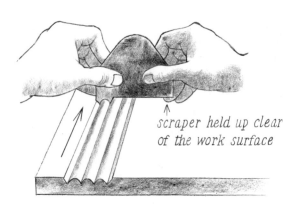

*scraper held up clear
of the work surface*

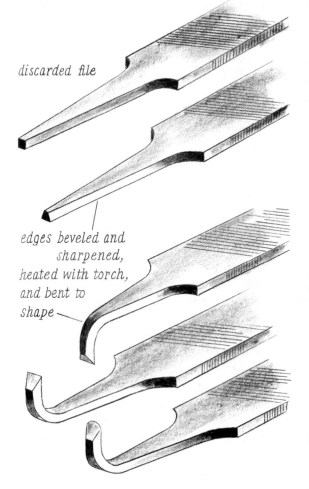

*discarded file*

*edges beveled and
    sharpened,
heated with torch,
and bent to
shape*

ANGLE AND PRESSURE    The two must work together. Aside from the necessity of keeping it sharp, a scraper must be held at an angle to the work while it is pushed or pulled under a certain amount of pressure, the exact angle having a direct effect on the kind of work it does. Heavy pressure combined with a nearly perpendicular angle cuts wood fast but doesn't necessarily make the smoothest surface. Holding it at a flatter angle makes the wood smoother but removes less of it. And at any angle, excessive pressure tends to rip and pluck the wood or to raise flakes on the surface.

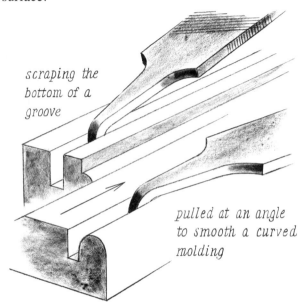

scraping the bottom of a groove

pulled at an angle to smooth a curved molding

# Flat Scrapers

Pushing a tool is more natural to the anatomy than pulling, makes better use of energy, and provides more precise control. Pushing a flat scraper with both hands puts the thumbs in sensitive touch with the way it is working, so that by the slightest muscle movement the angle can be changed to suit the condition of the wood. And for those times when you want to use a pull stroke, the hands make the switch without having to let go of the tool.

Flat scrapers are good for smoothing old or salvaged boards with surface irregularities and for finishing isolated low spots or removing individual blemishes, without the need to resurface an entire area. Spot scraping is often more useful than planing when working over erratic grain and knots. Specially shaped models like the shave hook and others that you make will clean moldings and remove paint more efficiently than sandpaper and with less danger of deforming their contours.

USING A FLAT SCRAPER     Hold the scraper almost perpendicular. Scrape with reasonably long strokes in one direction only: scrubbing back and forth will leave a "cut line" every place you stop or change direction. Push in the same direction in which the grain emerges at the surface. Try to make the strokes more of a fluid sweep. Let the scraper down on the wood and apply pressure only after it is in motion; and at the end of a stroke, lift it off before it stops, more in the manner of stroking it over the wood. On the return stroke lift it off the work to avoid dulling the edge.

*push and pull*

*pushing uses the muscles most efficiently, allows the greatest pressure and control*

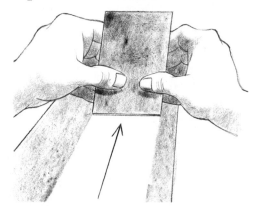

*keep thumbs low on the blade*

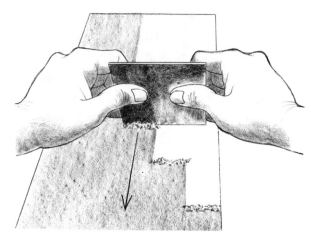

*cut narrow, overlapping swaths*

# Handled Scrapers

By design, handled scrapers have to be worked not just with two hands but both shoulders as well, one hand on the scraper up next to the blade for pressure, the other hand and shoulder providing the force to pull it. Because of this required hold and the mechanics involved, these scrapers are only effective when pulled. They are especially useful for heavy work such as removing layers of old paint or refinishing floors, where they get into corners that a sanding machine can't reach.

Although the replaceable blades dull quickly under the pressure, only a few strokes with a file are necessary to resharpen them the few times before they must be replaced.

REMOVING PAINT    The more layers of paint, the more muscle needed to maintain sufficient pressure while pulling at the same time. Start on the edge of a board and clean off one swath down to the bare wood. On the next swath, use only half the width of the blade, concentrating all the pressure to cut a correspondingly narrower swath. Sharpen the blade whenever necessary, as a dull edge is likely to skip suddenly over a patch of paint and then dig into the wood.

*the right amount of blade angle,*
*driving force, and pressure are what make any scraper work*

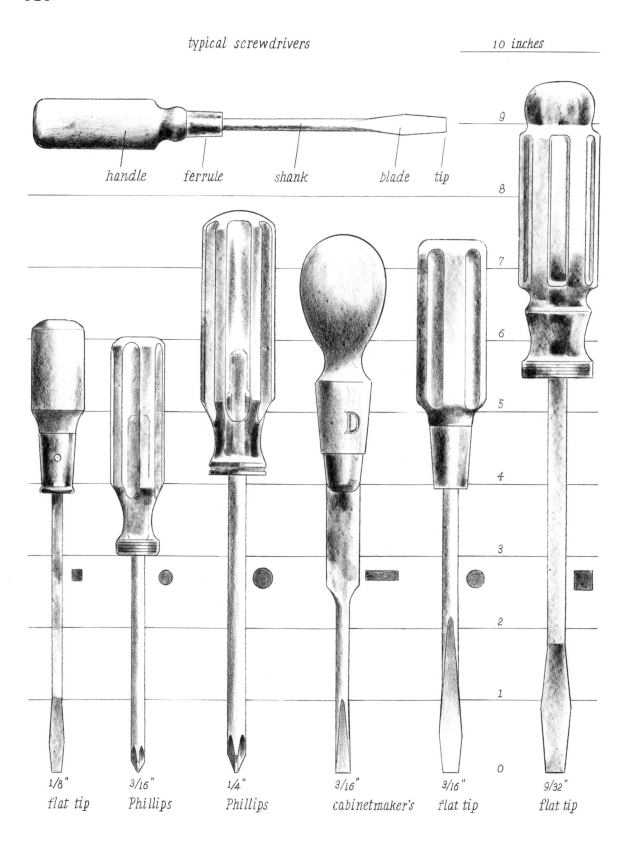

*typical screwdrivers*

*10 inches*

handle    ferrule    shank    blade   tip

1/8"
*flat tip*

3/16"
*Phillips*

1/4"
*Phillips*

3/16"
*cabinetmaker's*

9/16"
*flat tip*

9/32"
*flat tip*

# 27

# Screwdriver

## Mechanics of a Screwdriver

Think of a screwdriver as a steel shaft extension of the screw itself. One end fits into the screw slot and the other has a handle with which to turn it. The efficient working of this tool depends on five cooperative factors: (1) a good fit between screwdriver and screw slot; (2) sufficient handle diameter; (3) a firm hand grip; (4) proper alignment of screw, screwdriver, and hand; and (5) firm pressure.

Using a screwdriver of the wrong size and failing to keep it in alignment are the two most common causes of trouble. The tip of the screwdriver should be the same width as the screw slot and a snug fit the other way to prevent its climbing out, slipping off, and punching a hole in your work. Maintaining good alignment demands the joint efforts of hand, wrist, arm, elbow, and shoulder. Even though the hand and wrist provide sufficient torque for most work, without the stabilizing effect of the elbow and shoulder, the screwdriver collapses to one side and slips out of the slot. In principle, a weakly held screwdriver is like a stick with a joint in the middle. As long as the stick is supported at the joint, it can withstand a lot of end pressure. But without it the joint folds up under the least thrust.

When driving large screws whose greater circumference creates more friction in the wood, locking the wrist and forearm while swinging the elbow increases the leverage in an action similar to that of a bit brace. But at the same time, more pressure is called for to keep the screwdriver from working out of the screw slot.

Since screwdrivers are made in so many different sizes, it is easy to find three or four that will accommodate the general run of work. A basic collection should include a $^{1}/_{8}$-inch and $^{3}/_{16}$-inch flat tip and a couple of Phillips pattern. Pay attention to the handles. They are made in a number of styles, some smooth, some hexagonal, and others fluted

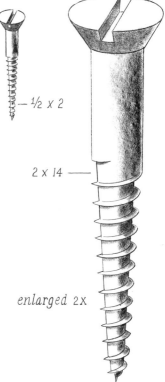

*not all screw slots are the same size*

— $^{1}/_{2}$ x 2

2 x 14 —

*enlarged 2x*

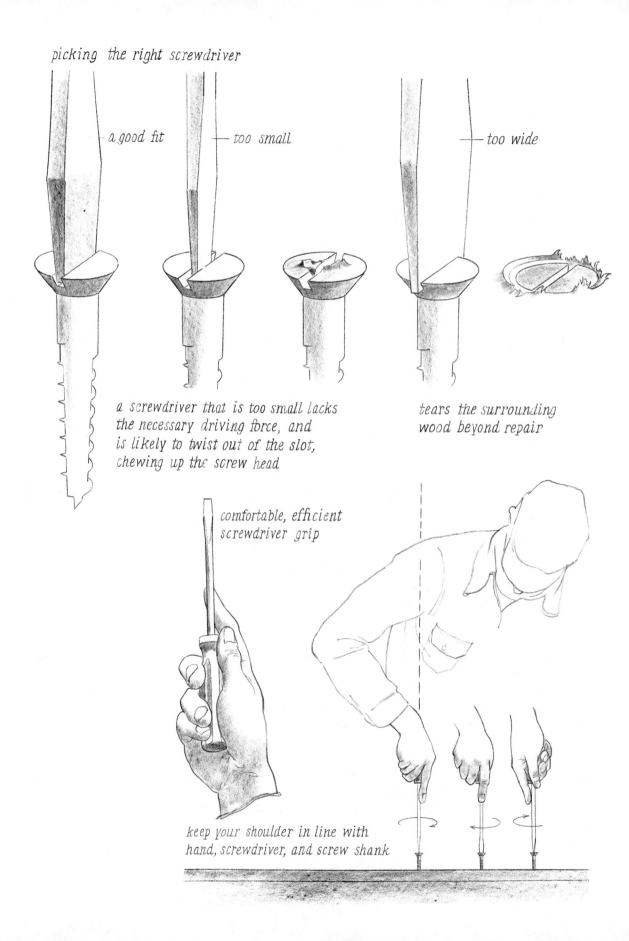

picking the right screwdriver

a good fit

too small

too wide

a screwdriver that is too small lacks
the necessary driving force, and
is likely to twist out of the slot,
chewing up the screw head

tears the surrounding
wood beyond repair

comfortable, efficient
screwdriver grip

keep your shoulder in line with
hand, screwdriver, and screw shank

to give a positive grip. Pick the ones that fit the size of your hand, bearing in mind that the larger the diameter the more torque it will generate. If you choose a wooden handle and you find that its end is rough, sand it good and smooth before using it, or it may raise blisters in the palm of your hand. And don't be tempted by the "Three for $1—regularly 79¢" screwdriver specials. They are worthless. A good quality screwdriver costs from $6 to $18 or $20, depending on its size.

# Starting a Screw

Whenever possible, hold the work in the vise or in clamps. Use both hands—one on the handle, the other to guide and steady the shank until the screw has made two or three turns into the wood and caught hold. Otherwise, your arm pressure will probably knock the screw over sideways. Insert the screw and give it a turn with your fingers, just to keep it upright. Set the screwdriver in the slot, holding it by the shank to support it and the screw. After two or three turns, continue to steady the shank as you apply more pressure.

*a cheap screwdriver will often twist or break*

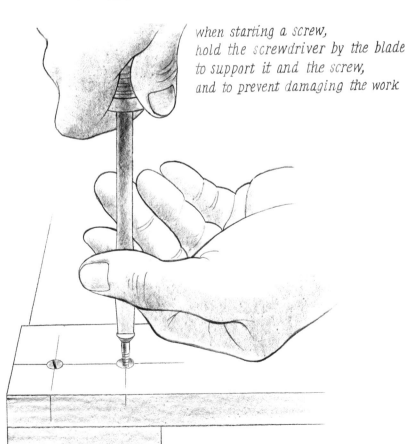

*when starting a screw, hold the screwdriver by the blade to support it and the screw, and to prevent damaging the work*

_anatomy of a wood screw_

head

slot

shank

root

threads

point

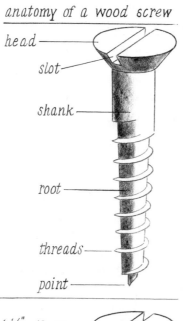

the threads pull the screw
into the wood and hold
it fast —
at the same time, the screw
can be withdrawn and
driven again in the original
threads, without much
weakening the fastening

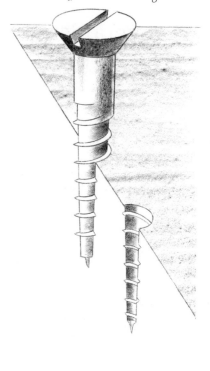

1 ¼" x No. 12

screw size
designated
by wire gauge
and length
from top of
head to point

12

1 ¼"

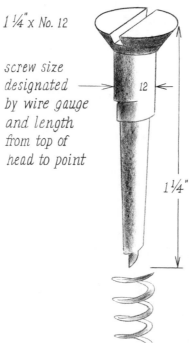

PILOT HOLES    In the majority of situations it is a good practice to drill pilot holes for screws. In softwood use a drill a little smaller than the diameter of the screw at its middle. This forces the screw to cut threads in the wood by which to pull itself in. In hardwood, however, it is safer to make the pilot hole with two drills of different sizes. Drill the first part of the hole to match the shank diameter of the screw; then deepen the hole with a smaller one to fit the threads. Without pilot holes the screw will tend to seize up tight when only partway in, and the screwdriver may twist out of the slot, chewing up the screw head in the process. Now it won't go in and you'll need pliers to get it out. Then, too, there is the strong probability that the screw will simply twist off from the stress.

Pilot holes are particularly necessary when driving brass screws into anything harder than pine, as brass overheats very fast and twists off under surprisingly little strain. It saves time and hardware to make trial holes in scraps of wood of the same kind you plan to use for the job in order to determine what size drill is needed. Start a brass screw into the hole. If it is the correct diameter, the screw should turn into the wood almost to the end of the threads before it feels tight. But if you feel it binding almost at once, the hole is too small.

*drilling screw pilot holes*

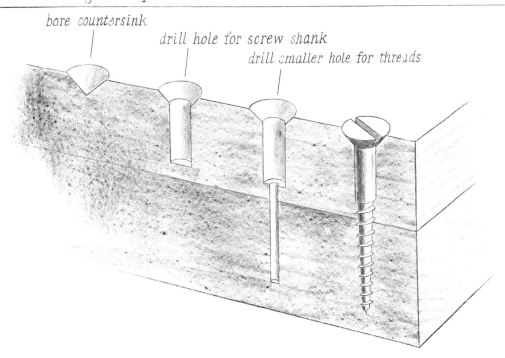

*bore countersink*

*drill hole for screw shank*

*drill smaller hole for threads*

A screw of any kind will pull its way into hardwood more easily if it is first stuck into a cake of soap or paraffin. This lubricates the threads, reduces friction, and helps prevent the screw from overheating.

STOP WHEN IT'S TIGHT    Make the final tightening turns slowly and avoid trying to draw the screw head below the surface to make it tighter. Too much leverage after the head has seated may strip out the threads in the wood, especially in end grain where screws have limited holding power at best.

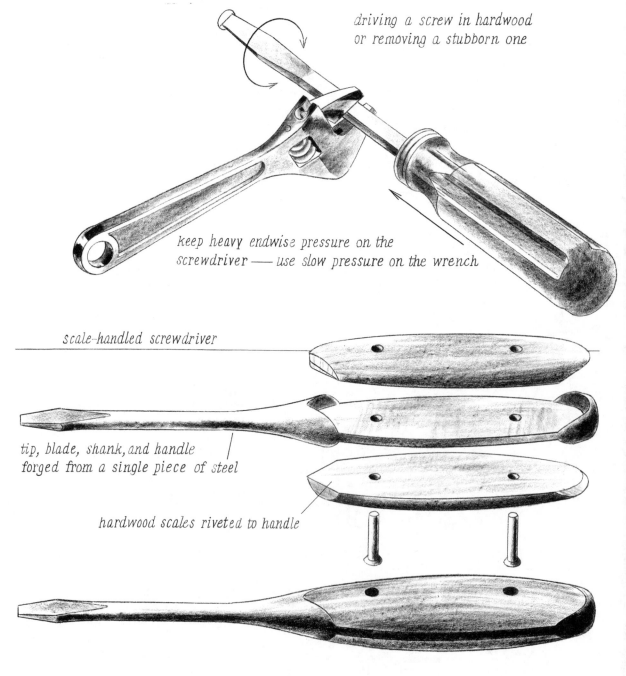

*driving a screw in hardwood or removing a stubborn one*

*keep heavy endwise pressure on the screwdriver — use slow pressure on the wrench*

*scale-handled screwdriver*

*tip, blade, shank, and handle forged from a single piece of steel*

*hardwood scales riveted to handle*

*damaged screwdriver tips*

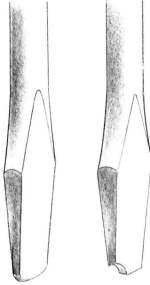

both of these will twist
out of the screw slot,
chew up the screw, and
probably damage the work

instead of filing the tip down
to fit a small screw ——
get a smaller screwdriver

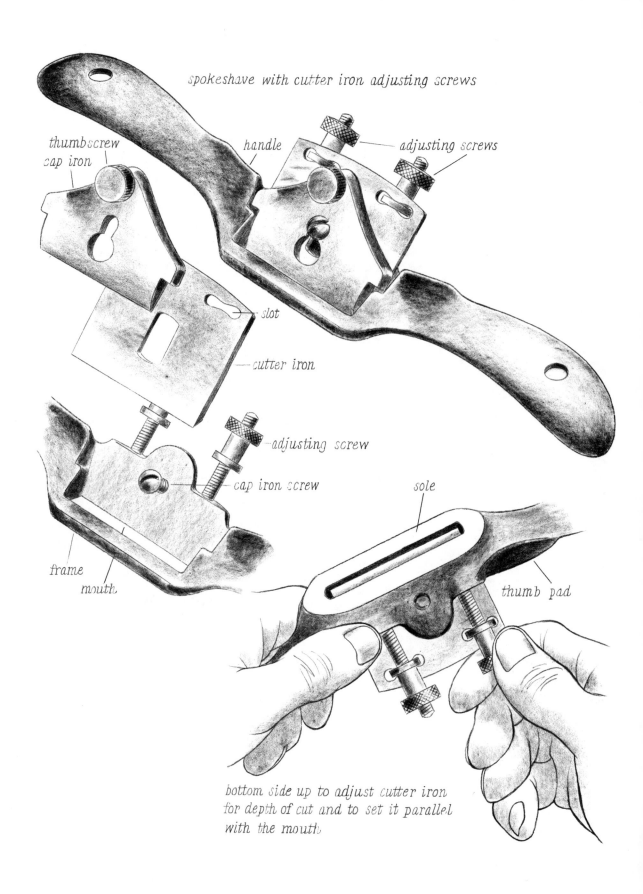

spokeshave with cutter iron adjusting screws

thumbscrew
cap iron

handle

adjusting screws

slot

cutter iron

adjusting screw

cap iron screw

frame

mouth

sole

thumb pad

bottom side up to adjust cutter iron
for depth of cut and to set it parallel
with the mouth

# 28

# Spokeshave

Wheelwrights used spokeshaves to round and shape the spokes for wagon wheels. This is a two-handed tool built on the same principle as a plane but with an extremely short sole, which is the feature that allows it to follow contours. A spokeshave is exactly what its name suggests—a tool for shaving wood rather than removing it in great amounts. It is used for shaping, smoothing, and finishing, following after the rough work done by such tools as the drawknife, chisel, and compass saw.

Spokeshaves are made in several patterns, but a good model for general work is the one with a straight cutter and a flat sole about $7/8$ inch long, shown in the illustrations. It does good work on flat surfaces and will shave round all but the sharpest curved edges. Be sure to get the model that has a pair of knurled thumbscrews for adjusting the cutter iron. This one costs a bit more than the plain version, which is adjusted by trial and error alone, but the ease and accuracy of thumb-screw adjustment is well worth the difference in price.

For working exceptionally tight curves there is another version with a sole curved fore-and-aft. There are also special models with curved cutter irons: one for rounding, as in the making of stair railings, another for scooping such pieces as chair seats.

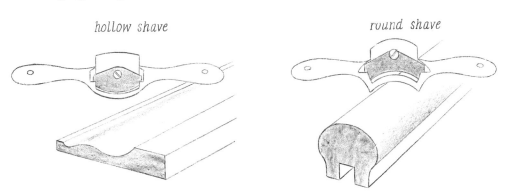

*hollow shave*          *round shave*

*cutaway views of flat and round sole spokeshaves*

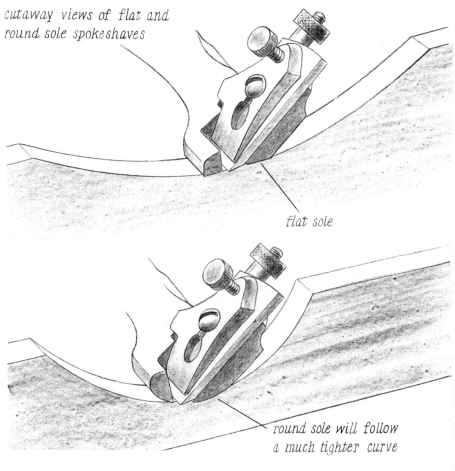

*flat sole*

*round sole will follow a much tighter curve*

*a spokeshave can be pulled as well as pushed*

ADJUSTING THE CUTTER IRON    The cutter iron should be sharp and set for a fine cut. It simply won't work when the iron is dull or set too deep. First loosen the thumbscrew an eighth of a turn. Turn the spokeshave bottom up and hold it in one hand. Use the other hand to turn the knurled adjusting screws—to the right for a deeper cut, to the left for a finer one. Sight across the sole to make sure the cutting edge of the iron is parallel with the mouth of the shave. Then tighten the thumbscrew—firmly, but by no means as tight as it will go. By using only medium pressure, the iron is free to slide up and down, and can be further adjusted as you work without loosening the screw each time. Finally, turn the knurled screws gently until they come up snug against the forward side of the slots. This prevents the iron from working back and out of adjustment when you begin work. Make a few trial shavings on scrap wood to verify the setting.

# Operating the Spokeshave

Take the shave in both hands. It can be pulled as well as pushed, but the push stroke is generally better because the natural thrust of hands and arms is down—down against the wood. The two thumb pads are cast in the frame for exactly this reason. Set your thumbs firmly into the pads and wrap your fingers around the handles. The thumbs transmit the pushing effort right next to the cutter iron where it's needed for good control. The fingers give a rocking motion to the shave which enables you to keep the sole in proper relation to the work as the shave slides over a curved cut.

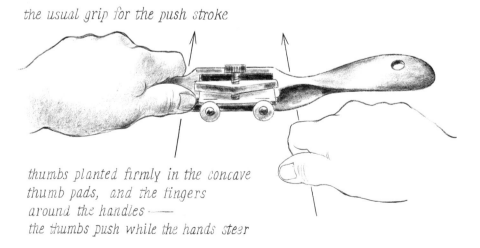

the usual grip for the push stroke

thumbs planted firmly in the concave
thumb pads, and the fingers
around the handles ——
the thumbs push while the hands steer

*another handgrip that gives good control of delicate shaving*

*thumbs firmly in thumb pads*        *index fingers on corners of frame*

Stiffen your forearms and keep a good firm pressure on the shave. Don't be timid. Pushing it halfheartedly will make it skip and chatter. As a shaper, the spokeshave will quickly transform a square stick into a dowel by cutting chamfers on the four edges to make the stick octagonal, and then chamfering all eight edges. In certain situations it may be necessary to pull the shave instead of pushing, but you will probably have to bear down on the tool more consciously in order to counteract its tendency to lift off of the wood. In good hands a spokeshave can be made to leave a finish that often needs no sanding at all.

SHEAR CUTTING     Any cutting tool generally makes the cleanest cut and with the least effort if the blade is run at an angle to the direction of push. It is this sliding, shearing cut that does the trick.

What is true of other tools applies no less to a spokeshave. Its complete workings are discovered only through trial and error. You must take it up, try it out dozens of times and on as many different jobs in order to see the good work it will perform.

*pulling the shave at an angle to get good shearing action*

*work*

*basic design of early spokeshave*

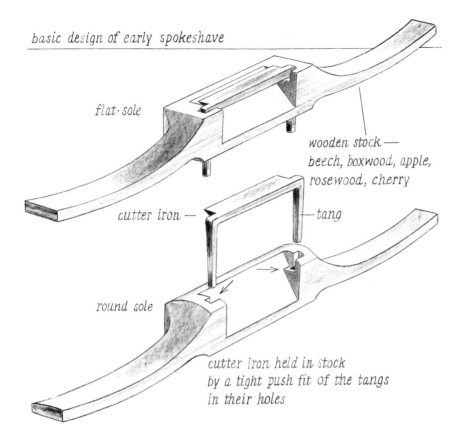

*flat·sole*

*wooden stock —
beech, boxwood, apple,
rosewood, cherry*

*cutter iron —*          *tang*

*round sole*

*cutter iron held in stock
by a tight push fit of the tangs
in their holes*

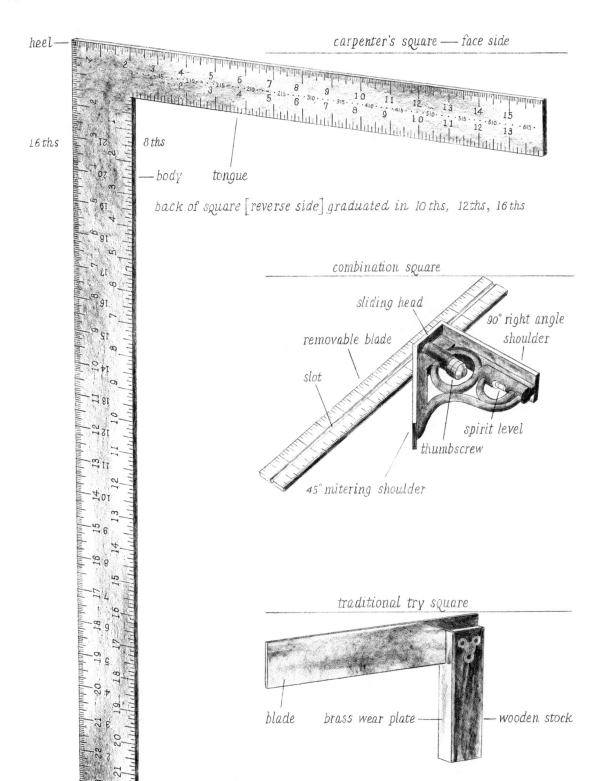

heel

carpenter's square — face side

16 ths

8 ths

body

tongue

back of square [reverse side] graduated in 10 ths, 12 ths, 16 ths

combination square

sliding head

90° right angle shoulder

removable blade

slot

spirit level

thumbscrew

45° mitering shoulder

traditional try square

blade

brass wear plate

wooden stock

# 29

# Square

Because successful woodworking depends in large measure on saw cuts and joints that are square, this foundation tool is indispensable when laying out the work, making saw cuts, planing them true, and when putting all the pieces together. If the first piece of wood is out of square, it will be next to impossible to measure and cut the next one so that it fits with the first. If, on the other hand, everything is made square from start to finish, there is a much better chance that the work will come out as planned.

Always use a square to mark off for a saw cut, however crude or preliminary you may consider the work to be. This habit makes for better quality work, saves time and lumber, and avoids frustration. Saw the pieces square to begin with, check your clean-up plane work with the square, and use it again as the pieces are assembled.

Two squares are almost a necessity: a combination square for small work at the bench, and a 16″×24″ carpenter's square for wide boards, glued up sections, furniture-making, and any construction beyond the limited 10-inch reach of the combination square.

## Combination Square

This small square does the same work as the traditional try square, which was used to "try it on the work" to see if it was square. Whereas the try square with wooden stock and metal blade was limited to just this one job, the combination is a much more versatile tool. It is made with a cast steel head that slides to any position on a flat blade, one face of the head at a 90-degree right angle to the blade and the other at a 45-degree angle for mitering. Some of these squares are supplied with an extra centering head which is used to find the center of round stock such a dowels. Both heads can be removed, leaving the blade free as an accurate straightedge.

*the mechanics of the combination square*

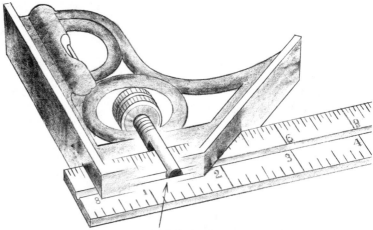

*dog on end of lock pin engages in groove*
*to lock blade securely to the head*

These features make the combination especially useful not only as a square but also as a gauging tool, for marking along the edge of a board for a ripsaw cut, marking out for a rabbet or mortise and tenon joint, or marking for a 45-degree miter cut. In working a mortise and tenon joint, the combination square also serves as a gauge to determine the depth of the mortise.

When planing the flat side of a board this square can be used as a straightedge set on the surface to check its flatness by observing light showing under the blade.

Most combination squares have a spirit level built into the head, but this feature is of negligible value since the part of the head containing the level is only about 4 inches long—much too short a bearing surface for any degree of accuracy.

ADJUSTING THE COMBINATION SQUARE    To adjust the sliding blade, hold the square in one hand and loosen the thumbscrew. Slide the blade with the other hand and then retighten the screw. Tighten it no more than is possible while holding the square and operating the thumbscrew with the one hand.

To remove the blade, simply loosen the thumbscrew and slide the blade out of the head. To put it back on, start the blade into the head, then push in against the spring pressure of the thumbscrew until the dog on the end of the lock pin engages the slot in the blade. Slide the blade in. A slight turn of the thumbscrew will again lock the head to the blade.

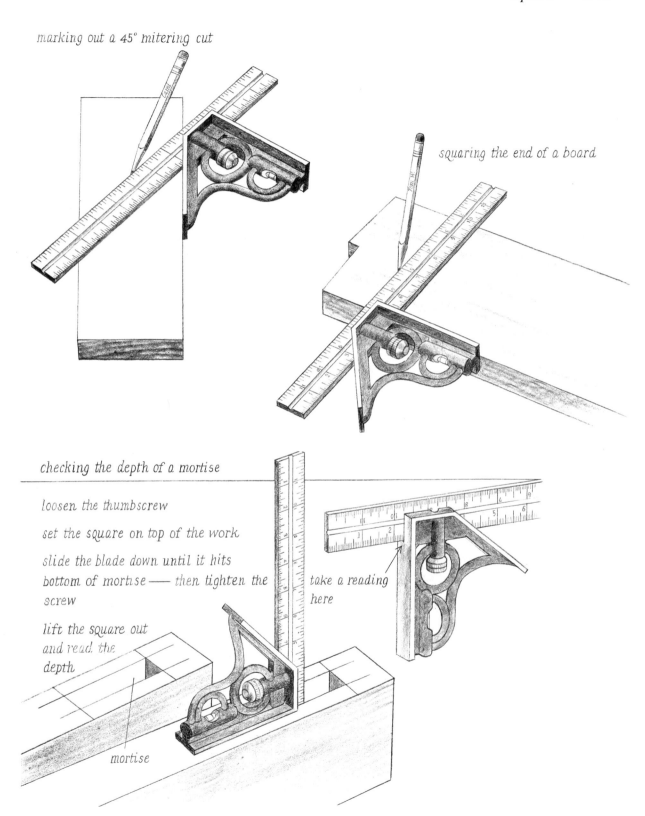

marking out a 45° mitering cut

squaring the end of a board

checking the depth of a mortise

loosen the thumbscrew

set the square on top of the work

slide the blade down until it hits
bottom of mortise — then tighten the
screw

lift the square out
and read the
depth

take a reading
here

mortise

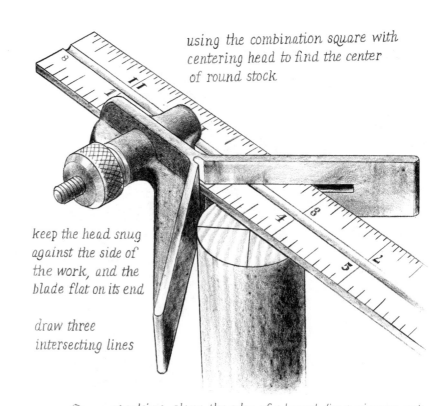

using the combination square with centering head to find the center of round stock

keep the head snug against the side of the work, and the blade flat on its end

draw three intersecting lines

marking along the edge of a board for a ripsaw cut

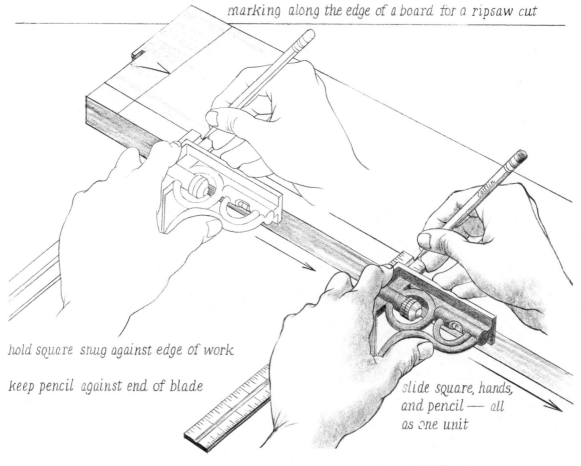

hold square snug against edge of work

keep pencil against end of blade

slide square, hands, and pencil — all as one unit

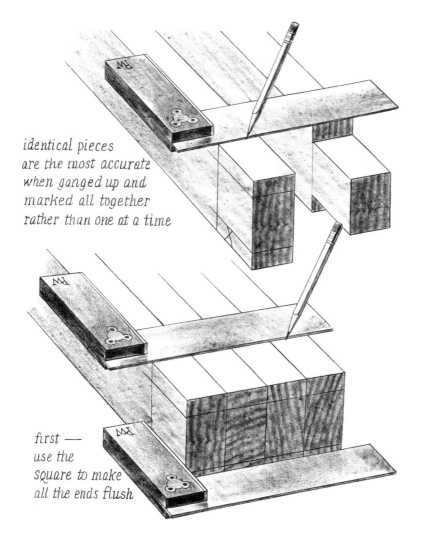

*identical pieces
are the most accurate
when ganged up and
marked all together
rather than one at a time*

*first —
use the
square to make
all the ends flush*

checking the end of a board for square

*the most accurate way —
light showing under the blade reveals at once
where the inaccuracy is*

*the least accurate way —— difficult to
align the square exactly with the corner
of the board*

# Steel Squares

These big squares are made in two versions—the carpenter's and the rafter square. Made from a single piece of steel, they are extremely accurate. The chief difference between the two is in the tables of figures stamped on their sides, each set of which is intended for use with a particular type of work. The carpenter's square has the basic information necessary for fine work—inches graduated in 8ths, 10ths, 12ths, and 16ths. The rafter square, on the other hand, is graduated only in 8ths, and has a table of dimensions used to calculate the angles for rafters and other framing members commonly used in construction work. The details of using these time-saving tables are explained in an instruction booklet that comes with the square.

When assembling and squaring up a large piece of work such as a tabletop, or when laying out saw cuts on wide boards, the longer the arms of the square, the more exact the work will be. For example, if you are marking a cutoff on a 12-inch board, the carpenter's square is more accurate than the combination because of its longer contact with the work. Hold the 24-inch body against the edge of the board, and draw the saw-cut line against the 16-inch tongue.

*squaring the end of a wide board*

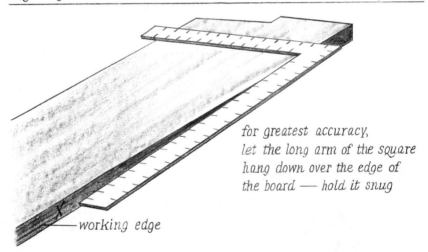

for greatest accuracy,
let the long arm of the square
hang down over the edge of
the board — hold it snug

—working edge

On very large work—let's say a 36-inch tabletop—it is a good practice to check the square of the work from both sides before making your saw cuts. Lay the square on the mark at one edge and draw a line. Then flop the square over to the opposite edge. If the board has been properly jointed and its two edges are truly parallel, both squared lines should coincide exactly.

Both these squares are precision instruments that need special care. Drop a square on the floor, step on it by mistake, or treat it as you might more excusably treat a tough tool such as a hammer, and it may be damaged enough to make it totally useless. A square that is not quite square will consistently produce poor work. Squares should be kept clean and wiped now and then with an oily rag to retard rusting. At least once a year, take the combination square apart, clean the screw threads of the lock pin, and lubricate it with a drop or two of light machine oil. The carpenter's square should be stored on a simple rack rather than stood on the floor or laid on the bench.

Handled with common sense, either of these squares will last for several generations, square and useful even after the scale of inches has been obliterated by rust, dirt, and time.

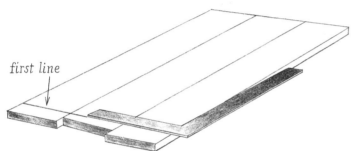

first line

flop square over to the other edge —
if the edges of the panel were jointed parallel, the square
should exactly align with the first line

using the carpenter's square to lay out a 45° angle on a wide board

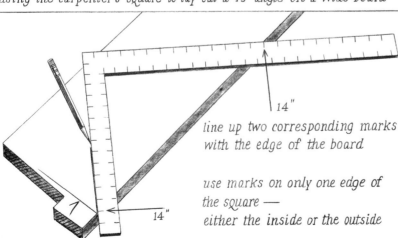

14"

line up two corresponding marks
with the edge of the board

use marks on only one edge of
the square —
either the inside or the outside

14"

*brassbound T-bevel with wooden stock*

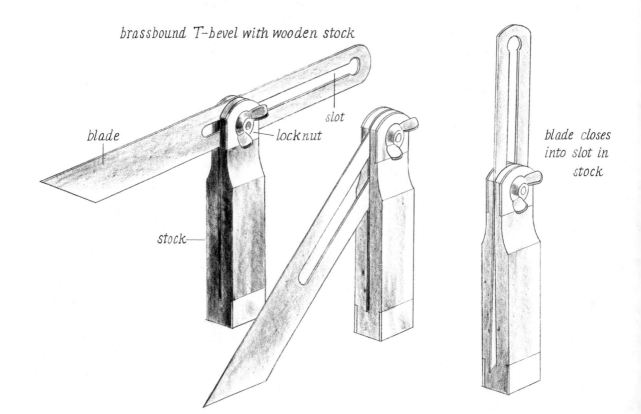

*blade*

*slot*

*lock nut*

*stock*

*blade closes into slot in stock*

# 30

# T-Bevel

This is an ingenious tool for measuring, verifying, and setting out angles. It consists of a stock and a slotted steel blade that slides on a bolt. The position of the blade is secured by a simple locknut which when tightened squeezes together the split ends of the stock. When not being used, the blade closes into the slot in the stock, and the tool may be hung up by the hole in the end of the blade.

When the locknut is loosened, the blade can be moved into any position to measure an existing angle that is to be marked out and reproduced in new work. Lay the stock against one side of the angled work and move the blade until it touches the other. Tighten the lock-

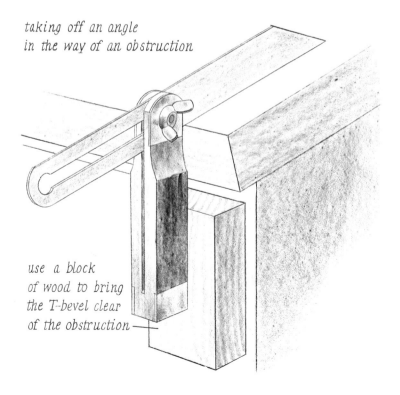

*taking off an angle
in the way of an obstruction*

*use a block
of wood to bring
the T-bevel clear
of the obstruction*

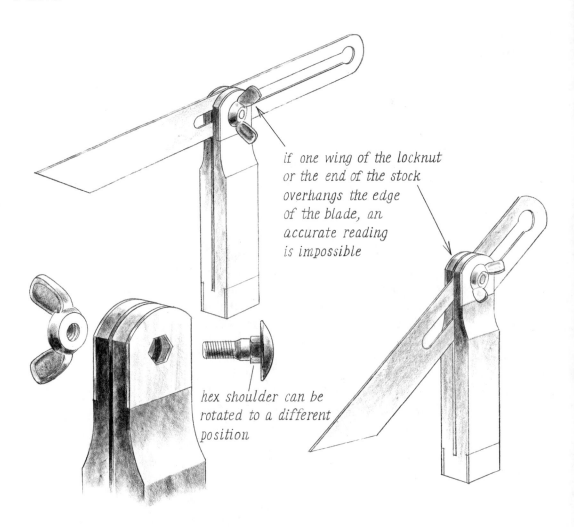

if one wing of the locknut
or the end of the stock
overhangs the edge
of the blade, an
accurate reading
is impossible

hex shoulder can be
rotated to a different
position

taking an angle
from a protractor

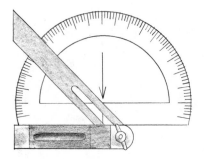

blade must intersect base of
protractor exactly on center

nut a bit, but only enough to just keep the blade from slipping. Set the T-bevel into the angle again to make certain that the setting is correct: the stock and blade both touching wood. Any final adjustment can now be made without loosening the nut. Then tighten it. A mere fraction of a turn is enough. Very little pressure is needed to immobilize the blade.

Occasionally it happens that the stock or blade is prevented from seating properly against the work because one wing of the locknut sticks out in the way. To fix this, loosen the nut and push the bolt in so the head disengages from the hex hole in the stock. Then rotate the hex bolt a sixth of a turn. This will alter the position of the wing nut when it is fully tightened.

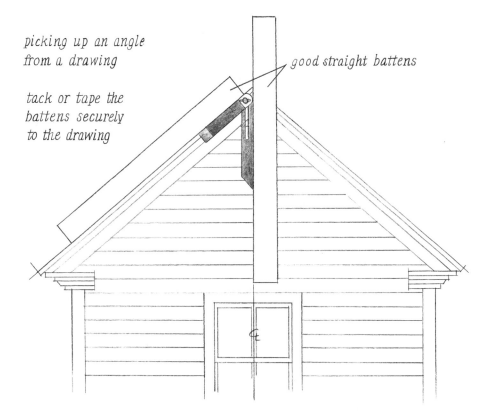

*picking up an angle from a drawing*

*good straight battens*

*tack or tape the battens securely to the drawing*

The stock itself may accidentally get in the way of accurately taking off an angle. There is a fair amount of slop in the slotted blade, enough to allow the stock to slide out past the edge of the blade a 16th of an inch or so. In this case, just pull the stock clear of the blade.

The T-bevel can be used to pick up angles from large-scale drawings, or—when a specific angle is wanted—to be taken directly from a protractor, which at the same time provides reciprocal angles.

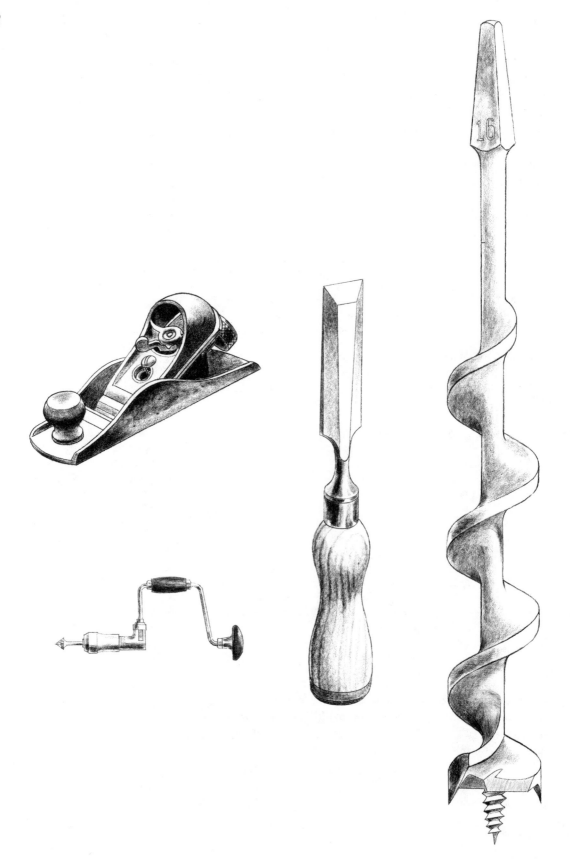

# 31

# Sharpening

*for delicate sharpening—*
*extra fine silicon carbide*
*paper glued to the*
*blank end of an auger*
*bit file*

A set of sharp tools and the ability to keep them so are at the very root of good workworking. Sharp tools are easier to use and return a greater satisfaction in the improved workmanship they tend to produce. By the same token, even the highest degree of skill is pretty much wasted on dull tools. Naturally, the more they are used and handled, the more often tools will have to be sharpened. The kind of stuff you use them on has a major influence on this as well. An edge tool dulls faster in rock maple than in pine, and it suffers even more from being run through knots and grit-dirty lumber.

Sharpening is neither easy nor impossibly difficult. It is a process that takes time, patience, and practice. The best results are undoubtedly obtained when you are in a relaxed, deliberate frame of mind and have nothing else to do.

The time to sharpen a tool is when you see that it is working dull, not after it is worn blunt. A neglected tool takes three or four times as long to properly recondition it. Whatever tools need it, plan to sharpen them in off-hours rather than in the middle of a job that is absorbing all of your attention. You will do a better job and avoid the trap of thinking, "I'll just touch it up for now," which can catch you in the ruination of an edge that will require a major overhaul sometime later when you least want it. Fixing several tools at one session is also better because skill is cumulative: the knack you develop by sharpening one tool will improve the job you do on the next one.

Whatever the tool—saw, plane, chisel, or auger bit—the principle of sharpening is simple: remove only as much metal as it takes to restore the cutting edge—and no more.

# Sharpening Single-Bevel Tools

In this group are the chisel, plane, spokeshave, drawknife, and inshave. The blades or cutter irons of these tools are flat on one side and ground to a bevel on the other to form the cutting edge. Sharpening consists of three basic operations: (1) coarse grinding to remove any nicks and to reshape the bevel; (2) fine grinding to smooth and bring the bevel to a sharp edge; and (3) honing to refine the edge.

EQUIPMENT    The essential piece of equipment is a combination oilstone about 1″×2″×8″ with gray Crystolon on one side for coarse grinding, and brown India on the other for the fine grinding necessary to actually produce the edge. The stone should be firmly anchored to

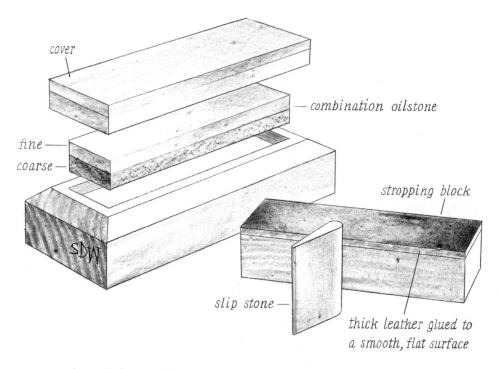

cover

— combination oilstone

fine —
coarse —

stropping block

slip stone —

thick leather glued to
a smooth, flat surface

keep it from sliding around during grinding. The simplest solution to this is a heavy wooden tray and cover made to fit the stone. It can be put in the vise for sharpening tools, and when not in use the cover protects the stone from accumulated dirt that clogs its pores and impairs its grinding efficiency.

For honing, use a hard Arkansas slip stone or a leather strop. Slip stones are about 2″×4″ with one side beveled to a thin, rounded edge which is very handy for touching up the cutting edges of auger bits and other small tools. A piece of thick leather belting glued to a 2-inch block of wood makes a good solid stropping surface. You will also need a can of light machine oil of the sewing machine variety and another of kerosene, either of which are suitable for grinding, although the thicker machine oil is preferable because it doesn't run off or sink into the stone as quickly. Have some clean, absorbent rags on hand to wipe the stone clean of oil and metal particles when you're finished.

Where a major grinding is not needed to reshape a cutting tool or to remove nicks in the edge, extra fine waterproof silicon carbide paper can be used instead of an oilstone. Tape the paper tight over a flat, smooth block of wood, or wrap and tape a smaller piece of the paper around a slender stick for sharpening such small tools as auger bits, countersinks, and reamers. This paper can be used dry or lubricated with oil. In the case of the wrapped stick, use two hands to maintain the best control for delicate sharpening in close quarters.

How an Oilstone Works   A sharpening oilstone consists of thousands of tiny, harder than steel sharp-edged points with spaces in between. As a tool is pushed over the stone under pressure, these points

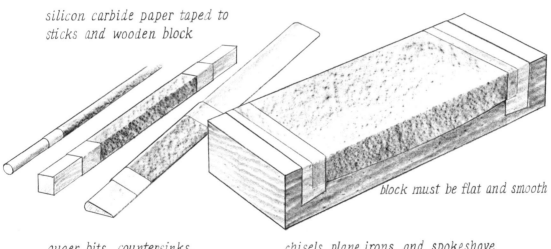

*silicon carbide paper taped to sticks and wooden block*

*block must be flat and smooth*

*auger bits, countersinks, and reamers*

*chisels, plane irons, and spokeshave*

grind off particles of steel. On the coarse side of the stone the points are relatively large and far apart. This initial grinding removes metal rapidly but leaves the surface, and more particularly the edge, rough and ragged. At this stage, the tool may feel sharp and indeed for a time may cut better than it did before. However, such an edge produces a cut that is more chewed than sliced, and will soon break down again.

It is the job of the fine side of the stone to grind away enough more metal to eliminate the scratches and ridges from the bevel, and to cut down the ragged metal along the cutting edge. To see the importance of these three sharpening operations and their relationship to the fin-

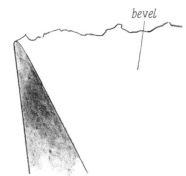

*cutting edge of a dull chisel, greatly magnified*

bevel

*before sharpening*

*after coarse grinding*

*after fine grinding*

*honed and ready to use*

ished edge, inspect your work each step of the way under a high-powered lens. For example, before you have begun sharpening it, the cutting edge of a dull chisel may look as crude as a stone ax. After the preliminary coarse grinding it will probably resemble a range of jagged mountain peaks. But when you've ground it on the fine side of the stone, the edge should appear as a straight, comparatively clean line, needing only a bit of honing to remove the few remaining flecks of steel.

COARSE GRINDING     Have your rags and oilcan ready. With the stone laid coarse side up in its tray, put the tray in the vise. Squirt some oil along the stone. Pick up the tool with the bevel side next to the stone. Wrap your fingers around the tool as close to the cutting edge as possible in a controlled grip that is firm but not tense. Set the bevel down on the stone and rock it fore-and-aft a bit so that you can feel when the whole bevel is touching. The object is to keep the full

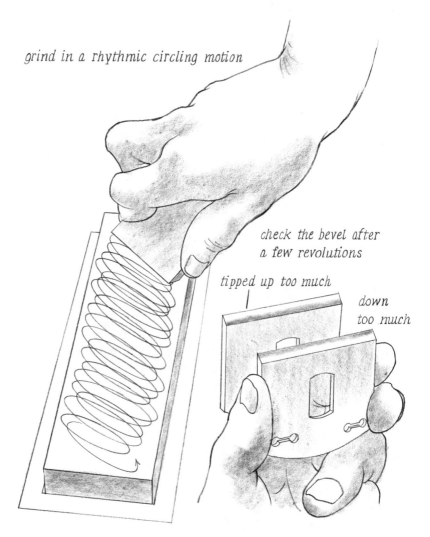

*grind in a rhythmic circling motion*

*check the bevel after a few revolutions*

*tipped up too much*

*down too much*

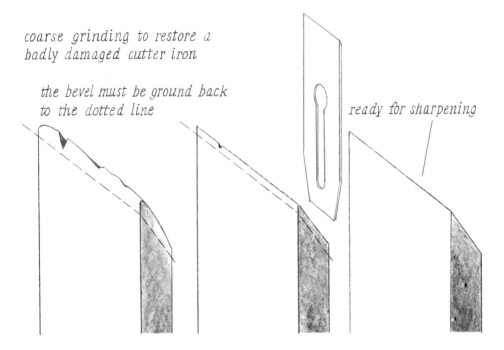

*coarse grinding to restore a badly damaged cutter iron*

*the bevel must be ground back to the dotted line*

*ready for sharpening*

area of the bevel in contact with the stone in order to remove metal evenly, and to maintain its original manufactured angle.

Move hand and tool over the stone in a constant circling motion, traveling from one end of the stone to the other to avoid wearing it hollow. Try to get a rhythm as regular as the moderate turning of a wheel. After five or six revolutions stop for an inspection. Without changing your grip on the tool, lift it off the stone and turn it bevel up. Wipe off the oil and have a look. If the entire bevel is bright, you are grinding at the correct angle. But if either the edge or the heel is bright and the rest of the bevel is dull, adjust the angle as you go back to continue grinding.

Use plenty of oil throughout the grinding process—both coarse and fine. It is necessary to float away the steel particles, and maintaining good circular motion is easier on a lubricated surface than a dry one. Continue grinding until the entire cutting edge shows a rough burr. Depending on the condition of the tool when you started, this first grinding may take a considerable length of time, anywhere from fifteen minutes to an hour or more.

FINE GRINDING    Turn the stone over in the tray and continue grinding on the fine side, being careful to hold the tool in the same grip and at the same angle. When enough more metal has been removed, a feather edge should appear along the cutting edge—a thin flap of metal that indicates sharpening is nearly done. Turn the blade of the tool over and lay it *flat* on the stone. Then draw it along the stone

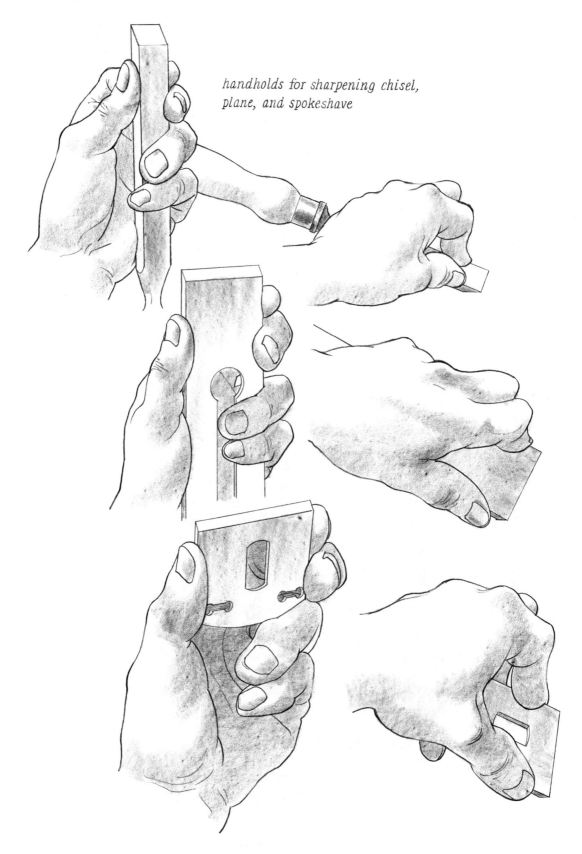

handholds for sharpening chisel,
plane, and spokeshave

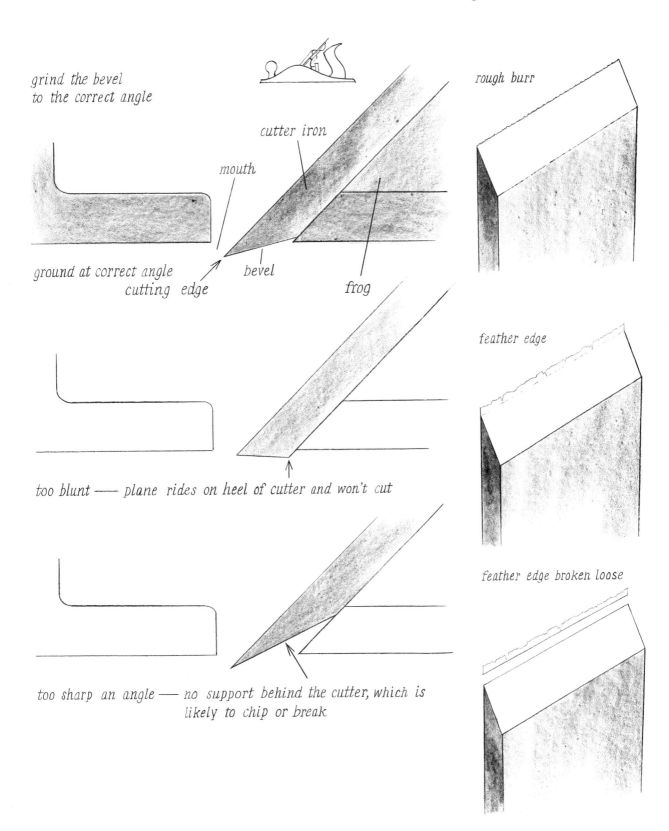

*grind the bevel
to the correct angle*

*cutter iron*

*mouth*

*ground at correct angle
cutting edge*

*bevel*

*frog*

*rough burr*

*too blunt —— plane rides on heel of cutter and won't cut*

*feather edge*

*too sharp an angle —— no support behind the cutter, which is
likely to chip or break*

*feather edge broken loose*

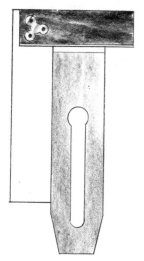

*a plane iron should be
ground square to its sides*

*match plane irons*

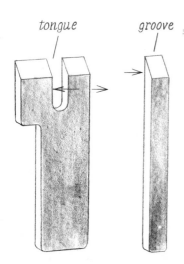

tongue                groove

*never grind the sides of
these cutters, as the widths
of tongue and groove
would no longer match*

toward you—once. Again turn it over and give the bevel a few more light strokes. This bending back and forth should break loose the feather edge, or most of it. If not, drawing it across the edge of a scrap of wood will usually remove the remaining flecks of the feather edge.

HONING     This simply carries the grinding process to a more refined degree, and although it actually removes microscopic particles of metal, it is more of a polishing action to create a longer-lasting edge. A hard Arkansas stone does the best job, although a leather strop accomplishes much the same thing. Draw the bevel two or three times the length of an oiled strop. Then flop the cutter iron and draw its back flat along the strop.

# Small Plane Irons

The cutter irons of such planes as the grooving, plow, rabbet, combination, Stanley 45 and 55, and the multiplane are of course sharpened according to the same principles as used for the larger bench planes. But because their irons are so short and narrow they cannot be ground with any degree of accuracy when simply held in the thumb and fingers of one hand. It is impossible to hold the cutter iron steadily at the correct angle to the oilstone throughout grinding.

One of the most efficient ways to sharpen these miniature irons accurately is with a grinding palm. This is a simple wooden block with a slot of the correct angle cut in one side, into which the cutter iron is clamped. To adjust the grinding palm, loosen the setscrews and put the cutter in the slot with its cutting edge projecting slightly below the sole of the palm. Tighten the setscrews just enough to keep the cutter from moving. Push or tap the cutter down until it barely shows below the sole. Now try it out. Set the palm on the stone and slide it back

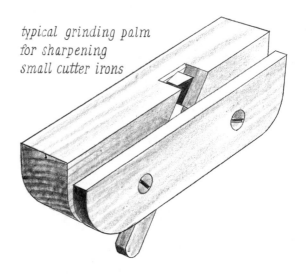

*typical grinding palm
for sharpening
small cutter irons*

and forth once. If this trial brightens the steel of the cutter's bevel, tighten the setscrews and proceed with sharpening. If not, tap the cutter a bit lower and make another trial.

While sharpening with the palm, keep its sole *flat on the stone* at all times. Use plenty of oil, and to avoid grooving the stone use its full length as well as traveling slowly from one edge of the stone to the other.

A grinding palm will do a professional sharpening job so long as it is made with care and precision. The slot must be cut at the same angle as the bevel of the cutter iron; the front and rear surfaces of the slot must be square with the side of the palm; and there should be a snug push-fit of the cutter in the slot.

Since the sizes and bevels of cutter irons differ from plane to plane, it is necessary to have one palm for each plane. Directions for making a typical grinding palm are given in the Appendix.

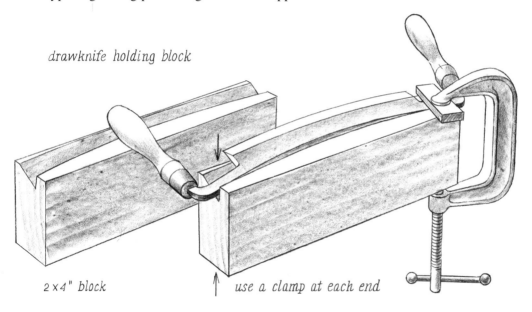

*drawknife holding block*

*2 x 4" block*          ↑ *use a clamp at each end*

# Drawknife and Inshave

The same grinding principles apply to these two tools, but because of their shapes they cannot be ground in a circular motion over a stationary oilstone with any satisfactory control, even when held in both hands. Instead, the tool must be held securely while the stone is used in one hand and moved about over the blade. With a drawknife the simplest procedure is to clamp it to a homemade wooden holding block that can be held in the vise. There are directions in the Appendix for making such a block.

To hold an inshave, put one arm of a Jorgensen clamp in the vise and then tighten the jaws over the back edge of the inshave. By tilting the clamp this way and that, every section of the curved blade can be reached.

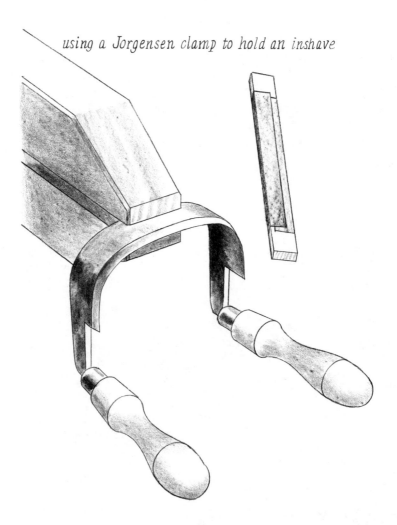

*using a Jorgensen clamp to hold an inshave*

With both these tools, the stone is worked in a circular rotation over the blade, working from one end to the other and back again so that all parts of the bevel get a uniform amount of grinding. When sharpening an inshave, however, the motions of the stone must be modified to a rounding, wiping attitude in order to follow the curvature of the blade.

# Saws

Sharpening is only one of three basic operations in saw maintenance which is better described as fixing: *jointing* to bring all the teeth to the same length; *setting* to give each tooth an identical outward bend; and *filing* to actually sharpen the teeth. Before fixing a saw it is helpful to compare the old one with a new saw of the same type and point size, in order to note the original shape of the teeth and the amount of set. You can make a similar comparison by looking at the teeth of the old saw at the extreme heel end, which gets almost no wear.

You need three tools to fix a saw. (1) *Saw vise*      This is a simple cast-iron vise with a lever that clamps the saw blade tight. It is generally screwed to a board so it can be held in a woodworking vise at a comfortable working height. As a substitute, two boards can be put in the vise with the saw blade sandwiched between them. (2) *Saw set*      The best job is done with this small one-handed tool with plier

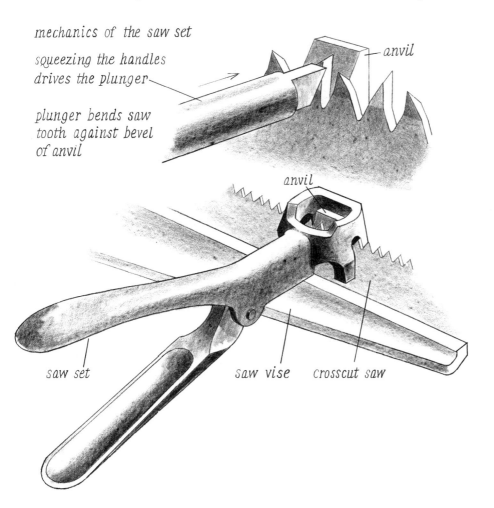

*mechanics of the saw set*

*squeezing the handles drives the plunger*

*plunger bends saw tooth against bevel of anvil*

anvil

anvil

saw set            saw vise      crosscut saw

grip and adjustments for saws of different point sizes. (3) *Files*    You will need an 8-inch mill bastard file for jointing, and two or three tapered triangular saw files for sharpening the teeth. Be sure to get the right file for the particular saw: a 6-inch slim taper for 7- and 8-point saws; a 5–6-inch slim taper for 10-point; and a $4\frac{1}{2}$–5-inch double extra slim for 12–14-point saws. If in any doubt, take your saw to the hardware store for assistance in making the selection.

JOINTING    Clamp the saw in the saw vise with the teeth up, leaving about 2 inches of blade projecting. Clamp a block of wood to the 8-inch mill file so that one of its edges overhangs the block. Lay the block flat against the side of the saw blade, with the edge of the file resting flat on top of the teeth. Start at the heel of the saw and run the file over the teeth clear to the toe. Then lift it off and come back to make another stroke. Don't file any more than is necessary. Stop filing when every tooth shows a shiny, flat tip. These are essential reference points that will be used later to file the teeth.

*jointing with a file clamped to a block of wood*

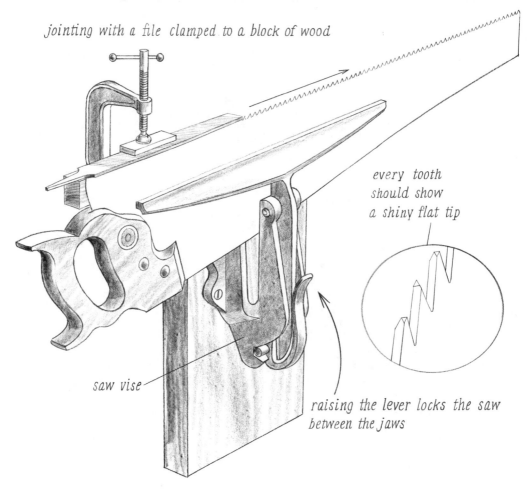

*every tooth should show a shiny flat tip*

*saw vise*

*raising the lever locks the saw between the jaws*

SETTING     To put set in a saw, the teeth are bent outward alternately to right and left, causing the saw to cut a kerf a shade wider than the thickness of the blade. This prevents the saw from binding in the cut and allows it to run easily. The hand-operated saw set bends one tooth at a time. First adjust the saw set for the correct point size. Then put the set over the saw blade with a tooth centered on the anvil of the saw set. Squeeze the plier handle hard—once. One squeeze for each tooth. Skip the next tooth—which will be set in the opposite direction—and set the next one. Continue along the length of the saw, setting every other tooth. Then turn the saw around in the vise and set alternate teeth in the opposite direction.

*filing a crosscut*

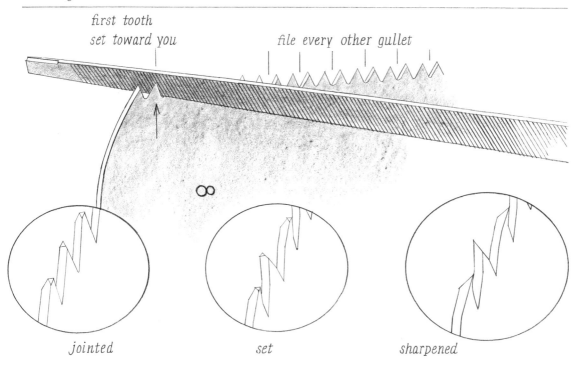

first tooth
set toward you          file every other gullet

jointed          set          sharpened

FILING A CROSSCUT     Lower the saw in the vise so that only $1/2$-inch of blade projects. Note the shiny flat tips left by jointing. These are used as guides to filing the teeth all to the same length. Both bevels of each tooth are filed until the shiny flat tip disappears to a point in the center of what was the shiny flat tip.

Knock a handle onto the tang of a file. It provides the best control. Hold the file in both hands, one on the handle and the other steadying the tip. Start at the heel of the saw—its handle to your left. Lay the end of the file in the gullet between the first tooth set toward you and the first tooth set away from you. The file should be pointing to your left at an angle of about 60 degrees to the saw blade. Hold the file handle up a bit, at an angle of about 15 degrees to 20 degrees. In this position the triangular file cuts the leading bevel of tooth one and the trailing bevel of tooth two, both at the same time. Push the file through the gullet nonstop, then lift it out. *Don't file on the return stroke.* Again set the file in the same gullet and make a second stroke. Keep the strokes smooth and positive. Very little pressure is needed as a good file cuts its own way. Keep a sharp eye on the shiny flat tip, and when it is half gone—stop. The other half will be cut away when you file the alternate teeth from the other side of the saw.

Now skip the next tooth and put the file in the next gullet. Continue filing every other gullet until you reach the toe of the saw. Then turn it end-for-end in the vise and again file alternate gullets along the other side. Since the saw handle will now be on your right, remember to point the file to your right on this return trip. When the file brings the shiny flat tip to a point—stop.

FILING A BACKSAW    A backsaw is a crosscut with very fine teeth. It is sharpened in exactly the same way as described above except that a much finer file must be used. Filing these saws is much easier if a spotlight and a magnifying glass are rigged up over the work.

FILING A RIPSAW    Before filing a ripsaw, see that it is first jointed and set in the usual way. The teeth of a ripsaw have no bevels, which makes sharpening somewhat simpler. Use a triangular file of the correct size and clamp the saw in the vise as low as possible, to prevent its chattering. Start at the heel. Lay the file in the gullet between the first and second teeth, holding the file level and at right angles to the saw blade. File straight across. One face of the file cuts the perpendicular front of tooth one while a second face cuts the sloping back of tooth two. After filing this first gullet, skip a tooth and file the next gullet. Keep a close watch on the shiny flat tips as before, and file away only half of them. Continue along the full length of the saw, then turn it around in the vise and file the alternate gullets. On this return trip the shiny flat tips should disappear, leaving the teeth sharp and all the same length.

# Auger Bits

A double-twist auger bit has four cutting edges: two spurs, or flukes that score the wood, and two cutters that follow along and remove it. The lead screw acts as an automatic feed, pulling the bit into the wood. Whereas a chisel can be sharpened for years without noticeably shortening its life, the cutting head of an auger bit has no metal to spare.

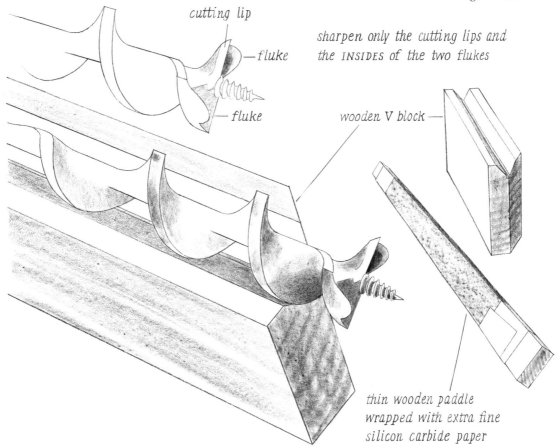

cutting lip

—fluke

—fluke

*sharpen only the cutting lips and the* INSIDES *of the two flukes*

wooden V block —

*thin wooden paddle wrapped with extra fine silicon carbide paper*

Bits should therefore be treated with fanatical restraint. Remove the least amount of metal necessary to restore the cutting edges.

A tapered auger bit file and a slip stone are the tools you need. They are made slim and small especially for this job. Don't use an ordinary 8-inch file; it is too thick, wide, and clumsy, and will damage the throat of the bit or undercut and weaken the lead screw. Don't stick the lead screw of a bit into the bench to hold it steady for sharpening! It cannot be sharpened. Use a simple homemade wooden V block that can be made from directions in the Appendix. Put the V block in the vise and lay the bit in the trough. The cutting end of the bit should hang out over the end of the block. Hold the bit firmly in the trough with one hand and use the other to manipulate the file or slip stone. In most cases a careful honing with the slip stone is enough to bring the cutting edges sharp again, but if a file must be used, use it with surgical delicacy. Two or three moderate strokes should suffice. File only the faces shown in the illustration. Never file the outsides of the flukes or the undersides of the main cutters. Finish the job by honing the edges with a few judicious strokes of the slip stone. Don't forget the oil.

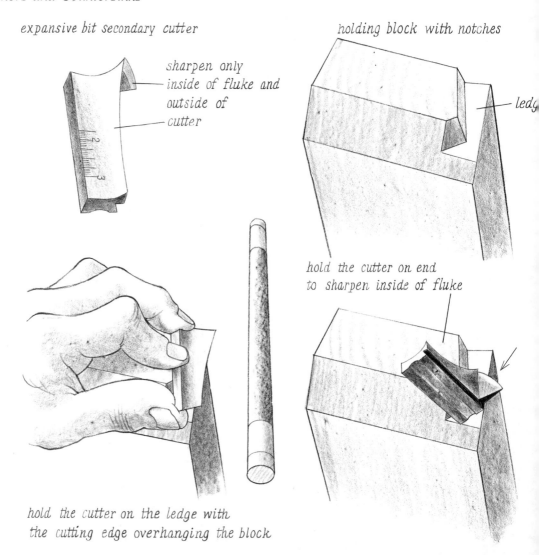

expansive bit secondary cutter

sharpen only
inside of fluke and
outside of
cutter

holding block with notches

ledge

hold the cutter on end
to sharpen inside of fluke

hold the cutter on the ledge with
the cutting edge overhanging the block

# Reamers and Countersinks

Reamers and rosehead countersinks are sharpened with an oilstone rather than a file, as the steel is very hard. Have a good light over the work, for the cutting facets are small and very close together. These bits can be secured with a C-clamp to one end of a length of wood held in the vise with the point of the tool toward you, or they can be clamped in a machinist's vise between two pieces of wood. Use the edge of the oilstone, running it along each cutting edge from the point to the back. Keep the stone at the same angle as the bevel and use slow, steady strokes. To prevent striking and dulling an adjacent cutting edge, hold a thin piece of wood over the edge to act as a guide fence.

The single-cutter countersink can be ground with a round stone or a length of dowel wrapped in a patch of extra fine emery paper. Some older countersinks were made with two cutters formed by a split cone of thin steel. These are usually soft enough to be sharpened with a fine, half-round jeweler's file.

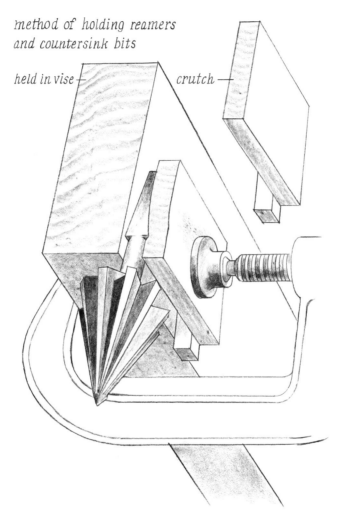

*method of holding reamers and countersink bits*

*held in vise*    *crutch*

# Jackknife

This is the most satisfactory method I have found for sharpening a knife. Put a 12-inch length of two-by-four end-up in the vise. Holding the knife in one hand, lay the blade on top of the stick and tip the cutting edge up at an angle. Use the other hand to stroke the oilstone along the bevel of the knife blade, working across it at a slight angle. The stick of wood provides firm support while the bevel of the knife is always in plain sight, reflecting the light as you grind it.

# Scrapers

CABINET SCRAPER    The cutting edge of this type of scraper is sharpened in two steps. First, the edge of the blade is filed straight and square using the draw filing method described on page 145. In the second step, a burr is formed on this edge. It is this sharp burr edge that does the scraping.

Put the scraper in the vise—preferably a machinist's vise—with the freshly filed edge up. Find a smooth, round steel rod about 14 inches long. An iron bolt will not work because it is too soft. Holding it by a hand on each end, set the middle of the rod on the edge of the scraper

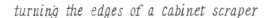

*turning the edges of a cabinet scraper*

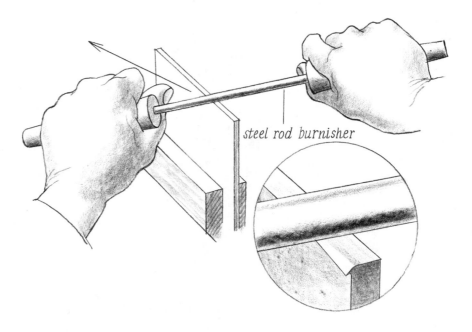

*steel rod burnisher*

at an angle of about 40 degrees. Slide it along and down against the edge of the scraper, traveling its full length. The object is to turn the steel of the scraper's edge over to form a slight hook. Use all the pressure you can bring to bear; a better hook results from one or two heavy passes than from several light ones because the steel is being bent over, and excessive bending will break it. This type of turned-burr cutting edge is very fine, wears out quickly, and must therefore be done over frequently. But it also scrapes a smooth surface indeed.

BEVEL-EDGED SCRAPERS    Shave hooks and homemade scrapers can best be sharpened with a file. Put the scraper in the vise and use an 8-inch mill bastard file, stroking it down, against, and along the bevel. Unlike the turned edge of a cabinet scraper, these edges should be fine-ground and honed in the same way that a chisel or plane iron is finished.

*sharpening a bevel-edged scraper*

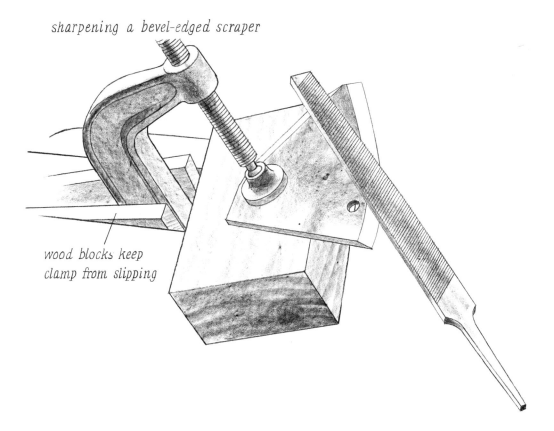

*wood blocks keep clamp from slipping*

# Twist Drills

It is not feasible to hand sharpen twist drills or brad point drills on an oilstone, for unless the low conical bevels of their cutting lips are ground at precisely the right angle they will cut nothing, not even wood. Take them to a machine shop that has the power equipment to do the job correctly, or refer to the manufacturer's specifications and use a bench grinder and one of the special attachments made for this work. Unless you have bought expensive, top quality drills, it may even be cheaper to simply buy new ones.

# Appendixes

A    TOOLMAKERS        374

B    TOOL CATALOGS        376

C    WORKBENCH PLANS        380

D    PLANS FOR BENCH TOOLS AND EQUIPMENT        385

E    FITTING A HAMMER HANDLE        401

F    CLOSET WORKBENCH PLANS        404

G    INVENTORY OF TYPICAL HAND TOOL SHOP        409

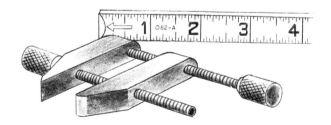

# A

## TOOLMAKERS

The manufacturer who makes a good tool marks it with his name as a warranty of quality. And depending on the particular tool it may also be marked with the model number, size, weight, type of steel, and in some cases the place of manufacture—stamped, cast, or etched in a conspicuous place. These markings are especially useful when buying old tools, and well worth the chore of cleaning off rust and grime to read them, particularly if you find something like this on the blade of a saw: "The result of more than 150 years sawmaking experience and today's latest improvements. This saw carries a full guarantee."

Bailey
John Berry & Son
Boker
Charles Buck
Buck Brothers
Cattaraugus
Cincinnati Tool Co.
Columbian
Craftsman
Crescent
Diamond Saw Co.
Henry Disston & Son
Estwing
Fuller
Garland Mfg. Co.
Groves & Sons
Hammacher Schlemmer
Hargrave
Heller
Irwin
Russell Jennings
Wm. Johnson
Sanderson Kayser

Keeth
M. Klein & Sons
Kraeuter
Lufkin
Marples
Millers Falls
Nicholson
North Bros.
I. K. Penfield & Co.
Pennsylvania Saw Co.
Peterson Mfg. Co.
Pexto
Plumb
Record
Shelton
Simonds
Spear & Jackson
Stanley
L. S. Starrett
Swan
Union Hardware
Union Tool Co.
S. K. Wayne
Weller
Wiss

# B

## Tool Catalogs

### DEALERS

These firms carry a general line of hand woodworking tools and other products as noted.

Brookstone Company
127 Vose Farm Road
Peterborough, New Hampshire 03458

Constantine
2050 Eastchester Road
Bronx, New York 10461
Hardwoods, veneers, moldings, furniture and
cabinet hardware, selected hand tools

The Fine Tool Shop
20 Backus Avenue
Danbury, Connecticut 06810

Frog Tool Company, Ltd.
700 West Jackson Boulevard
Chicago, Illinois 60606

John Harra Wood & Supply Company
511 West 25th Street
New York, New York 10001
Hardwoods, sandpaper, oils, finishes, shop
supplies

Leichtung, Inc.
4944 Commerce Parkway
Cleveland, Ohio 44128

The Princeton Company
P. O. Box 276
Princeton, Massachusetts 01541

The Tool Room
East Oxbow Road
Shelburne Falls, Massachusetts 01370

The Tool Works
76 Ninth Avenue
New York, New York 10011
Replacement parts for planes, spokeshaves,
saws, other tools; good range of files and
rasps; brass and bronze hardware

Garrett Wade
302 Fifth Avenue
New York, New York 10001

Woodcraft Supply Corporation
313 Montvale Avenue
Woburn, Massachusetts 01888

The Wooden Boat Shop
1007 Northeast Boat Street
Seattle, Washington 98105
Adhesives, marine hardware, paints, and var-
nishes

The Woodworkers' Store
21801 Industrial Boulevard
Rogers, Minnesota 55374
Hardwoods, veneers, moldings; cabinet and
furniture hardware


MANUFACTURERS

Adjustable Clamp Company
417 North Ashland Avenue
Chicago, Illinois 60622
Full line of wooden, steel, and web band
clamps; plans and dimensions for various
homemade clamps

Brink & Cotton Manufacturing Company
P. O. Box 3035
67 Poland Street
Bridgeport, Connecticut 06605
Clamps, machinist's vises

Buck Brothers, Inc.
Box 192
Millbury, Massachusetts 01527
Chisels, gouges, carving and lathe tools

Connecticut Valley Manufacturing Company
265 Newington Avenue
New Britain, Connecticut 06051
Scrapers, Forstner and expansive bits, cutters
and other parts

Disston
P.O. Box 3000
Danville, Virginia 24541

Greenlee Tool Division
Ex-Cell-O Corporation
2330 23rd Avenue
Rockford, Illinois 61101
Ship augers, brace bit extensions, chisels,
chisel handles, drawknives, bellhanger's drills

Millers Falls Division
Deerfield Industrial Park
South Deerfield, Massachusetts 01373

Stanley Tools
Division of the Stanley Works
600 Myrtle Street
New Britain, Connecticut 06050
Replacement parts for Stanley planes and
some of their other tools

L. S. Starrett Company
Athol, Massachusetts 01331
Primarily a manufacturer of machinists' tools,
Starrett's combination squares, levels, screw-
drivers, toolmaker's clamps, rules, nail sets,

and machinist's vises are of especially good
quality

Vaughan & Bushnell Manufacturing Company
135 South LaSalle Street
Chicago, Illinois 60603

Wetzler Clamp Company
43-15 11th Street
Long Island City, New York 11101
Complete line, all types of clamps

# C

## WORKBENCH PLANS

This is a strong and serviceable bench that can be built at reasonable cost from materials available in the average lumberyard and hardware store. Put together with screws and bolts—no nails are used—this design can be dismantled and reassembled with a screwdriver and two wrenches.

### MATERIALS

| Pieces | Part | | Dimensions |
|---|---|---|---|
| 2 | top planks | A | $2'' \times 12'' \times 72''$ |
| 1 | backboard | B | $1'' \times 12'' \times 72''$ |
| 1 | center brace | C | $2'' \times 4'' \times 24''*$ |
| 2 | ends | D | $2'' \times 4'' \times 24''*$ |
| 4 | legs | E | $2'' \times 4'' \times 33''**$ |
| 2 | end braces | F | $1'' \times 12'' \times 24''*$ |
| 1 | apron | G | $1'' \times 12'' \times 60''$ |
| 31 | screws | | $1^{1}/_{2}'' \times$ No.8 flat head |
| 12 | bolts | | $^{1}/_{4}'' \times 5^{1}/_{2}''$ machine (top planks) |
| 8 | bolts | | $^{1}/_{4}'' \times 4''$ machine (end units) |
| 40 | flat washers | | to fit $^{1}/_{4}''$ bolts |

\* cut to same dimension as width of top less $^{3}/_{4}$ inch
\*\* trim to same dimension as height of bench less actual thickness of the top planks you use

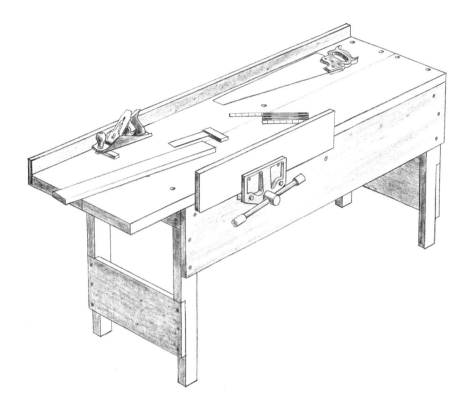

The dimension from floor to bench top, which is shown in the plans as 33 inches, has intentionally been made full to allow for shortening the legs to fit your particular size and requirements. For information on how to determine a comfortable bench height, see *Workbench and Vise,* page 16. According to the space you have available, the bench can be made shorter or longer by modifying the dimensions of parts A, B, and G. But if the bench is made longer than 60 inches, be sure there is one cleat for every 3 feet of bench length. The exact position of the cleats should be planned at the outset with the location of the vise in mind, even if it is to be installed at some later time.

When buying lumber for the bench, get stuff that is dry and flat—without twist, warp, or bow. This is especially important for the top, which should be as smooth and level as possible. Maple, oak, and beech are hard, dense, and quite stiff—ideal for the purpose. But pine and other less expensive woods are satisfactory if sensibly treated, and are generally easier to find. The rest of the bench can be made of pine, fir, or whatever dry stuff is available.

CONSTRUCTION NOTES

(1) Start with the top planks. Square their ends, joint their edges, and plane the good sides smooth. Give their undersides two coats of a good sealer or paint. Clamp them edge to edge and measure their combined width.

(2) Use this measurement to cut the ends, end braces, and center brace all the same length—equal to the exact width of the top less $3/4$ inch. Cut the notches in the legs for ends and end braces. Clamp the ends into the top notches of the legs, then bore $5/16$-inch holes clear through for the bolts. Put in the bolts but tighten the nuts only slightly. Use flat washers under the heads and nuts of all bolts. Clamp the end braces into the lower leg notches, checking to make things square, then drill $1/8'' \times 1''$ pilot holes through the end braces. Countersink the holes, drive the screws, then go back and tighten the bolts.

(3) Set up the frame. Clamp the backboard to the two end units, checking everything to keep it square. Drill and countersink holes for 4 screws (2 at each end) and drive them. Attach the apron in the same way, using the square and leaving the clamps on until the screws are driven.

(4) Attach the top planks. On the rear plank mark out the location of the bolt holes. Counterbore holes $11/16'' \times 5/16''$ deep to recess the washers and bolt heads. Lay the plank in position on the end units, tight against the backboard and flush at the ends. Clamp the plank down. Then drill $1/8'' \times 1''$ holes and drive 5 screws from the outside of the backboard into the back edge of the plank. Leave the clamps on and bore $5/16$-inch holes clear through plank and ends. Put in the bolts and make them tight. Next, clamp the center brace in position, bore $5/16$-inch holes through plank and brace, and insert and tighten the bolts. Drive 2 screws from the outside of the backboard into the back end of center brace, and 2 more from the outside of the apron into the front end of the center brace. Attach the front plank in the same way, using shims as necessary to bring the meeting surfaces of the planks flush and flat.

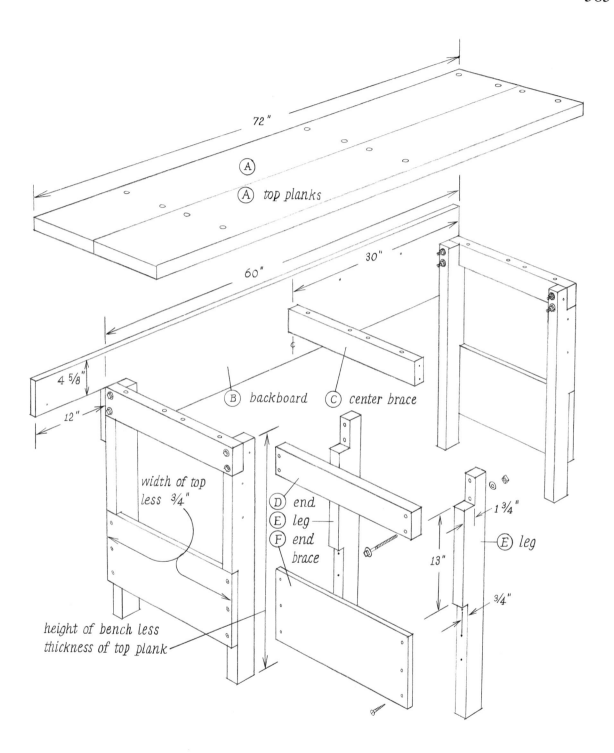

72 "

Ⓐ

Ⓐ top planks

60"  30"

4 5/8 "

12 "

Ⓑ backboard   Ⓒ center brace

width of top
less ¾ "

Ⓓ end
Ⓔ leg
Ⓕ end
brace

13"

1 ¾ "

Ⓔ leg

¾ "

height of bench less
thickness of top plank

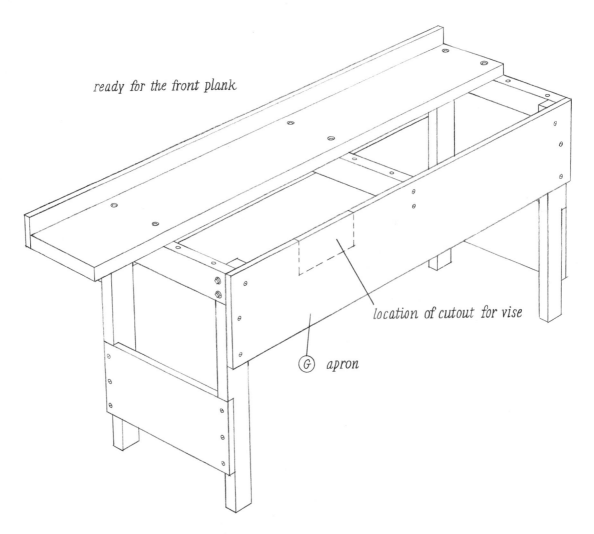

ready for the front plank

location of cutout for vise

Ⓖ apron

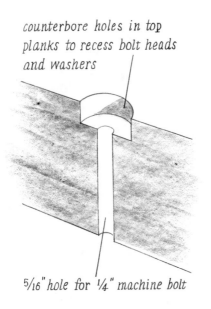

counterbore holes in top
planks to recess bolt heads
and washers

5/16" hole for 1/4" machine bolt

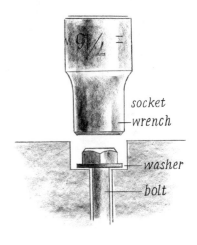

socket
wrench

washer

bolt

# D

## Plans for Bench Tools and Equipment

Few of these useful tools are available ready-made, but they are fairly simple to make. Use only well-seasoned hardwoods such as maple, oak, beech, and cherry. It isn't necessary to lay out a lot of money for a long board. Ends and scraps can usually be bought from a cabinet-making shop. Pieces as small as $1'' \times 6'' \times 16''$ are adequate for all these items except the saw horse, which in any case need not be built of hardwood. If you buy ends, make sure they are free of end checks and splits.

Since many of these tools are used in connection with precision work, take extra pains to measure, cut, plane, and fit as accurately as possible. To protect the finished tool from the damage of warping, give it a treatment of mineral or hot linseed oil. Apply it liberally—especially to the end grain—and let it stand overnight. Then wipe off any excess oil and rub it down with steel wool and a dry cloth to polish the surface. This treatment should be repeated in a week's time, and thereafter occasionally to keep the wood from drying out.

| | |
|---|---|
| Auger bit depth gauge | 386 |
| Auger bit V block | 387 |
| Bar clamp blocks | 387 |
| Bench hold-down | 388 |
| Bench hook | 389 |
| Drawknife holding block | 390 |
| Grinding palm | 391 |
| Inshave blade guard | 392 |
| Mallet | 393 |
| Miter block | 394 |
| Oilstone tray | 395 |
| Saw handles | 396 |
| Sawhorse | 398 |
| Saw table | 399 |
| Shooting board | 400 |

*auger bit depth gauge*

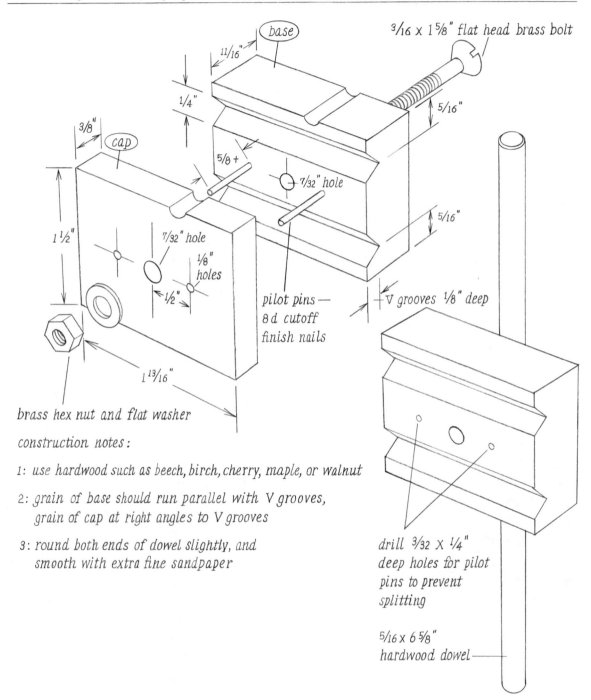

base

3/16 x 1 5/8" flat head brass bolt

11/16"

1/4"

5/16"

3/8"

cap

5/8 +

7/32" hole

1 1/2"

7/32" hole

1/8" holes

1/2"

5/16"

pilot pins — 8d cutoff finish nails

V grooves 1/8" deep

1 13/16"

brass hex nut and flat washer

construction notes:

1: use hardwood such as beech, birch, cherry, maple, or walnut

2: grain of base should run parallel with V grooves, grain of cap at right angles to V grooves

3: round both ends of dowel slightly, and smooth with extra fine sandpaper

drill 3/32 x 1/4" deep holes for pilot pins to prevent splitting

5/16 x 6 5/8" hardwood dowel

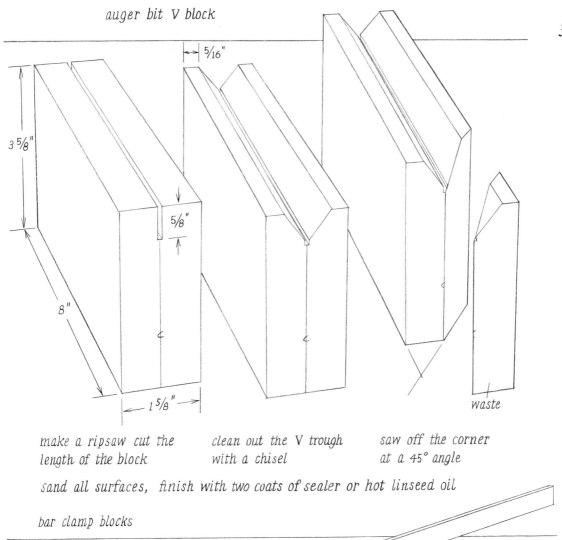

5/16"

3 5/8"

5/8"

8"

1 5/8"

waste

make a ripsaw cut the
length of the block

clean out the V trough
with a chisel

saw off the corner
at a 45° angle

sand all surfaces, finish with two coats of sealer or hot linseed oil

bar clamp blocks

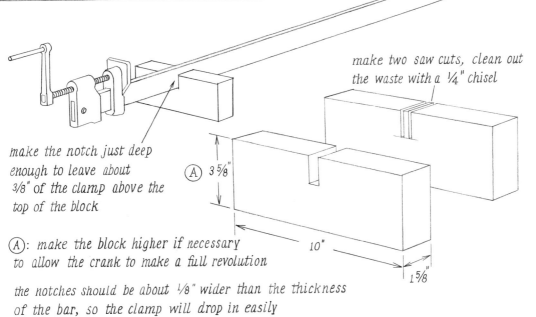

make two saw cuts, clean out
the waste with a 1/4" chisel

make the notch just deep
enough to leave about
3/8" of the clamp above the
top of the block

Ⓐ 3 5/8"

10"

1 5/8"

Ⓐ: make the block higher if necessary
to allow the crank to make a full revolution

the notches should be about 1/8" wider than the thickness
of the bar, so the clamp will drop in easily

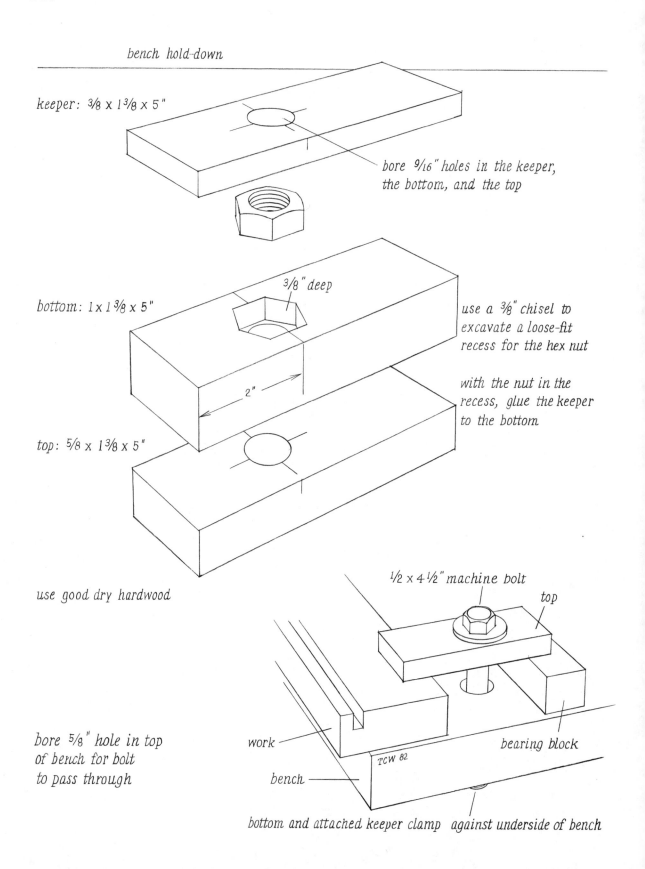

bench hold-down

keeper: 3/8 x 1 3/8 x 5"

bore 9/16" holes in the keeper,
the bottom, and the top

bottom: 1 x 1 3/8 x 5"

3/8" deep

use a 3/8" chisel to
excavate a loose-fit
recess for the hex nut

with the nut in the
recess, glue the keeper
to the bottom

2"

top: 5/8 x 1 3/8 x 5"

use good dry hardwood

1/2 x 4 1/2" machine bolt

top

bore 5/8" hole in top
of bench for bolt
to pass through

work

bench

TCW 82

bearing block

bottom and attached keeper clamp  against underside of bench

bench hook

table: ¾ x 6 x 11"     fence: ⅞ x 1½ x 4½"

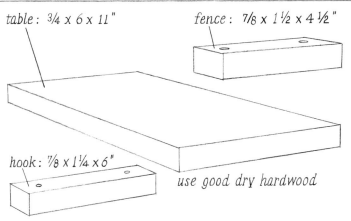

hook: ⅞ x 1¼ x 6"     use good dry hardwood

*the grain should follow the long dimension of all three parts*

1¼" x No. 8 flat head screws

countersunk holes

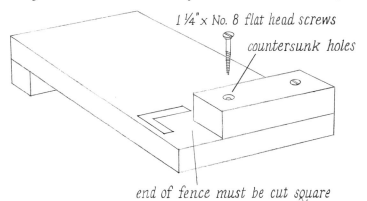

end of fence must be cut square

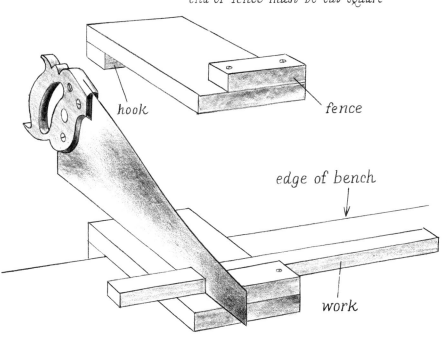

hook     fence

edge of bench

work

390

*drawknife holding block*

trace the contour of the knife's back
edge onto the block

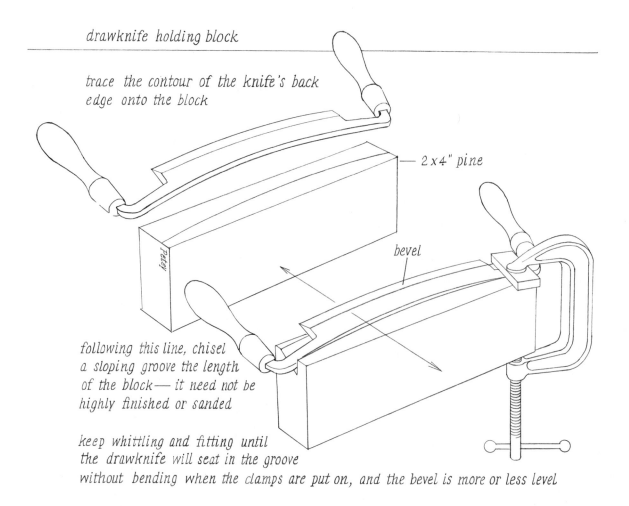

— 2 x 4" pine

*bevel*

following this line, chisel
a sloping groove the length
of the block — it need not be
highly finished or sanded

keep whittling and fitting until
the drawknife will seat in the groove
without bending when the clamps are put on, and the bevel is more or less level

*grinding palm to fit the cutters of a Stanley No. 248 grooving plane*

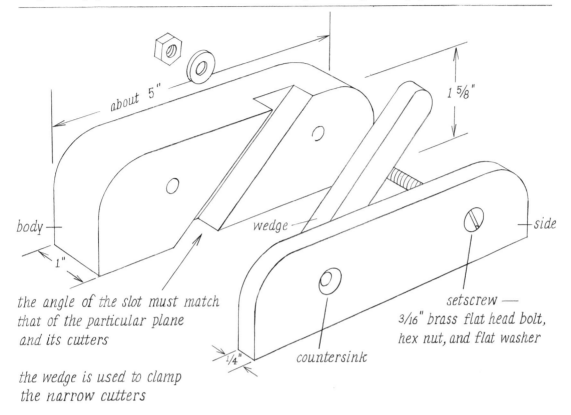

about 5"

1 5/8"

body

1"

wedge

side

the angle of the slot must match
that of the particular plane
and its cutters

1/4"

countersink

setscrew —
3/16" brass flat head bolt,
hex nut, and flat washer

the wedge is used to clamp
the narrow cutters

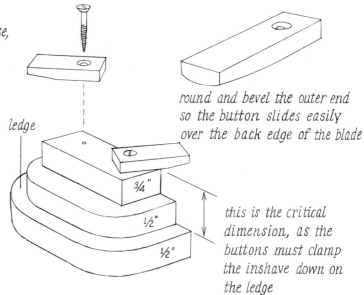

use pine for three-layer base,
one of the hardwoods
for the pair of buttons

round and bevel the outer end
so the button slides easily
over the back edge of the blade

ledge

assemble three
layers with glue
and clamps

drill oversize holes for
screws in the buttons so
that they will turn freely

¾"

½"

½"

this is the critical
dimension, as the
buttons must clamp
the inshave down on
the ledge

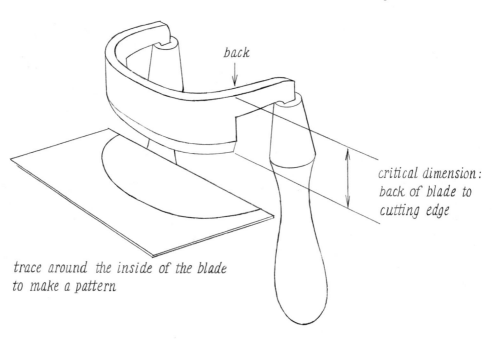

back

critical dimension:
back of blade to
cutting edge

trace around the inside of the blade
to make a pattern

*mallet : apple, beech, cherry*

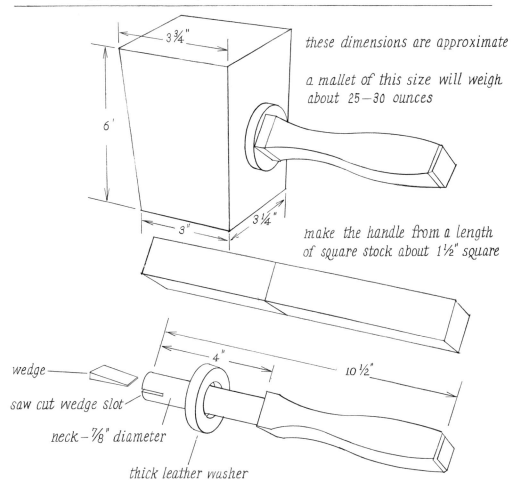

*these dimensions are approximate*

*a mallet of this size will weigh about 25—30 ounces*

3¾"

6'

3"

3¼"

*make the handle from a length of square stock about 1½" square*

wedge ——

4"

10½"

*saw cut wedge slot*

*neck – ⅞" diameter*

*thick leather washer*

1: *work the neck first, using the methods described in the File & Rasp section*

2: *shape the handle*

3: *cut the wedge slot, make a hardwood wedge and a washer*

4: *bore a ⅞" hole through the head*

5: *assemble — slip washer over neck, drive neck into head, drive the wedge* (*see Appendix : Fitting a Hammer Handle*)

6: *finish with at least two coats of sealer*

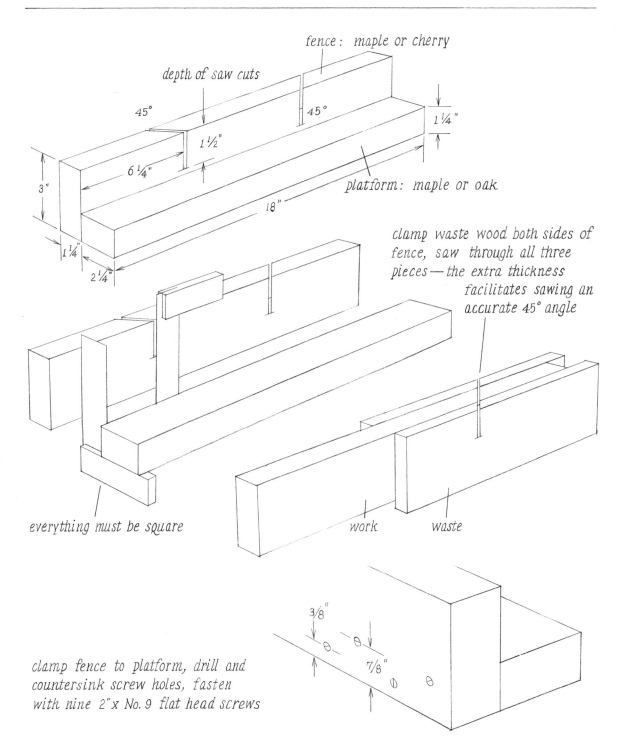

fence: maple or cherry

depth of saw cuts

45°

45°

1 ¼"

1 ½"

6 ¼"

platform: maple or oak

3"

18"

1 ¼"

2 ¼"

clamp waste wood both sides of
fence, saw through all three
pieces — the extra thickness
facilitates sawing an
accurate 45° angle

everything must be square

work

waste

3/8"

7/8"

clamp fence to platform, drill and
countersink screw holes, fasten
with nine 2"x No. 9 flat head screws

*oilstone tray for a  1 x 2 x 8" stone*

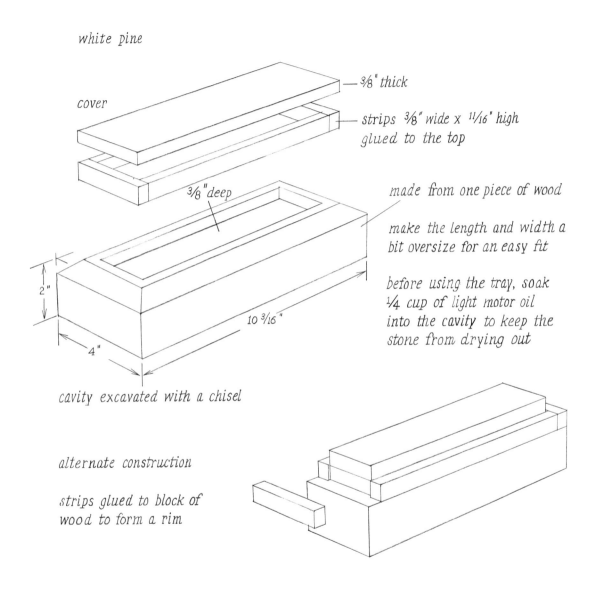

white pine

cover

3/8" thick

strips 3/8" wide x 11/16" high
glued to the top

made from one piece of wood

make the length and width a
bit oversize for an easy fit

before using the tray, soak
1/4 cup of light motor oil
into the cavity to keep the
stone from drying out

3/8" deep

2"

4"

10 3/16"

cavity excavated with a chisel

alternate construction

strips glued to block of
wood to form a rim

*full-scale pattern for a saw handle*

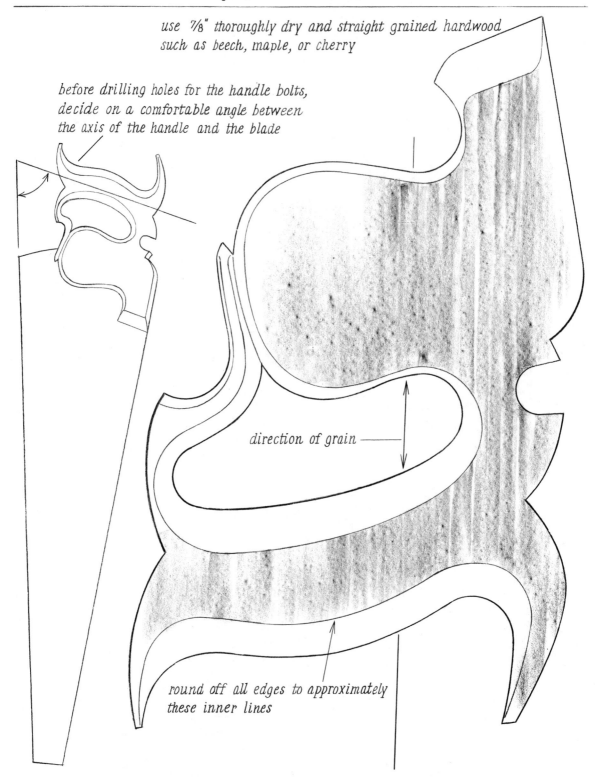

use ⅞" thoroughly dry and straight grained hardwood
such as beech, maple, or cherry

before drilling holes for the handle bolts,
decide on a comfortable angle between
the axis of the handle and the blade

direction of grain —

round off all edges to approximately
these inner lines

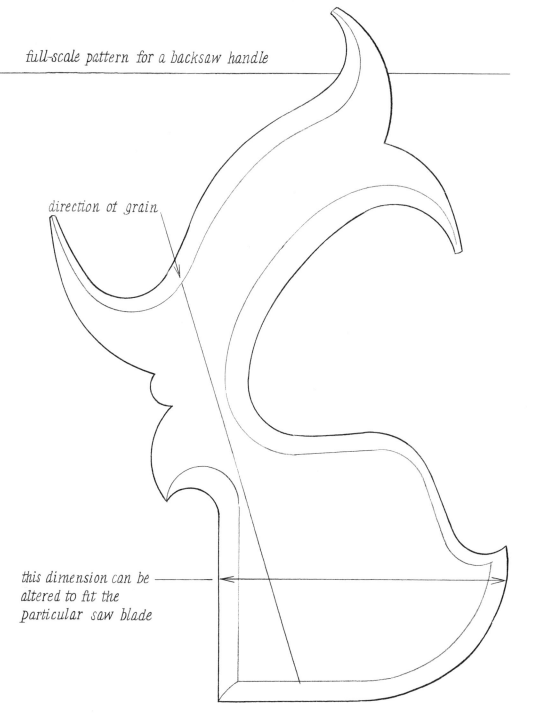

full-scale pattern for a backsaw handle

direction of grain

this dimension can be altered to fit the particular saw blade

sawhorse

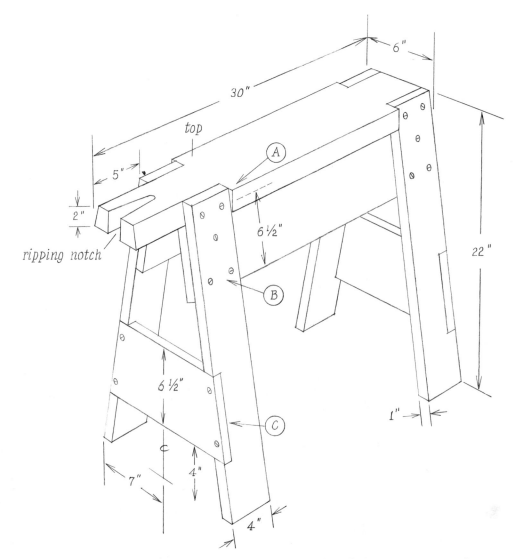

30"

top

6"

5"

2"

ripping notch

A

6 ½"

B

22"

1"

6 ½"

C

C

7"

4"

4"

use good dry lumber, as straight grained and clear as you can find

top: hardwood        legs and braces: pine

fasten all joints with glue and screws

(A)  1½" x No. 8  flat head    (B) &(C)  1¼" x No. 7 flat head

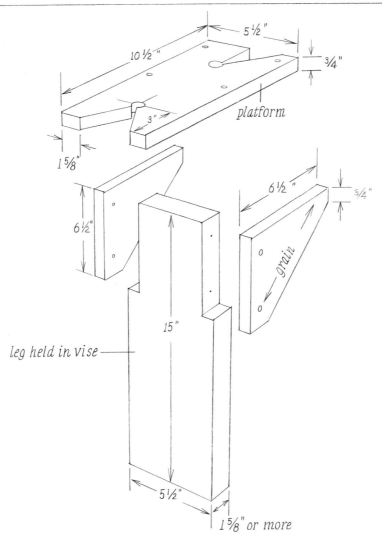

*saw table*

5 ½"

10 ½"

¾"

3"

*platform*

1 ⅝"

6 ½"

¾"

6 ½"

*grain*

15"

*leg held in vise*

5 ½"

1 ⅝" *or more*

*platform : hardwood or plywood*

*leg and braces : pine*

*assemble with glue and 1½"x No.7 flat head screws*

*shooting board : 45°/ 90°*

*plan*

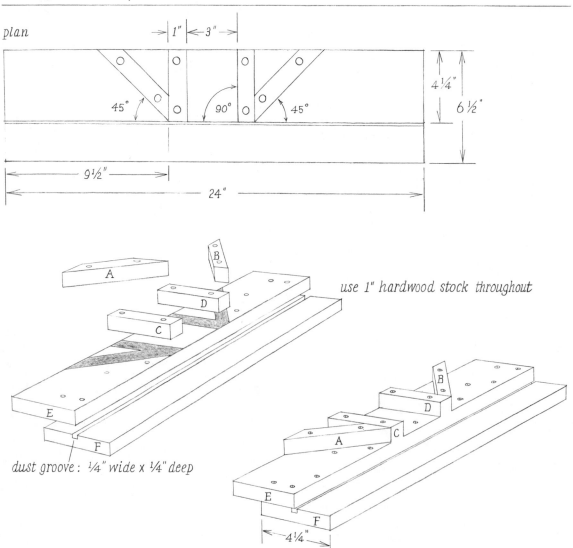

*use 1" hardwood stock throughout*

*dust groove : ¼" wide x ¼" deep*

*fasten the four stops A B C D with 1½" x No. 8 flat head screws*

*clamp each piece—one at a time—to part E; check the angle exactly with the combination square until it is perfect; then drill screw pilot holes, countersink the holes, and drive the screws    leave clamps on until screws are driven*

*attach C and D first, then A and B*

*fasten E to F with 1½" x No. 8 flat head screws*

# E

### Fitting a Hammer Handle

A hammer handle generally breaks just back of the head, leaving the eye full of wood and wedges. All this has to be cleaned out. First saw off the protruding wood with a hacksaw as close to the head as possible. Put the hammer head in a 300°F. oven for an hour or so. The heat shrinks the wood and at the same time expands the iron without drawing its temper. Have a pair of hardwood blocks ready to set it on. When it comes out of the oven, lay the hammer head across the blocks with the eye suspended over the free space underneath. Also have a $1/2$-inch machine bolt ready to use as a punch. Set the head of the bolt on the old wood and drive it out. Save the iron wedges.

New handles are usually sold with a wooden wedge and a pair of iron ones, and with the wedge slot already cut in the handle. The head end of a store-bought handle is a good bit oversize and has to be shaved down to fit. Notice its shape: it has a swelling near the head end. This

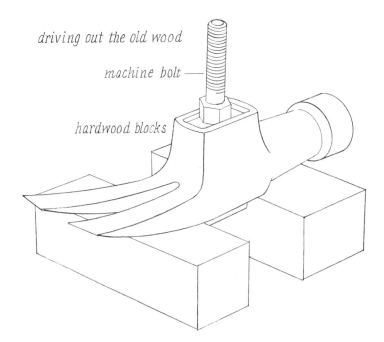

driving out the old wood

machine bolt

hardwood blocks

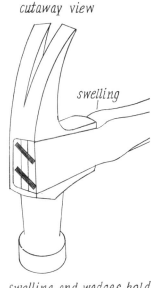

cutaway view

swelling

swelling and wedges hold the head on

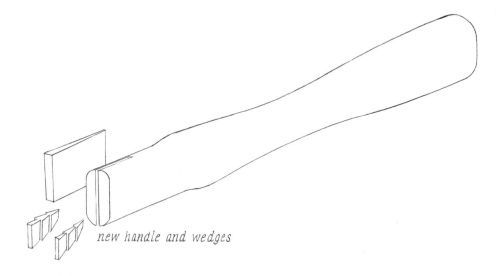

*new handle and wedges*

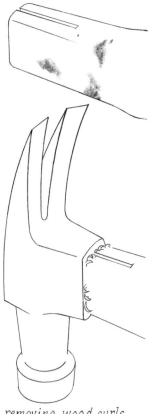

*removing wood curls and friction marks*

swelling and the wedges are what hold the head tight. The head is seated or drawn back against the swelling and the wedges hold it there. They spread the end of the handle to fill the outer end of the eye and prevent the head from moving in either direction. Therefore in fitting a handle, it is important to remove wood *from in front of the swelling only.*

This is a very picky job, so settle down with patience. Begin fitting by tapping the new handle in as far as it will go, which won't be much. Take it out, and, using a double-cut wood file, remove the wood that has curled up next to the hammer head. Don't use a wood rasp; it takes off too much too fast. Then tap the handle in again. Pull it out once more and again file off the peeled-back wood. Also file off any friction marks made by the inside of the head. File lightly and only where there are marks; leave the rest alone. A good fit depends on the wood touching the inside of the eye at every point.

Continue this process until the handle can be hand-pushed almost all the way through the eye. Stop there. Seating the head will pull it through the rest of the way.

SEATING THE HEAD    Seating the head simply means shucking it back tight against the swelling of the handle. To do this, hold the hammer by the handle with the head on top. Pound the butt of the handle down hard several times on the anvil or anything else as solid until the head is back as far as it will go. The weight of the head does most of the work. The same thing can be accomplished by pounding the butt of the handle with another hammer. The end of the handle may now stick out beyond the head $1/4$ inch or more. If so, saw it off flush with a hacksaw.

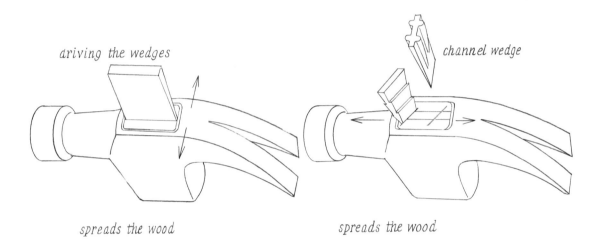

*driving the wedges*

*channel wedge*

*spreads the wood*

*spreads the wood*

DRIVING THE WEDGES    Start with the wooden wedge. Push the thin end into the handle slot and give it a light tap just to get it started straight. Now set the butt of the handle on the anvil and drive the wedge in as tight as it will go. Use good solid blows and strike the wedge squarely or it may split or break. Stop pounding when you feel and hear the wood ringing to a different pitch. Then use the hacksaw to cut off the surplus wood flush.

Now the iron wedges. If they are the barbed-spear type, set them at an angle of 45 degrees to the wooden wedge in order to spread the wood in all four directions. Channel wedges can be set at right angles. Either of these iron wedges starts more easily in a slit made with a $1/2$-inch chisel. Tap one wedge into the slit, then set the handle butt on the anvil and drive the wedge in flush, using another hammer. Use good hard blows. When both wedges are driven, smooth off the work with a file and paint the handle end and wedges with two coats of sealer or paint.

# F

## Closet Workbench Plans

This is not a substitute for a full-scale workshop. Rather, it is a way to have a bench where none was thought possible. And despite the miniature size of its top, this bench provides the one thing most necessary in any shop—an absolutely solid work surface to which a vise can be attached. It has been designed to swing out and lock securely to the doorframe, using the rigidity of the wall for support. This bench can be built in with no defacement of property and when tipped back into the closet, the closed door makes it invisible. For complete security, a lock can be installed in the closet door if it doesn't already have one.

This bench will not necessarily fit into every closet. The critical measurement is the distance from the back wall of the closet to the inside of the closed door. The front-to-back dimension of the bench top is determined by this measurement. These plans were designed for a typical closet with a critical measurement of 29 inches. In a shallow closet, for example, one no deeper than 14 inches, the maximum depth of the bench top would be only 12 or 13 inches, and before proceeding to build a bench to such slim dimensions it would be wise first to work out the engineering on paper to determine if the scheme is practicable.

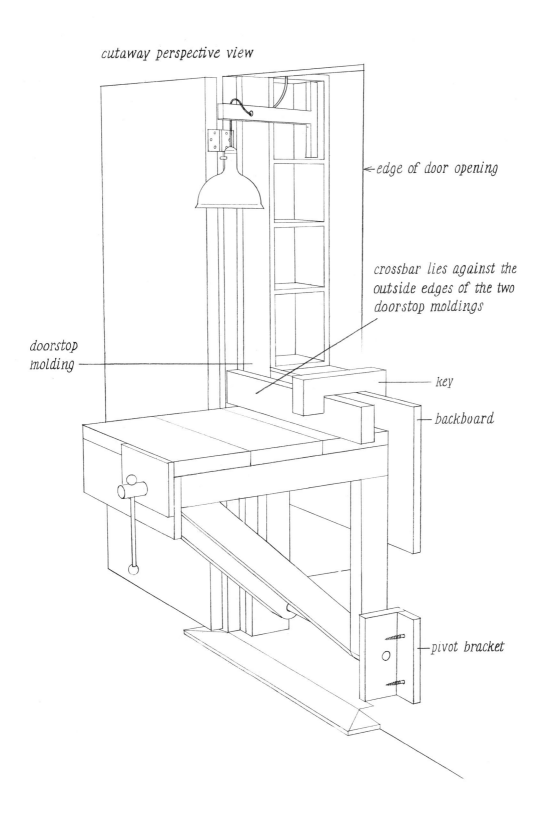

cutaway perspective view

←edge of door opening

crossbar lies against the
outside edges of the two
doorstop moldings

doorstop
molding

key

backboard

pivot bracket

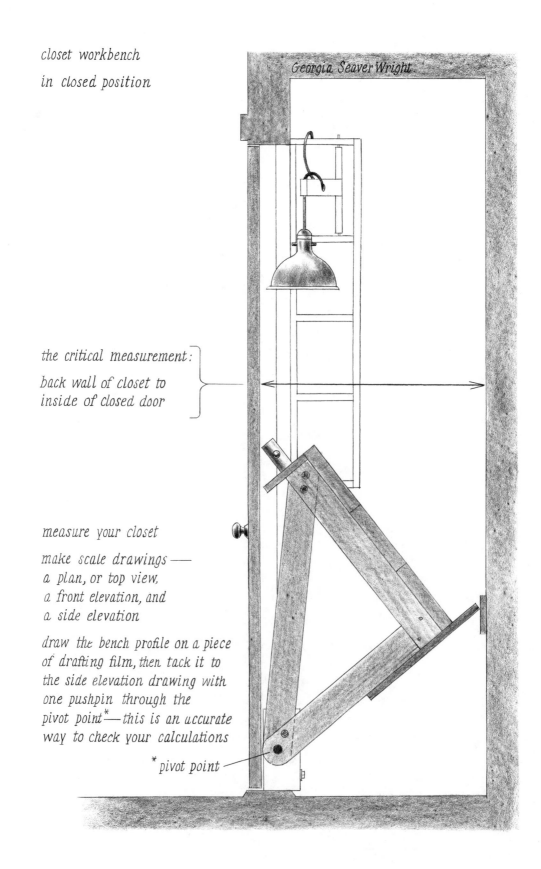

*closet workbench*
*in closed position*

*Georgia Seaver Wright*

*the critical measurement:*
*back wall of closet to*
*inside of closed door*

*measure your closet*

*make scale drawings —*
*a plan, or top view,*
*a front elevation, and*
*a side elevation*

*draw the bench profile on a piece*
*of drafting film, then tack it to*
*the side elevation drawing with*
*one pushpin through the*
*pivot point\*—this is an accurate*
*way to check your calculations*

*\* pivot point*

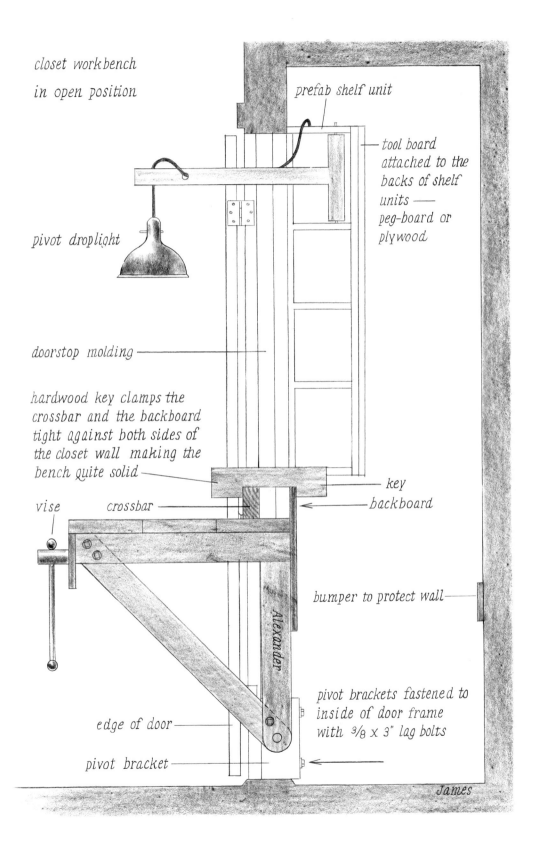

closet workbench
in open position

prefab shelf unit

tool board
attached to the
backs of shelf
units —
peg-board or
plywood

pivot droplight

doorstop molding

hardwood key clamps the
crossbar and the backboard
tight against both sides of
the closet wall making the
bench quite solid

vise

crossbar

key

backboard

bumper to protect wall

Alexander

pivot brackets fastened to
inside of door frame
with ⅜ x 3" lag bolts

edge of door

pivot bracket

James

construction of bench frame

legs and braces
2 x 4" pine

backboard
5/8" or 3/4" plywood
attached with glue
and screws

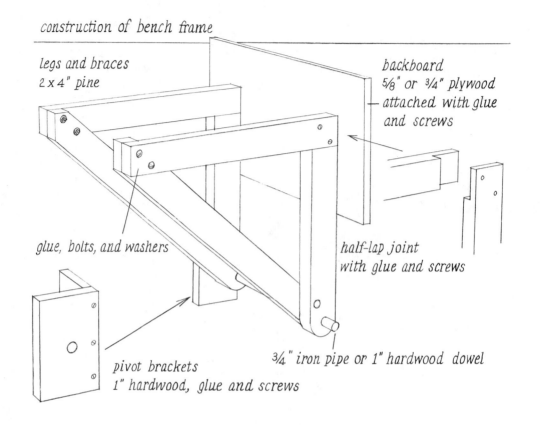

glue, bolts, and washers

half-lap joint
with glue and screws

pivot brackets
1" hardwood, glue and screws

3/4" iron pipe or 1" hardwood dowel

# G

Inventory of Typical Hand Tool Shop

10″×12″ quick-action vise
3½″ swivel base machinist's vise
Pair bench hold-downs
9-lb. anvil
Scratch awl
Bit braces, 4″ throw, 5″ throw, 5½″ throw
Auger bits, ¼, 5/16, 3/8, 7/16, ½, 9/16, 5/8, 11/16, ¾,
   13/16, 7/8, 15/16, 1″
Countersinks, ½″ single-cutter, 11/16″ rosehead, ½″ split cone
Expansive bits
Screwdriver bits, ¼″, 5/16″, 3/8″
Reamer, ¼″–1¼″
Wire brush
6″ calipers
Chisels, 1/8, ¼, 5/16, 3/8, ½, 5/8, ¾, 7/8, 1″, 2″
C-clamps, pair 4″, pair 4½″, pair 6″, 1–6¼″ deep throat,
   pair 8″, pair 10″
Carriage clamps, pair 3″, pair 4″
Pair 36″ furniture clamps
Pair 48″ furniture clamps
Pair 12″ Jorgensen
Pair toolmaker's parallel clamps
Pair 6″ spring clamps
8″ drawknife
Hand drill
Twist drills
   1/16″, 5/64″, 3/32″, 7/64″, 1/8″, 9/64″, 5/32″, 11/64″,
   3/16″, 13/64″, 7/32″, 15/64″, ¼″
   brad point, ½″
   3/8″×16″ bellhanger's
Assorted files and rasps, auger bit, chain saw, flat, half round, round
Hammers
   3-lb. smith's
   10-oz. Warrington

    12-oz. one-piece steel
    16-oz. full curved claw
    8-oz. casing
    10-oz. ball peen
    5-oz. magnetic tack
Inshave and blade guard
Jackknife
2-ft. laminated wood level
$1^1/_2'' \times 3''$ rawhide mallet
29-oz. applewood mallet
Stanley No. $64^1/_2$ marking gauge
Pair 6" dividers
Perfection miter box 45° and 90°, 9°, $22^1/_2°$, 30°, 36°
Oak miter block
Shooting board, 45°/90°
4 nail sets
Planes
    Stanley No. 4 smoothing
    Stanley No. 220, 7" block
    Stanley No. 10, 13" jack rabbet
    Stanley No. 6, 18" fore
    Bailey No. 27, 15" jack
    4" bullnose
    Stanley No. 248 grooving
    Stanley No. 148, $^7/_8''$ match plane
    Record No. 778 rabbet
    Stanley No. 45 combination
Pliers
    4" round nose wire loop
    $5^1/_2''$ needle-nose with side cutters
    $6^1/_2''$ do
    $5^1/_2''$ diagonal cutting
    $9^1/_2''$ lineman's with side and notch cutters
Pair spring leaf pry bars
6-ft. wooden extension rule
8-ft. do, with brass extension
6-ft. tape rule
Saws
    coping
    $7^1/_2$ pt–11" compass
    19 pt–6" do
    8 pt–$25^1/_2''$ crosscut
    9 pt–22" do
    10 pt–24" do

10 pt–26″ do
12 pt–14″ backsaw
14 pt–12″ do
$5^1/_2$ pt–23″ ripsaw
7 pt–26″ do
27 pt–5″ tenon
19 pt–$8^1/_2$″ do
Saw set & files
Saw vise
3 hook scrapers
Various homemade scrapers
Screwdrivers
    $^1/_8$″ flat tip–4″
    $^1/_8$″ do–7″
    $^3/_{16}$″ do–10″
    $^1/_4$″ do–10″
    $^3/_8$″ do–10″
    $^1/_2$″ do–13″
    $^3/_{16}$″ Phillips–$6^1/2$″
    $^5/_{16}$″ do–9″
    $^1/_4$″ flat tip stubby–$3^1/_4$″
Stanley No. 151 spokeshave
6″ try square
Combination square
16″×24″ rafter square
Do carpenter's square
T-bevel
Combination oilstone
Slip stones
Auger bit depth gauge
Auger bit V block
Pair bar clamp blocks
Grinding palm
$^7/_{16}$″ wooden doweling jig
4 sawhorses

# Index

Anvil, 37-39
Auger bits, 56-63
  cleaning clogged bit, 61
  countersink bits, 78-80
  damage, types of, 70
  depth gauge, 67
  depth gauge, plans for making, 386
  expansive bit, 72-75
  function of, 56, 57, 60, 61
  reamer bit, 79
  sharpening of bits, 366-368, 387
  V block for sharpening, 367
  V block, plans for making, 387
Awl, 40-43

Backsaw, 22, 304, 312
  cutting rabbets with, 265
  used with miter block, 199
  used with miter box, 197
Bead saw, 304, 319
Bench dog, 26, 33
Bench hold-down, 35
  plans for making, 388
Bench hook, plans for making, 389
Bench tools. *See* Workbench tools and equipment
Block plane, 234-244
  sharpening cutter irons, 354-360
Brace (bit brace), 23, 44-81
  boring at an angle, 71
  boring clean hole, 62, 63
  boring straight, 65-69
  boring without splitting, 71
  counterboring for screws, 80, 81
  driving and removing screws, 75-78, 80, 81
  lubrication, 53

  mechanics of, 45-52, 54
  positions and handholds, 57-59
  screw pilot holes, importance of, 331
Bradawl, 43
Brad point drill, 64, 65
Bullnose plane, 266-268

Cabinet scraper, 320, 321, 324
  sharpening, 370
Carpenter's square, 340, 346, 347
Center punch, 40
Chamfer
  with block plane, 237, 242-244
  with chisel, 102, 103
  examples of, 242, 271
Chisels, 86-103
  cleaning out a groove, 101
  cleaning out a rabbet, 98
  compass stroke, 94, 95, 102
  construction of, 87-90
  cutting a mortise, 99
  end grain work, 94, 95
  handholds, 88, 90-92, 95-100, 102, 103
  making a chamfer, 102, 103
  pressure, 88, 90, 91, 96, 97
  sharpening, 354-358, 360
  swan neck chisel, 86
  types and sizes, 86, 87, 89, 90
  used with gauge block, 98, 101
Clamps, 104-121, 240
  bar clamp holding blocks, 118
  bar clamp holding blocks, directions for making, 387
  bar clamps, 117, 118
  blocking used with, 104, 108-111, 119-121

Clamps (*continued*)
  C-clamps, 104-111, 121
  clamp fixtures, 117-119
  clamp substitutes, 120
  Jorgensen (handscrew), 22, 28,
    112-116, 240
  mechanics of, 112-116
  spar clamps, 117
  spring clamp, 119
  toolmaker's parallel clamp, 119
Closet workbench, plans for mak-
  ing, 404
Combination plane, 259
Combination square, 340-344
Compass saw, 304, 318
Coping saw, 304, 314-317
Countersink bits, 78-80
  sharpening, 368, 369
Crosscut saw, 296-301, 305

Depth gauge, auger bit, 67
  plans for making, 386
Donkey's ear, 200
Dovetail saw, 319
Dowel pegs, making, 171-173
Drawknife, 122-131
  construction, 122-124
  handholds, 125, 128, 129
  holding block, plans for making,
    390
  scoring method, 131
  sharpening, 361, 362, 390
  slicing stroke, 128

Expansive bit, 72-75
  sharpening, 368
Extension rule, 284

Files, 140-151
  cross filing, 144, 145
  draw filing, 145
  handholds, 143, 145, 146, 149
  reducing diameter of round stock,
    148
  round-and-round filing, 149, 150
  types, 142
  used to sharpen saws, 364-366
  used to sharpen scrapers, 371

Fore plane, 260, 261

Grinding palm, 360
  plans for making, 391
Grooving plane, 35, 248-254
  adjustments, 250-252
  sharpening cutter irons, 360, 361,
    391
  used with far-to-near method,
    253, 254

Hammer, 154-165
  construction, 154-159
  fitting handle, directions for, 401-
    403
  function and use, 157, 159-161,
    163-165
  types, 156, 158
Hand drill, 132-139
  adjustment, 134, 135
  construction, 132, 133
  gauging depth of hole, 139
  handholds, 135, 136, 138
  twist drill, anatomy of, 137
Handscrew. *See* Clamps, Jorgensen
Hold-down, 35
  plans for making, 388
Hook scrapers, 320

Inshave, 166-169
  blade guard, plans for making,
    392
  sharpening, 361, 362

Jackknife, 170-173
  sharpening, 369
Jack rabbet plane, 222-233
Jointer plane, 260, 261

Level, 174-183
  anatomy and construction, 174-
    177
  checking level of floor, 178, 179
  leveling a bookcase, 178-181
  leveling a kitchen cabinet, 180
  leveling a table on uneven floor,
    182, 183
Lineman's pliers, 276, 278

Machinist's vise. *See* Vise
Mallet, 184-187
  plans for making, 393
  rawhide mallet, 173, 187
  used in conjunction with hammer, 161
Marking gauge, 188-193
Match plane. *See* Tongue and groove plane
Miter block, 22, 198, 199
  plans for making, 394
Miter box, 196, 197
Mitering tools, 194-201
  donkey's ear, 200
  miter block, 198, 199
  miter boxes, 196, 197
  miter template, 201
  shooting board, 199, 200
Miter template, 201
Multiplane, 259

Nail set, 202-205
Needle-nose pliers, 274-276

Oilstone, 354-360
  tray, plans for making, 395

Planes, 206-273
  adjustments, 212-217, 246
  design and construction, 207-215
  lubrication points, 210
  sharpening plane irons, 354-361, 391
  TYPES OF PLANES
  block plane, 234-244
  bullnose, 266-268
  combination, multiplane, 259
  fore, 260, 261
  grooving, 35, 248-254
  jack rabbet, 222-233
  jointer, 260, 261
  rabbet, 262-267
  smoothing, 226-229, 245-248
  tongue and groove, 255-258
Planing
  bevels and chamfers, 237, 242-244
  end grain, 237-240

grooves, 253, 254
old lumber, 248
pressure, importance of, 220, 237, 245
rough-sawn lumber, 246, 247
round and tapered work, 268-272
swipe-and-lift technique, 245, 246
thin stock, 272, 273
to reduce thickness, 246
Planing stick, 273
Pliers, 274-278
  cutting, 276, 277
  lineman's, 276, 278
  needle-nose, 274-276
  to remove nails, 277
  used as wrench, 278
Pry bar, 279-281

Rabbet plane, 262-267
Rabbets, cutting, 230-232, 262-267
Rasps, 140-142, 151-153
  anatomy of, 140, 141
  flat and curved work, 152, 153
  types, 142
Reamer bit, 79
  sharpening, 368, 369
Ripsaw, 296-299
Rules, 282-289
  folding extension, 284-286
  tape rule, 287, 288

Sanding sticks, 291, 292, 295
  used in sharpening, 355, 367, 368
Sandpaper, 290-295
Saw handles, plans for making, 151, 396, 397
Sawhorse, plans for making, 398
  to hold board for planing, 104
  used when sawing, 306, 307
Saws, 296-319
  back, 22, 197, 199, 265, 304, 312
  bead, 304, 319
  compass, 304, 318
  coping, 304, 314-317
  crosscut, 296-301, 305
  dovetail, 319
  ripsaw, 296-299
  sharpening saws, 363-366

Saws (*continued*)
   tenon saw, 319
Saw set, 363
Saw table, for coping saw work, 315
   plans for making, 399
Saw vise, 364
Scrapers, 320-325
   homemade, 322
   sharpening, 370, 371
Scratch brush, 82-85
Screwdriver, 326-333
   screw pilot holes, importance of,
      331
Screwdriver bits, 75-77
   screw pilot holes, importance of,
      331
Sharpening of tools, 353-371
   auger bits, 366-368, 387
   chisels, 354-358, 360
   countersinks, 368, 369
   drawknife, 361, 362, 390
   equipment, 354, 355, 360, 361,
      363, 364, 367-370, 387, 390,
      391, 395
   inshave, 361, 362
   jackknife, 369
   plane irons, 354-361, 391
   principles and methods, 355-360
   reamers, 368, 369
   saws, 363-366
   scrapers, 370, 371
   spokeshave, 354-360
Shave hook, 320
Ship scraper, 320
Shooting board, 199, 200
   plans for making, 400
Six-foot rule, 284
Slipstone, sharpening, 354
Smoothing plane, 226-229, 245-248
Spokeshave, 334-339
   sharpening, 354-360
Square, 340-347
Steel square, 340, 346, 347
Stropping block, sharpening, 354
Swan neck chisel, 86

Tape rule, 287, 288
T-bevel, 348-351
Tenon saw, 319

Tongue and groove plane, 255-258
Tool catalogs, 376
Toolmakers, 374
Tools, buying of, 14
Tools, typical inventory of, 409
Try square, 43, 264, 340, 345
   as guide to boring straight, 68
Twist drill, anatomy of, 137

V block, to hold round workpiece,
      104
   for sharpening auger bits, 367
   plans for making, 387
Vise, 21-36
   blocking, importance of, 27
   faceplates, 25
   installation, 30, 31, 34-36
   machinist's vise, 29
   quick-action mechanism, 24, 25
   uses for, 20-23, 26-28, 308
   woodworking vise, 20-28

Wire brush, 82-85
Woodworking vise, 20-28
Workbench, 15-36
   care of, 36
   closet workbench, plans for, 404-
      408
   construction of, 17
   height, importance of, 16
   homemade, plans for, 380-384
   installation of, 18-20
Workbench tools and equipment,
      plans
   auger bit depth gauge, 386
   auger bit V block, 387
   bar clamp blocks, 387
   bench hold-down, 388
   bench hook, 389
   drawknife holding block, 390
   grinding palm, 391
   inshave blade guard, 392
   mallet, 393
   miter block, 394
   oilstone tray, 395
   saw handles, 396, 397
   sawhorse, 398
   saw table, 399
   shooting board, 400